1,000,000 Books

are available to read at

www.ForgottenBooks.com

Read online
Download PDF
Purchase in print

ISBN 978-1-330-04160-4
PIBN 10011143

This book is a reproduction of an important historical work. Forgotten Books uses state-of-the-art technology to digitally reconstruct the work, preserving the original format whilst repairing imperfections present in the aged copy. In rare cases, an imperfection in the original, such as a blemish or missing page, may be replicated in our edition. We do, however, repair the vast majority of imperfections successfully; any imperfections that remain are intentionally left to preserve the state of such historical works.

Forgotten Books is a registered trademark of FB &c Ltd.
Copyright © 2018 FB &c Ltd.
FB &c Ltd, Dalton House, 60 Windsor Avenue, London, SW19 2RR.
Company number 08720141. Registered in England and Wales.

For support please visit www.forgottenbooks.com

1 MONTH OF FREE READING

at

www.ForgottenBooks.com

By purchasing this book you are eligible for one month membership to ForgottenBooks.com, giving you unlimited access to our entire collection of over 1,000,000 titles via our web site and mobile apps.

To claim your free month visit:
www.forgottenbooks.com/free11143

* Offer is valid for 45 days from date of purchase. Terms and conditions apply.

English
Français
Deutsche
Italiano
Español
Português

www.forgottenbooks.com

Mythology Photography **Fiction** Fishing Christianity **Art** Cooking Essays Buddhism Freemasonry Medicine **Biology** Music **Ancient Egypt** Evolution Carpentry Physics Dance Geology **Mathematics** Fitness Shakespeare **Folklore** Yoga Marketing **Confidence** Immortality Biographies Poetry **Psychology** Witchcraft Electronics Chemistry History **Law** Accounting **Philosophy** Anthropology Alchemy Drama Quantum Mechanics Atheism Sexual Health **Ancient History Entrepreneurship** Languages Sport Paleontology Needlework Islam **Metaphysics** Investment Archaeology Parenting Statistics Criminology **Motivational**

BARNES ONE-TERM SERIES

A BRIEF HISTORY
OF
ANCIENT PEOPLES

WITH SOME ACCOUNT OF THEIR MONUMENTS, INSTITUTIONS,
ARTS, MANNERS AND CUSTOMS

BY

JOEL DORMAN STEELE, Ph.D., F.G.S.
AND
ESTHER BAKER STEELE, Lit.D.

NEW YORK ·:· CINCINNATI ·:· CHICAGO
AMERICAN BOOK COMPANY

BARNES BRIEF HISTORY SERIES.

12MO. ILLUSTRATED.

BY JOEL DORMAN STEELE AND ESTHER B. STEELE.

BARNES BRIEF HISTORY OF THE UNITED STATES,
FOR THE USE OF SCHOOLS AND FOR PRIVATE READING.

BARNES BRIEF HISTORY OF FRANCE, FOR THE USE
OF SCHOOLS AND FOR PRIVATE READING.

BARNES BRIEF HISTORY OF GREECE, WITH SELECT
READINGS FROM STANDARD AUTHORS.

BARNES BRIEF HISTORY OF ROME, WITH SELECT
READINGS FROM STANDARD AUTHORS.

BARNES BRIEF HISTORY OF ANCIENT PEOPLES,
FOR THE USE OF SCHOOLS AND FOR PRIVATE READING.

**BARNES BRIEF HISTORY OF MEDIÆVAL AND
MODERN PEOPLES,** FOR THE USE OF SCHOOLS AND
FOR PRIVATE READING.

**BARNES BRIEF GENERAL HISTORY; ANCIENT, ME-
DIÆVAL, AND MODERN PEOPLES.**

Copyright, 1881, *by A. S. Barnes & Co.*
Copyright, 1909, *by Esther Baker Steele.*

W. P. 11

PREFACE

THE plan of the Barnes Brief History Series has been thoroughly tested in the books already issued, and their extended use and approval are evidence of its general excellence. In this work the political history, which occupies most if not all of the ordinary school-text, is condensed to the salient and essential facts, in order to give room for some account of the literature, religion, architecture, character, and habits of the different nations. Surely, it is as important to know *something* about Plato as *all* about Cæsar; to learn how the ancients wrote their books as how they fought their battles; and to study the virtues of the old Germans and the dawn of our own customs in English home-life, as to trace the petty squabbles of Alexander's successors or the intricacies of the Wars of the Roses.

The general divisions on "Civilization" and "Manners and Customs" were prepared by MRS. J. DORMAN STEELE.

The chapters on "Manners and Customs" and "Scenes in Real Life" represent the people of history as men and women subject to the same wants, hopes, and fears as ourselves, and so bring the distant past near to us. The "Scenes," which are intended only for reading, are the result of a careful study of the monuments in foreign museums, of the ruins themselves, and of the latest authorities on the domestic life of the peoples of other lands and times. Though intentionally written in a semi-romantic style, they are accurate pictures of what *might* have occurred, and some of them are simple transcriptions of the details sculptured in Assyrian alabaster, or painted on Egyptian walls.

It should be borne in mind that the extracts here made from "The Sacred Books of the East" are not comprehensive specimens of their style and teachings, but only gems selected from a mass of matter, much of which is absurd, meaningless, and even revolting. It has not seemed best to cumber a book like this with selections conveying no moral lesson.

The numerous cross-references, the abundant dates in parentheses, the blackboard analyses, the pronunciation of the names in the index, the genealogical tables, the choice reading references at the close of each general subject, and the novel "Historical Recreations" in the appendix, will be of service to both teacher and pupil. An acknowledgment of indebtedness in the preparation of this history is hereby made to the works named in the reading references.

It is hoped that a large class of persons who desire to know something about the progress of historic criticism as well as the discoveries resulting from recent archæological excavations, but who have no leisure to read the ponderous volumes of Brugsch, Layard, Grote, Mommsen, Rawlinson, Ihne, Lanfrey, Froude, Martin, and others, will find this little book just what they need.

CONTENTS.

	PAGE
1. INTRODUCTION	9
2. EGYPT	15
3. BABYLONIA AND ASSYRIA	45
4. PHŒNICIA	73
5. JUDEA	80
6. MEDIA AND PERSIA	88
7. INDIA	105
8. CHINA	109
9. GREECE	113
10. ROME	203
11. APPENDIX:	
1. THE SEVEN WONDERS OF THE WORLD	i
2. THE SEVEN WISE MEN	i
3. HISTORICAL RECREATIONS	ii
4. INDEX	xi

LIST OF MAPS.

	PAGE
MAP OF EARLY RACES AND NATIONS	11
MAP OF ANCIENT EGYPT	16
MAP OF THE ASSYRIAN AND PERSIAN EMPIRES	45
MAP OF PHŒNICIA AND JUDEA IN SOLOMON'S TIME	74
MAP OF CANAAN AND THE WILDERNESS	81
MAP OF GREECE AND HER COLONIES	113
MAP OF HELLAS IN THE HEROIC AGE	118
MAP OF GREECE IN THE TIME OF THE PERSIAN WARS	125
MAP OF THE PLAIN OF MARATHON	126
MAP OF THE VICINITY OF THERMOPYLÆ	130
MAP OF THE VICINITY OF ATHENS AND SALAMIS	135
MAP ILLUSTRATING THE PELOPONNESIAN WAR	142
MAP OF THE EMPIRE OF ALEXANDER	153
MAP OF THE ROMAN EMPIRE AND ITS PROVINCES	203
MAP OF THE EARLY TRIBES AND CITIES OF THE ITALIAN PENINSULA	210
MAP ILLUSTRATING THE PUNIC WARS	228
MAP OF THE DIVISIONS OF ITALIA TO THE TIME OF AUGUSTUS	255
MAP OR PLAN OF ANCIENT ROME	299

ANCIENT PEOPLES.

Examine History, for it is "Philosophy teaching by Experience."
Carlyle.

"Truth comes down to us from the past, as gold is washed down from the mountains of the Sierra Nevada, in minute but precious particles—the *débris* of the centuries."

BLACKBOARD ANALYSIS.

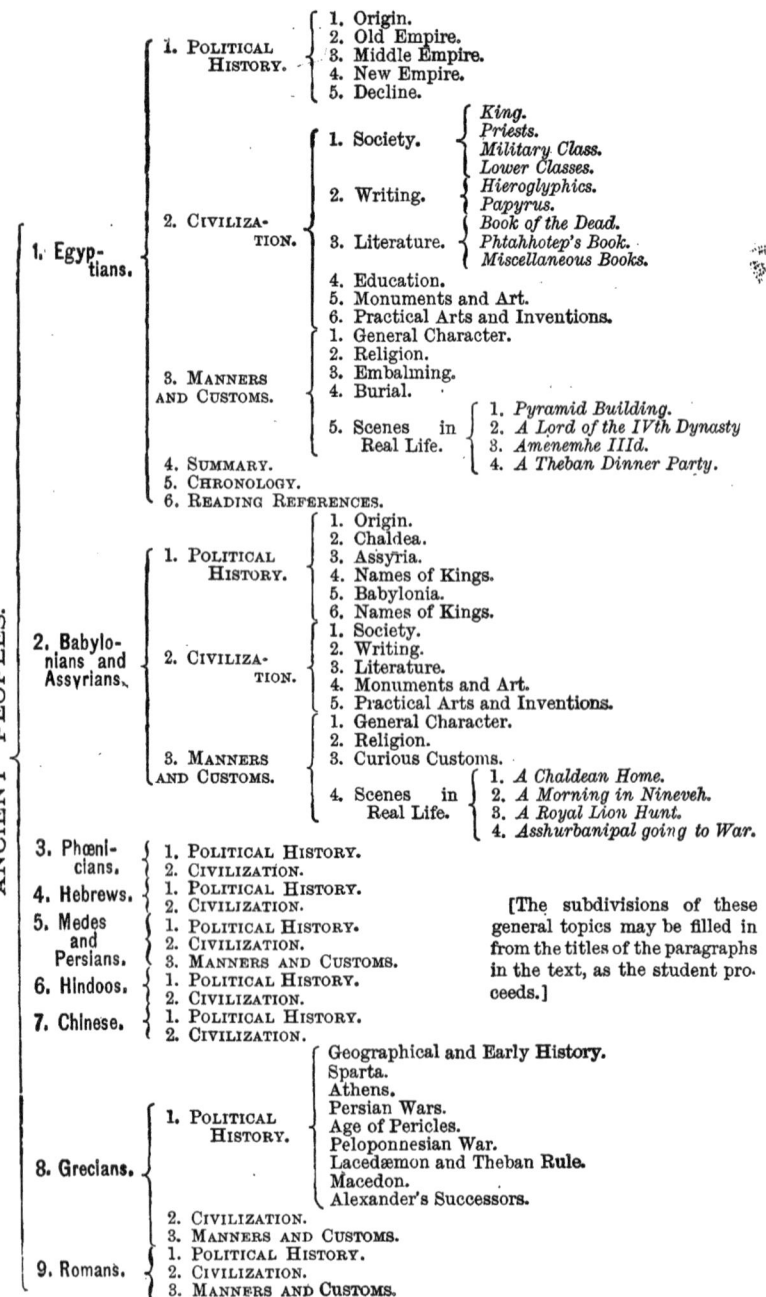

ANCIENT PEOPLES.
- 1. Egyptians.
  - 1. Political History.
    - 1. Origin.
    - 2. Old Empire.
    - 3. Middle Empire.
    - 4. New Empire.
    - 5. Decline.
  - 2. Civilization.
    - 1. Society. { King. Priests. Military Class. Lower Classes. }
    - 2. Writing. { Hieroglyphics. Papyrus. }
    - 3. Literature. { Book of the Dead. Phtahhotep's Book. Miscellaneous Books. }
    - 4. Education.
    - 5. Monuments and Art.
    - 6. Practical Arts and Inventions.
  - 3. Manners and Customs.
    - 1. General Character.
    - 2. Religion.
    - 3. Embalming.
    - 4. Burial.
    - 5. Scenes in Real Life. { 1. Pyramid Building. 2. A Lord of the IVth Dynasty. 3. Amenemhe IIId. 4. A Theban Dinner Party. }
  - 4. Summary.
  - 5. Chronology.
  - 6. Reading References.
- 2. Babylonians and Assyrians.
  - 1. Political History.
    - 1. Origin.
    - 2. Chaldea.
    - 3. Assyria.
    - 4. Names of Kings.
    - 5. Babylonia.
    - 6. Names of Kings.
  - 2. Civilization.
    - 1. Society.
    - 2. Writing.
    - 3. Literature.
    - 4. Monuments and Art.
    - 5. Practical Arts and Inventions.
  - 3. Manners and Customs.
    - 1. General Character.
    - 2. Religion.
    - 3. Curious Customs.
    - 4. Scenes in Real Life. { 1. A Chaldean Home. 2. A Morning in Nineveh. 3. A Royal Lion Hunt. 4. Asshurbanipal going to War. }
- 3. Phœnicians.
  - 1. Political History.
  - 2. Civilization.
- 4. Hebrews.
  - 1. Political History.
  - 2. Civilization.
- 5. Medes and Persians.
  - 1. Political History.
  - 2. Civilization.
  - 3. Manners and Customs.
- 6. Hindoos.
  - 1. Political History.
  - 2. Civilization.
- 7. Chinese.
  - 1. Political History.
  - 2. Civilization.

[The subdivisions of these general topics may be filled in from the titles of the paragraphs in the text, as the student proceeds.]

- 8. Grecians.
  - 1. Political History. { Geographical and Early History. Sparta. Athens. Persian Wars. Age of Pericles. Peloponnesian War. Lacedæmon and Theban Rule. Macedon. Alexander's Successors. }
  - 2. Civilization.
  - 3. Manners and Customs.
- 9. Romans.
  - 1. Political History.
  - 2. Civilization.
  - 3. Manners and Customs.

A Brief History of Ancient Peoples

Introduction

GREAT HALL OF KARNAK.

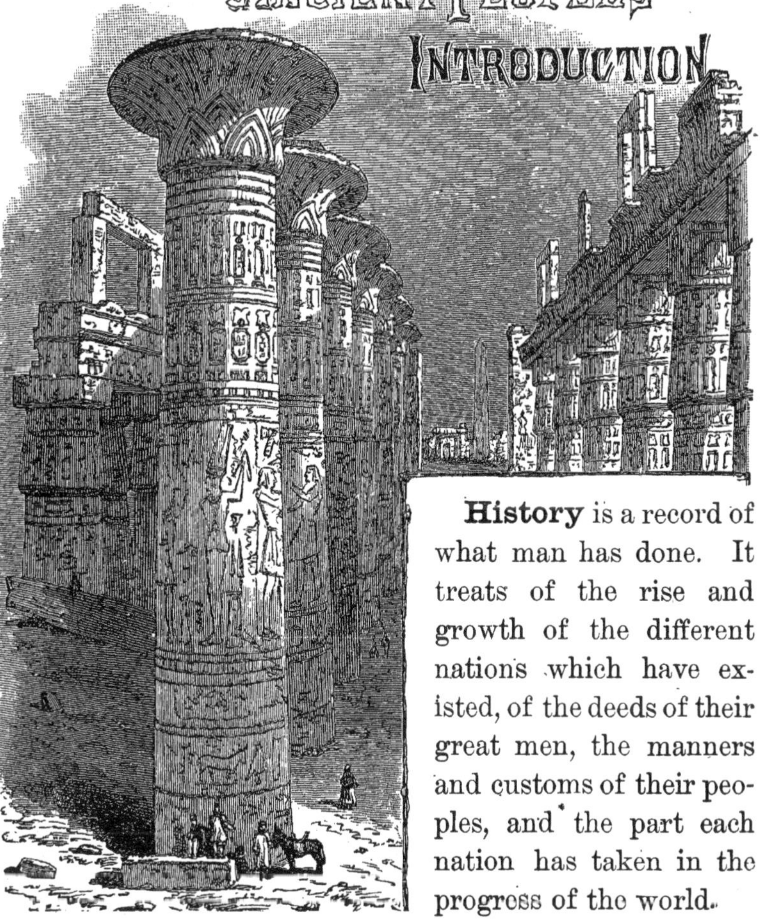

History is a record of what man has done. It treats of the rise and growth of the different nations which have existed, of the deeds of their great men, the manners and customs of their peoples, and the part each nation has taken in the progress of the world.

Dates are reckoned from the birth of Christ, the central point in history. Time before that event is denoted as B. C.; time after, A. D. (*Anno Domini*, in the year of our Lord).[1]

Three Divisions.—History is distinguished as Ancient, Mediæval, and Modern. Ancient history extends from the earliest time to the fall of the Roman Empire (476 A. D.); Mediæval, or the history of the Middle ages, covers about a thousand years, or to the close of the 15th century; and Modern history continues to the present time.

The only Historic Race is the Caucasian, the others having done little worth recording. It is usually divided into three great branches: the *Ar'yan*, the *Semit'ic*, and the *Hamit'ic*. The first of these, which includes the Persians, the Hindoos, and nearly all the European nations, is the one to which we belong. It has always been noted for its intellectual vigor. The second embraces the Assyrians, the Hebrews, the Phœnicians, and the Arabs. It has been marked by religious fervor, and has given to the world the three faiths—Jewish, Christian, and Mohammedan—which teach the worship of one God. The third branch[2] includes the Chaldeans and the Egyptians. It has been remarkable for its massive architecture.

Ancient Aryan Nation.—Asia was probably the birthplace of mankind. In a time far back of all history there lived in Bactria (map, p. 11) a nation that had made considerable progress in civilization. The people called them-

---

[1] This method of reckoning was introduced by Exiguus, a Roman abbot, near the middle of the 6th century. It is now thought that the birth of Christ occurred about four years earlier than the time fixed in our chronology. The Jews still date from the Creation, and the Mohammedans usually from the Hegira (p. 326), 622 A. D.

[2] The Chaldeans were a mixed people, and are variously classed as Semitic, Hamitic, or *Turanian*. Those nations of Europe and Asia that are not Aryan or Semitic are frequently termed Turanian. This branch would then include the Mongols, Chinese, Japanese, Turks, Tartars, Lapps, Finns, Magyars, etc. Iran (e'-rahn), or Aria, the old name of Persia (the "land of light"), is opposed to Turan, the barbarous region around (the "land of darkness"). The Aryan (Indo-European) and Semitic languages have certain resemblances, but the so-called Turanian dialects bear little resemblance to one another.

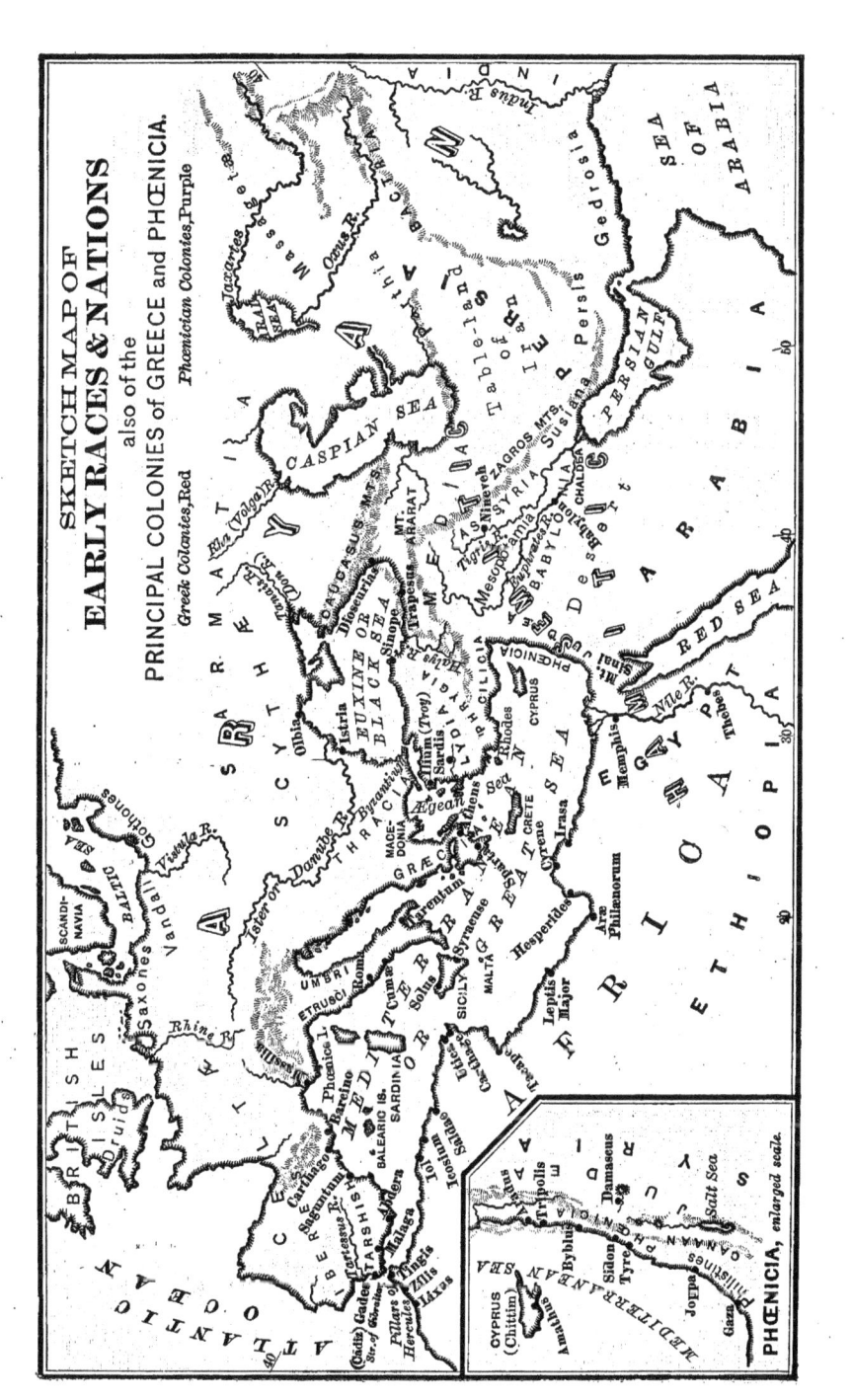

selves Aryas or Aryans,—those who go straight or upward. They dwelt in houses, plowed the soil, ground their grain in mills, rode in vehicles, worked certain metals, calculated up to 100, and had family ties, a government, and a religion.[1]

Aryan Dispersion.—How long our Aryan forefathers lived united in their early home, we have no means of knowing. As they increased in numbers, they would naturally begin to separate. When they moved into distant regions, the bond of union would become weaker, their language would begin to vary, and so the seeds of new tongues and new nations would be sown. To the south-east these Aryan emigrants pushed into Persia and northern India; to the west they gradually passed into Europe, whence, in a later age, they settled Australia and America. In general, they drove before them the previous occupants of the land. The peninsulas of Greece and Italy were probably earliest occupied. Three successive waves of emigration seem to have afterward swept over central Europe. First came the Celts (Kelts), then the Teutons (Germans), and finally the Slaves.[2] Each of these appears to have crowded the preceding one farther west, as we now find the Celts in Ireland and Wales, and the Slaves in Russia and Poland.

---

[1] These views are based on similarities of language. About 600,000,000 people—half the population of the globe—speak Aryan languages. These contain many words which have a family likeness. Thus, *night*, in Latin, is *noct;* in German, *nacht;* and in Greek, *nykt.* *Three*, in Latin, is *tres;* in Greek, *treis;* and in Sanscrit (the ancient language of the Hindoos), *tri.* All such words are supposed to have belonged to one original speech, and to suggest the life of that parent race. Thus we infer that the Aryans had a regular government, since words meaning *king* or *ruler* are the same in Sanscrit, Latin, and English; and that they had a family life, since the words meaning *father, mother, brother, sister,* etc., are the same in these kindred tongues. Some recent theories discredit successive western migrations, place the primitive Aryan home in Europe, and argue that the Indo-Iranians emigrated from Europe to Asia.

[2] This word originally meant "glorious," but came to have its present signification because at one time there were in Europe so many bondsmen of Slavonic birth.

INTRODUCTION. 13

The following table shows the principal peoples which have descended from the ancient races:—

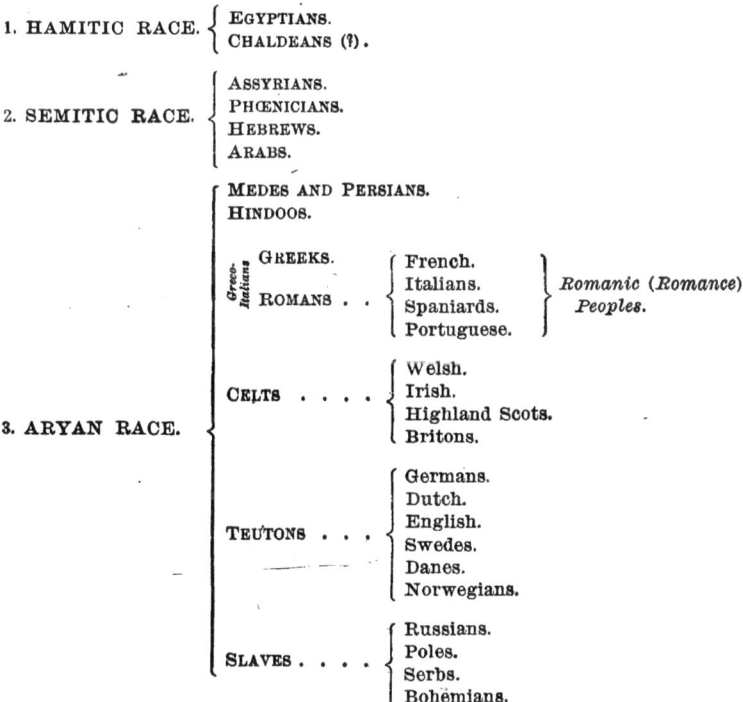

1. HAMITIC RACE. { EGYPTIANS. CHALDEANS (?). }

2. SEMITIC RACE. { ASSYRIANS. PHŒNICIANS. HEBREWS. ARABS. }

3. ARYAN RACE. {
  MEDES AND PERSIANS.
  HINDOOS.
  Græco-Italians { GREEKS. ROMANS .. { French. Italians. Spaniards. Portuguese. } } *Romanic (Romance) Peoples.*
  CELTS .... { Welsh. Irish. Highland Scots. Britons. }
  TEUTONS ... { Germans. Dutch. English. Swedes. Danes. Norwegians. }
  SLAVES .... { Russians. Poles. Serbs. Bohemians. }
}

Commencement of Civil History.—History begins on the banks of the Nile, the Tigris, and the Euphrates.[1] There the rich alluvial soil, the genial climate, and the abundant natural products of the earth, offered every inducement

---

[1] "The Nile valley and the Tigris-Euphrates basin were two great oases in the vast desert which extended from west to east very nearly across the eastern hemisphere. These favored spots were not only the two centers of early civilization, but they were rivals of each other. They were connected by roads fit for the passage of vast armies. Whenever there was an energetic ruler along the Nile or the Tigris-Euphrates, he at once, as if by an inevitable law, attempted the conquest of his competitor for the control of western Asia. In fact, the history of ancient as well as modern Asia is little more than one continuous record of political struggles between Egypt and Mesopotamia, ending only when Europe entered the lists, as in the time of Alexander the Great and the Crusaders."

ANCIENT HISTORY.

to a nomadic people to settle and commence a national life. Accordingly, amid the obscurity of antiquity, we catch sight of Memphis, Thebes, Nineveh, and Babylon,—the ear-

liest cities of the world. The traveler of to-day, wandering among their ruins, looks upon the records of the infancy of civilized man.

EGYPT.

1. THE POLITICAL HISTORY.

The Origin of the civilization which grew up on the banks of the Nile is uncertain. The earliest accounts represent the country as divided into *nomes*, or provinces, and having a regular government. About 2700[1] B. C. Menes (me'-neez), the half-mythical founder of the nation, is said to have conquered Lower Egypt and built Memphis, which he made his capital. Succeeding him, down to the conquest of Egypt by the Persians under Camby'ses (527 B. C.), there were twenty-six dynasties of Pharaohs, or kings. The history of this long period of over 2000 years is divided into that of the Old, Middle, and New Empires.

1. The Old Empire (2700–2080 B. C.).—During this

Geographical Questions.—Locate the capitals of the five early kingdoms of Egypt This, Elephantine (fan'-tē-nā), Mem'phis, Heracleop'olis, Thebes; the Pyramids of Gizeh; the Nile's first cataract. Why is southern Egypt called Upper? Describe Egypt. *Ans.* A flat valley, 2 to 10 miles wide, skirted by low, rocky hills; on the west, the desert; on the east, a mountainous region rich in quarries, extending to the Red Sea. Through this narrow valley, for 600 miles, the Nile rolls its muddy waters northward. About 100 miles from the Mediterranean the hills recede, the valley widens, and the Nile divides into two outlets,—the Damietta and Rosetta. These branches diverge until they enter the sea, 80 miles apart. Anciently there were seven branches, and the triangular space they inclosed was called the Delta, from the Greek letter Δ. As the Nile receives no tributary for the last 1100 miles of its course it becomes smaller toward its mouth.

[1] Before the discoveries of the last century, the chief sources of information on Egypt were (1) Herodotus, a Greek historian who traveled along the Nile about 450 B. C.; (2) Diodo'rus Sic'ulus, another Greek historian, who visited Egypt in the 1st century B. C.; and (3) Man'etho, an Egyptian priest (3d century B. C.) of whose history only fragments now remain. Manetho, who compiled his accounts from archives preserved in the Egyptian temples, has been the main authority on chronology. How many dynasties were contemporaneous is a subject of dispute

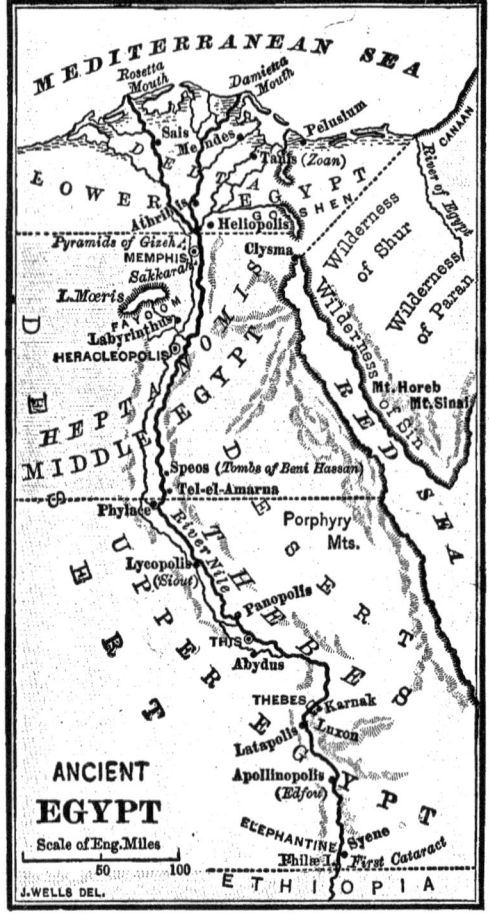

epoch the principal interest clusters about the IVth or Pyramid dynasty, so called because its chief monarchs built the three great pyramids at Gizeh (ghe'-zeh). The best-known of these kings was *Khu'fu*, termed *Cheops* (ke'-ops) by Herodotus. In time, Egypt broke up into kingdoms, Memphis lost its preëminence, and Thebes became the favorite capital.

2. The Middle Empire (2080 B. C.– 1525 B. C.).—When the hundred-gated city, Thebes, rose to sovereign power, a new epoch began in Egyptian history. The XIIth dynasty claimed all the district watered by the Nile, and under its

among Egyptologists, who differ over 3000 years—from 5702 B. C. to 2691 B. C.—on the date for Menes. As the Egyptians themselves had no continuous chronology, but reckoned dates from the ascension of each king, the monuments furnish little help. Of the five recovered lists of kings, only one attempts to give the length of their respective reigns, and this is in 164 fragments. All early Egyptian dates are therefore extremely uncertain, although most Egyptologists differ less than 200 years on those following the foundation of the New Empire. The Egyptian Exploration Fund (founded 1883) and the Archæological Survey (1890) are now systematically investigating monuments and papyri. In this book, what is called the "**Short Chronology**" has been followed.

great kings, the *Sesorta'sens* and the *Amenem'hes*, Ethiopia was conquered. To this dynasty belong the famous Lake Mœris and the Labyrinth (p. 39). The brilliant XIIth dynasty was followed by the weak XIIIth. The divided country invited attack, and the Hyksos ("shepherd kings"), a rude, barbarous race that had already conquered Lower Egypt, finally overran the whole region, and ruled it for 400 years. When at last they were driven out, they left to Egypt a strong, centralized government.

3. The New Empire (1525–527 B. C.).—The native kings having been restored to the throne, Egypt became a united people, with Thebes for the capital. Then followed a true national life of 1000 years. The XVIIIth and XIXth dynasties exalted Egypt to the height of its glory. *Thothmes* I. (tot'-meez) began a system of great Asiatic expeditions, which lasted 500 years. *Thothmes* III.,[1] the Egyptian Alexander the Great, was a magnificent warrior-king. In the sculptures, Nineveh and Babylon pay him tribute; while his ships, manned by Phœnician sailors, sweep the Mediterranean. The Great Temple of Karnak (p. 26) was largely built by him. *Am'unoph* III. was also a famous warrior and builder. Among his structures there remains the Vocal Memnon, which was said to sing when kissed by the rising sun. *Khu-en-A'ten*, the heretic king, rejected the Theban gods for the one-god (*Aten*) sun-worship of his foreign mother. He founded a new capital (now Tel-el-Amarna ruins), but neither capital nor religion long survived him. *Seti* (Mineptah I.) subdued Mesopotamia, and built the Great Hall of Columns at Karnak. At an early age his son,

---

[1] In 1881, between 30 and 40 royal mummies, including those of Thothmes III., Seti I., and Rameses II., were found in a concealed mummy pit near Thebes. The official records on the cases and bandages show that these precious relics had been moved from tomb to tomb, probably for safety, until at some crisis they had been hurriedly deposited here. The **great Rameses** had thus been shifted many times,

Ram'eses II., was made joint king with him, and they reigned together until Mineptah's death. *Rameses* II., the Sesostris the Great of the Greek historians, carried his conquering arms far into Africa. The greatest builder[1] of all the Pharaohs, his gigantic enterprises exhausted the nation. Annual slave-hunting expeditions were made into Ethiopia; prisoners of war were lashed into service; and the lives of the unhappy Hebrews were made "bitter with hard bondage, in mortar, and in brick" (Exod. i. 14). He founded a library inscribed "The Dispensary of the Soul," and gathered about him many men of genius, making his time a golden age of art and literature.

The Decline of Egypt began with the XXth dynasty, when it was no longer able to retain its vast conquests. The tributary peoples revolted, and the country was subdued in turn by the Ethiopians and the Assyrians (p. 49). After nearly a century of foreign rule, *Psammetichus* of the XXVIth dynasty threw off the Assyrian yoke, and restored the Egyptian independence. This monarch, by employing Greek

---

only to land at last in the Gizeh museum, where "his uncovered face now lies for the whole world to gaze upon." In 1891, over 60 mummies of the same period (XVIIth to XXIst dynasties) were found in another tomb near the first. These had escaped the eyes of modern trafficking thieves, and were found as they were left over 3000 years ago. In 1892, Khu-en-Aten's tomb was uncovered. His enemies had shattered his sarcophagus, torn his mummy-wrappings to shreds, and effaced every token of his hated religion. Babylonian clay-tablet dispatches (p. 65) dug up in 1887 at Tel-el-Amarna fix Khu-en-Aten's reign at about 1430 B. C.

[1] Though most of the monuments in Egypt bear his name, it is often inscribed over the erased cartouch (p. 22) of a previous king. One of his first acts after Seti's death was to complete the unfinished temple of Ab'ydus, where his father was buried. A long inscription which he placed at the entrance, ostensibly in praise of the departed Seti, is a good example of his own boastfulness and habit of self-glorification. He says, "The most beautiful thing to behold, the best thing to hear, is a child with a thankful breast, whose heart beats for his father. Wherefore my heart urges me to do what is good for Mineptah. *I will cause them to talk forever and eternally of his son*, who has awakened his name to life." The filial zeal of Rameses so declined in his later years, that, true to his ruling propensity, he chiseled out his father's name and memorials in many places on the temple walls, and substituted his own in their place. **Rameses II. is supposed to be the Pharaoh of the Israelitish Oppression, and his son, Mineptah II., to be the Pharaoh of the Exodus.**

troops, so offended the native warriors that 200,000 of them mutinied, and emigrated to Ethiopia. His successor, *Necho* (Pharaoh-Necho of the Scriptures), maintained a powerful fleet. Under his orders the Phœnician ships rounded the Cape of Good Hope.[1]

The internal prosperity of Egypt still continued, as is shown by the magnificent monuments of this period; but the army was filled with mercenaries, and the last of the Pharaohs fell an easy prey to the fierce-fighting Persians under Cambyses. Egypt, like Babylon (p. 51), was now reduced to a Persian province governed by a satrap.

2. THE CIVILIZATION.

Egyptian Society was divided into distinct classes, so that ordinarily no man could rise higher than the station in which he was born.[2] The priestly and military classes, which included the king, princes, and all men of rank, were far above the others.

The King received the most exalted titles, and his authority was supposed to come direct from the gods. The courtiers, on approaching him, fell prostrate, rubbing the ground with their noses; sometimes, by his gracious consent, they were permitted to touch his sacred knee.[3] That he might be kept pure, he was given from childhood only the choicest and most virtuous companions, and no

---

[1] Twice during this voyage, says Herodotus, the crews, fearing a want of food, landed, drew their ships on shore, sowed grain, and waited for a harvest. The pupil will notice that this was over 2000 years before Vasco da Gama (Hist. U. S., p. 41), to whom is generally accorded the credit of first circumnavigating Africa.

[2] There seems to have been an exception in favor of talented scribes. "Neither descent nor family hampered the rising career of the clever. Many a monument consecrated to the memory of some nobleman who had held high rank at court has the simple but laudatory inscription, 'His ancestors were unknown people.'"—*Brugsch*. Royal preferment was also without restriction.

[3] "When they had come before the king, their noses touched the ground, and their feet lay on the ground for joy; they fell down to the ground, and with their hands they prayed to the king. Thus they lay prostrate and touching the earth before the king, speaking thus: 'We are come before thee, the lord of heaven, lord of the earth, sun, life of the whole world, lord of time, creator of the harvest, dispenser of breath to all men, animator of the gods, pillar of heaven, threshold of the earth, weigher of the balance of the two worlds,'" etc. (Inscription of Rameses II. at Abydus).

hired servant was allowed to approach his person. His daily conduct was governed by a code of rules laid down in the sacred books, which prescribed not only the hourly order and nature of his occupations, but limited even the kind and quantity of his food. He was never suffered to forget his obligations; and one of the offices of the High Priest at the daily sacrifice was to remind him of his duties, and, by citing the good works of his ancestors, to impress upon him the nobility of a well-ordered life. After death he was worshiped with the gods.

The Priests were the richest, the most powerful, and the only learned body of the country. They were not limited to sacred offices, and in their caste comprised all the mathematicians, scientists, lawyers, and physicians of the land. Those priests who "excelled in virtue and wisdom" were initiated into the *holy mysteries*,— a privilege which they shared only with the king and the prince-royal. Among the priesthood, as in the other classes, there were marked distinctions of rank. The High Priests held the most honorable station. Chief among them was the Prophet, who offered sacrifice and libation in the temple, wearing as his insignia a leopard-skin over his robes. The king himself often performed the duties of this office. The religious observances of the priests were rigid. They had long fasts, bathed twice a day and twice in the night, and every third day were shaven from head to foot, the most devout using water which had been tasted by the sacred Ibis. Beans, pork, fish, onions, and various other articles of diet, were forbidden to them; and on certain days, when a religious ceremony compelled every Egyptian to eat a fried fish before his door, the priests burned theirs instead. Their dress was of linen: woolen might be used for an outer, but never for an inner garment, nor could it be worn into a temple. The influence of the priests was immense, since they not only ruled the living, but were supposed to have power to open and shut the gates of eternal bliss to the dead. They received an ample income from the state, and had one third of the land free of tax,—

EGYPTIAN PROPHET.
(From Monument at Thebes.)

an inheritance which they claimed as a special gift from the goddess Isis.

The Military Class also possessed one third of the land, each soldier's share being about eight acres. The army, which numbered 410,000 men, was well disciplined and thoroughly organized. It comprised archers, spearmen, swordsmen, clubmen, and slingers. Each soldier furnished his own equipments, and held himself in constant readiness for duty. He wore a metal coat of mail and a metal or cloth helmet, and carried a large shield made of ox-hide drawn over a wooden frame. The chariots, of which great use was

EGYPTIAN WAR CHARIOT (THEBES).

made in war, were sometimes richly ornamented and inlaid with gold. The king led the army, and was often accompanied by a favorite lion.

Lower Classes.—All the free population not belonging to the priesthood or the military was arbitrarily classified; each trade or occupation having its own rank in the social scale, and inhabiting a certain quarter in the town,—a custom still observed in Cairo. Scribes and architects, whose profession gave them access to temples and palaces, and who had thus a chance to win royal favor, naturally stood highest. Swine-herds were the most despised of all men; the Egyptian, like the Hebrew, Mohammedan, and Indian, considering the pig an unclean animal. Swine-herds were forbidden to enter a temple. As the entire land of Egypt was owned by the king, the priests, and the soldiers, the lower classes could hold no real estate; but they had strongly marked degrees of importance, depending upon the relative rank of the trade to which they were born, and their business success. According to Herodotus, no artisan could engage in any other employment than the one to which he had been brought up. He also tells us that every man was obliged to have some regular means of subsistence, a written declaration of which was deposited periodically with the magistrate. A false account or an unlawful business was punished by death.

Writing.— *Hieroglyphics* [1] (sacred sculptures).—The earliest Egyptian writing was a series of object pictures analogous to that still used by the North American Indians (Brief Hist. U. S., p. 13). Gradually this primitive system was altered and abbreviated into (1) *hieratic* (priestly) writing, the form in which most Egyptian literature is written, and which is read by first resolving it into the original hieroglyphs; and (2) *demotic* (writing of the people), in which all traces of the original pictures are lost. During these changes many meanings became attached to one sign, so that the same hieroglyph might represent an idea, the symbol of an idea, or an abstract letter, syllable, or word. An Egyptian scribe used various devices to explain his meaning. To a hieroglyphic word or syllable he would append one or more of its letters; then, as the letter-signs had different meanings, he

THE NAME OF EGYPT IN HIEROGLYPHICS.

---

[1] So called by the Greeks, who thought them to be mystic religious symbols understood only by the priests. Neither the Greeks nor Romans attempted to decipher them. The discovery of the Rosetta stone (1799) furnished the first clew to their reading. A French engineer, while digging intrenchments on the site of an old temple near the Rosetta mouth of the Nile (Brief Hist. France, p. 229), unearthed a black basalt tablet inscribed in three languages,—hieroglyphic, demotic, and Greek. It proved to be a decree made by the priests in the time of Ptolemy V. (196 B. C.), whom it styled the "god Epiphanes," increasing his divine honors, and ordering that the command should be engraved in the three languages, and placed in all the chief temples. By a comparison of the Greek and Egyptian texts, a principle of interpretation was finally established. Hieroglyphics had hitherto been supposed to represent only ideas or symbols. Twenty-three years after the discovery of the Rosetta stone, the great French scholar François Champollion announced that they express both ideas and sounds. The Egyptians inclosed their royal names and titles in an oval ring or cartouch. Out of the four cartouches, Ptolemaios, Berenike, Kleopatra, and Alexandros, Champollion obtained a partial alphabet, which was completed by subsequent analyses.

would add a picture of some object that would suggest the intended idea. Thus, for the word *bread* 🐦 ◦ he would write the syllable 🐦 (*AQ*) then its complement ◦ (*Q*) and finally, as a determinative, give the picture of a loaf (◦). One would suppose that the form of the loaf would itself have been sufficient, but even that had several interpretations. In like manner the scribe appended the determinative 𓀁 not only to words signifying actions of the mouth, as *eating, laughing, speaking*, etc., but to those of the thought, as *knowing, judging, deciding*. To understand hieroglyphics, a knowledge of the peculiar ideas of the Egyptians is also necessary. It is easy to see that 𓀃 means worship, and 𓀠 crime; but we should hardly interpret 𓅬 as son, or 𓅐 as mother, unless we knew that geese were believed to possess a warm filial nature, and all vultures to be females. Besides these and other complications in hieroglyphic writing, there was no uniform way of arranging sentences. They were written both horizontally and perpendicularly; sometimes part of a sentence was placed one way, and part the other; sometimes the words read from right to left, sometimes from left to right, and sometimes they were scattered about within a given space without any apparent order.

Papyrus.—Books were written and government records kept on papyrus [1] (hence, paper) rolls. These were generally about ten inches wide and often one hundred and fifty feet long. They were written upon with a frayed reed dipped into black or red ink. As the government had the monopoly of the papyrus, it was very costly.

---

[1] The papyrus, or paper reed, which flourished in ancient times so luxuriantly that it formed jungles along the banks of the Nile, is no longer found in Egypt. ("The paper reeds by the brooks, by the mouth of the brooks, . . . shall wither, be driven away, and be no more."—Isa. xix. 7.) It had a large, three-sided, tapering stem, two to three inches broad at the base. The reed was prepared for use by peeling off the smooth bark, and cutting the inner mass of white pith lengthways into thin slices, which were laid side by side with their edges touching one another. A second layer having been placed transversely upon the first, and the whole sprinkled with the muddy Nile water, a heavy press was applied which united them into one mass. It was then dried, and cut into sheets of the required size. Papyrus was in use until the end of the 7th century A. D., when it was superseded by parchment (prepared skins). The latter was also used in Egypt at a very early period; and though it is generally supposed to have been invented by Eumenes, King of Pergamus, in the 2d century B. C., "records written upon skins and kept in the temple" are mentioned in the time of the XVIIIth dynasty, 1200 years before Eumenes (p. 156).

EGYPT.

THE PAPYRUS REED.

For common purposes, therefore, the people used bits of broken pottery, stones, boards, the bark and leaves of trees, and the shoulder-bones of animals.

Literature.—*Book of the Dead.*—The most celebrated Egyptian book is the "Book of the Manifestation to Light," often called the "Book of the Dead." It is a ritual for the use of the soul in its journeys[1] after death, and a copy more or less

---

[1] After death the soul was supposed to descend into the lower world, where, in the great Hall of Justice, before Osiris and his forty-two assessors (p. 34), it was weighed in the infallible scales of Truth. The soul's defense before Osiris is elaborately detailed in the Ritual. If accepted, it became itself an "Osiris," and roamed the universe for three thousand years, always maintaining a mysterious connection with its mummied body, which it visited from time to time. In its wanderings it assumed different forms at will, and the Ritual gives instructions by means of which it could become a hawk, heron, lotus-flower, serpent, crocodile, etc., all emblems of Deity. Various incantations are also given by which it could vanquish the frightful monsters that assailed it in the nether world. The Soul, the Shadow, and the *Ka* were at last reunited to the body in a blissful immortality. The *Ka* (p. 38) was a man's mysterious "double," an ethereal counterpart distinct from the soul, which dwelt in

complete, according to the fortune of the deceased, was inclosed in the mummy-case. This strange book contains some sublime passages, and many of its chapters date from the earliest antiquity. As suggestive of Egyptian morals, it is interesting to find in the soul's defense before Osiris such sentences as these:—

"I have not been idle; I have not been intoxicated; I have not told secrets; I have not told falsehoods; I have not defrauded; I have not slandered; I have not caused tears; I have given food to the hungry, drink to the thirsty, and clothes to the naked."

Phtah-ho'tep's Book.—Good old Prince Phtah-hotep, son of a king of the Vth dynasty, wrote a moral treatise full of excellent advice to the young people of 4000 years ago. This book, now preserved in Paris, is believed to be the oldest in the world. The following extracts are noticeable:—

On Filial Obedience. "The obedient son shall grow old and obtain favor; thus have I, myself, become an old man on earth and have lived 110 years in favor with the king, and approved by my seniors."

On Freedom from Arrogance. "If thou art become great, after thou hast been humble, and if thou hast amassed riches after poverty, being because of that the first in thy town; if thou art known for thy wealth and art become a great lord, let not thy heart become proud because of thy riches, for it is God who is the author of them. Despise not another who is as thou wast; be towards him as towards thy equal."

On Cheerfulness. "Let thy face be cheerful as long as thou livest; has any one come out of the coffin after having once entered it?"

Miscellaneous Books.—Several treatises on medicine have been deciphered. They generally abound in charms and adjurations. Works on rhetoric and mathematics, and various legal and political documents, are extant. Epistolary correspondence is abundant. A letter addressed by a priest to one of the would-be poets of the time contains this wholesome criticism:—

"It is very unimportant what flows over thy tongue, for thy compositions are very confused. Thou tearest the words to tatters, just as it comes into thy mind. Thou dost not take pains to find out their force for thyself. If thou rushest wildly forward thou wilt not succeed. I have struck out for thee the end of thy composition, and I return to thee thy descriptions. It is a confused medley when one hears it; an uneducated person could not understand it. It is like a man from the lowlands speaking with a man from Elephantine."

A few works of fiction exist which belong to the XIIth dynasty, and there are many beautiful hymns addressed to the different gods. A long and popular poem, the *Epic of Pentaur*, which celebrated

the tomb with his mummy while his soul performed its appointed pilgrimage. The soul which was rejected by Osiris and his forty-two assessors, took the form of a pig or other unclean animal, and, if incorrigible, was finally annihilated.

the deeds of Rameses II., won the prize in its time as an heroic song, and was engraved on temple walls at Abydus, Luxor, Karnak, and the Ramesseum. It is sometimes styled "The Egyptian Iliad."

Education was under the control of the priesthood. Great attention was paid to mathematics and to writing, of which the Egyptians were especially fond. Geometry and mensuration were important, as the yearly inundation of the Nile produced constant disputes concerning property boundaries. In music, only those songs appointed by law were taught, the children being carefully guarded from any of doubtful sentiment. As women were treated with great dignity and respect in Egypt, reigning as queens and serving in the holiest offices of the temple, they probably shared in the advantages of schooling. The common people had little education, except what pertained to their calling. Reading and writing were so difficult as to be considered great accomplishments.

QUEEN AIDING KING IN TEMPLE SERVICE (THEBES).

Monuments and Art.—Stupendous size and mysterious symbolism characterize all the monuments of this strange people. They built immense pyramids holding closely hidden chambers: gigantic temples [1] whose massive entrances, guarded by great stone statues, were approached by long avenues of colossal sphinxes; vast temple-courts, areas, and halls in which were forests of carved and painted columns; and lofty obelisks, towers, and sitting statues,[2]

---

[1] The temples were isolated by huge brick inclosures, and wore an air of solemn mystery. None but priests could enter the holy precincts. The Great Temple of Karnak (see ill. p. 9) was 1200 feet long by 360 wide; its Great Hall, 340 by 170 feet, contained 134 painted columns, some of them 70 feet high and 12 feet in diameter. This temple was joined to one at Luxor by an avenue of sphinxes two miles long. Other famous monuments are the *Memnonium*, built by Amunoph III.; the *Ramesseum*, by Rameses II.; and the *Medinet-Abou* palace of Rameses III. The construction and various reparations of some of these vast piles of stone cover immense periods of time. Excavations made in 1887 at Tell-Basta, the ancient Bubastis, show that a temple to Pasht, the cat-headed goddess (p. 30), existed there from the time of the Pyramid dynasty down to 150 B. C.

[2] Rameses II. reared gigantic self-statues all over Egypt. A wall-painting discovered at Luxor in 1891 shows six colossi in front of the temple at its dedication. His sitting statue at the Memnonium was 22 feet across the shoulders, and weighed nearly 900 tons; his standing statue at Tanis towered 92 feet above the plain.

which still endure, though desert winds and drifting sands have beaten upon them for thousands of years.

Sculpture, Painting, Statuary.—Egyptian granite is so hard that it is cut with difficulty by the best steel tools of to-day; yet the ancient sculptures are sometimes graven to the depth of several inches, and show an exquisite finish and accuracy of detail. Painting was usually combined with sculpture, the natural hue of the objects represented being crudely imitated. Blue, red, green, black, yellow, and white were the principal colors. Red, which typified the sun, and blue, the color of the sky reflected in the Nile, were sacred tints. Tombs, which were cut in the solid rock, had no outer ornamentation, but the interior was gayly painted with scenes from every-day life. Sarcophagi and the walls which inclosed temples were covered both inside and outside with scenes or inscriptions. The painted scenes were sometimes taken from the "Book of the Dead"; often they were vivid delineations of the royal conquests. The proportion, form, color, and expression of every statue were fixed by laws prescribed by the priests, the effect most sought being that of immovable repose.[1] A wooden statue found at Sakkarah, and belonging to one of the earliest dynasties, is remarkable for its fine expression and evident effort at portraiture.[2]

SON OF RAMESES III.
(Thebes.)

Mode of Drawing, Perspective.—In drawing the human form, the entire body was traced, after which the drapery was added (see cut). Several artists were employed on one picture. The first drew squares of a definite size, upon which he sketched in red an outline of the desired figure; the next corrected and improved it in black; the sculptor then followed with his chisel and other tools; and finally the most important artist of all laid on the prescribed colors. The king was drawn on a much larger scale than his subjects, his dignity being suggested by his colossal size. Gods and

[1] All Egyptian statues have a stiff, rigid pose, and are generally fastened at the back to a pillar. In standing statues the arms are held close to the sides; in seated, the knees are pressed together, and the hands spread out upon them, palms down.

[2] When Mariette discovered in the Memphite necropolis this now famous statue of a man standing and holding in his hand the *baton* of authority, the *fellahs* (peasants) saw in it a wonderful resemblance to their own rustic tax-assessor, the dignitary of the place. An astonished fellah shouted out, "It's the Sheikh-el-Beled!" His companions took up the cry, and the statue has been called by that name ever since. This incident illustrates the persistency of national type.

goddesses were frequently represented with the head of an animal on a human form. There was no idea of perspective, and the general effect of an Egyptian painted scene was that of grotesque stiffness.

Practical Arts and Inventions.—We have seen how the Egyptians excelled in cutting granite. Steel was perhaps in use as early as the IVth dynasty, as pictures on the Memphite tombs seem to represent butchers sharpening their knives on a bar of that metal. Great skill was shown in alloying, casting, and soldering metals. Some of their bronze implements, though buried for ages, and since exposed to the damp of European climates, are still smooth and bright. They possessed the art of imparting elasticity to bronze or brass, and of overlaying bronze with a rich green by means of acids.

Glass bottles are represented in the earliest sculptures, and the Egyptians had their own secrets in coloring, which the best Venetian glass-makers of to-day are unable to discover. Their glass mosaics were so delicately ornamented that some of the feathers of birds and other details can be made out only with a lens, which would imply that this means of magnifying was used in Egypt. Gems and precious stones were successfully imitated in glass; and Wilkinson says, "The mock pearls found by me in Thebes were so well counterfeited that even now it is difficult with a strong lens to detect the imposition."

EGYPTIAN EASY-CHAIR.

Goldsmiths washing and working gold are seen on monuments of the IVth dynasty; and gold and silver wire were woven into cloth and used in embroidery as early as the XIIth dynasty. Gold rings, bracelets, armlets, necklaces, ear-rings, vases, and statues were common in the same age, the cups being often beautifully engraved and studded with precious stones. Objects of art were sometimes made of silver or bronze inlaid with gold, or of baser metals gilded so as to give the effect of solid gold.

Veneering was extensively practiced, and in sculptures over 3300 years old workmen are seen with glue-pot on the fire, fastening the rare woods to the common sycamore and acacia. In cabinet-work Egypt excelled, and house-furniture assumed graceful and elegant forms.

THE CIVILIZATION.

Flax and Cotton were grown, and great perfection was reached in spinning and weaving. Linen cloth of exquisite texture has been found in Memphite tombs, and the strong flax-strings used

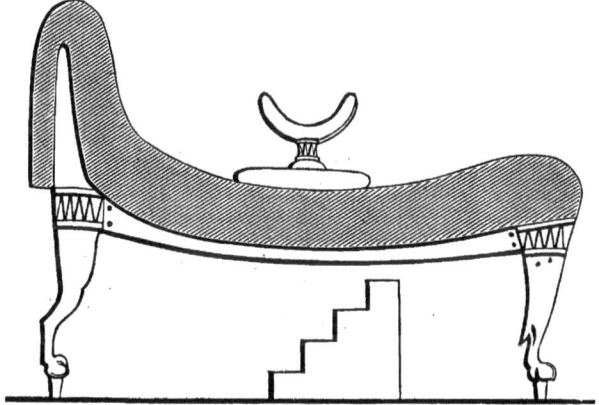

EGYPTIAN COUCH, PILLOW, AND STEPS.

for fowling-nets were so finely spun that it was said "a man could carry nets enough to surround a whole wood." Finally, wooden hoes, shovels, forks, and plows, toothed sickles, and drags aided the farmer in his work; the carpenter had his ax, hammer, file, adz, hand-saw, chisel, drill, plane, right angle, ruler, and plummet; the glass-worker and gem-cutter used emery powder, if not a lapidary's

EGYPTIAN MUSICIANS
(THE GUITAR, HARP, AND DOUBLE PIPE).

wheel; the potter had his wheel upon which he worked the clay after he had kneaded it with his feet; the public weigher had stamped weights and measures, and delicate scales for balancing the gold and silver rings used as currency; musicians played on pipes, harps, flutes,[1] guitars, lyres, tambourines, and cymbals; while drum and trumpet cheered the soldier in his march.

---

[1] In 1889 several flutes were found in an Egyptian tomb. These instruments, which are over three thousand years old, give the exact sounds of our diatonic scale.

3. THE MANNERS AND CUSTOMS.

General Character.—The Egyptians were mild in disposition, polite in manners, reverential to their elders and superiors, extremely loyal and patriotic, and intensely religious. They have been called a gloomy people, but their sculptures reveal a keen sense of humor and love of caricature. They were especially fond of ceremonies and of festivals. Their religion formed a part of their every-day life, and was interwoven with all their customs.

Religion.—The Egyptian priests believed in one invisible, over-ruling, self-created God; the immortality of the soul; a judgment after death; the final annihilation of the wicked; and the ultimate absorption of the good into the eternal Deity.

"*God* created his own members, which are *the gods,*" they said; and so out of one great God grew a host of lesser ones, regarded by the priests as only His attributes and manifestations, but becoming to the people distinct and separate divinities. Natural objects and principles were thus deified,—the soil, the sky, the east, the west, even the general idea of time and space. Each month and day had its own god. The Nile, as the source of the country's fertility, was especially revered; and the conflict of God with sin was seen in the life-giving river, and the barren, encroaching desert.

The Sun, especially in later times, was the great exponent of Deity. His mysterious disappearance each night, and his return every morning to roll over the heavens with all the splendor of the preceding day, were events full of symbolic meaning. The rising sun was the beautiful young god Horus. In his mid-day glory he was Ra, as he neared the western horizon he became Tum, and during the night he was Amun. Each of these gods, as well as the many others connected with the sun, had his own specific character. This complex sun-god was imagined to float through the sky in a boat, accompanied by the souls of the Supremely Blest, and at night to pass into the regions of the dead.

Triad of Orders.—There were three orders of gods. The first [1]

---

[1] In Thebes, *Amun-Ra* (the "Concealed God" or "Absolute Spirit") headed the deities of the first order. He was represented as having the head of a ram, the hieroglyphic of a ram signifying also concealment. In Memphis, *Phtah* ("Father of the Beginnings"), the Creator, was chief. his symbol was the *Scarabæus,* or beetle, an image of which was placed on the heart of every mummy. Phtah was father of *Ra,* the sun-god. Ra was, in the mystic sense, that which is to-day, the existing present. The hawk was his emblem. *Pasht,* his sister, one of the personifications of the sun's strong rays, sometimes healthful, sometimes baneful, was both loved and feared. She was especially worshiped at Bubastis; but her statues, having the head

was for the priesthood, and represented the ideal and spiritual part of the religion; the second impersonated human faculties and powers; and the third—the most popular of all among the people—was made up of forms and forces in nature.

Triads of Gods.—Each town or city had its specially honored triad of deities to whom its temples were dedicated. The triads often consisted of father, mother, and son, but sometimes of two gods and a king. *Osiris*, who with *Isis* and *Horus* formed the most celebrated of these triads, was worshiped throughout the land. So popular were these deities that it has been said, "With the exception of Amun and Neph, they comprise all Egyptian mythology."[1]

Animal Worship.—As early as the II[d] dynasty certain animals had come to be regarded as emblems or even incarnations of the gods. The bull Apis, whose temple was at Memphis, was supposed to be inhabited by Osiris himself, and the sacred presence of the god to be attested by certain marks on the body of the animal. Apis was consulted as an

BRONZE FIGURE OF APIS.

---

of a cat, are common all over Egypt. *Neph*, often confounded with Amun, and, like him, wearing the ram's head, was the Divine Breath or Spirit pervading matter; sheep were sacred to him. *Thoth*, son of Neph, was god of intelligence; the ibis was his emblem. *Sate*, the wife of Neph and one of the forms of Isis, was the goddess of vigilance; she was the eastern sky waiting for the morning sun. *Athor*, goddess of love, was the beautiful western sky, wife of the evening sun, taking the wearied traveler to rest in her arms after each day's labor; the cow was her emblem. *Neith*, wife of Phtah, was goddess of wisdom; she was the night sky which induces reflection. *Maut*, the Mother Goddess and greatest of the sky divinities,—which were all feminine,—was the cool night sky tenderly brooding over the hot, exhausted earth; the shrew-mouse was sacred to her. *Typhon* was the common enemy of all the other gods; his emblems were the pig, the ass, and the hippopotamus.

[1] It was related that Osiris once went about the earth doing good; that he was slain by Set (Typhon), his brother; that his wife, Isis, by prayers and invocations, assisted in his resurrection; and that finally Horus, his son, avenged his wrongs and destroyed Set. In this myth Osiris represents Divine Goodness; Isis is the Love of Goodness; Set, the principle of Evil; and Horus, Divine Triumph. Osiris had a multitude of characters. He was the Nile; he was the sun; he was the judge of the dead; from him all souls emanated, and in him all justified souls were swallowed up at last. To know "the mysteries of Osiris" was the glory of the priesthood. Isis, too, appeared in many forms, and was called by the Greeks "she of the ten-thousand names." Mystic legends made her the mother, wife, sister, and daughter of Osiris; while Horus was their son and brother, and was Osiris himself.

oracle, and his breath was said to confer upon children the gift of prophecy. When an Apis died, great was the mourning until the priests found his successor, after which the rejoicing was equally demonstrative. The cost of burying the Apis was so great as sometimes to ruin the officials who had him in charge.[1] The calf Mnevis at Heliopolis, and the white cow of Athor at Athribis, were also reverenced as incarnations of Deity. Other animals were considered as only emblems. Of these, the hawk, ape, ibis, cat,[2] and asp were everywhere worshiped; but crocodiles, dogs, jackals, frogs, beetles, and shrew-mice, as well as certain plants and vegetables, were venerated in different sections of the country. Those sacred in one nome were often in others hated and hunted or used for food. Thus, at Thebes the crocodile and the sheep were worshiped, while the goat was eaten; at Mendes the sheep was eaten and the goat worshiped; and at Apollinopolis the crocodile was so abhorred as an emblem of the evil spirit, that the people set apart an especial day to hunt and kill as many crocodiles as possible, throwing the dead bodies before the temple of their own god.

The *crocodile* was principally worshiped about Lake Mœris in the Fayoom. A chosen number of these animals was kept in the temples, where they were given elegant apartments, and treated to every luxury, at public expense. Let us imagine a crocodile fresh from a warm, sumptuous bath, anointed with the most precious ointments, and perfumed with fragrant odors, its head and neck glittering with jeweled ear-rings and necklace, and its feet with bracelets, wallowing on a rich and costly carpet to receive the worship of intelligent human beings. Its death was mourned as a public calamity; its body, wrapped in linen, was carried to the embalmers, attended by a train of people, weeping, and beating their breasts in grief; then, having been expensively embalmed and bandaged in gayly colored mummy-cloths, amid imposing ceremonies it was laid away in its rock sepulcher.

Embalming.—This art was a secret known only to those priests

---

[1] Ancient authorities state that no Apis was allowed to live over twenty-five years. If he attained that age, he was drowned with great ceremony in the Nile. The following inscription upon a recently discovered memorial stone erected to an Apis of the XXII^d dynasty, shows that at least one Apis exceeded that age: "This is the day on which the god was carried to his rest in the beautiful region of the west, and was laid in the grave, in his everlasting house and in his eternal abode." . .

"His glory was sought for in all places. After many months he was found in the temple of Phtah, beside his father, the Memphian god Phtah." . . . "The full age of this god was 26 years."

[2] When a cat died in any private dwelling, the inmates shaved their eyebrows; when a dog died, they shaved their entire bodies. The killing of a cat, even accidentally, was reckoned a capital offense. All sacred animals were embalmed, and buried with impressive ceremonies.

who had it in charge. The mummy was more or less elaborately prepared, according to the wealth and station of the deceased. In the most expensive process the brain and intestines were extracted, cleansed with palm-wine and aromatic spices, and either returned to the body or deposited in vases which were placed in the tomb with the coffin.[1] The body was also cleansed, and filled with a mixture of resin and aromatics, after which it was kept in niter for seventy days. It was then wrapped in bands of fine linen smeared on the inner side with gum. There were sometimes a thousand yards of bandages on one mummy. A thick papyrus case, fitted while damp to the exact shape of the bandaged body, next inclosed it. This case was richly painted and ornamented, the hair and features of the deceased being imitated, and eyes inlaid with brilliant enamel inserted. Sometimes the face was covered with heavy gold leaf. Often a network of colored beads was spread over the body, and a winged scarabæus (p. 30) placed upon the breast. A long line of hieroglyphics extending down the front told the name and quality of the departed. The inner case was inclosed in three other

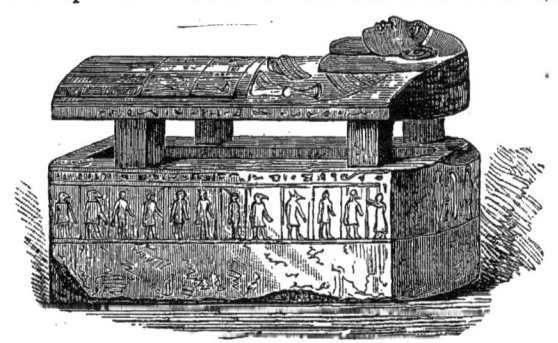

A MUMMY IN BANDS.

AN EGYPTIAN SARCOPHAGUS.

cases of the same form, all richly painted in different patterns. A wooden or carved stone sarcophagus was the final receptacle in the tomb.[2]

[1] "So careful were the Egyptians to show proper respect to all that belonged to the human body, that even the sawdust of the floor where they cleansed it was tied up in small linen bags, which, to the number of twenty or thirty, were deposited in vases, and buried near the tomb."—*Wilkinson.*

[2] In a less expensive mode of embalming, the internal parts were dissolved by oil of cedar, after which the body was salted with niter, as before. The ordinary

34   EGYPT.

Burial.—When any person died, all the women of the house left the body and ran out into the streets, wailing, and throwing dust upon their heads. Their friends and relatives joined them as they went, and if the deceased was a person of quality, others accompanied them out of respect. Having thus advertised the death, they returned home and sent the body to the embalmers. During the entire period of its absence they kept up an ostentatious show of grief, sitting unwashed and unshaven, in soiled and torn garments, singing dirges and making lamentation. After the body was restored to them, if they wished to delay its burial, they placed it in a movable wooden closet standing against the wall of the principal room in the house. Here, morning and evening, the members of the family came to weep over and embrace it, making offerings to the gods in its behalf. Occasionally it was brought out to join in festivities given in its honor (p. 42). The time having come to entomb it, an imposing procession was formed, in the midst of which the mummy was drawn upright on a sledge to the sacred lake adjoining every large city. At this point forty-two chosen officials—emblematical of the forty-two judges in the court of Osiris (p. 24)—formed a semicircle around the mummy, and formal inquiries were made as to its past life and character. If no accusation was heard, an eulogium was pronounced, and the body was passed over the lake. If, however, an evil life was proven, the lake could not be crossed, and the distressed friends were compelled to leave the body of their disgraced relative unburied, or to carry it home, and wait till their gifts and devotions, united to the prayers of the priesthood, should pacify the gods. Every Egyptian, the king included, was subjected to the "trial of the dead," and to be refused interment was the greatest possible dishonor. The best security a creditor could have was a mortgage on the mummies of his debtor's ancestors. If the debt were not paid, the delinquent forfeited his own burial and that of his entire family.

A WOMAN EMBRACING HER HUSBAND'S MUMMY.
(Thebes.)

mummy-cloth was coarse, resembling our sacking. The bodies of the poor were simply cleansed and salted, or submerged in liquid pitch. These black, dry, heavy, bad-smelling relics are now used by the fellahs for fuel. It is a fact that few mummies of children have been discovered. The priests had the monopoly of everything connected with embalming and burial, and they not only resold tombs which had been occupied, but even trafficked in second-hand mummy-cases.

The mummies of the poorer classes were deposited in pits in the plain or in recesses cut in the rock, and then closed up with masonry; those of the lowest orders were wrapped in coarse cloth mats, or a bundle of palm-sticks, and buried in the earth or huddled into the

THE FUNERAL OF A MUMMY (AFTER BRIDGEMAN).

general repository. Various articles were placed in the tombs, especially images of the deceased person, and utensils connected with his profession or trade (p. 38). Among the higher classes these objects were often of great value, and included elegant vases, jewelry, and important papyri.

SCENES IN REAL LIFE.

Scene I.—*Pyramid Building* (IVth dynasty).[1]—Let us imagine ourselves in Egypt about 2400 B. C. It is the middle of November. The Nile, which, after its yearly custom, began to rise in June, changing its color rapidly from a turbid red to a slimy green and then again to red, overflowed its banks in early August, and, spreading its waters on either side, made the country to look like an immense lake dotted with islands. For the last month it has been gradually creeping back to its winter banks, leaving everywhere behind it a fresh layer of rich brown slime. Already the farmers are out with their light wooden

[1] Over seventy Egyptian pyramids have been discovered and explored, all situated on the edge of the desert, west of the Nile. The three Great Pyramids of Gizeh built by Khufu and his successors are the most celebrated. The Great Pyramid built in steps at Sakkarah, and said to date from the Ist or IId dynasty, is believed by many to be the oldest monument in Egypt.

plows and hoes, or are harrowing with bushes the moist mud on which the seed has been thrown broadcast, and which is to be trampled down by the herds driven in for the purpose. The first crop of clover is nearing its harvest; by proper care and a persistent use of the *shadoof*,[1] three more crops will be gathered from the same ground. The crocodile and the hippopotamus haunt the river shores; in the desert the wolf, jackal, and hyena prowl; but the greatest scourge and torment of the valley are the endless swarms of flies and gnats which rise from the mud of the subsiding Nile.

A MODERN SHADOOF.

King Khufu of the IVth dynasty is now on the throne, and the Great Pyramid, his intended tomb, is in process of erection near Memphis, the city founded by Menes three hundred years ago. One hundred thousand dusky men are toiling under a burning sun, now quarrying in the limestone rock of the Arabian hills, now tugging at creaking ropes and rollers, straining every nerve and muscle under the rods of hard overseers, as along the solid causeway [2] and up the inclined plane they drag the gigantic stones they are to set in place. Occasionally a detachment is sent up the river in boats to Syene to bring fine red granite, which is to be polished for casings to the inner passages and chambers. Not a moment is lost from work save when they sit down in companies on the hot sand to eat their government rations of "radishes, onions, and garlics," the aggregate cost of which is to be duly inscribed upon the pyramid itself. So exhausting is this forced and unpaid labor that four times a year a fresh levy is needed to take the place of the worn-out toilers. When this pyramid is finished,—and it will continue to grow as long as the king shall live,[3]—it will stand

---

[1] The pole and bucket with which water was drawn from the Nile to irrigate the land. It is still in use in Egypt.

[2] It took ten years to build the causeway whereon the stone was brought. The construction of the pyramid required twenty years more. Herodotus thought the causeway as great a work as the pyramid itself, and described it as built of polished stone, and ornamented with carvings of animals.

[3] As soon as a Pharaoh mounted his throne, he gave orders to some nobleman to plan the work and cut the stone for the royal tomb. The kernel of the future edifice

480 feet high, with a base covering 13 acres. Its sides, which exactly face the four cardinal points, will be cased with highly polished stone fitted into the angles of the steps; the workmen beginning at the apex and working downward, leaving behind them a smooth, glassy surface which cannot be scaled. There will be two sepulchral chambers with passages leading thereto, and five smaller chambers,[1] built to relieve the pressure of so great a mass of stone. The king's chamber, which is situated in the center of the pyramid and is to hold the royal sarcophagus, will be ventilated by air-shafts, and defended by a succession of granite portcullises. But Khufu will not rest here, for his oppression and alleged impiety have so angered the people that they will bury him elsewhere, leaving his magnificently planned tomb, with its empty sarcophagus, to be wondered and speculated over, thousands of years after his ambitious heart has ceased to beat.

Meantime other great public works are in progress.[2] Across the arm of the Red Sea, on the peninsula of Sinai,—not sacred Sinai yet, for there are centuries to come before Moses,—are the king's copper and turquoise mines. Sculpture is far advanced; and images of gold, bronze, ivory, and ebony are presented to the gods. The whole land swarms with a rapidly increasing population; but food is abundant,[3] raiment little more than a name, and lodging free on the warm earth. Besides, the numbers are kept down by a royal policy which rears enormous monuments at the price of flesh and blood. The overwrought gangs constantly sink under their burdens, and hasten on to crowd the common mummy-pits in the limestone hills.

---

was raised on the limestone soil of the desert in the form of a small pyramid built in steps, of which the well constructed and finished interior formed the king's eternal dwelling, with the stone sarcophagus lying on the rocky floor. A second covering was added, stone by stone, on the outside of this kernel, a third to this second, and to this a fourth, the mass growing greater the longer the king lived. Every pyramid had its own proper name. That of Khufu bore a title of honor, "The Lights."—*Brugsch's Egypt.*

[1] In one of these small chambers, Colonel Vyse, who was the first to enter them, found the royal name scrawled in red ocher on the stones, as if done by some idle overseer in the quarry. It is a proof of the architectural skill of the Egyptians, that in such a mass of stone they could construct chambers and passages which, with a weight of millions of tons pressing upon them, should preserve their shape without crack or flaw for thousands of years.

[2] Near Khufu's Pyramid is the Great Sphinx, a massive union of solid rock and clumsy masonry, 146 feet long. This recumbent, human-headed lion, an image of the sun-god Horus, is believed to be older than the pyramid itself. Under the sand close by lies a vast temple constructed of enormous blocks of black or rose-colored granite and oriental alabaster without sculpture or ornament. Here, in a well, were found fragments of splendid statues of Shafra, the successor of Khufu.

[3] "The whole expense of a child from infancy to manhood," says Diodorus, "is not more than twenty drachmas" (about four dollars).

Scene II.—*A Lord of the IVth Dynasty* has large estates managed by a host of trained servants. He is not only provided with baker, butler, barber, and other household domestics, but with tailor, sail-maker, goldsmith, tile-glazer, potter, and glass-blower.[1] His musicians, with their harps, pipes, and flutes, his acrobats, pet dogs, and apes, amuse his leisure hours. He has his favorite games of chance or skill, which, if he is too indolent to play himself, his slaves play in his presence. He is passionately fond of hunting, and of fishing in the numerous canals which intersect the country and are fed from the Nile. He has small papyrus canoes, and also large, square-sailed, double-masted boats, in which he sometimes takes out his wife and children for a moonlight sail upon the river; his harpers sitting cross-legged at the end of the boat, and playing the popular Egyptian airs. But he does not venture out into the Mediterranean with his boats. He has a horror of the sea, and to go into that impure region would be a religious defilement. On land he rides in a seat strapped between two asses. He has never heard of horses or chariots, nor will they appear in Egypt for a thousand years to come. He wears a white linen robe, a gold collar, bracelets and anklets, but no sandals. For his table he has wheaten or barley bread, beef, game, fruits and vegetables, beer, wine, and milk. His scribes keep careful record of his flocks and herds, his tame antelopes, storks, and geese, writing with a reed pen on a papyrus scroll. He has his tomb cut in the rocks near the royal pyramid, where he sometimes goes to oversee the sculptors and painters who are ornamenting the walls of its entrance-chambers with pictures[2] of his dignities, riches, pleasures, and manner of life. Directly below these painted rooms, perhaps at a depth of seventy feet, is the carefully hidden mummy-pit. Here, in recesses cut

---

[1] Such a household must have been a center of practical education; and an enterprising Egyptian boy, dearly as he loved his games of ball and wrestling, was likely to be well versed in the processes of every trade. (See Brief Hist. France, p. 33.)

[2] These pictures, with various articles stored in the tomb, served a magical purpose, for the benefit of the *Ka* (p. 24). In the paintings on the walls, the Ka saw himself going to the chase, and he went to the chase; eating and drinking with his wife, and he ate and drank with her. The terra-cotta statuettes, armed with hoe, flail, and seed-sack, worked the fields, drew the water, and reaped the grain, in his phantom life of industry, while the painted workmen on the papyri made his shoes, cooked his food, and carried him to hunt in the desert or to fish in the marshes. Besides the periodical offerings of fresh baked meats, wine, and fruits brought by ministering friends, the Ka was sometimes furnished with mummied meats packed in sealed hampers; and, to make sure of an abundance, a magical formula, placed on the funerary tablet in the entrance-chamber of the tomb, insured to him ghostly supplies of "thousands of loaves, thousands of beeves, thousands of geese," etc., down to the end of the weary cycle of waiting. If, finally, when that glad hour came, the mummy had perished, its place could be supplied by a portrait statue, which was snugly concealed behind the solid masonry.

in the sides and bottom, will finally be placed the mummies of this lord and his family. Meantime he strives to be true to his gods, obedient to his king, and affectionate to his household; for thus he hopes to pass the rigid ordeals which follow death, and to rest at last in the Boat of the Sun.

Scene III.—*Amenemhe III., the Labyrinth, and Lake Mœris* [1] (XIIth dynasty, about B. C. 2080–1900).—Over four centuries have passed since Khufu's Pyramid was finished, and now toward the southwest, on an oasis in the midst of the desert, we see rising a magnificent group of palaces, built about an immense twelve-courted rectangle. The stone roofs and walls are covered with carvings Here are three thousand chambers, large and small, half of which are under ground and are to sepulcher mighty kings and sacred crocodiles. This marvelous Labyrinth, where one "passes from courts into chambers, and from chambers into colonnades, from colonnades into fresh houses, and from these into courts unseen before," is surrounded by a single wall, and incloses three sides of the large central rectangle. On the fourth side stands a pyramid, engraven with large hieroglyphics, and entered by a subterranean passage. Amenemhe III. does not leave his identity as the founder of this grand palace tomb to the chance scrawls of a quarry workman, as did Khufu with his pyramid, but has his cartouch properly inscribed on the building-stones.

Lake Mœris.—There have been some grievous famines [2] in Egypt produced by the variable inundations of the Nile, and Amenemhe

---

[1] These descriptions of the Labyrinth and Lake Mœris are founded on Herodotus Strabo located the Labyrinth "between two pyramids." Prof. Petrie, who spent nearly three years (1888–90) exploring the Fayoom, states that he "found between two pyramidal structures an immense bed of fine white limestone concrete, upon which lie thousands of tons of limestone and red granite, fragments of the destroyed walls of some enormous structure." Profs. Sayce and Maspero believe that in "Lake Mœris" Herodotus saw only an overflow into a natural depression. All Egyptologists concede, however, that Amenemhat III., in *some* way, greatly increased the amount of arable land in this region. Petrie found here several inscribed fragments of Amenemhat's statues and pyramidal pedestals.

[2] "All Egypt is the gift of the Nile," wrote Herodotus. The river, however, was not left to overflow its banks without restrictions. The whole country was intersected with canals and protected by dikes, Menes himself, according to Herodotus, having constructed a dike and turned aside the course of the Nile in order to found Memphis. The rise of the river was closely watched, and was measured by "Nilometers" in various parts of the country; and the proper moment for cutting away the dams and opening the canals was awaited with intense anxiety, and decided by auspicious omens. "A rise of fourteen cubits caused joy, fifteen security, sixteen delight." Twelve cubits foretold a famine. An excessive Nile was as disastrous as a deficient one. A "Good Nile" brought harvests so abundant as to make Egyptian storehouses the granary of the eastern world. For this reason, when the famine arose in Canaan, Abram and Sarai came to Egypt, probably during the reign of the XIth dynasty.

causes to be constructed not far from the Labyrinthine Palace a gigantic lake, with one canal leading to the great river, and another terminating in a natural lake still farther to the west. He thus diverts the waters of an excessive Nile, and hoards those of a deficient one to be used at need on the neighboring lands. He stocks this lake with fish, and so provides for the future queens of Egypt an annual revenue of over $200,000 for pin-money. The banks of Lake Mœris are adorned with orchards, vineyards, and gardens, won by its waters from the surrounding desert. Toward the center of the lake, rising three hundred feet above its surface, stand two pyramids, and on the apex of each sits a majestic stone figure. But pyramid-building is going out of favor in Egypt, and the fashion of obelisks has come in. These are made of single blocks of beautiful red granite from Syene, and are covered with delicately carved hieroglyphs. Memphis is losing her precedence. Thebes is shining in her first glory, and the Temple of Karnak, which is to become the most splendid of all times and countries, is begun; while, down the river, at Beni Hassan,[1] the powerful princes have built tombs which, like cheerful homes, spread their pillared porches in the eastern rocky heights.

OBELISK.

Scene IV.—*A Theban Dinner-Party* (time of Rameses II., 1311–1245 B. C.).—The Labyrinth has stood for nearly seven centuries. During this time the shepherd kings have had their sway and been expelled. The XVIIIth dynasty, including the long and

---

[1] The tombs of Beni Hassan in Middle Egypt are remarkable for their architecture, the prototype of the Grecian Doric (p. 182). They are also noticeable for being east of the Nile, and for not being concealed, as was the almost universal custom. A recent visitor to these tombs writes: "Having ascended the broad road which leads gradually up to the entrances, we found ourselves on a sort of platform cut in the cliff nearly half-way to the top, and saw before us about thirty high and wide doorways, each leading into one chamber or more, excavated in the solid rock. The first we entered was a large square room, with an open pit at one end,— the mummy-pit; and every inch of the walls was covered with pictures. Coming into this tomb was like getting hold of a very old picture-book, which said in the beginning, 'Open me and I will tell you what people did a long time ago.' Every group of figures told a separate story, and one could pass on from group to group till a whole life was unfolded. Whenever we could find a spot where the painted plaster had not been blackened or roughened, we were surprised at the variety of the colors, — delicate lilacs and vivid crimsons and many shades of green." Though these pictures on the walls of tombs were supposed to serve the dead, they were no less representations of real life. Were it not for them, we should never have learned the secrets of those homes along the Nile where people lived, loved, and died over four thousand years ago.

brilliant reign of Thothmes III., has passed away, leaving behind it temples, obelisks, and tombs of marvelous magnificence. Thebes is at the height of that architectural triumph which is to make her the wonder of succeeding ages. Meantime, what of the people? Let us invite ourselves to a dinner-party in Theban high life. The time is mid-day, and the guests are arriving on foot, in palanquins borne by servants, and in chariots. A high wall, painted in panels, surrounds the fashionable villa, and on an obelisk near by is inscribed the name of the owner. We enter the grounds by a folding-gate flanked with lofty towers. At the end of a broad avenue bordered by rows of trees and spacious water-tanks stands a stuccoed brick[1] mansion, over the door of which we read in hieroglyphics, "The Good House." The building is made airy by corridors, and columns, and open courts shaded by awnings, all gayly painted and ornamented with banners Its extensive grounds include flower-gardens, vineyards, date-orchards, and sycamore-groves. There are little summer-houses, and artificial ponds from which rises the sweet, sleepy perfume of the lotus-blossom; here the genial host sometimes amuses his guests by an excursion in a pleasure-boat towed by his servants. The stables and chariot-houses are in the center of the mansion, but the cattle-sheds and granaries are detached.

We will accompany the guest whose chariot has just halted. The Egyptian grandee drives his own horse, but is attended by a train of servants; one of these runs forward to knock at the door, another takes the reins, another presents a stool to assist his master to alight, and others follow with various articles which he may desire during the visit. As the guest steps into the court, a servant receives his sandals and brings a foot-pan that he may wash his feet. He is then invited into the festive chamber, where side by side on a double chair, to which their favorite monkey is tied, sit his placid host and hostess, blandly smelling their lotus-flowers and beaming a welcome to each arrival. They are dressed like their guests. On his shaven head the Egyptian gentleman wears a wig with little top-curls, and long cues which hang behind. His beard is short—a long one is only for the king His large-sleeved, fluted robe is of fine white linen, and he is adorned with necklace, bracelets, and a multitude of finger-rings. The lady by his side wears also a linen robe over one of richly colored stuff. Her hair falls to her shoulders front and back, in scores of crisp and glossy braids. The brilliancy of her eyes is heightened by antimony; and amulet beetles,[2] dragons, asps, and strange symbolic eyes dangle from

---

[1] The bricks were made of Nile mud mixed with chopped straw, and dried in the sun.

[2] The beetle was a favorite emblem for ornaments. No less than 180 kinds of scarabæi are preserved in the Turin Museum alone. It was also engraved on the precious stones used as currency between Egypt and neighboring countries.

her golden ear-rings, necklace, bracelets, and anklets. Having saluted his entertainers, the new-comer is seated on a low stool, where a servant anoints his bewigged head with sweet-scented ointment, hands him a lotus-blossom, hangs garlands of flowers on his neck and head, and presents him with wine. The servant, as he receives back the emptied vase and offers a napkin, politely remarks, "May it benefit you." This completes the formal reception.

Each lady is attended in the same manner by a female slave. While the guests are arriving, the musicians and dancers belonging to the household amuse the company, who sit on chairs in rows and chat, the ladies commenting on each other's jewelry, and, in compliment, exchanging lotus-flowers. The house is furnished with couches, armchairs, ottomans, and footstools made of the native acacia or of ebony and other rare imported woods, inlaid with ivory, carved in animal forms, and cushioned or covered with leopard-skins. The ceilings are stuccoed and painted, and the panels of the walls adorned with colored designs. The tables are of various sizes and fanciful patterns. The floor is covered with a palm-leaf matting or wool carpet. In the bedrooms are high couches reached by steps; the pillows are made of wood or alabaster (see cut, p. 29). There are many elegant toilet conveniences, such as polished bronze mirrors, fancy bottles for the *kohl* with which the ladies stain their brows and eyelids, alabaster vases for sweet-scented ointments, and trinket-boxes shaped like a goose, a fish, or a human dwarf. Everywhere throughout the house is a profusion of flowers, hanging in festoons, clustered on stands, and crowning the wine-bowl. Not only the guests but the attendants are wreathed, and fresh blossoms are constantly brought in from the garden to replace those which are fading.

And now the ox, kid, geese, and ducks, which, according to custom, have been hurried into the cooking-caldrons as soon as killed, are ready to be served. After hand-washing and saying of grace, the guests are seated on stools, chairs, or the floor, one or two at each little low, round table. The dishes, many of which are vegetables, are brought on in courses, and the guests, having neither knife nor fork, help themselves with their fingers. Meantime a special corps of servants keep the wine and water cool by vigorously fanning the porous jars which contain them. During the repast, when the enjoyment is at its height, the Osiris—an image like a human mummy—is brought in and formally introduced to each visitor with the reminder that life is short, and all must die. This little episode does not in the least disturb the placidity of the happy guests. There is one, however, to whom the injunction is not given, and who, though anointed and garlanded, and duly installed at a table, does not partake of the delicacies set before him. This is a real mummy, a dear, deceased member of the family, whom the host is keeping some months before burial, being loath to part with him. It is in his honor, indeed, that the relatives and friends are assembled, and the presence of a beloved mummy, whose soul is journeying toward the Pools of Peace, is the culminating pleasure of an Egyptian dinner-party.

4. SUMMARY.

1. Political History.—Our earliest glimpse of Egypt is of a country already civilized. Menes, the first of the Pharaohs, changed the course of the Nile and founded Memphis. His successor was a physician, and wrote books on anatomy. Khufu, Shafra, and Menkara, of the IVth dynasty, built the three Great Pyramids at Gizeh. In their time there were already an organized civil and military service and an established religion. From the VIth to the XIth dynasty the monuments are few and history is silent. Thebes then became the center of power. The XIIth dynasty produced Lake Mœris and the Labyrinth, and waged war against the Ethiopians. Meanwhile the Hyksos invaded Lower Egypt and soon conquered the land. At last a Theban monarch drove out the barbarian strangers. The XVIIIth and XIXth dynasties raised Egypt to the height of her glory. Thothmes, Amunoph, Seti, and, chief of all, Rameses II., covered the land with magnificent works of art, and carried the Egyptian arms in triumph to the depths of Asia. After the XXth dynasty Egypt began to decline. Her weak kings fell in turn before the Ethiopians, the Assyrians, and, finally, the Persians. The illustrious line of the Pharaohs was at length swallowed up in the Empire of Persia (see note, p. 46).

2. General Character of Egyptian Civilization.—In summing up our general impressions of Egypt, we recall as characteristic features her Pyramids, Obelisks, Sphinxes, Gigantic Stone Statues, Hieroglyphics, Sacred Animals, and Mummies. We think of her worshiped kings, her all-powerful priests, and her Nile-watered land divided between king, priests, and soldiers. We remember that in her fondness for inscriptions she overspread the walls of her palaces and the pillars of her temples with hieroglyphics, and erected monuments for seemingly no other purpose than to cover them with writing. We see her tombs cut in the solid rock of the hillside and carefully concealed from view, bearing on their inner walls painted pictures of home life. Her nobility are surrounded by refinement and luxuries which we are startled to find existing 4000 years ago; and her common people crowd a land where food is abundant, clothing little needed, and the sky a sufficient shelter.

We have found her architecture of the true Hamite type, colossal, massive, and enduring; her art stiff, constrained, and lifeless; her priest-taught schools giving special attention to writing and mathematics; her literature chiefly religious, written on papyrus scrolls, and collected in libraries; her arts and inventions numerous, including weaving, dyeing, mining and working precious metals, making glass and porcelain, enameling, engraving, tanning and embossing leather, working with potter's clay, and embalming the dead. Seeing her long valley inundated each year by the Nile, she made herself proficient in mathematics and mensuration, erected dikes, established Nilometers, appointed public commissioners, and made a god of the river which, since it seldom rains in Egypt, gives the land its only fertility. Her religion, having many gods growing out of One, taught a judgment after death, with immortality and transmigration of soul; its characteristic form was a ceremonial worship of animals as emblems or incarnations of Deity. Finally, as a people, the Egyptians were in disposition mild, unwarlike, superstitiously religious, in habits cleanly, luxurious, and delighting in flowers; in mind subtle, profound, self-poised; in social life talkative, given to festivals, and loud in demonstrations of grief; having a high conception of morals, a respect for woman, a love of literature, and a domestic affection which extended to a peculiar fondling of their mummied dead.

READING REFERENCES.

Brugsch's Egypt under the Pharaohs.—Bunsen's Egypt's Place in the World's History.—Birch's Egypt from the Earliest Times, and Egypt from the Monuments.—Wilkinson's Manners and Customs of the Ancient Egyptians.—Herodotus, Rawlinson's Translation with Notes.—Rawlinson's Origin of Nations, and Manual of Ancient History.—Lenormant and Chevallier's Ancient History of the East.—Records of the Past (New Series).—Egypt over 3300 Years Ago (Illustrated Library of Wonders).—Lübke's History of Art.—Westropp's Handbook of Archæology.—Fergusson's History of Architecture.—Early Egyptian History for the Young (Macmillan, London).—Zerffi's Historical Development of Art.—George Ebers's Egypt (illustrated); and An Egyptian Princess, The Sisters, and Uarda (historical romances).—Mariette's Monuments of Upper Egypt.—Perrot and Chipiez's History of Ancient Egyptian Art.—Goodyear's Grammar of the Lotus.—Books of the Egypt Exploration Fund and Archæological Survey.—Biblia (a current magazine).

COMPARATIVE CHRONOLOGY, "LONG" AND "SHORT."

	B. C.	B. C.
Menes	5700	2700
Old Empire	5700–3450	2700–2080
Middle Empire	3450–1750	2080–1525
Hyksos Rule	2325–1750	1900–1525
New Empire	1750– 525	1525– 527
Persian Conquest	525	527

ASSYRIAN EMPIRE
700 B.C.

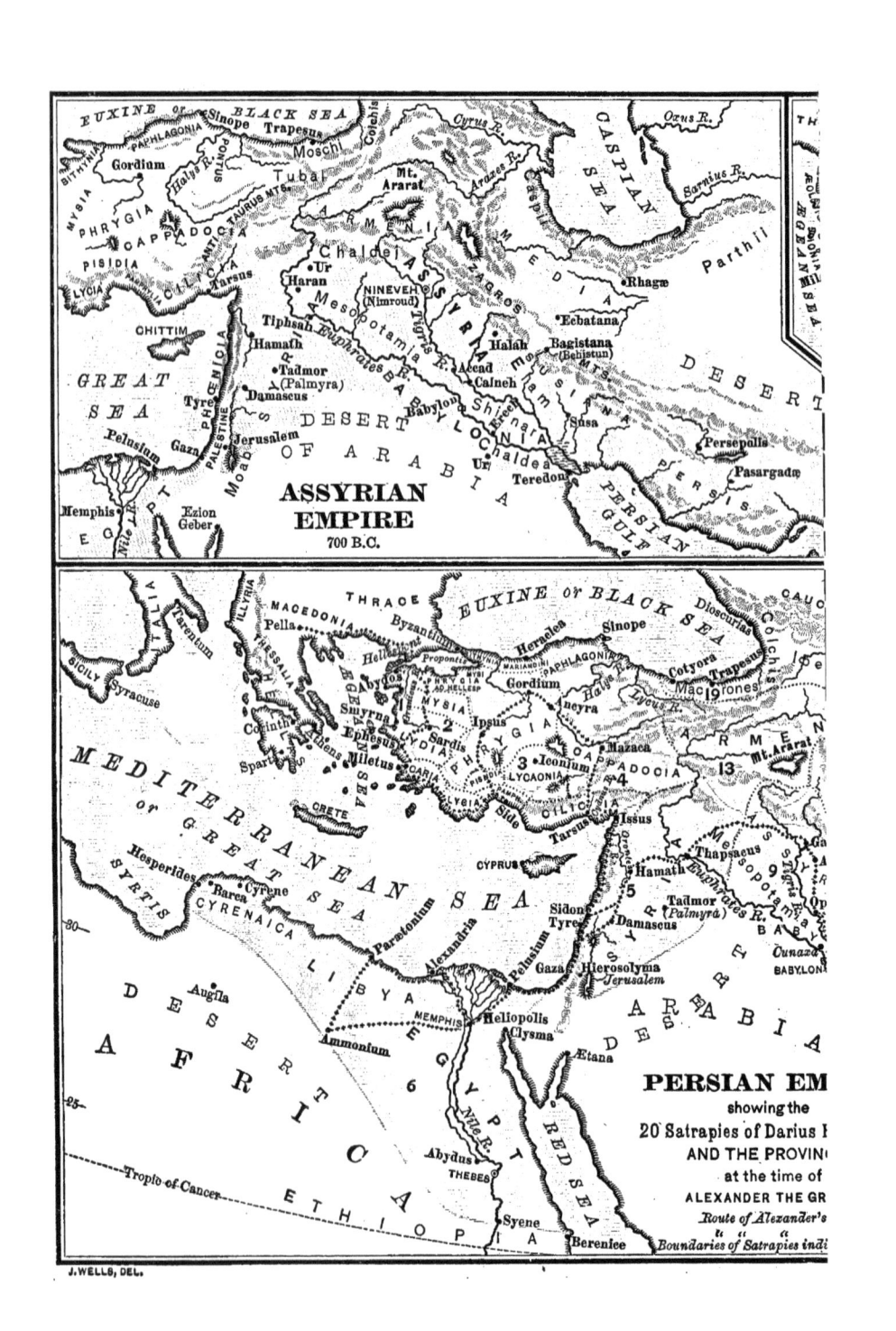

PERSIAN EM...
showing the
20 Satrapies of Darius...
AND THE PROVIN...
at the time of
ALEXANDER THE GR...
Route of Alexander's...
Boundaries of Satrapies indi...

J. WELLS, DEL.

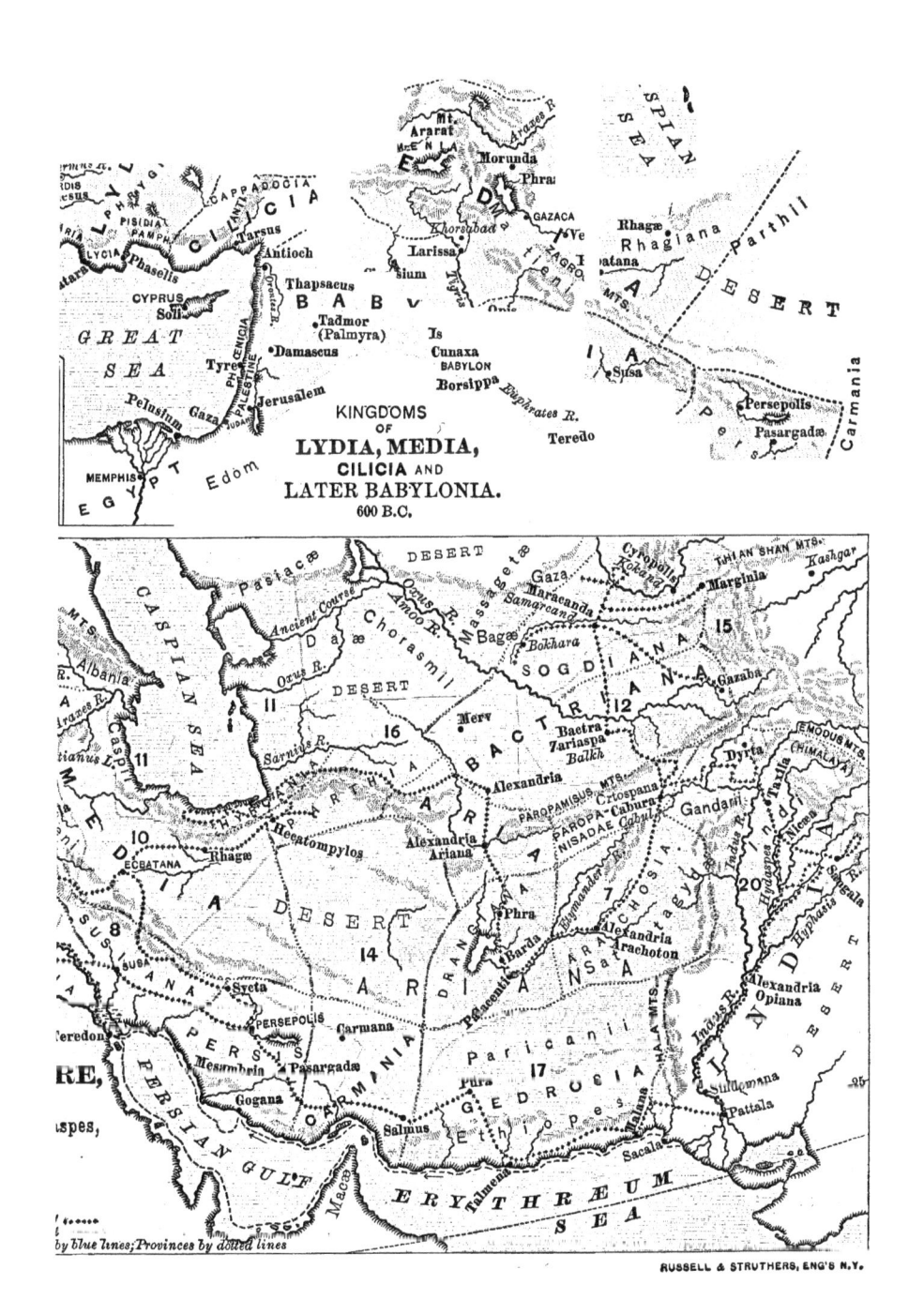

KINGDOMS OF LYDIA, MEDIA, CILICIA AND LATER BABYLONIA.
600 B.C.

*

BABYLONIA AND ASSYRIA.

1. THE POLITICAL HISTORY.

The Origin of the civilization along the Tigris and Euphrates may rival the Egyptian in antiquity; recent discoveries seem to remove far into the remote past that patriarchal civilization called Accadian, Sumerian, or Sumero-Accadian.

1. Chaldea.—Our earliest political glimpse of this country shows us a Turanian people with important cities; each city governed by a priest-king, and containing a temple sacred to some particular deity. Semitic peoples then enter the land. These have less culture but greater intellectual capacity than the Accadians. During the many centuries which follow—how many no one knows—*Sargon I.*, King of Accad, emerges from the mist of antiquity as a builder of palaces and temples, an editor of ancient Accadian literature, and a founder of libraries; *Ur-ea* (Uruch, p. 64), King of Ur, scatters gigantic, rudely constructed temples all over Chaldea; and *Khammuragus*, patron of science and litera-

---

Geographical Questions.—Locate Nineveh, Babylon, Tadmor, Accad, Erech, and Calneh. How far was it by direct line from Babylon to Memphis? To Thebes? Describe the Tigris and Euphrates Rivers. Locate and describe Mesopotamia, Assyria, Chaldea or Babylonia, and Susiana. *Ans.* Mesopotamia is a name given by the Greeks to the entire rolling plain between the Tigris and the Euphrates.; Assyria was an arid plateau cut up by rocky ridges, stretching north of Babylonia to the Armenian Mountains; Babylonia was a rich alluvial plain formed by the deposit of the Tigris and Euphrates in the shallow waters of the Persian Gulf; Susiana lay south east of Assyria and east of Babylonia. Northern Chaldea was called Accad; Southern Chaldea, Shumir. The alluvium was marvelously fertile. In it wheat grew so rank, that, to make it ear, the people mowed it twice, and then fed it off with cattle. The yield was enormous,—fifty-fold at the least, and often a hundred-fold.

ture, unites Accad and Shumir into one kingdom and makes Babylon the capital. All this occurs before 2000 B. C.[1] The ever-nomadic Semites push northward, and, later, people the middle Tigris, where they build great cities and lay the foundations of the Assyrian Empire.

As Chaldea had no natural boundary or defense, it was singularly open to attack. There were constant wars with the fast-rising power of Assyria, and in the 13th century B. C. the Chaldeans were conquered by their northern rival. The period of their servitude lasted nearly seven centuries, during which they became thoroughly Assyrianized in language and customs. Being, however, a sturdy, fiery, impetuous, warlike race, they often revolted. At one time —known in history as the *Era of Nabonassar* (747 B. C.)— they achieved a temporary independence, and on the fall of Nineveh (606? B. C.) they at once rose to power, founding the second Babylonian Empire.

2. Assyria, for nearly seven centuries (1298–606 B. C.),— from the conquest of Babylon to the overthrow of Nineveh, its own capital,—was the great empire[2] of south-western Asia. It attained its glory under Sargon and his descendants,—the Sargonidæ. The Assyrian sway then reached to the Mediterranean Sea, and included Syria, Media, Babylonia, Mesopotamia, Phœnicia, Palestine, and parts of Arabia and Egypt. These conquered nations retained their laws,

---

[1] Early Chaldean chronology is as uncertain as Egyptian. Berosus, a Babylonian, wrote (4th century B. C.) a history of his country, founded on the records in the temple of Belus. His work, like Manetho's, is known only by portions quoted in other books. Archæological research is now as enthusiastically pressed in Chaldea as in Egypt. A recently discovered cylinder at Sippara, near Accad, points to the remote date of 3800 B. C. for Sargon I.

[2] This was the first of the successive "World-Empires." Following it was the Persian under Cyrus. This was conquered by Alexander, who founded the Macedonian; and it in turn gave place to the grandest of all,—the Roman. Out of its ruins grew up the Mohammedan of Asia and Africa, and Charlemagne's in Europe. The former was shattered by the Turks, and the latter was broken up into several of the kingdoms of modern Europe.

kings, and religion, but, being required to pay tribute and furnish a military contingent to the royal army, they were always ripe for revolt. The history of Assyria is therefore the record of an empire constantly falling to pieces, and as often restored through the genius of some warrior-king.

ASSYRIAN HEADS (FROM NIMROUD).

About 606 B. C. Nineveh was captured by the combined forces of the Babylonians and Medes. Tradition says that its effeminate king Sar'-a-cus, taking counsel of his despair, burned himself in his palace with all his treasures. The conquerors utterly destroyed the city, so that there remained only a heap of ruins.[1]

The Names of the Assyrian Kings are tedious, and the dates of their reigns uncertain. Authorities differ greatly even in the spelling of the names. Some of the monarchs are notable from their connection with Grecian or Jewish history. *Tig'-lathi-nin* (worship be to Nin, p. 62) is supposed to be the Greek Ninus; on his signet-ring was inscribed "The Conqueror of Babylon," which connects him with the overthrow of Chaldea, already mentioned. *Tiglath-Pile'ser* I. (1110 B. C.) may be called "The Religious Conqueror." He built temples, palaces, and castles, introduced

---

[1] Xenophon, during the famous retreat of the Ten Thousand, only two centuries after this catastrophe, passed the site of Nineveh, yet does not even mention the fact in his history, so perfectly had Nineveh disappeared.

foreign cattle and vegetable products, and constructed canals. He multiplied the war-chariots, and carried the Assyrian arms to the Persian mountains on the east and to northern Syria on the west;[1] but he was repulsed by the Babylonians, who bore off his idols to their capital, where they were kept four hundred years. *Asshur-izir-pal* (Sardanapalus I., 883–858), a cruel but magnificent king, made many conquests, but is chiefly to be remembered in connection with the arts, which he raised to a point never before attained. He lined his palace walls (Nimroud) with great alabaster slabs, whereon were sculptured in spirited bas-relief the various glories he had achieved. He was a hunter as well as a warrior and an art patron, and kept a royal menagerie, where he gathered all the wild beasts he could procure from his own and foreign lands.

Shalmane'ser[2] II. was contemporary with Ahab and Jehu, kings of Israel; he personally conducted twenty-four military campaigns. *Vul-lush* III. (810–781) married Sammuramit, heiress of Babylon, and probably the original of

---

[1] A lengthy document written by Tiglath-Pileser, narrating some events of his reign, has been discovered. He writes: "The country of Kasiyara, a difficult region, I passed through. With their 20,000 men and their five kings I engaged. I defeated them. The ranks of their warriors in fighting the battle were beaten down as if by the tempest. Their carcasses covered the valleys and the tops of the mountains. I cut off their heads. Of the battlements of their cities I made heaps, like mounds of earth. Their movables, their wealth, and their valuables I plundered to a countless amount. Six thousand of their common soldiers I gave to my men as slaves." Having restored two ancient temples, he invokes the support of the gods, and adds: "The list of my victories and the catalogue of my triumphs over foreigners hostile to Asshur I have inscribed on my tablets and cylinders. Whoever shall abrade or injure my tablets and cylinders, or shall moisten them with water, or scorch them with fire, or expose them to the air, or in the holy place of God shall assign them to a place where they cannot be seen or understood, or shall erase the writing and inscribe his own name, or shall divide the sculptures and break them off from my tablets, may Anu and Vul, the great gods, my lords, consign his name to perdition! May they curse him with an irrevocable curse! May they pluck out the stability of the throne of his empire! May not his offspring survive him! May his servants be broken! May his troops be defeated! May his name and his race perish!"

[2] In connection with Shalmaneser and the following kings, read carefully 2 Kings, xv-xix.

the mythical "Semiramis." According to the legend, this queen, having conquered Egypt and part of Ethiopia, invaded India with an army of a million men, but was beaten back by elephants; she adorned Babylon with wonderful works, and at last took the form of a dove and flew away. *Tiglath-Pileser* III. (745–727) captured Damascus and conquered Ahaz, King of Judah. *Shalmaneser* IV. (727–722) laid siege to Samaria, which was taken by his successor, *Sargon* (722–705), who carried off its inhabitants and supplied their place with captive Babylonians.

Sargon founded the house of the Sargonidæ, who were the most brilliant of the Assyrian kings, and who made all the neighboring nations feel the weight of their conquering arms. He himself so subdued the Egyptians that they were never afterward the powerful nation they had been; he also reduced Syria, Babylonia, and a great part of Media and Susiana. His son, the proud, haughty, and self-confident *Sennacherib* (sen-nak'-e-rib, 705–681), captured the "fenced cities of Judah," but afterward lost 185,000 men, "smitten by the angel of the Lord" in a single night. The sculptures represent him as standing in his chariot personally directing the forced labor of his workmen, who were war-captives, often loaded with fetters. *Esarhaddon*, Sargon's grandson, divided Egypt into petty states, took Manasseh, King of Judah, prisoner to Babylon (2 Chron. xxxiii. 11), and more fully settled Samaria with colonists from Babylonia, Persia, and Susiana *Asshur-bani-pal* (Sardanapalus II., 668–626 ?),[1] Sargon's great-grandson, was a famous warrior, builder, and art patron. He erected a magnificent palace at Nineveh, in which he founded a royal library. His

---

[1] As the Greeks confounded several Egyptian monarchs under the name of Sesostris the Great, so the Assyrian king whom they called Sardanapa'lus seems to have been a union of Asshurizirpal, Asshurbanipal, and Asshuremedilin. The Greek ideal Sardanapalus is celebrated in Byron's well-known play of that name.

son, *Asshur-emed-ilin*, or Saracus, as he was called by some Greek writers (p. 47), was the last Assyrian king.

3. Later Babylonian Empire (606–538).—*Nabopolas'sar*, a favorite general under Saracus, obtained from his master the government of Babylon. Here he organized a revolt, and made an alliance with Cyaxares, King of the Medes; in 606 B. C. their combined forces captured Nineveh. The conquerors divided the spoils between them, and to

BABYLONIAN HEADS (FROM THE SCULPTURES).

Nabopolassar fell Phœnicia, Palestine, Syria, Susiana, and the Euphrates valley. Babylon, after the ruin of its rival, became again the capital of the East. It held this position for nearly a century, when it was captured by Cyrus the Great (538 B. C.).

The Names of two of its kings are familiar to every Bible reader. *Nebuchadnezzar* (604–561), the son of Nabopolassar, gave the new empire its character and position. Without him Babylon would have had little if any history worth recording. A great warrior, he captured Jerusalem,[1] overran Egypt, and, after a thirteen-years' siege, subdued Tyre. A great builder, he restored or repaired almost every temple and city in the country. By his marvelous energy Babylon became five or six times the present size of London;

. [1] "Israel is a scattered sheep; .. first the king of Assyria hath devoured him; and last this Nebuchadrezzar king of Babylon hath broken his bones."—*Jer.* l. 17.

and its walls and hanging gardens (p. 58) were among the Seven Wonders of the World (Appendix). Immense lakes were dug for retaining the water of the Euphrates, whence a net-work of canals distributed it over the plain to irrigate the land, while quays and breakwaters were constructed along the Persian Gulf for the encouragement of commerce.[1] *Belshazzar* held the throne jointly with his father, Nabona′dius, the last king of Babylon. *Cyrus*, ruler of the rising empire of the Medes and Persians, invaded the country "with an army wide-spreading and far-reaching, like the waters of a river." Having defeated the army in the open field, he besieged Babylon. One night when the Babylonians were celebrating a festival with drunken revelry, the Persians seized the unguarded gates and captured the place. From that time Babylon was a province of the Persian Empire, and its glory faded. Semitic power had succumbed to Aryan enterprise. To-day the site of the once great city is marked only by shapeless mounds scattered over a desolate plain.

2. THE CIVILIZATION.

Society.—*In Assyria* there were no castes or hereditary aristocracy, but all subjects, foreign and native, had equal privileges, dependent upon the one absolute royal will.

The King, though not worshiped as a god, as in Egypt, was considered "the earthly vicegerent of the gods," having undisputed authority over the souls as well as the bodies of his people.

The chief courtiers were eunuchs, who directed the public affairs, leaving the king undisturbed to enjoy his sports and pleasures. They, however, held their offices at his caprice, and were liable at any moment to be removed. The people had the privilege of

---

[1] Read the Scriptural account of Babylon and its kings in Daniel, Isaiah (chaps. x., xi., xiii., xiv., xxi., xlv., xlvi., xlvii., and especially xix., xxiii.), Jeremiah (chaps. xlix., l., and li.), 2 Kings (chaps. xxiv., xxv.), and Ezra (chaps. i.-vi.).

direct petition to the king in case of public wrong or neglect.[1]

In Babylonia, where there was a mixed population, society was divided into castes, of which the highest, the ancient Chaldean, was not unlike that of the Egyptian priesthood. The CHALDEANS read the warnings of the stars, interpreted dreams and omens, gave instructions in the art of magic and incantation, and conducted the pompous religious ceremonies. They also decided politics, commanded the armies, and held the chief state offices. From them came all the royal rulers of Babylon.

The king was as despotic as in Assyria, and Babylonian nobles at every slight offense trembled for their heads. The whole Chaldean caste were once ordered to be exterminated because they could not expound the dream of a king which he himself could not recall (Dan. ii. 12).

Merchants, artisans, and husbandmen formed each a caste. The fishermen of the marshes near the Persian Gulf corresponded to the swine-herds in Egypt, as being lowest in the social scale. They lived on earth-covered rafts, which they floated among the reeds, and subsisted on a species of cake made of dried fish.

Writing.—*Cuneiform Letters* (*cuneus*, a wedge).—*Clay Tablets.*—The earliest form of this writing, invented by the Turanians, was, like the Egyptian, a collection of rude pictures, with this peculiarity, that they were all straight-lined and angular, as if devised to be cut on stone with a chisel. The Chaldeans, having no stone in their country, made of the clay in which it abounded tiny pillow-shaped tablets, from one to five inches long. Upon these soft, moist tablets they traced

---

[1] A tablet in the British Museum thus exposes an official peculation in the time of Asshurbanipal: "Salutation to the king, my lord, from his humble petitioner, Zikar Nebo. To the king, my lord, may Asshur, Shamash, Bel, Zarpanit, Nebo, Tashmit, Ishtar of Nineveh, Ishtar of Arbela, the great gods, protectors of royalty, give a hundred years of life to the king, my lord, and slaves and wives in great number to the king, my lord. The gold that in the month Tashrit the minister of state and the controller of the palace should have given me—three talents of pure gold and four talents of alloyed gold—to make an image of the king and of the mother of the king, has not yet been given. May my lord, the king, give orders to the minister of state and to the controller of the palace, to give the gold, to give it from this time, and do it exactly."

THE CIVILIZATION. 53

the outline of the original object-picture in a series of distinct, wedge-like impressions made by the square or triangular point of a small bronze or iron tool. As in Egypt, the attempt to preserve the picture outline was gradually abandoned, and the characters, variously modified by the different-speaking races inhabiting Assyria, came to have a variety of meanings.[1] Cuneiform writing has been found even more difficult to interpret than Egyptian hieroglyphics. It has some of the peculiarities of that writing, but has no letter-signs, the cuneiform-writing nations never advancing so far as to analyze the syllable into vowels and consonants. Nearly three hundred different characters have been deciphered, and a large number remain yet unknown.[2]

Other Writing Materials, as Alabaster Slabs, Terra-cotta Cylinders, Cylinder Signets, etc.—The Assyrian clay tablets were generally larger than the Chaldean, and for the royal records slabs of fine stone were preferred.

ASSYRIAN CLAY TABLET.

[1] Generally all trace of the original picture disappeared, but in a few cases, such as , the outline is still visible. A curious example of the pictorial origin of the letters is furnished by the character , which is the French *une*, the feminine of "one." This character may be traced back through several known forms to an original picture on a Koyunjik tablet where it appears as a double-toothed comb. As this was a toilet article peculiar to women, it became the sign of the feminine gender.

[2] The *Behistun Inscription* furnished the key to Assyrian literature, as did the Rosetta stone to Egyptian. This inscription was carved by order of Darius Hystasp'es (p. 91) on the precipitous side of a high rock mountain in Media, 300 feet above its base. It is in three languages,—Persian, Median, and Assyrian. The Persian, which is the simplest of the cuneiform writings, having been mastered, it became, like the Greek on the Rosetta stone, a lexicon to the other two languages. Honorably connected with the opening-up of the Assyrian language in the present century, are the names of Sir Henry Rawlinson, who at great personal risk scaled the Behistun Mountain and made a copy of the inscription, which he afterward published; and M. Oppert, who systematized the newly discovered language, and founded an Assyrian grammar for the use of modern scholars.

These slabs were used as panels in palace walls, where they set forth the glorious achievements of the Assyrian monarchs. Even where figures were sculptured upon the panels, the royal vanity was not deterred, and the self-glorifying narrations were carried uninterruptedly across mystic baskets, sacred trees, and the dresses of worshiping kings and eagle-headed deities. The colossal alabaster bulls and lions which guarded the palace portals were also inscribed, and formal invocations to the gods were written on hollow terra-cotta cylinders, from eighteen to thirty-six inches high, which were placed in the temple corners. The lines are sometimes more closely compacted than those in this paragraph, and the characters so fine that a magnifying glass is required to read them. Little cylinders made of jasper, chalcedony, or other stone were engraved and used as seals by rolling them across the clay tablets. There is no positive proof that anything like paper or parchment was ever in use among the Assryians, though the ruins furnish indirect testimony that it may have been employed in rare instances.

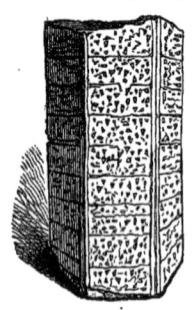

A TERRA-COTTA CYLINDER.

Literature.—*Libraries.*—An Assyrian or Babylonian book consisted of several flat, square clay tablets written on both sides, carefully paged, and piled one upon another in order. Asshurbanipal, who as patron of arts and literature was to Assyria what Rameses II. had been to Egypt 600 years before, established an extensive public library[1] in his palace at Nineveh. Many of the books were copied from borrowed Babylonian tablets, but a large number were evidently composed under his royal patronage. He gathered works on geography, history, law, mathematics, astronomy, astrology, botany, and zoölogy. Complete lists of plants, trees, metals, and minerals were prepared; also a catalogue of every known species of animals, classified in families and genera. "We may well be astonished," says Lenormant, " to learn that the Assyrians had already invented a scientific nomenclature, similar in principle to that of

---

[1] "Palace of Asshurbanipal, king of the world, king of Assyria, to whom the god Nebo and the goddess Tashmit (the goddess of wisdom) have given ears to hear and eyes to see what is the foundation of government. They have revealed to the kings, my predecessors, this cuneiform writing, the manifestation of the god Nebo, the god of supreme intelligence. I have written it upon tablets, I have signed it, I have placed it in my palace for the instruction of my subjects" (*Inscription*). One of the bricks of this library contains a notice that *visitors are requested to give to the librarian the number of the book they wish to consult, and it will be brought to them.*

Linnæus." Here, also, were religious books explaining the name, functions, and attributes of each god; magical incantations with which to charm away evil spirits; and sacred poems, resembling in style the Psalms of David. Among the records copied from Babylonian tablets, which were already antiquities in the time of Asshurbanipal, were the Chaldean accounts of the Creation, the Deluge, and the Tower of Babel, which are strikingly like the narrative in Genesis, though written hundreds of years before Moses was born. Most numerous of all were the various grammatical works. The Assyrians found their own language so complex, that lexicons and grammars were multiplied in efforts to explain and simplify it; and these books, written to aid the Assyrian learner over 2500 years ago, have been found invaluable in opening the long-lost language to the student of to-day. All this vast collection of tablets, gathered with so much care by Asshurbanipal, fell with the palace in its destruction under his son, Saracus, and were mostly broken into fragments. [1]

Monuments and Art.—As the *Chaldeans* had no stone, they made their edifices of burnt or sun-dried bricks, strengthening the walls by layers of reed matting cemented with bitumen. Their temples were built in stories, each one smaller in area than the one below, thus forming an irregular pyramid. In later times the number of stories increased, and the outer walls of Babylonian temples were painted in colors consecrated to the heavenly bodies. That of Nebo at Borsippa [2] had its lowest stage black (Saturn); the next orange (Jupiter); then red (Mars), gold (the sun), yellow (Venus), blue (Mercury), and silver (the moon). The gold and

---

[1] "The clay tablets lay under the ruined palace in such multitudes that they filled the chambers to the height of a foot or more from the floor. The documents thus discovered at Nineveh probably exceed in amount of writing all that has yet been afforded by the monuments of Egypt" (Layard's Nineveh). To Austen Henry Layard, an English archæologist, we are chiefly indebted for the wonderful discoveries made in exploring the mounds which mark the site of Nineveh. The British Museum has a magnificent collection of Assyrian antiquities recovered from these mounds, whole rooms being lined with the alabaster slabs exhumed from the ruins of the palaces of Asshurizirpal at Nimroud, Sennacherib and his grandson Asshurbanipal at Koyunjik, and Sargon at Khorsabad. Most of the remains of Sargon's palace, however, are deposited in the Louvre at Paris, having been excavated for the French government by M. Botta, who has the honor of having made (in 1843) the first discovery of an Assyrian monument.

[2] Borsippa was a town near Babylon. Some authorities include the ruins of this temple, now called the Birs-i-Nimrud, within the outer wall of Babylon, and believe it to have been the true Temple of Belus (p. 59), if not the actual Tower of Babel. A mound called Babil, near the Great Palace, is the other disputed site.

silver stages seem to have been covered with thin plates of those metals. Either the sides or the angles of these structures exactly faced the cardinal points, and the base was strengthened by brick buttresses scientifically arranged. The royal name and titles were engraved upon each building-brick.

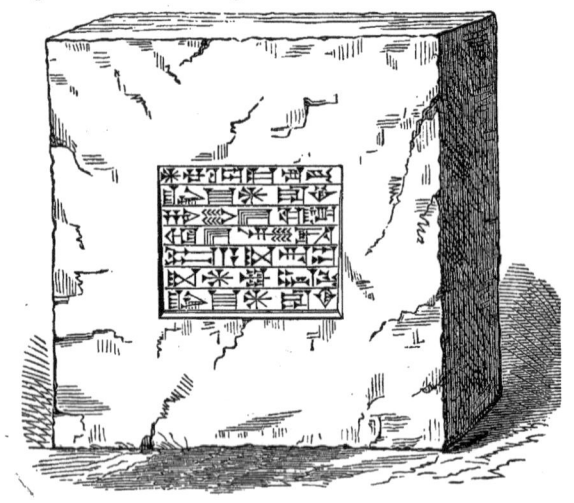

BABYLONIAN BRICK.

The Assyrians made their temples simple adjuncts to their palaces, where they were used as observatories. Here the priestly astrologers consulted the stars, and no enterprise was undertaken, however it might otherwise promise success, unless the heavens were declared favorable. Following the example of their Chaldean instructors, the Assyrians continued to build with brick, though they had an abundance of excellent stone. Their edifices, placed, like those in Chaldea, upon high artificial mounds of earth, were incased with bricks used while still soft, so that they adhered to one another without cement, and formed a single, compact mass. As their palaces were constructed of this same weak material, which was liable to disintegrate within twenty or thirty years, they were obliged to make the walls enormously thick, the halls narrow and low as compared with their length, and to limit the height to one story. The roof was loaded with earth as a protection from the fierce summer sun and the heavy winter rains. Their building-plan was always the same. Around immense square courts were arranged halls or chambers of different sizes opening into one another. These halls, though never more than 40 feet wide, were sometimes 180 feet in length. The sides were lined with alabaster slabs, from eight to fifteen feet high, covered with elaborate sculptures illustrating the sports, prowess, and religious devotion of the king; above these were enameled bricks. The court-yards were paved with chiseled stone or painted bricks, and the beams of Lebanon cedar were sometimes overlaid with silver or gold. The courts themselves were ornamented by gigantic sculptures, and the artificial mound was edged by a terraced wall. Sennacherib's palace at Koyunjik was only second in size and grandeur to the palace temple at Karnak. The ruling idea in Assyrian architecture, however, was not, as in the Egyptian, that of magnitude, much less of durability, but rather of close and finished ornamentation; the bas-reliefs being wrought out with a minuteness of detail which extended to the flowers and rosettes on a king's garment or the intricate pattern of his carved footstool. But Assyrian alabaster was far easier to manage than Egyptian granite, and where masses of hard stone like basalt were used, to which

BLACK OBELISK FROM NIMROUD.

the Egyptians would give the finish of a cameo, the Assyrians produced only coarse and awkward effects. A few stone obelisks have been found — one only, the Black Obelisk of Nimroud, being in perfect preservation. In statuary, the Assyrians signally failed, and in drawing they had no better idea of perspective than the Egyptians. In their water-scenes the fishes are as large as the ships, and the birds in the woods are half as tall as the men who hunt them. They excelled in bas-relief, in which they profusely detailed their religious ideas, home life, and royal greatness. As compared with Egyptian art,[1] the Assyrian was more progressive, and had greater freedom, variety, and taste.

Walls, Temple, Palaces, and Hanging Gardens of Babylon. — The wall of this great city formed a square, each side of which was, according to Herodotus, 14 miles long, 85 feet thick, and 335 feet high.[2] Twenty-five brass gates opened from each of the four sides upon straight, wide streets, which extended across the city, dividing it into squares. A space was left free from buildings for some distance next the walls; within that, beautiful gardens, orchards, and fields alternated with lofty dwellings. The broad Euphrates, instead of skirting the city as did the Tigris at Nineveh, ran midway through the town, and was guarded by two brick walls with brass gates opening upon steps which led down to the water. The river-banks were lined throughout with brick-and-bitumen quays, and the stream was crossed by ferries, and, during the day, by a movable drawbridge resting on stone piers.

On either side of the Euphrates rose a majestic palace, built upon a high platform, and surrounded by triple walls a quarter of a mile apart. The outer wall of the larger palace was nearly seven miles in circumference. The inner walls were faced with enameled brick, representing hunting scenes in gayly colored figures larger than life. The glory of the palace was its *Hanging Gardens*, imitated from those in Assyria, and built by Nebuchadnezzar to please his Median queen, who pined for her native hills. They consisted of a series of platforms resting on arches, and rising one above the other till the summit overtopped the city walls. The soil with which they were covered was deep enough to sustain not only flowers and shrubs, but the largest trees, so that the effect was that of a mountain clothed in verdure. The structure was ascended by broad stairs, and on the several terraces, among fountains, groves, and fragrant shrubs, were stately apartments, in whose cool shade

---

[1] The Chaldean tomb (p. 65) is without inscription, bas-relief, or painting (contrast with Egyptian tomb). No Assyrian sepulcher has yet (1892) been found.

[2] Other authorities reduce this estimate. In Alexander's time the wall still stood over seventy feet high. Curtius asserts that "nine tenths of Babylon consisted of gardens, parks, fields, and orchards."

the queen might rest while making the tour of her novel pleasure-ground. The *Temple of Belus* was also surrounded by a wall having brass gates. Within the sacred inclosure, but outside the building, were two altars for sacrifice, one of stone and one of gold. At the base of the tower—which was a huge, solid mass of brick-work—was a chapel containing a sitting image of Bel, a golden stand and table, and a human figure eighteen feet high, made of solid gold. The ascent was from the outside, and on the summit was the sacred shrine, containing three great golden images of Bel, Beltis, and Ishtar (p. 61). There were also two golden lions, two enormous silver serpents, and a golden table forty feet long and fifteen broad, besides drinking-cups, censers, and a golden bowl for each deity.

Practical Arts and Inventions.—*Agriculture* was carried to a high degree of perfection in both countries, and the system of irrigation was so complete that it has been said "not a drop of water was allowed to be lost." Their brilliantly dyed and *woven stuffs*, especially the Babylonian carpets, were celebrated throughout the ancient world; and the elaborate designs of their embroideries served as models for the earliest Grecian vases. In *metal-work* they were far advanced, and they must have possessed the art of casting vast masses, since their town and palace gates are said to have been of bronze. Where great strength was required, as in the legs of tripods and tables, the bronze was cast over iron, an ingenious art unknown to moderns until it was learned and imitated from Assyrian antiquities. The beams and furniture of palaces were often cased with bronze, and long bronze friezes with fantastic figures in relief adorned the palace halls. *Gold, silver, and bronze vases*, beautifully chased, were important articles of commerce, as was also the Assyrian pottery, which, being enameled by an entirely different process from that of Egypt, and having a finer paste, brighter hue, and thinner body, was largely exported to the latter country during the XVIIIth dynasty. Mineral tints were used for coloring. Assyrian *terra cotta* was remarkably fine and pure.

Transparent glass was in use in the time of Sargon. A rock-crystal lens has been found at Nimroud, the only object of its kind as yet discovered among the remains of antiquity. In gem-cutting the Assyrians decidedly excelled the Egyptians, and the exceeding minuteness of some work on seals implies the use of powerful magnifiers.

Most of the mechanical powers whereby heavy weights have commonly been moved and raised among civilized nations were understood.[1] The Assyrians imported their steel and iron tools from the neighboring provinces of the Caucasus, where steel had long been manufactured; the carved ivories which ornamented their palaces probably came from Phœnicia. It will be seen that in all the common arts and appliances of life the Assyrians were at least on a par with the Egyptians, while in taste they greatly excelled not only that nation, but all the Orientals. It must not be forgotten, however, that Egyptian civilization was over a thousand years old when Assyria was in its infancy.

3. THE MANNERS AND CUSTOMS.

General Character.—The *Assyrians* were brave, cruel,[2] and aggressive. Isaiah calls them a "fierce people," and Nahum speaks of Nineveh as "full of lies and robbery." The mixed people of Babylonia were more scholarly and less warlike than the purely Semitic Assyrians, but they, also, were "terrible and dreadful, going through the breadth of the land" with chariots "like the whirlwind," and "horses swifter than the leopards and more fierce than the evening wolves." In war savage and pitiless, in peace they were "tender and delicate, given to pleasures, exceeding in dyed attire upon their heads." Their covetousness and luxurious indulgences became a proverb. They were fond of giving banquets in their brilliantly painted saloons, where their visitors, clothed in scarlet robes and resplendent in cosmetics and jewelry, trod on carpets which were the envy of the ancient world, and were served with rich meats and luscious fruits on gold and silver plates. In Babylonia the guests were not formally garlanded, as in Egypt, but a profusion of flowers in elegant vases adorned the rooms. Meantime, while the air was filled with music and heavy with perfumes, the merry revelers drank deeply of the abundant wine, and loudly sang the praises of their favorite gods.

In pleasant contrast to their dissipation appear their learning, enter,

---

[1] The Assyrians wrought all the elaborate carvings of their colossi before moving them. They then stood the figure on a wooden sledge, supporting it by heavy framework, and bracing it with ropes and beams. The sledge was moved over rollers by gangs of men, levers and wedges being used to facilitate its progress. The entire process of transporting a colossal stone bull is graphically pictured in an extensive bas-relief found at Koyunjik, and now in the British Museum.

[2] The horrible atrocities inflicted on war captives are exultantly detailed on royal inscriptions. It is significant of the two civilizations that while Assyrian kings were thus mutilating and flaying alive their defenseless prisoners, Egypt had abolished the death penalty as a punishment for crime.

prise, and honesty in trade. In their intercourse with strangers they are said to have cultivated calmness of manner, a virtue probably not natural to them, but which was founded upon an intense pride in their superior culture and scientific attainments.

Religion.—The Assyrians and Babylonians were both, in an idolatrous way, religious nations, though much less so than the Egyptians. The sun, moon, and planets were conspicuous among their gods. Their ideas of one First Cause or Deity were even more obscure than those of the Egyptians, and although *Il* or *Ra*, who stood at the head of the Chaldean Pantheon, was vaguely considered as the fount or origin of Deity, there were several other self-originated gods, each supreme over his own sphere. *Il* was too dimly comprehended to be popular, and had apparently no temple in Chaldea.

Two Triads were next in rank. The first comprised *Ana*, the lord of spirits and demons, who represented original chaos; *Bel* or Bel-Nimrod, the hunter, lord and organizer of the world; and *Hoa*, the lord of the abyss, and regulator of the universe. The second triad embraced *Sin*, the moon-god; *San* (called in Assyria *Shamas*), the sun-god; and *Vul*, the air-god. Each god had a wife, who received her share of divine honors. After these came the five planetary deities: *Nin* or Saturn, sometimes called the *fish-god*—his emblem in Assyria being the man-bull; *Bel-Merodach* or Jupiter; *Nergal* or Mars—the man-lion of Assyria; *Ishtar* or Venus; and *Nebo* or Mercury. A host of inferior gods made up the Pantheon. In the later Babylonian empire, Bel, Merodach, Nebo, and Nergal were the favorite deities, the last two receiving especial worship at Babylon. The most popular goddesses were *Beltis*, wife of Bel-Nimrod, and "mother of the great gods;" and *Ishtar*, "queen of the gods," who shared with Beltis the titles of goddess of fertility, of war, and of hunting.[1] The gods were symbolized by pictorial emblems, and also by mystic numbers. Thus,

MOON-GOD. (From a Cylinder.)

Hoa = 40, emblem a serpent ; Sin = 30, emblem the moon ; San = 20, emblem the sun .

---

[1] In all the Pagan religions the characteristics of one deity often trench upon those of another, and in Chaldea the most exalted epithets were divided between a number of gods. Thus, Bel is the "father of the gods, the king of the spirits;" Ana and Merodach are each "the original chief" and "the most ancient;" Nebo is the "lord of lords, who has no equal in power;" Sin is "the king of the gods and the lord of spirits," etc. The same symbol also stands for different gods. Hoa and Nebo, each as the "god of intelligence," "teacher and instructor of men," have for one of their emblems the wedge or arrowhead characters used in cuneiform writing.

Among the emblems symbolizing other, and to us unknown, **gods, is** a double cross, generally repeated three times. Religious etiquette erected honorary shrines to outside gods in temples consecrated to one chosen favorite; and a Babylonian gentleman wore on his cylinder seal, besides the emblem of his chosen god patron, the complimentary symbols of other deities.

In Assyria, Il was known as *Asshur*,[1] and was the supreme object of worship. He was the guardian deity of king and country, and in the sculptures his emblem is always seen near the monarch. In the midst of battle, in processions of victory, in public worship, or in the pleasures of the chase, Asshur hovers over the scene, pointing his own arrow at the king's enemies, uplifting his hand with the king in worship, or spreading his wings protectingly over the scene of enjoyment. In bas-reliefs representing worship, there also appear a "sacred tree," whose true symbolism is unknown,[2] and winged eagle-headed deities or genii who hand to the king mysterious fruit from a sacred basket. *Sin* and *Shamas* were highly honored in Assyria, and their emblems were worn by the king on his neck. Upon the cylinders they are conjoined, the sun resting in the crescent of the moon.

Bel was also a favorite god;[3] but *Nin* and *Nergal*, the winged bull and lion, the gods who "made sharp the weapons" of kings, and who presided over war and hunting, were most devotedly worshiped. The race of kings was traditionally derived from Nin, and his name was given to the mighty capital (Nineveh).

Below the Great Gods were countless inferior ones, each city having its local deities which elsewhere received small respect. Good and evil spirits were represented as perpetually warring with one another. Pestilence, fever, and all the ills of life, were personified, and man was like a bewildered traveler in a strange land, exposed to a host of unseen foes, whom he could subdue only by charms and exorcisms.

The Assyrians apparently had no set religious festivals. When a feast was to be held in honor of any god, the king made special proclamation. During a fast, not only king, nobles, and people abstained from food and drink, clothed themselves in sackcloth, and sprinkled

---

[1] In the original language, the name of the country, of the first capital, and the term "an Assyrian," are all identical with the name of this god.

[2] Recent theories identifying the Egyptian lotus with all classic ornamentation assert that the "sacred tree" was a conventional arrangement of lotus palmettes and buds, that the mysterious cone-like fruit was a lotus-bud, and that the Assyrian "rosette" was the ovary stigma of the lotus-flower,—all being symbols of sun-worship. (See Goodyear's Grammar of the Lotus.)

[3] It was common for both Assyrian and Babylonian kings to signify their favorite god by associating his name with their own. The gods most frequently allied with royal names in Assyria were Asshur, Bel, and Nebo; in Babylonia, Nebo and Merodach.

THE MANNERS AND CUSTOMS. 63

ashes on their heads, but all the animals within the city walls were made to join in the penitential observance (see Jonah iii. 5-9).

Image Worship.—The stone, clay, and metal images which adorned the temple shrines of Assyria and Babylonia were worshiped as real gods. So identified was a divinity with its idol, that, in the inscriptions of kings where the great gods were invoked in turn, the images of the same deity placed in different temples were often separately addressed, as Ishtar of Babylon, Ishtar of Arbela, Ishtar of Nineveh, etc. In worship, living sacrifices and offerings were made and oblations poured, the king taking the chief position, instead of the priest, as in Egypt.

Curious Babylonish Customs.—If we are to believe Herodotus, the Babylonians buried their dead in honey, and married their daughters by auction, the money brought by the handsome ones being given as a dowry to their less favored sisters. The marriage festival took place once a year, and no father could give his daughter at any other time or in any other way. Each bride received a clay model of an olive, on which were inscribed her name and that of her husband, with the date of the ceremony; this was to be worn on her neck. Unlike the Egyptians, the Babylonians had no regular physicians; the sick and infirm were brought out into the market-place, where the passers-by prescribed remedies which had proved effectual in their own experience or that of their friends; it being against the law to pass by a sick person without inquiring into the nature of his disease.

ASSYRIAN LAMPS.

Every summer the slaves had a festival, called *Sacees*, when for five days they took command of their masters, one of them, clothed in a royal robe, receiving the honors of a king.

SCENES IN REAL LIFE.

Scene I.—*A Chaldean Home.*—Let us visit the home of an ancient Chaldean as we should have found it over 3500 years ago. Before us rises a high brick platform, supporting an irregular cross-shaped house built of burnt or sun-dried bricks cemented with mud or bitumen. The outside is gayly adorned with colored terra-cotta cones embedded in mud or plaster. Entering, we find long, narrow rooms opening one into another. If there are windows, they are set high, near the roof or ceiling. Upon the plastered walls, which are often broken by little recesses, are cuneiform inscriptions, varied by red, black, and white bands, or rude, bright-red figures of men and birds.[1] The chairs or stools, of soft, light date-wood, have legs modeled after those of an ox. The invaluable palm-tree, as useful in Chaldea as in Egypt, has not only supplied the table itself, but much of the food upon it. Its fresh or dried fruit appears as bread or sweetmeats; its sap, as wine, vinegar, and honey. The tableware is clay or bronze. The vases which contain the wine are mostly of coarse clay mixed with chopped straw; but here and there one of a finer glaze shows the work of the potter's wheel and an idea of beauty. The master of the house wears a long linen robe, elaborately striped, flounced, and fringed, which, passing over one shoulder, leaves the other bare, and falls to his feet. His beard is long and straight, and his hair either gathered in a roll at the back of his head or worn in long curls. He does not despise jewelry on his own person, and his wife revels in armlets and bracelets, and in rings for the fingers and toes. Bronze and iron—which is so rare as to be a precious metal—are affected most by the Chaldean belle, but her ornaments are also of shell, agate, and sometimes of gold. For the common people, a short tunic tied around the waist and reaching to the knee is a perpetual fashion, suitable for a temperature which ranges from 100° to 130° F. in summer. In the severest winter season, when the thermometer falls to 30° above zero, the Chaldean hunter dons an extra wrap, which covers his shoulders and falls below his tunic; then, barefooted, and with a skull-cap or a camel's-hair band on his head, he goes out, with his bronze arrowhead and bronze or flint knife, to shoot and dissect the wild boar. Our Chaldean gentleman makes out

SIGNET CYLINDER OF URUCH.[2]
(The earliest Chaldean king, of whom many definite remains have been found. Date, perhaps, 2800 B. C. See p. 45.)

---

[1] This description is based upon the only two Chaldean residences which have as yet, so far as is known, been exhumed. They are supposed to date from between 1800 and 1600 B. C.

[2] Uruch, King of Ur, lived perhaps before Babylon was founded. He was the first to call himself "King of Shumir and Accad." From his cylinder we learn that the Chaldeans at this early date dressed in delicate fabrics elaborately trimmed, and had tastefully fashioned household furniture.

a deed or writes a letter with a small bronze or ivory tool suited to his minute, cuneiform script, on a bit of moist clay shaped like a tiny pillow (p. 52). He signs it by rolling across the face the little engraved jasper or chalcedony cylinder, which he wears attached by a string to his wrist. Having baked it, he incloses it in a thin clay envelope, upon which he repeats his message or contract, and bakes it again. When the Chaldean dies, his friends shroud him in fine linen, and incase him in two large stone jars, so that the upper part of his body rests in one, and the lower part in the other, after which they cement the two jars together with mud or bitumen; or they lay him upon a brick platform with a reed matting beneath him, and place over him a huge, burnt-clay cover,—a marvel of pottery, formed of a single piece, and shaped like a modern tureen cover; or they put him on the mat in the family arched vault, pillowing his head on a sun-dried brick covered with a tapestry cushion. About him they arrange his ornaments and favorite implements; vases of wine are within his reach, and in the palm of his left hand they rest a bronze or copper bowl filled with dates or other food to strengthen him in his mysterious journey through the silent land.

A CYLINDER SEAL.

Scene II.—*A Morning in Nineveh.*—The Assyrian was a cedar in Lebanon, exalted above all the trees of the field, so that all the trees that were in the garden of God envied him, and not one was like unto him in his beauty (Ezek. xxxi.). Six centuries and a half have passed since Chaldea was humbled by her northern neighbor; and Assyria, not dreaming that her own fall is so near, is in the fullness of her splendor and arrogance. It is about the year 650 B. C., and the proud Asshurbanipal is on the throne—Asshurbanipal, who has subdued the land of the Pyramids and the Labyrinth, and made Karnak and Luxor mere adjuncts to his glory. Nineveh, with her great walls one hundred feet in height, upon which three chariots can run abreast, lies before us. The bright spring sun of the Orient looks down upon a country luxuriant with a rich but short-lived verdure. Green myrtles and blossoming oleanders fringe the swollen streams, and the air is filled with the sweet odors of the citron-trees. The morning fog has loaded the dwarf oak with manna, and the rains have crowded the land with flowers. The towers, two hundred feet high, which mark the various city gates, throw long shadows over rows of windowless houses, topped with open domes or high, steep, cone-like roofs. Out from these houses come the people, dressed according to their several stations: bareheaded and barefooted laborers, clothed in one garment, a plain, short-sleeved tunic reaching to the knee; prosperous folk in sandals and fringed tunics, and the wealthy, in long

AN ASSYRIAN PALACE RESTORED.

THE MANNERS AND CUSTOMS. 67

fringed and elegantly girdled robes. Only the higher orders are privileged to cover their heads with a cap, but all, even the meanest, glory in long, elaborately dressed hair. In the dwellings of the rich we may see furniture of elegant design: canopied beds and couches, and curtains of costly tapestry; carved stools and tables with feet fashioned like gazelle-hoofs; and, in the palace, luxurious chairs, and articles sacred to gods and the king. In the west end of the city, abutting the swift-flowing Tigris, is a high platform covering one hundred acres, on which stands the magnificent palace of Asshurbanipal. Near it is the still larger one built by Sennacherib, his grandfather, and about it are parks and hanging gardens. The palaces have immense portals guarded by colossal winged and human-headed bulls and lions; great court-yards paved with elegantly patterned slabs; and arched doorways, elaborately sculptured and faced by eagle-headed deities. We miss the warm, glowing colors so generously lavished on Egyptian temples. There are traces of the painter, but his tints are more subdued and more sparingly used. It is the triumphant day of the sculptor and the enameler. Asshurbanipal sits on his carved chair, arrayed in his embroidered robe and mantle. On his breast rests a large circular ornament wrought with sacred emblems; golden rosettes glitter on his red-and-white tiara, and rosettes and crescents adorn his shoes. He wears a sword and daggers, and holds a golden scepter. Necklaces, armlets, bracelets, and ear-rings add to his costume. Behind him is his parasol-bearer, grasping with both hands a tall, thick pole supporting a fringed and curtained shade. His Grand Vizier—who interprets his will to the people, and whose dress approaches his own in magnificence—stands before him in an attitude of passive reverence to receive the royal orders; the scribes are waiting to record the mandate, and a host of attendants are at hand to perform it.

COLOSSAL HUMAN-HEADED WINGED BULL.

Scene III.—*A Royal Lion-hunt.*—To-day it is a lion-hunt. At the palace gates, surrounded by a waiting retinue, stands the king's chariot, headed by three richly caparisoned horses, champing bronze bits and gayly tinkling the bells on their tasseled collars, while grooms hold other horses to be placed before the chariots of high officials, after the monarch shall have mounted. As the king steps into the box-like chariot, his two favorite eunuchs adjust the well-stocked quivers, put in the long spears, and enter behind him; the charioteer loosens the reins, and the horses start at full speed. At the park, or "paradise," a large circuit is inclosed by a double rampart of spearmen and archers, and a row of hounds held in leashes. Here the lions kept for the king's sport wait in their cages. Having arrived at the park and received a ceremonious salute, the king gives the order to release the wild beasts. Cautiously creeping out from their cages, they seem at first to seek escape; but the spearmen's large shields and bristling weapons dazzle their eyes; the fierce dogs, struggling in their leashes, howl in their ears; and the king's well-aimed arrows quickly enrage them to combat. Swifter and swifter fly the darts. The desperate beasts spring at the chariot sides only to receive death-thrusts from the spears of the attendants, while the excited king shoots rapidly on

THE ROYAL LION-HUNT (FROM THE SCULPTURES).

in front. Now one has seized the chariot-wheel with his huge paws, and grinds it madly with his teeth; but he, too, falls in convulsions to the ground. The sport fires the blood of the fierce Asshurbanipal. He jumps from his chariot, orders fresh lions to be released, grasps his long spear, selects the most ferocious for a hand-to-hand combat, furiously dispatches him, and, amid the deafening shouts of his admiring courtiers, proclaims his royal content. The hunt is over; the dead lions have been collected for the king's inspection, and are now borne on the shoulders of men in a grand procession to the palace, whither the king precedes them. The chief officers of the royal household come out to welcome him; the cup-bearer brings wine, and, while the king refreshes himself, busily plies his long fly-whisk about the royal head, the musicians meantime playing merrily upon their harps. It remains to offer the finest and bravest of the game to the god of the chase; and four of the largest lions are accordingly selected and arranged side by side before the altar. The king and his attendants, all keeping time to formal music, march in stately majesty to the shrine, where Asshurbanipal raises the sacred cup to his lips, and slowly pours the solemn libation. A new sculpture depicting the grand event of the day is ordered, and beneath it is inscribed,—

"I, Asshurbanipal, king of the nations, king of Assyria, in my great courage, fighting on foot with a lion terrible for its size, seized him by the ear, and in the name of Asshur and of Ishtar, Goddess of War, with the spear that was in my hand I terminated his life."

Scene IV.—*Asshurbanipal going to War.*—The king goes to war in his chariot, dressed in his most magnificent attire, and attended by a retinue of fan-bearers, parasol-bearers, bow, quiver, and mace-bearers. About these gather his body-guard of foot-spearmen, each one brandishing a tall spear and protected by scale-armor, a pointed helmet, and a great metal shield. The detachment of horse-archers which follows is also dressed in coats of mail, leather breeches, and jackboots. Before and behind the royal *cortége* stretches the army—a vast array of glancing helmets, spears, shields, and battle-axes; warriors in chariots, on horse, and on foot; heavy-armed archers in helmet and armor, with the strung bow on the shoulders and the highly decorated quiver filled with bronze or iron-headed arrows on the back; light-armed archers with embroidered head-bands and short tunics, and bare arms, limbs, and feet; spearmen who carry great wicker shields, which are made, in case of need, to join and furnish boats; and troops of slingers, mace-bearers, and ax-bearers. The massive throne of the king is in the cavalcade; upon this, when the battle or siege is ended, he will sit in great state to receive the prisoners and spoil. Here, too, are his drinking-cups and washing-bowls, his low-wheeled pleasure-chair, his dressing-table, and other toilet luxuries. Battering-rams, scaling-ladders, baggage-carts, and the usual paraphernalia of a great army make up the rear, where also in carefully closed *arabas* are the king's wives, who, with the whole court, follow him to war. The Ninevites come out in crowds to see the start; the musicians—who, however, remain at home—play a brisk farewell on double-pipes, harps, and drum; the women and children, standing in procession, clap their hands and sing; and so, amid "the noise of the rattling of the wheels, and of the prancing horses, and of the jumping chariots" (Nahum iii. 2), the Assyrian army sets off.

Scene V.—*A Royal Banquet.*—After many days the host comes back victorious (the sculptors never record defeats), bringing great spoil of gold, silver, and fine furniture, countless oxen, sheep, horses, and camels, prisoners of war, and captured foreign gods. Rejoicing and festivities abound. A royal feast is given in the most magnificent of the sculptured halls, where the tables glitter with gold and silver stands laden with dried locusts, pomegranates, grapes, and citrons.

There are choice meats, hare, and game-birds, and an abundance of mixed wine in the huge vases from which the busy attendants fill the beakers of the guests. Afterward the king invites the queen from her seclusion in the beautiful harem to sup with him in the garden. At this banquet the luxurious Asshurbanipal reclines on a couch, leaning his left elbow on a cushioned pillow, and holding in his hand a lotus, here, as in Egypt, the sacred flower. A table with dishes of incense stands by his couch, at the foot of which sits his handsome queen. Her tunic is fringed and patterned in the elaborate Assyrian style, and she is resplendent with jewelry. A grape-vine shelters the royal pair, and behind each of them stand two fan-bearers with long brushes, scattering the troublesome flies. Meantime the king and queen sip wine from their golden cups; the attendants bring in fresh fruits; the harpers play soft music; and, to complete the triumph of the feast, from a neighboring tree surrounded by hungry vultures dangles the severed head of the king's newly conquered enemy.

ASSYRIAN KING AND ATTENDANTS.

4. SUMMARY.

1· **Political History.**—Our earliest glimpse of Chaldea is of a Turanian people in temple cities. Later come the Semites, a nomadic people, who migrate northward, and finally build the Assyrian cities upon the Tigris. Henceforth war rages between the rival sections, and the seat of power fluctuates between Babylon and Nineveh. About 1300 B. C. Babylon is overwhelmed, and for nearly 700 years Nineveh is the seat of empire. Here the Sargonidæ—Sennacherib, Esarhaddon, and Asshurbanipal—develop the Golden Age of Assyrian rule. The Babylonians, however, continue to revolt, and in 747 B. C. Nabonassar ascends the Babylonian throne, destroys the records of all the kings before his time, and establishes a new era from which to reckon dates. In 606 B. C. Nineveh is finally overthrown by the Babylonians and the Medes, and Nabopolassar establishes the second Babylonian Empire. Nebuchadnezzar subdues the surrounding nations, humiliates Egypt, captures Tyre, crushes Judea, and with his captives brought back to Babylon makes that city the marvel of all eyes. It is, however, the last of her glory. Within the next quarter of a century Babylon is taken by the stratagem of Cyrus the Great, Belshazzar is slain, **and the mighty city falls, never again to rise to her ancient glory.**

SUMMARY. 71

2. Civilization.—*The Early Chaldeans* build vast temples of sun-dried brick cemented with bitumen; write in cuneiform characters on clay tablets; engrave signet cylinders; use implements of stone, flint, and bronze; manufacture cloth; make boats and navigate the sea. They are learned in astronomy and arithmetic; discover the equinoctial precession (Steele's Astronomy, p. 121); divide the day into twenty-four hours; draw maps, record phenomena, invent dials, and calculate a table of squares. They place their houses on high platforms, make their furniture of date-wood, and use tableware of clay or bronze. The palm-tree furnishes them food. Their dead are buried in large clay jars, or in dish-covered tombs, or are laid to rest in arched brick vaults.

INTERIOR COURT-YARD OF A MODERN ORIENTAL HOUSE

The Assyrians, their Semitic conquerors, are a fierce, warlike race, skillful in agriculture, in blowing glass and shaping pottery, in casting and embossing metals, and in engraving gems. They dye, weave, and are superior in plastic art. They build great palaces, adorning them with sculptured alabaster slabs, colossal bulls and lions, paved courts, and eagle-headed deities. They, too, write upon clay tablets, and cover terra-cotta cylinders with cuneiform inscriptions. Their principal gods are the heavenly bodies. They do not worship animals, like the Egyptians, but place images of clay, stone, or metal in their temples, and treat them as real deities. Magic and sorcery abound. There is no caste among the people, but all are at the mercy of the king. Women are not respected as in Egypt, and they live secluded in their own apartments. Clay books are collected and libraries founded, but most of the learning comes from the conquered race, and the Chaldean is the classic language.

BABYLONIA AND ASSYRIA.

The Babylonians are a luxurious people. Industries flourish and commerce is extensive. Babylonian robes and tapestries surpass all others in texture and hue. Far below Assyria in the art of sculptured bas-relief, Babylonia excels in brick-enameling, and is greatly the supe-

THE SITE OF ANCIENT BABYLON.

rior in originality of invention, literary culture, and scientific attainment. From her Assyria draws her learning, her architecture, her religion, her legal forms, and many of her customs.

"In Babylonia almost every branch of science made a beginning. She was the source to which the entire stream of Eastern civilization may be traced. It is scarcely too much to say that, but for Babylon, real civilization might not even yet have dawned upon the earth, and mankind might never have advanced beyond that spurious and false form of it which in Egypt, India, China, Japan, Mexico, and Peru, contented the aspirations of the people."—*Rawlinson's Ancient Monarchies.*

READING REFERENCES.

Rawlinson's History of Ancient Monarchies.—Fergusson's History of Architecture, and Palaces of Nineveh and Persepolis Restored.—Layard's Monuments of Nineveh, and Nineveh and its Remains.—Records of the Past (New Series).—Sayce's Babylonian Literature; Assyria, its Princes, Priests, and People; and Fresh Lights from Ancient Monuments.—Perrot and Chipiez's History of Art in Chaldea and Assyria.—George Smith's Chaldean Account of Genesis (Revised); Assyrian Discoveries; and Early History of Assyria.—Loftus's Chaldea and Susiana.—Also the General Ancient Histories named on p. 44.

CHRONOLOGY.

	B. C.
Sargon I.	3800 ?
Ur-ĕa (Uruch)	2800 ?
Khammuragus	2280 ?
Rise of Assyria	1300
Era of Nabonassar	747
Fall of Nineveh	606 ?
Cyrus captured Babylon	538
Alexander captured Babylon	331

PHŒNICIA.

The Phœnicians were Semites. They inhabited a barren strip of land on the eastern shore of the Mediterranean, not more than one hundred and eighty miles long and a dozen broad. The country was never united under one king, but each city was a sovereignty by itself. A powerful aristocracy was connected with these little monarchies, but the bulk of the people were slaves brought from foreign countries. The principal cities were Sidon and Tyre,[1] which successively exercised a controlling influence over the others. The chief defense of the Phœnicians lay in their naval power. Situated midway between the east and the west, and at the junction of three continents, they carried on the trade of the world.[2] The Mediterranean became the mere highway of their commerce. They passed the Strait of Gibraltar on one hand, and reached India on the other.

They settled Cyprus, Sicily, and Sardinia. In Spain they founded Gades (now Cadiz); and in Africa, Utica and Carthage, the latter destined to be in time the dreaded rival of Rome. They planted depots on the Persian Gulf and the

Geographical Questions.—Bound Phœnicia. Locate Tyre; Sidon. Name the principal Phœnician colonies. Where was Carthage? Utica? Tarshish? Gades? The Pillars of Hercules?

[1] Tyre, which was founded by Sidonians, has been called the Daughter of Sidon and the Mother of Carthage.

[2] Read the 27th chapter of Ezekiel for a graphic account of the Phœnician commerce in his day.

Red Sea. They obtained tin from the British Isles, amber from the Baltic,[1] silver from Tarshish (southern Spain), and

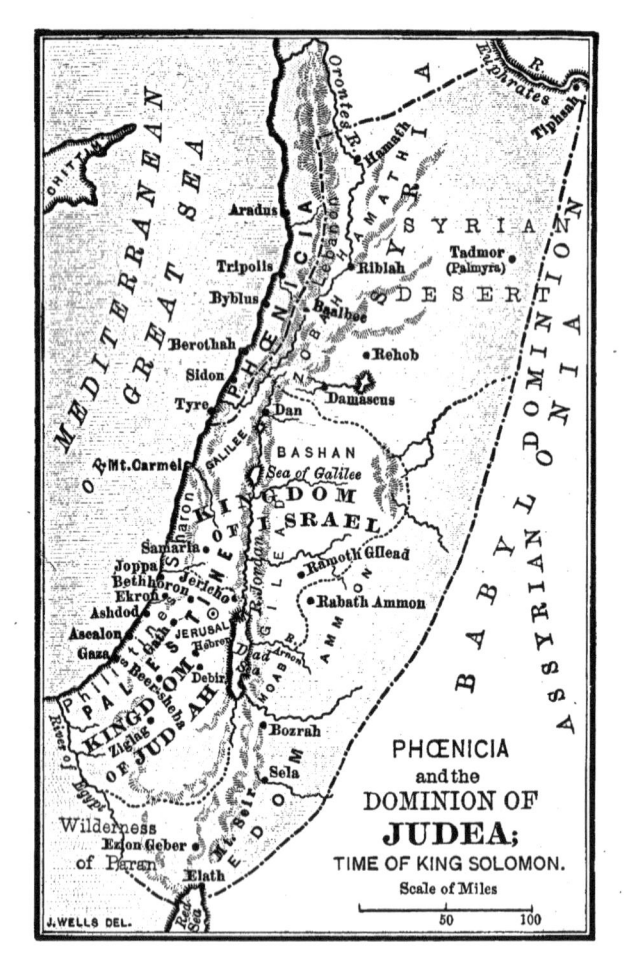

gold from Ophir (southeastern Arabia). In connection with their maritime trade they established great commercial

---

[1] Over their land trade routes. Amber also existed near Sidon. They carefully concealed the source of their supplies. An outward-bound Phœnician captain once found himself followed by a Roman ship. To preserve his secret and destroy his follower, he ran his own vessel on the rocks. The government made up his loss.

routes by which their merchants penetrated the interior of Europe and Asia. With the growth of Carthage and the rising power of Greece they lost their naval supremacy. But the land traffic of Asia remained in their hands; and their caravans, following the main traveled route through Palmyra, Baalbec, and Babylon, permeated all the Orient.

THE RUINS OF ANCIENT TYRE.

Loss of Independence.—Rich merchant cities were tempting prizes in those days of strife. From about 850 B. C., Phœnicia became the spoil of each of the great conquerors who successively achieved empire. It was made a province, in turn, of Assyria, Babylonia, Persia, Egypt, Greece, and finally Rome. The Phœnicians patiently submitted to the oppression of these various masters, and paid their tribute at Memphis or Nineveh, as the case might be. To them the mere question of liberty, or the amount of their taxes, was a small one compared with the opening or closing of their great routes of trade. The general avoidance of war, except as they entered the service of their foreign masters, must have arisen from self-interest, and not from cowardice, since the Phœnician navigator displayed a courage shaming that of the mere soldier.

Carthage,[1] the most famous Phœnician colony, was founded, according to legend, about 880 B. C., by Dido, who came thither with a body of aristocrats fleeing from the democratic party of Tyre. The location of Carthage was African, but its origin and language were Asiatic. The policy of the warlike daughter proved very unlike that of the peaceful mother. The young city, having gained wealth by commerce, steadily pushed her conquests among the neighboring tribes inch by inch, until, by the 7th century B. C., she reached the frontier of Numidia. No ancient people rivaled her in ability to found colonies. These were all kept subject to the parent city, and their tribute enriched her treasury. Of the history of Carthage we know little, and still less of her laws, customs, and life. No Punic orator, philosopher, historian, or poet has left behind any fragment to tell of the thoughts that stirred or the events that formed this wonderful people. Had it not been for the desolating wars that accompanied her fall, we should hardly know that such a city and such a nation ever existed.

[1] Carthage was built on a peninsula about three miles wide. Across this was constructed a triple wall with lofty towers. A single wall defended the city on every side next the sea. The streets were lined with massive houses lavishly adorned with the riches of the Punic traders. Two long piers reached out into the sea, forming a double harbor,— the outer for merchant ships, and the inner for the navy. In the center of the inner harbor was a lofty island crowned with the admiral's palace. Around this island and the entire circumference of the inner harbor extended a marble colonnade of Ionic pillars two stories high; the lower story forming the front of the curved galleries for the protection of the ships; and the upper, of the rooms for workshops, storehouses, etc. The limits of the city were twenty-three miles, and it was probably more populous than Rome. Its navy was the largest in the world, and in the sea-fight with Regulus comprised 350 vessels, carrying 150,000 men.

THE CIVILIZATION.

Civilization.—"Assyria and Egypt were the birthplaces of material civilization, and the Phœnicians were its missionaries." The depots of the Phœnician merchants were centers whence germs of culture were scattered broadcast. To Europe and Africa these traders brought the arts and refinements of the older and more advanced East.

Literature.—But the Phœnicians were more than mere carriers. To them we are said to owe the alphabet,[1] which came to us, with some modifications, through the Greeks and Romans. Unfortunately no remains of Phœnician literature survive. Treatises on agriculture and the useful arts are said to have been numerous; Debir, a Canaanite (probably Phœnician) town of Palestine, was termed the "book-city."

Arts and Inventions.—The Phœnicians were the first to notice the connection of the moon with the tides, and apply astronomy practically to navigation. They carried on vast mining operations, and were marvelous workers in ivory, pottery, and the metals, so that their bronzes and painted vases became the models of early Grecian art. The prize assigned by Achilles for the foot-race at the funeral of Patrocles (Iliad, XXIII., 471) was—

'A bowl of solid silver, deftly wrought,
That held six measures, and in beauty far
Surpassed whatever else the world could boast;
Since men of Sidon skilled in glyptic art
Had made it, and Phœnician mariners
Had brought it with them over the dark sea." [2]

---

[1] According to general belief, the Phœnicians selected from the Egyptian hieratic twenty-two letters, making each represent a definite articulation. Twelve of these we retain with nearly their Phœnician value. But the age and origin of the alphabet are still under discussion. Mr. Petrie says that the inscribed potsherds found by him (1890) in Egypt "point to the independent existence of the Phœnician and perhaps the Greek alphabet at least 2000 B. C.;" while Prof. Sayce, speaking of recent discoveries (1890) in Arabia, remarks, "Instead of seeking in Phœnicia the primitive home of our alphabet, we may have to look for it in Arabia."

[2] Until recently no specimen of pure Phœnician art was known to exist. Luigi Palma di Cesnola, former Consul to the Island of Cyprus, in his excavations on that island, uncovered the sites of seventeen cities, and opened many thousand tombs. Here he found countless Egyptian, Assyrian, Babylonian, Greek, and Phœnician treasures, dating from before the time of Thothmes III. (p. 17), whose official seal he exhumed. The Phœnician tombs were several feet below the Grecian; one city having perished and another sprung up, "which, in turn, buried its dead, unconscious of the older sepulcher below. Time had left no human remains except a few skulls, to some of which still adhered the gold leaf placed by the Phœnicians over the mouth of their dead."

78   PHŒNICIA.

Sidon was noted for its glass-working, in which the blow-pipe, lathe, and graver were used. The costly purple dye of Tyre, obtained in minute drops from shell-fish, was famous, the rarest and most beautiful shade being worn only by kings. The Phœnicians were celebrated for their perfumes, and had a reputation for nicety of execution in all ornamental arts. When Solomon was about to build the great Jewish Temple, King Hiram sent, at his request, "a cunning man of Tyre, skillful to work in gold, in silver,

SIDON.

in brass, in iron, in stone, and in timber; in purple, in blue, in crimson, and in fine linen; also to grave any manner of graving, and to find out every device which shall be put to him."

Their Religion resembled that of the Chaldeans and Assyrians, but was more cruel. *Baal* and *Moloch* were great gods connected with the sun. They were worshiped in groves on high places, amid the wild cries and self-mutilations of their votaries. Before and after a battle (if victorious) large numbers of human beings were sacrificed. *Melcarth*, the special god of Tyre, united the attributes of Baal and Moloch. He was a Hercules who pulled back the sun to the earth at the time of the solstices, moderated all extreme weather, and counteracted the evil signs of the zodiac; his symbol was that of the Persian Ormazd,—a never-ceasing flame (p. 98). *Astarte*, or Ashtaroth, goddess of fire and chief divinity of Sidon, became the wife of Melcarth; she symbolized the moon.

Children were the favorite offerings to Moloch. At Jerusalem (2 Kings xxiii. 10) the hollow metal image of the Tyrian god was heated by a fire beneath it, the priest placed the child in the idol's glowing hands, and drums were beaten to drown the little sufferer's cries. So common were such sacrifices, that one historian says the Phœnicians offered some relative on the occasion of any great calamity; and when the Carthaginians were besieged by Agathocles, tyrant of Sicily, they devoted two hundred of their noblest children in a public sacrifice. Even in Roman Carthage these horrible sights were revived, and infants were publicly offered till Tiberius, to put a stop to the revolting practice, crucified the priests on the same trees beneath whose shade they had performed these cruel rites.

READING REFERENCES.

The General Ancient Histories named on pp. 44 and 72.—Chevalier and Lenormant's Manual of Oriental History.—Capt. Mago's Adventures, a Phœnician Expedition 1000 B. C.—*Arnold's History of Rome, Vol. II., pp.* 455-467 (*Carthaginian Institutions*).—*Mommsen's History of Rome, Vol. II., p.* 261 (*Carthage*).—*Rawlinson's Phœnicia; and Church's Carthage* (*Story of the Nations Series*).—*Perrot and Chipiez's History of Art in Phœnicia*

CHRONOLOGY.

	B. C.
Sidon founded, about	1550
Rise of Tyre, about	1050
Carthage founded, about	880
Phœnicia conquered by Assyria, about	850
Tyre captured by Nebuchadnezzar	585
Tyre captured by Alexander	332

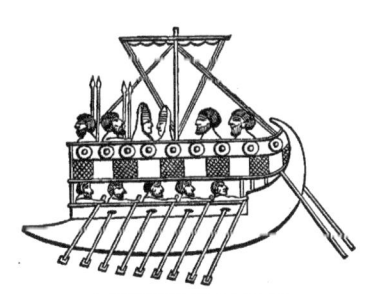

A PHŒNICIAN GALLEY.

JUDEA.

The Hebrews were Semites, and related to the Assyrians and the Phœnicians. Their history opens, in the 20th century B. C., with the coming of Abram from Chaldea into Canaan. There he and his descendants lived, simple shepherds, like the Arabs of to-day, dwelling in tents among their flocks and herds. By a singular fortune, Joseph, his great-grandson, became vizier of A-pe-pi II., one of the shepherd kings of Egypt (p. 17). Being naturally desirous of surrounding himself by foreigners who would support him against a revolt of the people, that monarch invited the Hebrews to settle in Egypt. Here they greatly prospered. But in time the native kings, who "knew not Joseph," were restored. During the XIXth dynasty, Rameses II. greatly oppressed them with hard service on his public works (p. 18). During the next reign (Mineptah's) Moses, one of the profoundest statesmen of history, who was versed in all the learning of the Egyptian court,—then the center of civilization,—rescued his people from their bondage.[1]

Geographical Questions.—Bound Palestine. Locate the Dead Sea; the Sea of Galilee; the Kingdom of Judah; the Kingdom of Israel. Describe the River Jordan. Where was Jerusalem? Samaria? Jericho? Damascus? Palmyra (Tadmor)? Joppa? Why, in going from Galilee to Jerusalem, did Jesus of Nazareth "needs pass through Samaria"? Name the five cities of the Philistines. *Ans.* Ashdod, Gaza, Ascalon, Gath, Ekron.

[1] The wonderful events by which this was accomplished are familiar to every Bible student. The design is here to give only the political history, omitting that

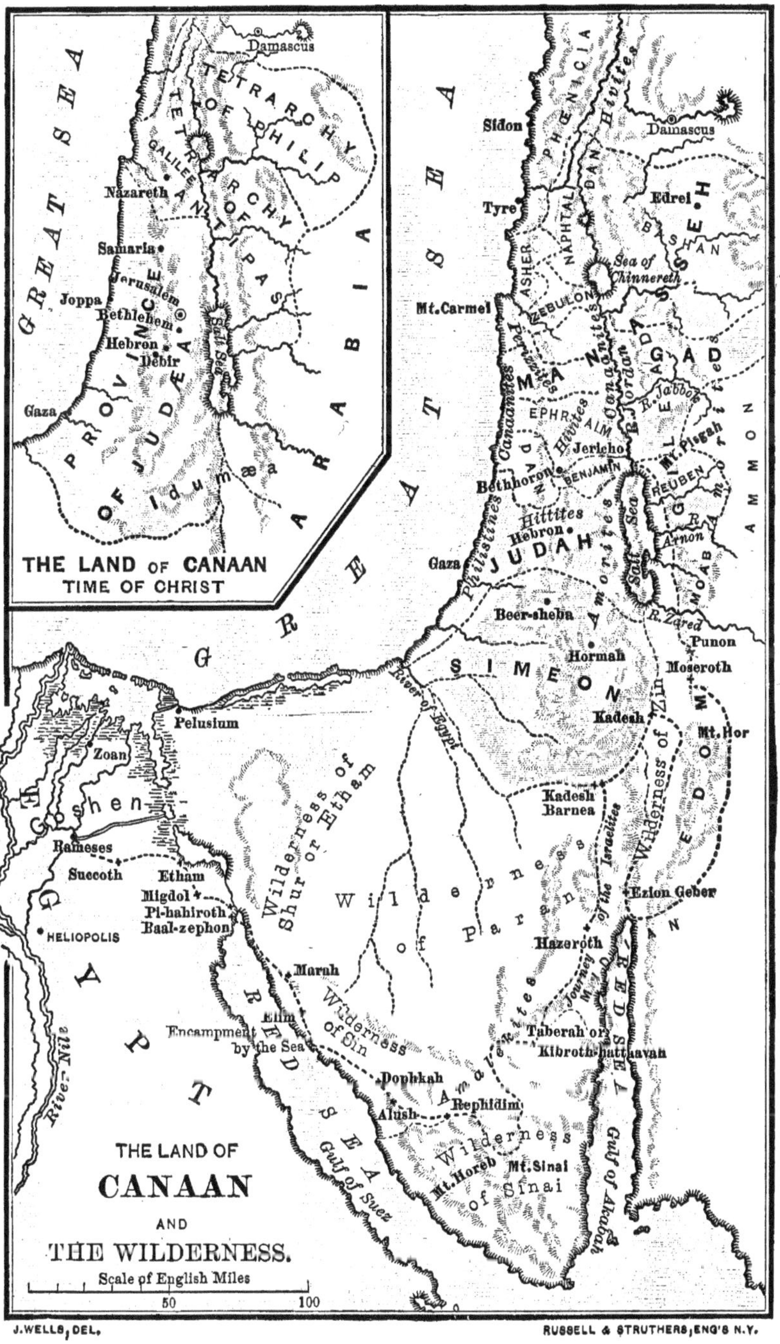

J. WELLS, DEL. RUSSELL & STRUTHERS, ENG'S N.Y.

The Exodus (about 1300 B. C.).[1]—For forty years Moses led the Jews through the wilderness until the 3,000,000 of slaves became assimilated into a nation of freemen, were won from Egyptian idolatries to the pure worship of the one God of their fathers, were trained to war, and made acquainted with the religious rites and the priestly government which were henceforth to distinguish them as a people.

The Conquest of Palestine was accomplished by Joshua,[2] successor to Moses, in six years of fierce fighting, during which thirty-one Canaanite cities were destroyed, and the country was allotted to the tribes.

The Judges.—Unfortunately, Joshua at his death did not appoint a new leader; and for want of a head, the tribes fell apart. The old spirit of enthusiasm, nationality, and religious fervor waned. Idolatry crept in. For a while the conquered Canaanites made easy prey of the disunited tribes. From time to time there arose heroic men who aroused their patriotism, inspired a new zeal for the Mosaic law, and induced them to shake off the yoke of servitude. These were the days of the Judges—Othniel, Ehud, Gideon, Samson, the prophetess Deborah, and the prophet Samuel.

Kingdom of Israel.—During the last days of the Judges, while the Jews and the Canaanites were at war, a new power grew up on their borders. The Philistines

---

providential oversight more often avowed in the case of the Jews, but not more real than in the life of every nation and individual. It is noticeable that Mineptah, the Pharaoh who, according to a common belief not supported by the Bible record, perished in the Red Sea, lived many years after that disaster, and died in his bed. (See 1 Kings vi. 1.)

[1] This is the date now generally accepted by Egyptologists. Usher, whose chronology is still preferred by some Bible students, says 1491 B. C. (See 1 Kings vi. 1.)

[2] Joshua's plan of crossing the Jordan, capturing Jericho, taking the heights beyond by a night-march, and delivering the crushing blow at Bethhoron (Joshua x. 9), was a masterpiece of strategy, and ranks him among the great generals of the world. His first movement placed him in the center of the country, where he could prevent his enemies from massing against him, and, turning in any direction, cut them up in detail.

formed a strong confederation of five cities along the coast south of Phœnicia, and threatened the conquest of Canaan. In order to make head against them, the people demanded a king. Accordingly, three monarchs were given them in succession,—*Saul, David,* and *Solomon.* Each reigned forty years. The first was merely a general, who obeyed the orders of God as revealed through the prophet Samuel. The second was a warrior king. He enlarged the boundaries of Palestine, fixed the capital at Jerusalem, organized an

TOMBS OF THE JUDGES.

army, and enforced the worship of Jehovah as the national religion. The third was a magnificent oriental monarch. His empire reached to the Euphrates, and the splendor of his court rivaled that of Egypt and Assyria. He married an Egyptian princess, built the temple on Mount Moriah in Jerusalem, erected splendid palaces, and sent expeditions to India and Arabia. This was the golden age of Judea, and Jerusalem overflowed with wealth.

The Two Kingdoms.—Luxury, however, brought enervation, commerce introduced idolatry, extravagance led to oppressive taxation. The people, on Solomon's death, demanded of his son a redress of their grievances. This being haughtily refused, a revolt ensued. The empire was rent into the two petty kingdoms of *Israel* and *Judah*,—the former containing ten tribes; the latter, two.

Israel (975 to 722 = 253 years) was idolatrous from the start. It was a continued scene of turmoil and wrong. Its nineteen kings belonged to nine different families, and eight met a violent death. Finally the Assyrians captured Samaria, the capital, and sent the people prisoners into Media. They vanished from history, and are known as the "Lost Tribes." The few remaining Israelites combined with the foreign settlers to form the Samaritans. With this mongrel people pure Hebrews had "no dealings" (John iv. 9).

Judah (975 to 586 = 389 years) retained the national religion. Its twenty kings, save one usurper, were all of the house of David in regular descent. But it lay in the pathway of the mighty armies of Egypt and Assyria. Thrice its enemies held Jerusalem. At last Nebuchadnezzar destroyed the city, and carried many of the principal inhabitants to Babylon.

The Captivity lasted about seventy years. The Jews prospered in their adopted country, and many, like Daniel, rose to high favor.

The Restoration.—Cyrus, after the capture of Babylon (p. 51), was friendly to the Jews,[1] and allowed those who chose to return to Judea and rebuild their temple. They were greatly changed by their bondage, and henceforth were faithful to their religion. While they had lost their native

---

[1] This was owing to (1) similarity in their religions; (2) the foretelling of the victories of Cyrus by the Jewish prophets; and (3) the influence of Daniel. Read Daniel, Nehemiah, and Ezra.

language, they had acquired a love for commerce, and many afterward went to foreign countries and engaged in trade, for which they are still noted.

Their Later History was full of vicissitude. They became a part of Alexander's World Empire (p. 151). When that crumbled, Palestine fell to the Ptolemies of Egypt (p. 154). In the 1st century B. C., Judea was absorbed in the universal dominion of Rome. The Jews, however, frequently rebelled, until finally, after a siege of untold horror, Titus captured Jerusalem and razed it to the ground. The Jewish nation perished in its ruins.

ORIENTAL SANDAL.

THE CIVILIZATION.

Civilization.—The Hebrews were an agricultural people. The Mosaic law discouraged trade and intercourse with foreign nations. The priests, who received a share of the crops, naturally favored the cultivation of the soil. There was no art or science developed. When the Temple was to be built, Solomon obtained not only skilled laborers from the Phœnicians (p. 78), but also sailors for his fleet. Yet this people, occupying a little territory 150 miles long and 50 broad, has, like no other, influenced the world's history. Its sacred books constitute the Bible; its religion has molded the faith of the most progressive and civilized nations; while from its royal family descended Jesus of Nazareth, the grandest factor in all history.

ANCIENT JEWISH BOOK.

The Hebrew Commonwealth was the first republic of which we have definite knowledge. The foundation was the house: thence the ascent was through the family or collection of houses, and the tribe or collection of families, to the nation. There were twelve heads of tribes, or princes, and a senate of seventy elders, but the source of power was the popular assembly known as the "Congregation of Israel," in which every Hebrew proper had a voice. This, like the centurion assembly of Rome (p. 215), formed the Jewish army.

The Mosaic Laws were mild, far beyond the spirit of the age. The cities of refuge modified the rigors of the custom of personal retaliation, and gave to all the benefits of an impartial trial. The slave was protected against excessive punishment, and if of Hebrew birth was set free with his children at the Jubilee year. Land could not be sold for more than fifty years, and the debtor could always expect on the Jubilee to go back to the home of his fathers. The stranger secured hospitality and kindness. Usury was prohibited. For the benefit of the poor, fruit was left on the tree, and grain in the field, the law forbidding the harvest-land or vineyard to be gleaned. Cruelty to animals was punished, and even the mother-bird with her young could not be taken.

HEBREW PRIEST OFFERING INCENSE.

Learning was held in high esteem. All Hebrews received what we should call a "common-school education." With this, the Levites, the hereditary teachers, blended instruction in the sacred history, the precepts of religion, and their duties to God and their country. Every boy was compelled to learn a trade. Ignorance of some kind of handicraft was discreditable, and the greatest scholars and statesmen had some regular occupation. After the captivity, education seems to have been made compulsory.

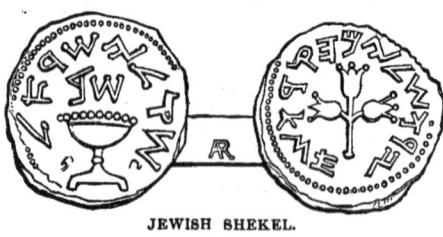

JEWISH SHEKEL.

The Hittites, mentioned in the Old Testament, inhabited the fertile valleys of the Orontes, and spread throughout southern Syria. They were a military and commercial nation, and made great advances in civilization and the fine arts. A court poet is mentioned

THE CIVILIZATION. 87

on the Egyptian monuments as having been among the retinue of a Hittite king, and the early art discovered in Cyprus by Di Cesnola is supposed to be largely derived from this people, who long resisted both the Assyrians and the Egyptians. The Egyptians called them the Kheta, and the victory of Rameses II. over the "vile chief of Kheta" is celebrated in the poem of Pentaur (p. 25). Some famous sculptured figures along the roads near Ephesus and from Smyrna to Sardis, attributed by Herodotus to Rameses II., prove now to be Hittite monuments. The language and various memorials of this once-powerful people are being eagerly investigated

ANCIENT KEY.

JERUSALEM IN EARLY TIMES.

by archæologists, who have already discovered the site of their commercial capital, Carchemish, in a huge mound on the lower Euphrates. In this mound—a mass of earth, fragments of masonry and *débris*, surrounded by ruined walls and broken towers— important remains with inscriptions are now being found.

CHRONOLOGY.

	B. C.
Abram migrated to Canaan, about	2000
The Exodus, about	1300
Monarchy established	1095
Reign of Solomon	1015-975
Division of the Kingdom	975
Sargon took Samaria	722
Nebuchadnezzar destroyed Jerusalem	588
Titus took Jerusalem	A. D. 70

MEDIA AND PERSIA.

1. THE POLITICAL HISTORY.

The Medes and Persians, two Aryan nations, were early conquered by the Assyrians. The Medes were the first to assert their independence. Under Cyax'ares they destroyed Nineveh (606 B. C.) and divided Assyria between themselves and the Babylonians, who had aided them in this conquest (p. 47). Asty'ages, successor of Cyaxares, had been acknowledged superior by the Persian king Cambyses, whose son, Cy'rus, became a hostage at the Median court. But the Medes were better fighters than organizers, and, besides, were soon enfeebled by the luxury that follows conquest.

Cyrus [1] was bold, athletic, and ambitious, and soon came

Geographical Questions.—Bound Persia; Media. Locate Persepolis; Susa; Pasargadæ. Name the countries of Asia Minor. Where was Lydia? Sardis? The river Halys? What was the extent of the Persian Empire at the time of Alexander the Great?

[1] According to one of many legends, Cyrus was the grandson, on his mother's side, of King Astyages. His future greatness, and through him that of Media's rival, Persia, were revealed to Astyages in a dream. Harpagus, who was ordered to kill the child, gave him to a herdsman to expose on a mountain (compare Greek and Roman customs, pp. 178, 286; and Romulus, p. 205). The herdsman, in pity, saved the child as his own. A boyish quarrel sent Cyrus before the Median king, who, struck by his noble bearing, sent for Harpagus, and, finally learning the truth, quietly directed him to send his son to be a companion for the young prince, and himself to attend a banquet at the palace. Cyrus was kept at court; but Harpagus, at the royal feast which he was directed to attend, was served with the roasted flesh of his own son. In time Harpagus roused Cyrus to revolt, betrayed the Median army to the young prince, and became his most devoted general.

to despise the now effeminate Medes. Arousing his warlike countrymen to revolt, he not only achieved their independence, but conquered Media and established the Medo-Persian, the second great empire of western Asia. His reign was a succession of wars and conquests. He defeated Crœsus, King of Lydia,[1] thus adding to his dominions all Asia Minor west of the Halys. He captured Babylon (p. 51) and overthrew the Assyrian Empire. With the fall of Babylon the fabric of Semitic grandeur was shattered, and Aryan Persia took the lead in all western Asia. When Cyrus died, the Medo-Persian kingdom reached from the borders of Macedonia to the banks of the Indus. The extensive conquests and noble character of this king won for him the title of Cyrus the Great.

A BAS-RELIEF OF CYRUS.

[1] Lydia was an exceedingly rich country. Her mountains abounded in precious ores, and the sands of the river Pactolus, which coursed her capital, Sardis, were heavy with electrum,—a mixture of gold and silver. Of this electrum, the first known coins were made in the 8th century B. C. Crœsus was so rich that his name has become proverbial. He was now doomed to die. Legend relates that, as he watched the flames surmounting his funeral pile, he exclaimed "Solon! Solon!" that in response to the queries of Cyrus he answered that the great Athenian statesman (p. 122) had once visited him, and had made light of his wonderful riches, saying, "No man can be judged happy till the manner of his death is known;" and that Cyrus, moved by the incident, thereupon released him, and became his faithful friend. Chronological difficulties in regard to Crœsus and Solon have discredited this legend, so charmingly told by Herodotus.

Cambyses (529 B. C.), his son, succeeded to the throne. He conquered Egypt (p. 19) in a single battle, using, it is said, the stratagem of placing before his army cats, dogs, and other animals sacred to the Egyptians. After this victory he invaded Ethiopia, but his army

CRŒSUS ON THE FUNERAL PYRE (FROM AN ANCIENT VASE).

nearly perished in the burning sands of the desert, and he returned, disgraced, to Memphis. On his journey back to Persia he died (522 B. C.) in Syria of a wound from his own sword.[1] The Persians called the gracious Cyrus "Father;" the reckless Cambyses was branded as "Despot."

---

[1] He had just learned of the assumption of the "False Smerdis" (p. 91). Hastily mounting his horse, his sword fell from its sheath, and, "killing himself, he died," says the Behistun Inscription. Differing authorities interpret this as a suicide or an accident.

Darius I. (521 B. C.)[1] organized the vast kingdom which Cyrus had conquered. There were twenty-three provinces, all restless and eager to be free. Insurrections were therefore frequent. Darius divided the empire into twenty great "satrapies," each governed by a satrap appointed by the king. The slightest suspicion of treachery was the signal for their instant death. To secure prompt communication with distant portions of the empire, royal roads were established with couriers to be relieved by one another at the end of each day's journey. Every satrapy paid a regular tribute, but retained its native king, laws, and religion.[2] The capital of the empire was fixed at Susa.

Darius I. is called the Second Founder of the Persian Monarchy. To his ability as an organizer was added the ambition of a conqueror. Having by one masterly move grasped the riches of India on the east, he essayed the conquest of Greece on the west. The story of his defeat we shall study in Greece.

The Later History of Persia presents the usual characteristics of oriental despotisms. There were scenes of cruelty, treachery, and fraud. Brothers murdering brothers, queens slaying their rivals, eunuchs bartering the throne and assassinating the sovereign, were merely ordinary events. At last the empire itself crumbled before the triumphant advance of Alexander.

---

[1] During the absence of Cambyses in Egypt, the Magi made one Gomates king, representing him to be Smerdis, the son of Cyrus. Cambyses, however, had secretly murdered this brother before his departure from Persia. Darius, conspiring with six other nobles, slew the "False Smerdis." The seven noblemen agreed to ride out at sunrise of the following day, and that he whose horse first neighed should become king. Darius secured the prize, Herodotus says, by a trick of his groom in placing a horse well known to his master's horse near where they were to pass.

[2] The satraps rivaled the king himself in the magnificence of their courts. Each had several palaces with pleasure gardens, or "paradises," as they called them, attached. The income of the satrap of Babylon is said to have been four bushels of silver coin per day.

2. THE CIVILIZATION.

Society.—*The King*, as in Assyria and Babylonia, held at his disposal the lives, liberties, and property of his people. He was bound by the national customs as closely as his meanest subject, but otherwise his will was absolute. His command, once given, could not be revoked even by himself: hence arose the phrase, "Unchangeable as the laws of the Medes and Persians." His every caprice was accepted without question. If he chose, in pure wantonness, to shoot an innocent boy before the eyes of his father, the parent, so far from expressing horror at the crime, would praise his skillful archery; and offenders, bastinadoed by royal order, declared themselves delighted that his majesty had condescended to notice them even with his displeasure. The king was the state. If he fell in battle, all was lost; if he were saved, it outweighed every calamity.

The Seven Princes (Esther i. 14; Ezra vii. 14) were grandees next to the king. One was of the royal family; the others were chiefs of the six great houses from which the king was legally bound to choose his legitimate wives. No one except the Seven Princes could approach the royal person unless introduced by a court usher. They sat beside the king at public festivals, entered his apartment at their pleasure, and gave him advice on public and private matters.

The Court was principally composed of *Magi* (p. 97), who judged all moral and civil offenses.

The People seem to have been divided into two general classes: those who lived in towns and cities and who generally cultivated the soil, and the roving or pastoral tribes. Social grades were strongly marked, and court etiquette was aped among all classes, special modes of salutation being prescribed for a man's superior, his equal, and his inferior. Trade and commerce were held in contempt, and the rich boasted that they neither bought nor sold.

Writing.— *Cuneiform Letters.*—The Persian characters were formed much more simply than the Assyrian. They were, so far as now known, less than forty in number, and were written from left to right. For public documents the rock and chisel were used; for private, prepared skin and the pen. Clay tablets seem never to have been employed, and papyrus brought from Egypt was too costly. As the cuneiform letters are not adapted to writing on parchment, it is probable that some cursive characters were also in use. The Persian writing which has survived is almost entirely on stone, either upon the mountain side or on buildings, tablets, vases, and signet cylinders.

Science and Literature.—To science the Persians contributed absolutely nothing. They had fancy, imagination, and a relish for poetry and art, but they were too averse to study to produce anything which required patient and laborious research. In this respect they furnish a striking contrast to the Babylonians.

The *Avesta*, or Sacred Text, written in Zend, the ancient idiom of Bactria, is all that remains to us of their literature. It is composed of eight distinct parts or books, compiled from various older works which have been lost, and purports to be a revelation made by Ormazd (p. 98) to Zoroaster,[1] the founder of the Persian religion. The principal books are the *Vendidad* and the *Yaçna:* the former contains a moral and ceremonial code somewhat corresponding to the Hebrew Pentateuch; the latter consists of prayers, hymns, etc., for use during sacrifice. The contents of the Zend-Avesta date from various ages, and portions were probably handed down by oral tradition for hundreds of years before being committed to writing.

FROM THE ZEND-AVESTA.

"Zoroaster asked Ahura Mazda: 'Ahura Mazda, holiest spirit, creator of all existent worlds, the truth loving! What was, O Ahura Mazda, the word existing before the heaven, before the water, before the earth, before the cow, before the tree, before the fire, the son of Ahura Mazda, before man the truthful, before the Devas and carnivorous beasts, before the whole existing universe, before every good thing created by Ahura Mazda and springing from truth?'

"Then answered Ahura Mazda: 'It was the All of the Creative Word, most holy Zoroaster. I will teach it thee. Existing before the heaven, before the water, before the earth,' etc. (as before).

"'Such is the All of the Creative Word, most holy Zoroaster, that even when neither pronounced, nor recited, it is worth one hundred other proceeding prayers,

---

[1] Zoroaster was a reformer who lived in Bactria, perhaps as early as 1500 B. C. Little is known of his actual history. The legends ascribe to him a seclusion of twenty years in a mountain cave, where he received his doctrines direct from Ormazd. His tenets, though overlaid by superstition, were remarkably pure and noble, and of all the ancient creeds approach the nearest to the inspired Hebrew faith. Their common hatred of idolatry formed a bond of sympathy between the early Persians and the Jews, Ormazd and Jehovah being recognized as the same Lord God (Isa. xliv. 28; Ezra i. 2, 3). At the time of the Persian conquest by Alexander, the Zoroastrian books were said to number twenty-one volumes. During the five hundred years of foreign rule they were scattered and neglected. Under the Sassanian kings (226-651 A. D.) the remaining fragments were carefully collected, and translated, with explanatory notes, into the literary language of the day. This translation was called Avesta-u-Zend (text and comments). By some mistake the word "Zend" was applied to the original language of the text, and is now generally used in that sense: hence "Zend-Avesta."

neither pronounced, nor recited, nor chanted. And he, most holy Zoroaster, who in this existing world remembers the All of the Creative Word, utters it when remembered, chants it when uttered, celebrates when chanted, his soul will I thrice lead across the bridge to a better world, a better existence, better truth, better days. I pronounced this speech containing the Word, and it accomplished the creation of Heaven, before the creation of the water, of the earth, of the tree, of the four-footed beast, before the birth of the truthful, two-legged man.'"

A Hymn.—" We worship Ahura Mazda, the pure, the master of purity.

"We praise all good thoughts, all good words, all good deeds which are or shall be; and we likewise keep clean and pure all that is good.

"O Ahura Mazda, thou true, happy being! We strive to think, to speak, and to do only such actions as may be best fitted to promote the two lives [*i. e.*, the life of the body and the life of the soul].

"We beseech the spirit of earth for the sake of these our best works [*i. e.*, agriculture] to grant us beautiful and fertile fields, to the believer as well as to the unbeliever, to him who has riches as well as to him who has no possessions."

Education.—"To ride, to draw the bow, and to speak the truth," were the great ends of Persian education. When a boy was five years old, his training began. He was made to rise before dawn, to practice his exercises in running, slinging stones, and the use of the bow and javelin. He made long marches, exposed to all weathers, and sleeping in the open air. That he might learn to endure hunger, he was sometimes given but one meal in two days. When he was seven years old, he was taught to ride and hunt, including the ability to jump on and off his horse, to shoot the bow, and to use the javelin, all with his steed at full gallop. At the age of fifteen he became a soldier. Books and reading seem to have formed no part of an ordinary Persian education. The king himself was no exception. His scribes learned his wishes, and then wrote his letters, edicts, etc., affixing the royal seal without calling upon him even to sign his name.[1]

Monuments and Art.—As the followers of Zoroaster worshiped in the open air, we need not look in Persia for temples, but must content ourselves with palaces and tombs. The palaces at Persepolis[2] were as magnificent as those at Nineveh and Babylon had been, though different in style and architecture. Like them they stood on a high platform, but the crude or burnt brick of Assyria

---

[1] "Occasionally, to beguile weary hours, a monarch may have had the 'Book of the Chronicles of the Kings of Persia and Media' read before him; but the kings themselves never opened a book or studied any branch of science or learning."—*Rawlinson.*

[2] Remains of a large palace have been discovered at Susa, which is supposed to be the identical one described in the Book of Esther. On the bases of the pillars it is stated that the palace was erected by Darius and Xerxes, but repaired by Artaxerxes Memnon, who added the inscriptions.

THE CIVILIZATION. 95

and Babylon gave place to enormous blocks of hewn stone,[1] fastened with iron clamps. The terraced platform, and the broad, gently sloping, elaborately sculptured staircases, wide enough to allow ten horsemen to ride abreast, were exceedingly grand and imposing. The subjects of sculpture were much like those in Assyria: the king in combat with mythical monsters, or seated on his throne surrounded by his attendants; long processions of royal guards, or of captives bringing tribute; and symbolical combats be-

PERSIAN SUBJECTS BRINGING TRIBUTE TO THE KING.

tween bulls and lions. Colossal winged and human-headed bulls, copied from Assyria, guarded the palace portals. For effect, the Persians depended upon elegance of form, richness of material, and splendor of coloring, rather than upon immense size, as did the Egyptians and Chaldeans. The Great Hall of Xerxes, however, was larger than the Great Hall of Karnak, and in proportion and design far surpassed anything in Assyria. What enameled brick was to Babylon, and alabaster sculpture to Assyria, the portico and pillar were to Persia. Forests of graceful columns, over sixty feet high, with richly carved bases and capitals, rose in hall and colonnade, between which were magnificent hangings, white,

[1] An idea borrowed from the conquered Egyptians.

green, and violet, "fastened with cords of fine linen and purple to silver rings and pillars of marble" (Esther i. 6). Pavements "of red, blue, white, and black marble," with carpets from Sardis spread for the king to walk upon; walls covered with plates of gold and silver; the golden throne of the king, under an embroidered canopy, supported by pillars of gold inlaid with precious stones; a golden palm-tree; gold and silver couches; and over the royal bed a golden vine, each grape being a precious stone of enormous value,—are recorded as appurtenances to the royal palace. The Persian king, like the Egyptian, attended during his lifetime to the building of his last resting-place. The most remarkable of the Persian tombs is that of Cyrus at Pasargadæ, which has been called "a house upon a pedestal." Upon a pyramidal base made of huge blocks of beautiful white marble was erected a house of the same material, crowned with a stone roof. Here, in a small chamber entered by a low and narrow door, were deposited in a golden coffin the remains of the great conqueror.

TOMB OF CYRUS AT PASARGADÆ.

A colonnade of twenty-four pillars, whose broken shafts are still seen, seems to have inclosed the sacred spot. With this exception, all the royal sepulchers that remain are rock tombs, similar in situation to those in Egypt. Unlike those, however, they were made conspicuous, as if intended to catch the eye of an observer glancing up the mountain side. A spot difficult of approach having been chosen, the recessed chamber was excavated in the solid rock, and marked by a porticoed and sculptured front, somewhat in the shape of a Greek cross. The sarcophagi, cut in the rock floor of the recesses, were covered by stone slabs.

Persian Architecture is distinguished for simplicity and regularity, in most buildings one half being the exact duplicate of the other. Although many ideas were borrowed from the nations we have already considered, Persian art, in its best features, such as the grand sculptured staircases and the vast groves of tall and slender

THE GREAT STAIRCASE AT PERSEPOLIS.

pillars,[1] with their peculiar ornamentation, was strikingly original. The Persian fancy seems to have run toward the grotesque and monstrous. When copying nature, the drawing of animals was much superior to that of the human form. Statuary was not attempted.

The Practical Arts and Inventions were almost entirely wanting. No enameling, no pottery, no metal castings, no wooden or ivory carvings, were made. A few spear and arrow heads, coins, and gem cylinders are all the small objects which have been discovered among the ruins. Persia thus presents a marked contrast to the other nations we have been studying. It was, indeed, the boast of the Persians that they needed not to toil, since by their skill in arms they could command every foreign production. "The carpets of Babylon and Sardis, the shawls of Kashmir and India, the fine linen of Borsippa and Egypt, the ornamental metal-work of Greece, the coverlets of Damascus, the muslins of Babylonia, and the multiform manufactures of the Phœnician towns," poured continually into Persia as tributes, gifts, or merchandise, and left among the native population no ambition for home industries.

3. THE MANNERS AND CUSTOMS.

General Character.—The Persian was keen-witted and ingenious, generous, warm-hearted, hospitable, and courageous. He was bold and dashing in war; sparkling, vivacious, and given to repartee in social life. Except in the presence of the king, where no sadness was allowed, he never checked the expression of his emotions, but childishly, regardless of all spectators, laughed and shouted when pleased, or wept and shrieked when in sorrow. In this he was very unlike the Babylonian gentleman, who studied calmness and repose of manner. He was self-indulgent and luxurious, but chary of debt. The early Persians were remarkable for truthfulness, lying being abhorred as the special characteristic of the evil spirit.

Religion.—That of the Persians was Mazdeism, from Ahura Mazda (Ormazd), their great and good god; it was also called Zoroastrianism, after its founder (p. 93). That of the Medes was Magism, so named from the priests, who were of a caste called Magi.

Mazdeism taught the existence of two great principles,—one good, the other evil,—which were in perpetual and eternal conflict.

---

[1] In Assyria the pillar was almost unknown, while in Egypt it was twice as broad in proportion to its height as in Persia.

Ormazd was the "all-perfect, all-powerful, all-wise, all-beautiful, all-pure; sole source of true knowledge, of real happiness; him who hath created us, him who sustains us, the wisest of all intelligences" (*Yaçna*). Having created the earth, he placed man thereon to preserve it. He was represented by the sun, fire, and light.

SYMBOL OF ORMAZD.
(Copied by the Persians from that of the Assyrian god Asshur.)

Ahriman was the author of evil and death, causing sin in man, and barrenness upon the earth. Hence the cultivation of the soil was considered a religious duty, as promoting the interests of Ormazd and defeating the malice of his opposer. Those who yielded to the seductions of Ahriman were unable to cross the terrible bridge to which all souls were conducted the third night after death; they fell into the gulf below, where they were forced to live in utter darkness and feed on poisoned banquets. The good were assisted across the bridge by an angel, who led them to golden thrones in the eternal abode of happiness. Thus this religion, like the Egyptian, contained the doctrine of the immortality of the soul and of future reward and punishment. Ormazd and Ahriman had each his councilors and emissaries, but they were simply genii or spirits, and not independent gods, like the lesser deities of the Egyptians and Assyrians.

Zoroastrian Worship consisted mainly in prayer and praises to Ormazd and his court, the recital of Gathas or hymns, and the Homa ceremony. In the last, during the recitation of certain prayers, the priests extracted the juice of a plant called "homa,"[1] formally offering the liquid to the sacrificial fire, after which a small portion was drunk by one of the priests, and the rest by the worshipers.

Magism taught not only the worship of Ormazd, but also that of Ahriman, who, under another name, was the serpent-god of the Turanians. In Media, Ahriman was the principal object of adoration, since a good god, so it was reasoned, would not hurt men, but an evil

---

[1] A kind of milkweed, sometimes called the "moon-plant." In India it was called "soma," and was similarly used.

one must be appeased by honor and sacrifice. Sorcery and incantations, which were expressly forbidden by Zoroaster, were the outgrowth of the Median faith.

The Magi apparently held their office by hereditary succession. In time, Magism and Mazdeism became so assimilated that the Magi were accepted as the national priests of Persia. As we have seen the Egyptian religion characterized by animal and sun worship, and the Chaldeo-Assyrian by that of the sun, moon, and planets, so we find the Persian distinguished by the *worship of the elements.* The sun, fire, air, earth, and water were all objects of adoration and sacrifice. On lofty heights, whence they could be seen from afar, stood the fire-altars, crowned by the sacred flame, believed to have been kindled from Heaven, and never suffered to expire. It was guarded by the Magi, who so jealously kept its purity that to blow upon it with the breath was a capital offense. By these holy fires, flickering on lonely mountain-tops, the Magi, clad in white robes and with half-concealed faces, chanted day after day their weird incantations, and, mysteriously waving before the awe-stricken spectators a bundle of tamarisk twigs (divining-rods), muttered their pretended prophecies.

Sacrifice was not offered at the altar of the eternal flame, but on fires lighted from it, a horse being the favorite victim. A small part of the fat having been consumed by the fire, and the soul of the animal having been, according to the Magi, accepted by the god, the body was cut into joints, boiled and eaten, or sold by the worshipers. Sacrifices to water were offered by the side of lakes, rivers, and fountains, care being taken that not a drop of blood should touch the sacred element. No refuse was allowed to be cast into a river, nor was it even lawful to wash the hands in a stream. The worship of these elements rendered the disposal of the dead a difficult matter. They could not be burnt, for that would pollute fire; nor thrown into the river, for that would defile water; nor buried in the ground, for that would corrupt earth. The Magi solved the problem by giving their own dead to be devoured by beasts of prey. The people revolted from this, and incased the lifeless bodies of their friends in a coating of wax; having made this concession to the sacred earth, they ventured to bury their dead in its bosom.

Domestic Life.—The early Persians were noted for their simple diet. They ate but one meal a day, and drank only water. With their successes their habits changed. They still ate only one meal each day, but it began early and lasted till night. Water gave place to wine, and each man prided himself on the quantity he could drink. Drunkenness at last became a sort of duty. Every serious family council ended in a debauch, and once a year, at the feast of Mithras, part of the royal display was the intoxication of the king. Love of dress increased, and to the flowered robes and tunics, embroidered trousers, tiaras, and shoes of their Median predecessors, the Persians now added the hitherto unwonted fineries of gloves and stockings. They wore massive gold collars and bracelets, and studded the golden sheaths and handles of their swords and daggers with gems. They not only drank wine from gold and silver cups, as did their fallen neighbors the Babylonians, but they plated and inlaid the tables themselves with the precious metals. Even the horses felt the growing extravagance and champed bits made of gold instead of bronze. Every rich man's house was crowded with servants, each confining himself to a single duty. Not the least of these were the "adorners," who applied cosmetics to their master's face and hands, colored his eyelids, curled his hair and beard, and adjusted his wig. The perfume-bearer, who was an indispensable valet, took charge of the perfumes and scented ointments, a choice selection of which was a Persian gentleman's pride.

ORDINARY PERSIAN COSTUME.

Women were kept secluded in their own apartments, called the harem or seraglio, and were allowed no communication with the other sex.[1] So rigid was etiquette in this respect, that a Persian wife might not even see her own father or brother. When she rode, her litter was closely curtained, yet even then it was a capital offense for a man simply to pass a royal litter in the street.[2]

The King's Household numbered 15,000 persons. The titles of some of his servants reveal the despotism and dangers of the times. Such were the "Eyes" and "Ears," who were virtually spies and detectives; and the "Tasters," who tried every dish set before the king, to prove it not poisoned. A monarch who held the life of his subjects so lightly as did the Persian kings might well be on the alert for treachery and conspiracy against himself. Hence the court customs and etiquette were extremely rigorous. Even to touch the king's carpet in crossing the

ANCIENT PERSIAN SILVER COIN

---

[1] Even at the present day it is considered a gross indecorum to ask a Persian after the health of his wife.

[2] It is curious to notice that the same custom obtained in Russia a few centuries ago. In 1674 two chamberlains were deprived of their offices for having accidentally met the carriage of the Tsaritsa Natalia.

courts was a grave offense; and to come into his chamber unannounced, unless the royal scepter was extended in pardon, was punished by instant death. Every courtier prostrated himself in the attitude of worship on entering the royal presence, and kept his hands hidden in his sleeve during the entire interview. Even the king was not exempt from restrictions of etiquette. He was required to live in seclusion; never to go on foot beyond the palace walls; and never to revoke an order or draw back from a promise, however he might desire it. He took his meals alone, excepting occasionally, when he might have the queen and one or two of his children for company. When he gave a great banquet, his guests were divided into two classes; the lower were entertained in an outer court, and the higher, in a chamber next his own, where he could see them through the curtain which screened himself. Guests were assigned a certain amount of food; the greater the number of dishes, the higher the honor conferred; what was left on their plates they were at liberty to take home to their families. Sometimes at a "Banquet of Wine," a select number were allowed to drink in the royal presence, but not of the same wine or on the same terms with the king; he reclined on a golden-footed couch, and sipped the costly wine of Helbon; they were seated on the floor, and were served a cheaper beverage.

The Persians in War.—*Weapons, etc.*—The Persian footman fought with bow and arrows, a sword and spear, and occasionally with a battle-ax and sling. He defended himself with a wicker shield, similar to the Assyrian, and almost large enough to cover him. He wore a leather tunic and trousers, low boots, and a felt cap; sometimes he was protected by a coat of mail made of scale-armor, or of quilted linen, like the Egyptian corselet. In the heavy cavalry, both horse and horsemen wore metal coats of mail, which made their movements slow and hesitating; the light cavalry were less burdened, and were celebrated for quick and dexterous maneuvering. The special weapon of the horseman was a javelin,—a short, strong spear, with a wooden shaft and an iron point. Sometimes he was armed with a long leather thong, which he used with deadly effect as a lasso. The war-chariots, which we have seen so popular in Egyptian and Assyrian armies, were regarded by the Persians with disfavor. Kings and princes, however, rode in them, both on the march and in action, and sometimes a chariot force was brought into the field. The wheels of the Persian chariot were armed with scythes, but this weapon does not seem to have caused the destruction intended, since, as it was drawn by from two to four horses, and always contained two or more occupants, it furnished so large a mark for the missiles of the enemy, that a chariot advance was usually checked before reaching the opposing line of battle. Military engines seem rarely if ever used, and the siege-towers and battering-rams, so familiar in Egyptian and Assyrian sculptures, are never mentioned in Persian inscriptions. Elephants were sometimes employed in battle; and at Sardis, Cyrus gained his victory over Crœsus by frightening the Lydian horses with an array of camels.

Organization of the Army.—The Persians trusted for success mainly to numbers. The army was commanded personally by the king, or some one appointed by him. In the division of men under officers a decimal system prevailed, so that, grading upward, there were the captains of tens, of hundreds, of thousands, and of tens of thousands. Sometimes a million men were brought into service.[1]

PERSIAN FOOT-SOLDIERS.

On the March.—The Persians, like the Assyrians, avoided fighting in winter, and led out their armies in early spring. They marched only by day, and, as before the time of Darius there were neither roads nor bridges, their immense cavalcade made slow progress. The baggage-train, composed of a vast multitude of camels, horses, mules,

---

[1] The troops were drawn from the entire empire, and were marshaled in the field according to nations, each tribe accoutered in its own fashion. Here were seen the gilded breastplates and scarlet kilts of the Persians and Medes; there the woolen shirt of the Arab, the leathern jerkin of the Berber, or the cotton dress of the native of Hindustan. Swart savage Ethiops from the Upper Nile, adorned with a war-paint of white and red, and scantily clad with the skins of leopards or lions, fought in one place with huge clubs, arrows tipped with stone, and spears terminating in the horn of an antelope. In another, Scyths, with their loose, spangled trousers and their tall pointed caps, dealt death around from their unerring blows; while near them Assyrians, helmeted, and wearing corselets of quilted linen, wielded the tough spear or the still more formidable iron mace. Rude weapons, like cane bows, unfeathered arrows, and stakes hardened at one end in the fire, were seen side by side with keen swords and daggers of the best steel, the finished productions of the workshops of Phœnicia and Greece. Here the bronze helmet was surmounted with the ears and horns of an ox; there it was superseded by a fox-skin, a leathern or wooden skull-cap, or a head-dress fashioned out of a horse's scalp. Besides horses and mules, elephants, camels, and wild asses diversified the scene, and rendered it still more strange and wonderful to the eye of a European.—*Rawlinson.*

oxen, etc., dragging heavy carts or bearing great packs, was sent on in advance, followed by about half the troops in a long, continuous column. Then, after a considerable break, came a picked guard of a thousand horse and a thousand foot, preceding the most precious treasures of the nation,—its sacred emblems and its king. The former consisted of the holy horses and cars, and perhaps the silver altars on which flamed the eternal fire. The monarch followed, riding on a car drawn by Nisæan steeds. After him came a second guard of a thousand foot and a thousand horse; then ten thousand picked foot— probably the famous *"Immortals"* (p. 130)—and ten thousand picked horsemen. Another break of nearly a quarter of a mile ensued, and then the remainder of the troops completed the array. The wives of the chief officers often accompanied the army, and were borne in luxurious litters amid a crowd of eunuchs and attendants. On entering a hostile land, the baggage-train was sent to the rear, horsemen were thrown out in front, and other effective changes made.

In Battle the troops were massed in deep ranks, the bravest in front. Chariots, if used, led the attack, followed by the infantry in the center, and the cavalry on the wings. If the line of battle were once broken, the army lost heart; the commander usually set the example of flight, and a general stampede ensued.

4. SUMMARY.

1. Political History.—In the 7th century B. C. the hardy Medes threw off the Assyrian yoke and captured Nineveh. But the court of Astyages became as luxurious as that of Asshurbanipal had been, and the warlike Persians pushed to the front. Under Cyrus they conquered Media, Lydia, Babylonia, and founded an empire reaching from India to the confines of Egypt. Cambyses, helped by Phœnicians, subdued Egypt, but most of his army perished in the Ethiopia desert. Meanwhile a Magian usurped the throne in the name of Smerdis, the murdered brother of Cambyses. Darius unseated the Pseudo-Smerdis, and organized the empire which Cyrus had conquered. He invaded India, Scythia, and finally Greece, but his hosts were overthrown on the field of Marathon (see p. 126).

2. Civilization.—Every Persian, even though one of the Seven Princes, held his life at the mercy of the king. Truthful and of simple tastes in his early national life, he grew in later days to be luxurious and effeminate. Keen-witted and impulsive, having little love for books or study, his education was with the bow, on the horse, and in the field. In architecture he delighted in broad, sculptured **staircases, and tall,** slender columns. He expressed some original taste **and de-**

sign, but his art was largely borrowed from foreign nations, and his inventions were few or none. He wrote in cuneiform characters, using a pen and prepared skins for epistles and private documents; his public records were chiseled in stone. He had little respect for woman, and kept his wife and daughters confined in the harem. He went to war with a vast and motley cavalcade, armed by nations, and relied upon

THE RUINS OF PERSEPOLIS.

overwhelming numbers for success. He worshiped the elements, and the Magi—his priests—guarded a holy flame on mountain heights. When he died, his friends incased his body in wax and buried it, or exposed it to be destroyed by the vultures and wild beasts.

READING REFERENCES.

The General Ancient Histories named on pp. 44 and 72.—Rawlinson's Five Great Monarchies.—Vaux's Nineveh and Persepolis.—Fergusson's Palaces of Nineveh and Persepolis restored.—Loftus's Chaldea and Susiana.—Haug's Essays on the Sacred Language, Writings, and Religion of the Parsees.—Ebers's Egyptian Princess (p. 44) contains a vivid description of the times of Cambyses and the Pseudo-Smerdis.—Rawlinson's Translation of Herodotus.—Müller's Sacred Books of the East (Vols. IV. and V.).—Benjamin's Story of Persia.—Media and Persia in the various Cyclopædias.

CHRONOLOGY.

	B. C.
Cyaxares destroyed Nineveh	606?
Cyrus subdued the Medes	558
Cyrus defeated Crœsus, and captured Sardis	547?
Cyrus subdued the far East	553–540
Cyrus captured Babylon	538
Cambyses ascended the Throne	529
Cambyses conquered Egypt	527
Darius Hystaspes ascended the Throne	521
Darius invaded Greece	490

INDIA.

The Hindoos, like the Persians, were Aryans. In all respects, except color, they resemble the Europeans. They are thought to have emigrated from Iran (p. 12) earlier than 1500 B. C. They never materially influenced the steady flow of history,[1] and are only incidentally mentioned when foreigners went thither for purposes of trade or conquest. The first authentic event recorded is that of the invasion of Darius (518 B. C.), and the next that of Alexander (p. 152).

THE CIVILIZATION.

Civilization.—The character of their civilization was early stereotyped. By mixing with the dark races of the country, the fair-skinned invaders lost the Aryan progressiveness and energy. What Alexander found in India meets the traveler there to-day,— a teeming, peaceable population; fabulous riches; arts and industries passing unchanged from generation to generation; and a religion whose rigorous rules and ceremonies regulate all the details of life. The products of Indian looms were as eagerly sought anciently as now; and the silks, pearls, precious stones, spices, gold, and ivory of India have in successive ages enriched Phœnicia, the Italian republics, and England.

Society.—*Castes* were established by the early Aryans: (1) the *Brahmans*, or priests, who had the right of interpreting the sacred books, and possessed a monopoly of knowledge; (2) the *Kshatriyas*,

---

[1] There is little, if anything, in the Indian annals worthy the name of history. The Hindoo mind, though acute and intelligent, is struck, not by the reasonableness or truth of a statement, but by its grandeur. Thus, in the Brahman mythology we hear of Râhu, an exalted being, 76,800 miles high and 19,200 miles across the shoulders. While the Egyptian engraved on stone the most trivial incident of daily life, the Hindoo disregarded current events, **and was** absorbed in metaphysical subtleties.

or soldiers; (3) the *Vaisya,* or traders and farmers; and (4) the *Sudras*, or laborers, who consisted of the conquered people, and were slaves. The *Pariahs*, or outcasts, ranked below all the others, and were condemned to perform the most menial duties. Intermarriage between the castes was forbidden, and occupations descended rigidly from father to son.

Literature.—*The Sanskrit* (perfected), the language of the conquerors, is preserved among the Hindoos, as is the Latin with us, through grammars and dictionaries. Its literature is rich in fancy and exalted poetry, and embalms the precious remains of that language which was nearest the speech of our Aryan forefathers. Thousands of Sanskrit works are still in existence. No man's life is long enough to read them all. A certain Hindoo king is said to have had the contents of his library condensed into 12,000 volumes! A portion of the VEDAS, the sacred books of Brahma, was compiled 1200 B. C. The Rig-Veda contains 1028 hymns, invoking as gods the sun, moon, and other powers of nature. The following extract is a beautiful litany:—

1. "Let me not yet, O Varuna [the god of water], enter into the house of clay. Have mercy, Almighty, have mercy!
2. "If I go along trembling, like a cloud driven by wind, have mercy, Almighty, have mercy!
3. "Through want of strength, thou Strong One, have I gone to the wrong shore. Have mercy, Almighty, have mercy!
4. "Thirst came on the worshiper, in the midst of the waters. Have mercy, Almighty, have mercy!
5. "Wherever we men, O Varuna, commit an offense before the heavenly host; wherever we break thy law through thoughtlessness, have mercy, Almighty, have mercy!"

Religion.—*Brahmanism*, the Hindoo faith, teaches *pantheism*,[1] a system which makes God the soul of the universe, so that "whatever we taste, or see, or smell, or feel, is God." It also contains the doctrine of the transmigration of souls; *i. e.*, that after death good spirits will be absorbed into the Supreme Being, but wicked ones will be sent back to occupy the bodies of animals to begin afresh a round of purification and elevation. The idea of prayer, meditation, sacrifice, and penance,[2] in order to secure this final

---

[1] The doctrine of the Hindoo Trinity, *i. e.*, that God reveals himself in three forms,—Brahma the creator, Vishnu the preserver, and Siva the destroyer,—is now known to be a modern one. It grew out of an attempt to harmonize all the views that were hostile to Buddhism.

[2] Travelers tell us that Hindoo fanatics carry this idea of penance to such an extent as to keep their hands clinched until the nails grow through the palms, and to hold their arms upright until they become paralyzed.

absorption which is the highest good, constitutes the key to Brahmanism, and explains why in its view the hermit and devotee are the truly wise. By acts of benevolence and sacrifice performed in different stages of transmigration, one may accumulate a vast stock of merit, so as finally to attain to a godlike intelligence. Several of these divine sages are believed to have arisen from time to time.

Buddhism (500 B. C.) was an effort to reform Brahmanism by inculcating a benevolent and humane code of morals. It teaches the necessity of a pure life, and holds that by the practice of six transcendent virtues —alms, morals, science, energy, patience, and charity—a person may hope to reach Nirvana or eternal repose. BUDDHA, the founder of this system, is said to have "previously existed in four hundred millions of worlds. During these successive transmigrations he was almost every sort of fish, fly, animal, and man. He had acquired such a sanctity millions of centuries before as to permit him to enter Nirvana, but he preferred to endure the curse of existence in order to benefit the race." Buddha is an historic character. His life was marvelously pure and beautiful; but his religion was a practical atheism, and his teachings led to a belief in annihilation and not absorption in Brahma, or God, as the chief end of existence. The Buddhists were finally expelled from India. But they took refuge in Ceylon; their missionaries carried their doctrines over a large part of the East, and Buddhism now constitutes the religion of

BUDDHIST PRIESTS.

108   INDIA.

over one fourth of the world's population. There are almost endless modifications of both these faiths, and they abound in sentiments imaginative and subtle beyond conception. Mingled with this lofty ideality is the grossest idolatry, and most grotesque images are the general objects of the Hindoo worship.

The Sacred Writings of the Hindoos contain much that is simple and beautiful, yet, like all such heathen literature, they are full of silly and repulsive statements. Thus the *Institutes of Vishnu* declare that "cows are auspicious purifiers;" that "drops of water falling

A BRAHMAN AT PRAYER.

from the horns of a cow have the power to expiate all sin;" and that "scratching the back of a cow destroys all guilt." The Brahmans assert that prayer, even when offered from the most unworthy motives, compels the gods to grant one's wishes. The *Institutes of Gautama* (Buddha) forbid the student to recite the text of the Veda "if the wind whirls up the dust in the day-time." The Buddhists declare that all animals, even the vilest insects, as well as the seeds of plants, have souls.

READING REFERENCES.

Müller's Sacred Books of the East, and History of Ancient Sanskrit Literature.—Whitney's Oriental and Linguistic Studies.—Lenormant's Manuel, etc., Vol. III.—Johnson's Oriental Religions, India.—Taylor's Student's Manual of the History of India.—Bayard Taylor's India, China, and Japan.—Articles on India, etc., in Appletons', Zell's, and Johnson's Cyclopædias, and Encyclopædia Britannica.

CHINA.

The Chinese were Turanians (p. 10). Their historical records claim to reach far back of all known chronology, but these are largely mythical. Good authorities place the foundation of the empire at about 2800 B. C. Since then more than twenty dynasties of kings have held sway. From early times the country has been disturbed by incursions of the Tartars (Huns or Mongols). The Emperor Che Hwang-te, the Chinese national hero, expelled these wild barbarians, and to keep them out began (214 B. C.) the Great Wall of China along the northern frontier. This wall is fifteen to thirty feet high, wide enough for six horsemen to ride abreast upon the top, and extends over mountains and valleys a distance of over twelve hundred miles. Che Hwang-te died six years before it was finished.

In the 13th century the great Asiatic conqueror Genghis Khan invaded the empire, and paved the way for the establishment of the first Mongol dynasty, which held the kingdom for nearly one hundred years. During this period the famous traveler Marco Polo (Brief Hist. U. S., p. 19) visited China, where he remained seventeen years. On his return to Europe he gave a glowing description of the magnificence of the Eastern monarch's court. Again, in the 17th century, the Tartars obtained the throne, and founded the dynasty which now governs the empire.

THE CIVILIZATION.

Civilization.—The Chinese have always kept themselves isolated from the other nations: consequently China has influenced history even less than has India. Law and tradition have done for the former what a false religion has for the latter. Everything came to a stand-still ages ago.[1] The dress, the plan of the house, the mode of bowing, the minutest detail of life, are regulated by three thou-

THE GREAT WALL OF CHINA.

sand ceremonial laws of almost immemorial usage. No man presumes to introduce any improvement or change. The only hope is to become as wise as the forefathers by studying the national classics.

---

[1] Herodotus says that in dealing with foreigners the Chinese were wont to deposit their wool or silk in a certain place, and then go away. The merchants came up, laid beside the goods the sum of money they were willing to pay, and retired. The Chinese then ventured out again, and, if satisfied, took the money and left the goods; if not, they left the money and carried off the goods. There is a marked resemblance between this people and the ancient Egyptians. Both have the same stereotyped character, the same exceptional mode of writing, the same unwillingness to mingle with surrounding nations, the same mode of reckoning time by dynasties, and the same enjoyment in the contemplation of death.

THE CIVILIZATION. 111

Such is the esteem in which agriculture is held, that once a year the emperor exhibits himself in public, holding a plow. The ingenuity of the Chinese is proverbial. They anticipated by centuries many of the most important inventions of modern Europe, such as gunpowder, printing, paper, porcelain, and the use of the compass. A Chinese chart of the stars represents the heavens as seen in that country 2300 B. C., thus showing how early astronomy was cultivated by this people.

The Literature is very extensive. The writings of Confucius (551–478 B. C.) are the chief books perused in the schools. All appointments to the civil service are based on examinations, which include the preparation of essays and poems, and the writing of classical selections.

Three Religions, Buddhism, Taôism or Rationalism, and Confucianism, exist. Such is the liberty of faith, that a man may believe in them all, while the mass of the people will pray in the temples of any one indiscriminately. All these faiths agree in the worship of one's ancestors. *Buddhism* was introduced from India (p. 107), and by its gorgeous ritual and its speculative doctrines, powerfully appeals to the imagination of its devotees. *Taôism* is a religion of the supreme reason alone. *Confucianism* is named from its founder, who taught a series of elevated moral precepts, having reference solely to man's present, and not his future state. Confucius died eight years before the birth of the Greek philosopher Socrates (p. 174).

TRADITIONAL LIKENESS OF CONFUCIUS.

SAYINGS OF CONFUCIUS.—" He who exercises government by means of his virtue may be compared to the north polar star which keeps its place, and all the (other) stars turn towards it."

" What you do not like when done to yourself, do not do to others."

" I am not concerned that I have no place (office); I am concerned how I may fit myself for one. I am not concerned that I am not known, I seek to be worthy to be known."

"Slow in words and earnest in action. Act before speaking, and then speak according to your actions."

112 CHINA.

EXTRACT FROM THE CLASSIC OF FILIAL PIETY.—"The services of love and reverence to parents when alive, and those of grief and sorrow to them when dead:— these completely discharge the fundamental duty of living men."

The Chinese call their country the "Middle Kingdom," from a notion that it is in the center of the world. Their map of the globe is a parallelogram, of the habitable part of which China occupies nine tenths or more. "I felicitate myself," says a Chinese essayist, "that I was born in China, and not beyond the seas in some remote part of the earth, where the people, far removed from the converting maxims of the ancient kings, and ignorant of the domestic relations, are clothed with the leaves of plants, eat wood, and live in the holes of the earth."

READING REFERENCES.

Doolittle's Social Life of the Chinese.—Loomis's Confucius and the Chinese Classics.—Collie's Four Books (a Translation of Chinese Classical Works).—Thornton's History of China.—Williams's Middle Kingdom.—Legge's Religions of China.—Johnson's Oriental Religions; China.—Articles on China and Confucius in Appletons', Zell's, and Johnson's Cyclopædias and Encyclopædia Britannica.

CHINESE TEMPLE.

HELLAS or GREECE
AND THE COLONIES

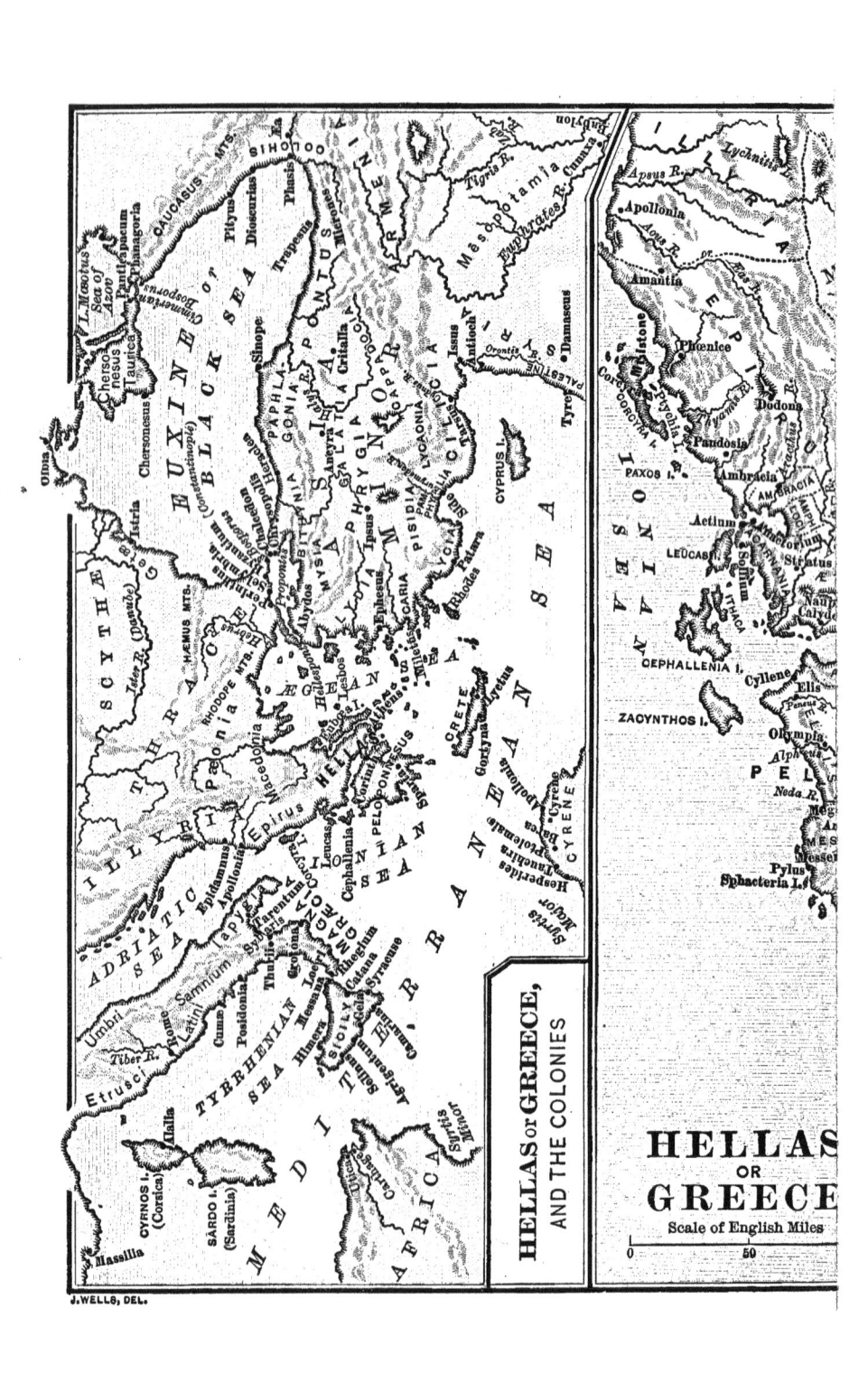

HELLAS
OR
GREECE

Scale of English Miles
0   50

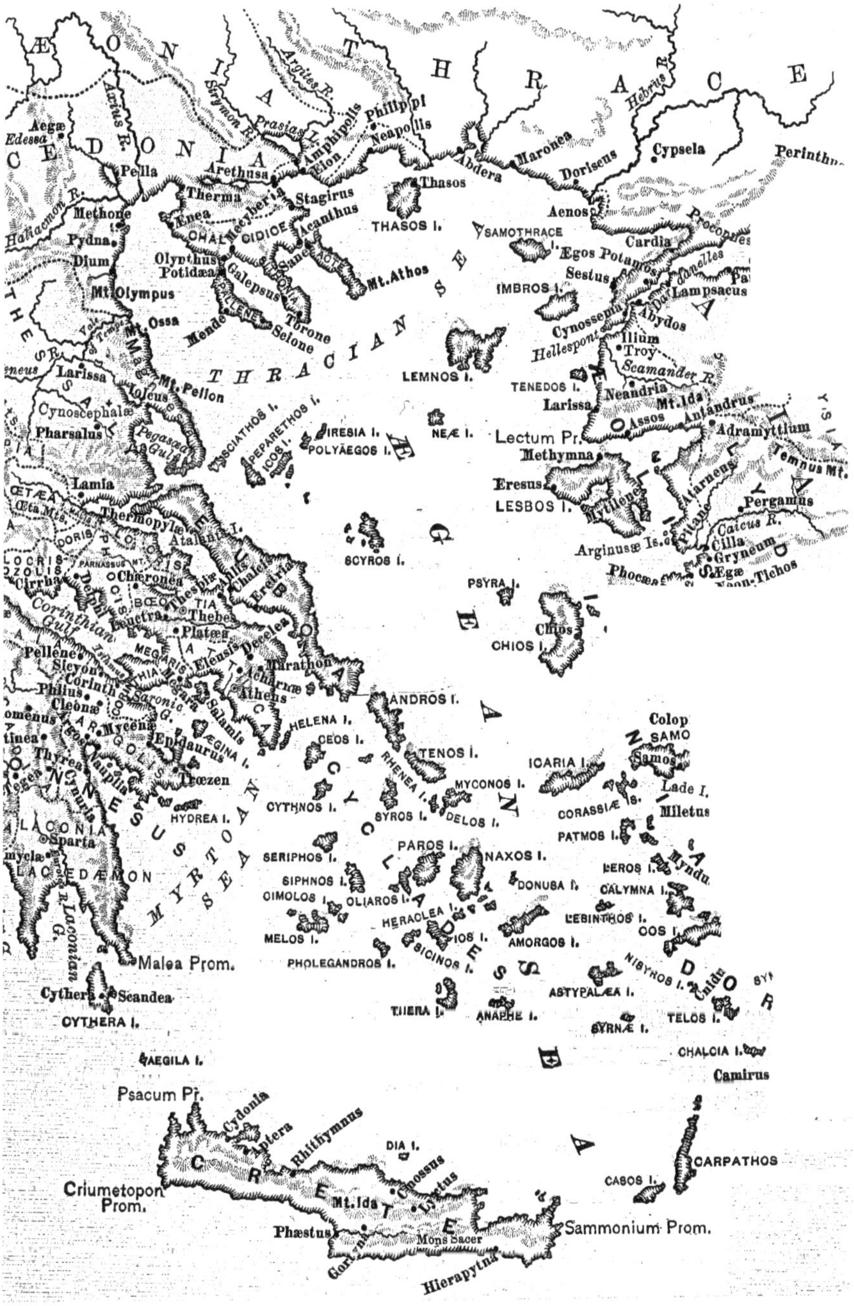

RUSSELL & STRUTHERS, ENG'S N.Y.

GREECE.

1. THE POLITICAL HISTORY.

Seat of Civilization Changed.—Thus far we have traced the beginnings of civilization among the oldest peoples of antiquity. Our study has been confined to the Orient. We now turn to Europe. Its history, so far as we know, began in Greece. The story of that little peninsula became, about the time of the Persian wars (p. 91), the record of civilization and progress, to which the history of the East is thenceforth but an occasional episode.

The Difference between Eastern and Western Civilization is marked. The former rose to a considerable height, but, fettered by despotism, caste, and polygamy, was soon checked. The monarchs were absolute, the empires vast, and the masses passive. In Greece, on the contrary, we find the people astir, every power of the mind in full play, and little states all aglow with patriotic ardor. Assyrian art, Egyptian science, and the Phœnician alphabet were absorbed, but only as seeds for a new and better growth. Much of the life we live to-day, with its political, social, and

---

Geographical Questions—Bound Greece. Name the principal Grecian states; the principal Grecian colonies (map, p 11); the chief islands in the Ægean Sea. Locate the Peloponnesus; Arcadia. Where was Ionia? Æolis? Athens? Sparta? Thebes? Argos? Corinth? Delphi? Marathon? Platæa? The pass of Thermopylæ? Ilium? The Hellespont? The isle of Rhodes? Mount Parnassus? Vale of Tempe? Mount Ossa? Mount Pelion? Salamis Island? Syracuse? Magna Græcia? Chæronea?

intellectual advantages, its music, painting, oratory, and sculpture; its thirst for knowledge, and its free institutions,—was kindled on the shores of the Æge'an Sea, was transmitted by the Greek to the Roman, by him to the Teuton, and so handed down to us.

The Geographical Features of Greece had much to do with fixing the character of its inhabitants. The coast was indented, like no other, with bays having bold promontories reaching far out to sea, and forming excellent harbors. Nature thus afforded every inducement to a sea-faring life. In striking contrast to the vast alluvial plains of the Nile and the Euphrates, the land was cut up by almost impassable mountain ranges, isolating each little valley, and causing it to develop its peculiar life. A great variety of soil and climate also tended to produce a versatile people.

The Early Inhabitants were our Aryan kinsfolk (p. 12). The Pelasgians,[1] a simple, agricultural people, were the first to settle the country. Next the Helle'nes, a warlike race, conquered the land. The two blended, and gave rise to the Grecian language and civilization, as did in later times the Norman and Anglo-Saxon to the English.

Hellas and Hellenes.—The Greeks did not use the name by which we know them, but called their country Hellas, and themselves Hellenes. Even the settlements in Asia Minor, and in the isles of the Æge'an and Mediterranean, were what Freeman happily styles "patches of Hellas." All those nations whose speech they could not understand they called Barbarians.

Grecian Unity.—The different Grecian states, though always jealous and often fighting, had much in common.

---

[1] Remains of the Pelasgian architecture still survive. They are rude, massive stone structures. The ancients considered them the work of the Cyclops,—a fabulous race of giants, who had a single eye in the middle of the forehead.

THE POLITICAL HISTORY. 115

All spoke the same language, though there were several dialects. They had many common customs, and a common inheritance in the poems of Homer (p. 162) and the glory of the Hellenic name. There were, moreover, two great "holding-points" for all the Greeks. One was the half-yearly meeting of the Amphictyonic Council,[1] and the other the national games or festivals (p. 186). All Hellenes took part in the latter, and thus the colonies were united to the parent state. The Grecian calendar itself was based on the quadrennial gathering at Olympia, the FIRST OLYMPIAD dating from 776 B. C.[2]

Legendary History.—The early records of Greece are mythical. It is not worth the effort to pick out the kernels of truth around which these romantic legends grew. They chronicle the achievements of the Heroic Age of the poets. Then occurred the Argonautic Expedition in search of the Golden Fleece, the Twelve Labors of Hercules, the Siege of "Troy divine," the Hunt of the Calydonian Boar, and the exploits of heroes whose adventures have been familiar to each succeeding age, and are to-day studied by the youth of every civilized land.[3]

---

[1] In early times twelve tribes in the north agreed to celebrate sacrifices together twice a year,—in the spring to Apollo at Delphi, and in the autumn to Ceres at Anthela, near Thermopylæ. Their deputies were called the Amphictyonic Council (council of the neighbors or co-religionists), and the meetings, from being at first purely religious, became great centers of political influence. The temple at Delphi belonged to all the states, and the Delphic Oracle attained celebrity not only among the Greeks, but also among foreign nations.

[2] This was twenty-nine years before the era of Nabonassar (p. 46), and half a century before the Captivity of the Ten Tribes by Sargon (p 84)

[3] Thus read the legends: (1) *Jason*, a prince of Thessaly, sailed with a band of adventurers in the good ship Argo. The Argonauts went through the Dardanelles, past the present site of Constantinople, to the eastern coast of the Euxine Sea Jason there planted a colony, took away the famous Golden Fleece, carried off the beautiful princess Medea, and returned to Thessaly in triumph. (2) *Hercules* was the son of Jupiter and Alcmena Juno, Queen of Heaven, sent two serpents to strangle him in his cradle, but the precocious infant killed them both, and escaped unharmed. Afterward his half brother, Eurystheus, imposed upon him twelve difficult undertakings, all of which he successfully accomplished. (3) Soon after the return of the

116   GREECE.

Primitive Governments.—In legendary times, as we learn from the Iliad, each little city or district had its hereditary king, supposed to be descended from the gods. He

THE DEPARTURE OF ACHILLES (FROM AN ANCIENT VASE).

was advised by the *Council of the Elders* and the *Assembly,* the latter being a mass meeting, where all the citizens gath-

Argonautic expedition several of the Grecian warriors—Meleager, Theseus, and others—joined in an Æolian war, which the poets termed the "Hunt of the Calydonian Boar." Æneus, king of Calydon, father of Meleager, having neglected to pay homage to Diana, that goddess sent a wild boar, which was impervious to the spears of ordinary huntsmen, to lay waste his country. All the princes of the age assembled to hunt him down, and he was at last killed by the spear of Meleager. (4) The story of the Siege of Troy is the subject of Homer's Iliad. Venus had promised Paris, son of Priam, King of Troy, that if he would pronounce her the most beautiful of the goddesses, he should have for wife the handsomest woman of his time, Helen, wife of Menelaus, King of Sparta. Paris granted the boon, and then going to Sparta carried off Helen to Troy. Menelaus, smarting under this wrong, appealed to the Grecian princes for help. They assembled under his brother Agamemnon, King of Mycenæ. A hundred thousand men sailed away in eleven hundred and eighty-six ships across the Ægean, and invested Troy. The siege lasted ten years. Hector, "of the beamy helm," son of Priam, was the bravest leader of the Trojans. Achilles, the first of Grecian warriors, slew him in single combat, and dragged his body at his chariot-wheels in insolent triumph around the walls of the city. But the "lion-hearted" Achilles fell in turn

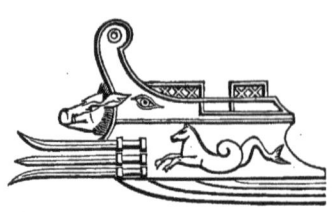

PROW OF AN EARLY GREEK SHIP.

"for so the Fates had decreed." Troy was finally taken by stratagem. The Greeks feigned to retire, leaving behind them as an offering to Minerva a great wooden horse. This was reported to be purposely of such vast bulk, in order to prevent the Trojans from taking it into the city, as that would be fatal to the Grecian cause. The deluded

ered about the king and the elders to discuss political[1] affairs. The power of the kings gradually diminished until most of the cities became republics, or commonwealths. In some cases the authority was held by a few families. If good, it was styled an *aristocracy* (*aristos*, best); but if bad, an *oligarchy* (*oligos*, few). In a *democracy* any citizen could hold office and vote in the assembly. At Sparta there were always two kings, although in time they lost most of their power.

The Dorian Migration was one of the first clearly defined events of Grecian history. After the Trojan war the ties which had temporarily held the princes together were loosed, and a general shifting of the tribes ensued. The Dorians—a brave, hardy race—descended from the mountains, and moved south in search of new homes.[2] They conquered the Achæans in the Peloponnesus, and occupied the chief cities,—Argos, Corinth, and Sparta. This was about the 11th century B. C.

Grecian Colonies.—Hellas was greatly extended in consequence of these changes. A part of the Achæans fled northward, dispossessing the Ionians, many of whom emigrated to Asia Minor, where they founded the *Ionic colonies*,[3] among which were Ephesus (Acts xix. 1; xx. 15) and Mile′-

---

inhabitants fell into the snare, and eagerly dragged the unwieldy monster within their walls. That night a body of men concealed in the horse crept out, threw open the gates, and admitted the Grecians, who had quietly returned. From the terrible massacre which ensued, Æne′as, a famous Trojan chief, escaped with a few followers. His subsequent adventures form the theme of Virgil's Æne′id. Homer's Odyssey tells the wanderings of the crafty Ulysses, king of Ithaca, on his journey home from Troy, and the trials of his faithful wife Penelope during his absence.

[1] The word "politics" is derived from the Greek word for city, and meant in its original form only the affairs of the city. The Hellenes, unlike most other Aryans (except the Italians), from the very first gathered in cities.

[2] This event is known in Grecian history as "The Return of the Heraclei′dæ." The Dorians were induced by the descendants of Hercules to support their claim to the throne of Argos, whence their ancestor had been driven by the family of Pelops.

[3] Some authorities make the Ionic colonies the parents of Greece.

tus. Similarly, the Æolians had already founded the *Æolic colonies*. Finally the Dorians were tempted to cross the sea and establish the *Doric colonies*, chief of which was Rhodes (map, p. 11). In subsequent times of strife many Greek citizens grew discontented, and left their homes to try their fortune in new lands. The colonial cities also soon became strong enough to plant new settlements. Every opportunity to extend their commerce or political influence was eagerly seized by these energetic explorers. In the palmy days of Greece, the Euxine and the Propontis (Sea of Marmora) were fringed with Hellenic towns. The Ionian cities, at the time of the Persian conquest (p. 125), "extended ninety miles along the coast in an almost uninterrupted line of magnificent quays, warehouses, and dwellings." On the African shore was the rich Cyrene, the capital of a prosperous state. Sicily, with her beautiful city of Syracuse, was like a Grecian island. Southern Italy was long called Magna Græcia (Great Greece). The Phœnicians, the seamen and traders of these times, almost lost the commerce of the eastern Mediterranean. On the western coast the Greeks possessed the flourishing colony of Massilia (Marseilles), and, had it not been for the rising power of Carthage, would have secured nearly the entire shore, and transformed the Mediterranean into a "Grecian lake."

Wherever the Greek went, he remained a Greek. He carried with him into barbarian lands the Hellenic language, manners, and civilization. In the colonies the natives learned the Grecian tongue, and took on the Grecian mode of thought and worship. Moreover, the transplanted Greek matured faster than the home growth. So it happened that in the magnificent cities which grew up in Asia Minor, philosophy, letters, the arts and sciences, bloomed even sooner than in Greece itself.

HELLAS or GREECE.
IN THE HEROIC AGE.

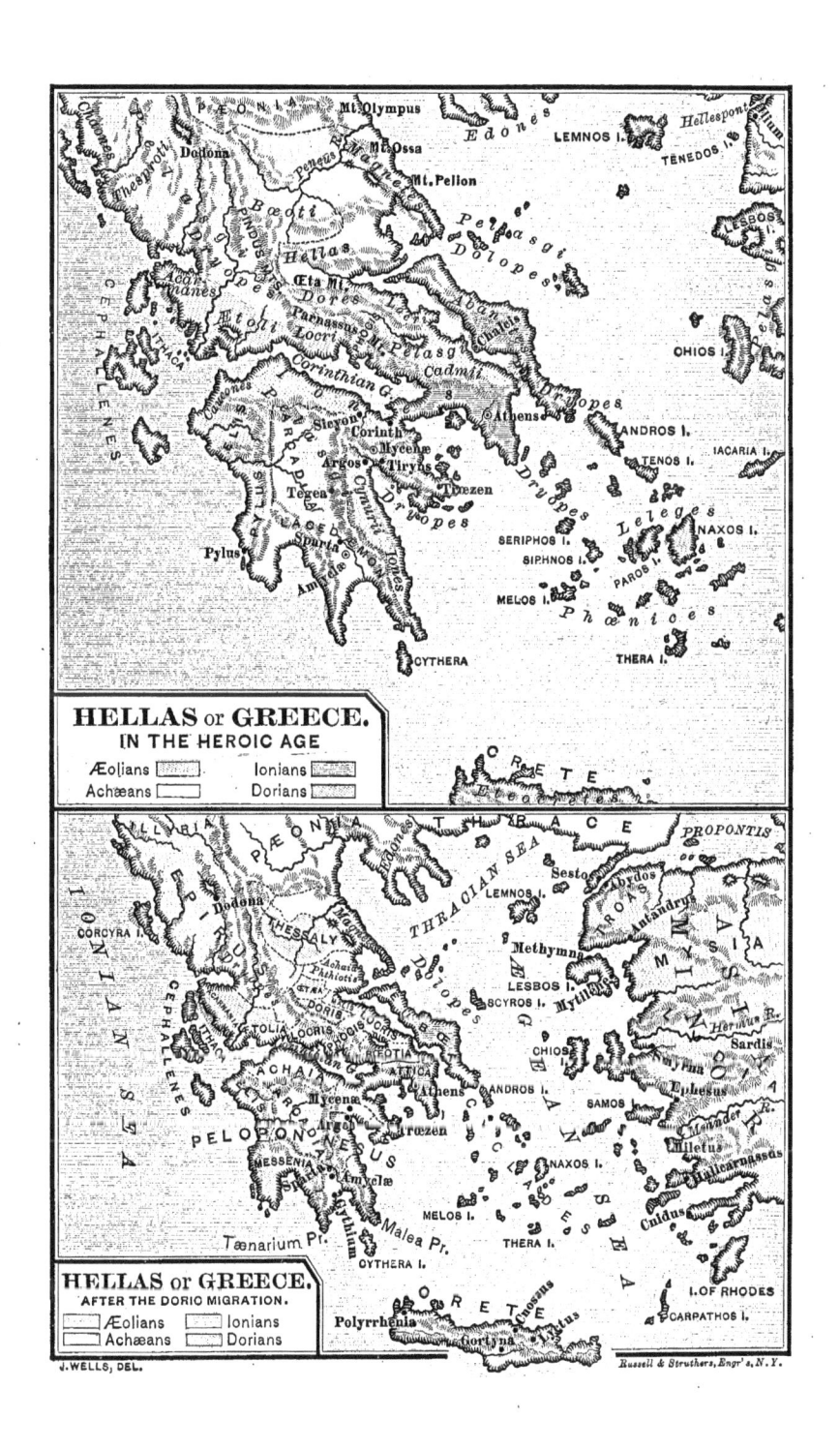

Æolians Ionians
Achæans Dorians

HELLAS or GREECE.
AFTER THE DORIC MIGRATION.

Æolians Ionians
Achæans Dorians

J. WELLS, DEL. Russell & Struthers, Engr's, N.Y.

Sparta and Athens.—The Dorians and the Ionians came to be the leading races in Greece. Their diverse characteristics had a great influence on its history. The Dorians were rough and plain in their habits, sticklers for the old customs, friends of an aristocracy, and bitter enemies of trade and the fine arts. The Ionians, on the other hand, were refined in their tastes, fond of change, democratic, commercial, and passionate lovers of music, painting, and sculpture. The rival cities, Sparta and Athens, represented these opposing traits. Their deep-rooted hatred was the cause of numerous wars which convulsed the country; for in the sequel we shall find that the Grecians spent their best blood in fighting among themselves, and that Grecian history is mostly occupied with the doings of these two cities.

SPARTA.

Early History.—One of the Dorian bands occupied Lacedæmon, called also Sparta from its grain-fields (*spartē*, sown land). The former owners (termed *periœ'ki*, dwellers-around) were allowed to keep the poorest of the lands, and to be tradesmen and mechanics. But they could neither have voice in the government nor intermarry with their Dorian conquerors, who now came to be called Spartans. The latter took the best farms, and compelled their slaves (helots) to work them. The helots were captives or rebels, and were at first few, but in the succeeding wars rapidly increased. The Spartans (only nine thousand strong in the time of Lycurgus), planted thus in the midst of a hostile population, were forced to live like soldiers on guard.

In the rest of the Peloponnesus the Dorians betook themselves to peaceful pursuits, and mingled with the natives. But in Sparta there was no relaxation, no blending. The Dorians there kept on their cold, cruel way. They were constantly quarreling among themselves, and so little gain did they make, that two centuries and a half passed and the Achæans were still fortified only little over two miles away from Sparta.

Lycurgus,[1] according to tradition, was a statesman of royal birth who crystallized into a constitution all the peculiarities of the Spartan character. His whole aim was to make the Spartans a race of soldiers. Trade and travel were prohibited. No money was allowed except cumbrous iron coins, which no foreigner would take. Most property, as slaves, horses, dogs, etc., was held in common. Boys were removed from home at the age of seven, and educated by state officers. The men ate at public tables, slept in barracks, and only occasionally visited their homes. Private life was given up for the good of the state, and devoted to military drill.

The two kings were retained; but their power was limited by a senate of twenty-eight men over sixty years old, and an assembly of all the citizens. The five *ephors* (overseers) chosen annually by the assembly were the real rulers. No popular discussion was allowed, nor could a private citizen speak in the assembly without special leave from a magistrate. Thus the government became in fact an oligarchy under the guise of a monarchy. The people having promised to live under this constitution until he should return, Lycurgus left Sparta, never to return.

The Supremacy of Sparta dates from this time. "A mere garrison in a hostile country, she became the mistress

---

[1] Lycurgus, like many other legendary heroes, has been banished by modern critics into the region of myth. There seems, however, good evidence that he existed about the 9th century B. C. Just what his laws included, and how far they were his own creations, is uncertain.

of Laconia." The conquest of Messenia, in two long, bloody wars, made her dominant in the Peloponnesus. This was preceded and followed by several minor wars, all tending to increase her territory and establish her authority over her neighbors. At the beginning of the 5th century B. C. the Spartans had already repeatedly carried their arms across the isthmus into Attica, and were ready to assert their position as the leaders in Grecian affairs, when, at this juncture, all Greece was threatened by the Persian forces (p. 124).

ATHENS.

Early History.—Athens, like the other Grecian cities, was governed for a time by kings. *Cecrops*, the first ruler, according to the legends, taught the people of Attica navigation, marriage, and the culture of the olive. *Codrus*, the last monarch, fell (1050 B. C.) while resisting the Dorians. After his death the nobles selected one of the royal family as *archon*, or chief. At first the archon ruled for life; afterward the term was shortened to ten years, and finally to one, the nobles choosing nine archons from their own number. Thus Athens became an aristocratic republic.

Draco's Code (621 B. C.).—But democratic spirit was rife. The people complained that they got no justice from the nobles, and the demand for *written laws* became so urgent that Draco was directed to prepare a code. His laws were so merciless that they were said to have been written

COIN OF ATHENS.

in blood, every offense being punished with death. To avoid the popular indignation, Draco fled, and his name is to this day synonymous with cruelty. His code shows (1) the barbarity of the age, and its lack of sympathy with the poor; (2) the growing spirit of democracy.

Solon's Constitution[1] (594 B. C.).—Party strife was now prevalent. The state being threatened with anarchy, Solon was appointed to draft a new constitution. He repealed the harsh edicts of Draco; relieved debtors;[2] redeemed many slaves; forbade parents to sell or pawn their children; ordered every father to teach his sons a trade; and required sons to support their aged father if he had educated them. He aimed to weaken the nobles and strengthen the people. He therefore gave every free-born native of Attica a vote in the assembly, where laws were enacted, archons elected, and the conduct of officers reviewed. The business presented in this assembly was prepared by a senate of four hundred, selected annually by lot.

SOLON'S TABLETS.

Property, instead of birth, now gave rank. The people were divided into four classes, according to their income. Only the three richest classes could hold office, but they had to pay the taxes and to equip themselves as soldiers. The wealthiest could serve as archons; those who had thus served were eligible to the Court of Areopagus.[3] This court

---

[1] This famous Athenian lawgiver, descended from the ancient kings, was forced by poverty to earn a livelihood. He gained a fortune by commerce, retired from business, and then traveled to the East in search of knowledge. He was reckoned one of the Seven Wise Men of Greece (Appendix).

[2] In that age a debtor might be sold into slavery (Nehemiah v. 3, 5; 2 Kings iv. 1).

[3] So called because it met on the hill known by that name (Acts xvii. 19).

repealed laws hurtful to the state, looked after public morals, and rebuked any person who was not properly bringing up his children, or who otherwise lived unworthy an Athenian

Tyrants.[1]—Athens prospered under Solon's wise management. The people got their rights The mortgage-pillars[2] disappeared. But moderate measures pleased neither extreme of society. Class factions strove for power. One day *Pisis'tratus*, a noble aspiring to office, rushed, besmeared with blood, into the market place, and, pointing to his self-inflicted wounds, asked for a guard, pretending that the other nobles had attacked him because he was the people's friend.[3] Solon detected the sham, but the people granted the request. Pisistratus soon seized the Acropolis (p. 194), and became the first tyrant of Athens. His use of his craftily secured place was beneficent. He established Solon's laws, erected beautiful public buildings, encouraged art, and founded the first library.

The *Pisistrat'idæ*, Hippias and Hipparchus, trod in their father's steps. But the assassination of Hipparchus imbittered his brother, so that he became moody and cruel. His enemies, led by the Alcmæon'idæ,[4] bribed the oracle

[1] The Greeks applied this name at first to a person who became king in a city where the law did not authorize one. Afterward the Tyrants became cruel, and the word took on the meaning which we now give it

[2] A mortgaged farm was known by a stone pillar marked with amount of loan and name of lender.

[3] Solon, though under obligations to his kinsman, Pisistratus, resisted his ambitions. He now exclaimed: "You are but a bad imitation of Ulysses He wounded himself to delude his enemies, you to deceive your countrymen."

[4] At the time Draco's laws aroused so much feeling, a noble named Cylon attempted to make himself tyrant. He seized the Acropolis, but was defeated, and his followers, half dead with hunger, were forced to take refuge at the altars of the gods. The archon Megăcles induced them to surrender on the promise of their lives, but they had scarcely left the altars, when his soldiers cut them down. Soon afterward a plague broke out, and the Athenians, believing that a judgment had fallen on their city, forced the Alcmæonidæ (the clan of Megăcles) into exile. To atone for their impiety, the Alcmæonidæ, who were rich, rebuilt the burned temple at Delphi. The contract called for common stone, but they faced the building with fine marble, and thus gained the favor of the Delphic oracle.

at Delphi, so that when the Lacedæmonians consulted the priestess, they received the reply, "Athens must be freed." The Spartans accordingly invaded Attica and drove away the tyrant (510 B. C.). Hippias went over to the Persian court, and was henceforth the declared enemy of his native city. We shall hear from him again.

Democracy Established.—Aristocratic Sparta had only paved the way for a republic. Solon's work now bore fruit. *Cleis'thenes*, an Athenian noble, head of the Alcmæonidæ but now candidate of the people's party, became archon. All freemen of Attica were admitted to citizenship. To break up the four old tribes, and prevent the nobles from forming parties among the people of their clans, or according to local interests, he divided the country into districts, and organized ten new tribes by uniting non-adjacent districts; each tribe sent fifty representatives to the senate, and also chose a *strategus*, or general, the ten generals to command the army in daily turn. To protect the rising democracy from demagogues, he instituted ostracism,[1] or banishment by popular vote (p. 129).

The triumph of democracy was complete. Four times a month all Athens met to deliberate and decide upon questions affecting the public weal. "The Athenians then," says Herodotus, "grew mighty, and it became plain that liberty is a brave thing."

It was now near the beginning of the 5th century B. C. Both Sparta and Athens had risen to power, when all Greece was threatened by a new foe. The young civilization of the West was for the first time called to meet the old civilization of the East. In the presence of a common danger, the warring states united. The next twenty years were stirring ones in the annals of freedom.

---
[1] Strangely enough, Cleisthenes was the first man ostracized.

THE PERSIAN WARS.

Cause.—The Persian empire now reached the borders of Thessaly. The Grecian colonies in Asia Minor had fallen into the hands of Cyrus; and the conquering armies of Darius were already threatening the freedom of Greece itself, when an act of Athens hastened the struggle. The

Ionian cities having tried to throw off the Persian yoke, the mother city sent them aid.[1] The Great King subdued the Ionic revolt, and then turned to punish the haughty foreign-

---

[1] During the brief campaign of the Athenians in Asia Minor, Sardis, the capital of Lydia, was accidentally burned. When Darius received this news, he took a bow and shot an arrow to the sky, with a prayer to Ahura Mazda (p. 93) for help; and that he might not forget the insult, he ordered that at dinner each day a servant should call out thrice, "Master, remember the Athenians."

ers who had dared to meddle in the affairs of his empire, and also to force the Athenians to receive back Hippias (p. 124) as their tyrant.

The First Expedition (493 B. C.) against Greece was sent out under Mardonius, the son-in-law of Darius. The land troops were defeated in Thrace, and the fleet was shattered while rounding Mount Athos. Mardonius returned without having set foot into the region he went to conquer.

The Second Expedition.—Darius, full of fury, began at once raising a new army. Meanwhile heralds were dispatched to demand the surrender of the Grecian cities. Many sent back earth and water, the oriental symbols of submission; Sparta and Athens refused, Sparta throwing the envoys into a deep well, and bidding them find there the earth and water they demanded.

Battle of Marathon (490 B. C.).—The Persian fleet of six hundred triremes (p. 192) safely crossed the Ægean, and landed an army of over a hundred thousand on the field of Marathon, twenty-two miles from Athens. Miltiades (to whom the other strategi had been led by Aristides to surrender their command) went out to meet them with but ten thousand soldiers. The usual prayers and sacrifices were offered, but it was late in the day before the auspices became favorable to an attack. Finding that the Persians had placed their best troops at the center, Miltiades put opposite them a weak line of men, and stationed heavy files of his choicest soldiers on the wings. Giving the enemy no time to hurl their jave-

VIEW OF THE PLAINS OF MARATHON.

lins, he immediately charged at full speed, and came at once to a hand-to-hand fight. The powerful wings swept everything before them, and then, wheeling, they fell upon both flanks of the victorious Persian center. In a few moments the Asiatic host were wildly fleeing to their ships.[1]

---

[1] The Spartans had promised aid, but from religious scruples the troops were unwilling to march until the full moon, and so did not arrive till after the battle. A thousand men from Plataea—all the little city had—stood by the side of the Athenians on that memorable day. When the victory was gained, Eucles, the swiftest runner in Greece, ran with the tidings, and, reaching Athens, had breath only to tell the news, when he fell dead in the street. Seven of the Persian vessels were captured by the pursuing Greeks. The brother of Æschylus, the poet, is said to have caught a trireme by the stern, and to have held it until his hand was hacked off by the enemy. Hardly had the Persians and Athenians separated from the last conflict on the beach, when the attention of both was arrested by a flash of light on the summit of Mount Pentelicus. It was the reflection of the setting sun on the glittering surface of an uplifted shield. Miltiades at once saw in this a signal from the traitors in Athens, inviting the fleet to join them before he returned. Not a moment was to be lost, and he ordered an instant march to the city. When the Persian ships arrived, they found the heroes of Marathon drawn up on the beach, awaiting them.

The Effect[1] of this victory was to render the reputation of Athens for valor and patriotism equal, if not superior, to that of Sparta. The Persian invasion had made a union of the Hellenic states possible, and Marathon decided that Athens should be its leader.

Greece was saved, and her deliverer, Miltiades, was for a time the favorite hero; but a disgraceful expedition to the Isle of Paros cost him his popularity, and soon after his return he died.

Themistocles and Aristides, generals associated with Miltiades at Marathon, now came to be the leading men in Athens. The former was an able but often unscrupulous statesman; the latter, a just man and an incorruptible patriot. Themistocles foresaw that the Persians would make another attempt to subdue Greece; and that Athens, with its excellent harbor and commercial facilities, could be far stronger on sea

---

[1] "So ended what may truly be called the birthday of Athenian greatness. It stood alone in their annals. Other glories were won in after times, but none approached the glory of Marathon. It was not merely the ensuing generation that felt the effects of that wonderful deliverance. It was not merely Themistocles whom the marble trophy of Miltiades would not suffer to sleep. It was not merely Æschylus, who, when his end drew near, passed over all his later achievements in war and peace, at Salamis, and in the Dionysiac theater, and recorded in his epitaph only the one deed of his early days,—that he had repulsed the 'long-haired Medes at Marathon.' It was not merely the combatants in the battle who told of supernatural assistance in the shape of the hero Theseus, or of the mysterious peasant, wielding a gigantic plowshare. Everywhere in the monuments and the customs of their country, and for centuries afterward, all Athenian citizens were reminded of that great day, and of that alone. The frescoes of a painted portico—the only one of the kind in Athens—exhibited in lively colors the scene of the battle. The rock of the Acropolis was crowned on the eastern extremity by a temple of Wingless Victory, now supposed to have taken up her abode forever in the city; and in its northern precipice, the cave, which up to this time had remained untenanted, was consecrated to Pan, in commemoration of the mysterious voice which rang through the Arcadian mountains to cheer the forlorn messenger on his empty-handed return from Sparta. The one hundred and ninety-two Athenians who had fallen on the field received the honor—unique in Athenian history—of burial on the scene of their death (the tumulus raised over their bodies by Aristides still remains to mark the spot), their names were invoked with hymns and sacrifices down to the latest times of Grecian freedom; and long after that freedom had been extinguished, even in the reign of Trajan and the Antonines, the anniversary of Marathon was still celebrated, and the battle-field was believed to be haunted night after night by the snorting of unearthly chargers and the clash of invisible combatants."

than on land. He therefore urged the building of a fleet. Aristides, fond of the old ways, condemned this measure. Themistocles, dreading the opposition, secured the ostracism [1] of his rival.

Third Expedition.—Darius died before he could make a new attempt to punish Athens. But his son Xerxes assembled over a million soldiers, whom he led in person across the Hellespont and along the coast of Thrace and Macedonia. A fleet of twelve hundred war-ships and three thousand transports kept within easy reach from the shore.[2]

Battle of Thermopylæ (480 B. C.).—At the Pass of Thermopylæ his march was checked by seven thousand Greeks under Leonidas, a Spartan. Xerxes sent a messenger to demand their arms. He received the laconic reply, "Come and take them." For two days the Greeks repulsed every attack, and the terrified Persians had to be driven to the assault with whips. On the third day, a traitor having pointed out to Xerxes a mountain-path, he sent the Immortals over it, to the rear of the Grecian post. Spartan law bade a soldier to die rather than yield. So Leonidas, learning of the peril, sent away his allies, retaining only three hundred Spartans and seven hundred Thespians, who wished to share in the glory of the day. The little band prepared

---

[1] For the origin of ostracism see p. 124. Into an urn placed in the assembly any citizen could drop a shell (*ostrakon*) bearing the name of the person he wished exiled. Six thousand votes against a man banished him for ten years. It is said that on this occasion a countryman coming to Aristides, whom he did not know, asked him to write Aristides on his shell. "Why, what wrong has he done?" inquired the patriot. "None at all," was the reply, "only I am tired of hearing him called the Just." Six years later Aristides was recalled.

[2] Two magnificent bridges of boats which he built across the Hellespont having been injured in a storm, the story is that Xerxes ordered the sea to be beaten with whips, and fetters to be thrown into it to show that he was its master. The vast army was seven days in crossing. The king sat on a throne of white marble, inspecting the army as it passed. It consisted of forty six different nations, each armed and dressed after its own manner, while ships manned by Phœnicians covered the sea. Xerxes is said to have burst into tears at the thought that in a few years not one of all that immense throng would be alive.

for battle,—the Spartans combing their long hair, according to custom,—and then, scorning to await the attack, dashed

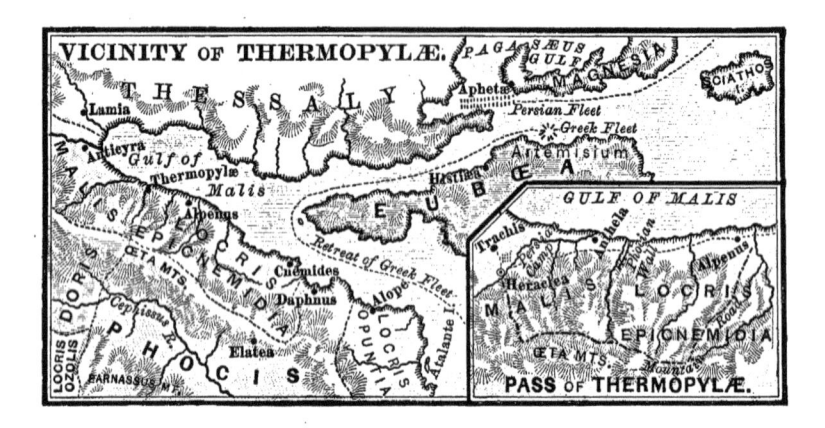

down the defile to meet the on-coming enemy. All perished, fighting to the last.[1]

---

[1] "Xerxes could not believe Demaratus, who assured him that the Spartans at least were come to dispute the Pass with him, and that it was their custom to trim their hair on the eve of a combat. Four days passed before he could be convinced that his army must do more than show itself to clear a way for him. On the fifth day he ordered a body of Median and Cissian troops to fall upon the rash and insolent enemy, and to lead them captive into his presence. He was seated on a lofty throne from which he could survey the narrow entrance of the Pass, which, in obedience to his commands, his warriors endeavored to force. But they fought on ground where their numbers were of no avail, save to increase their confusion, when their attack was repulsed: their short spears could not reach their foe; the foremost fell, the hinder advancing over their bodies to the charge; their repeated onsets broke upon the Greeks idly, as waves upon a rock. At length, as the day wore on, the Medians and Cissians, spent with their efforts and greatly thinned in their ranks, were recalled from the contest, which the king now thought worthy of the superior prowess of his own guards, the ten thousand Immortals. They were led up as to a certain and easy victory; the Greeks stood their ground as before; or, if they ever gave way and turned their backs, it was only to face suddenly about, and deal tenfold destruction on their pursuers. Thrice during these fruitless assaults the king was seen to start up from his throne in a transport of fear or rage. The combat lasted the whole day; the slaughter of the barbarians was great; on the side of the Greeks a few Spartan lives were lost; as to the rest, nothing is said. The next day the attack was renewed with no better success; the bands of the several cities that made up the Grecian army, except the Phocians, who were employed in defending the mountain-path by which the defile was finally turned, relieved each other at the post of honor; all stood equally firm, and repelled the charge not less vigorously than before. The confidence of Xerxes was changed into despondence and perplexity."

[480 B. C.] THE POLITICAL HISTORY. 131

The Sacrifice of Leonidas became the inspiration of all Greece, and has been the admiration of the lovers of freedom in every age. The names of the three hundred were

LEONIDAS AT THE PASS OF THERMOPYLÆ.

familiar to their countrymen, and, six hundred years after, a traveler spoke of seeing them inscribed on a pillar at Sparta. Upon the mound where the last stand was made a marble lion was erected to Leonidas, and a pillar to the three hundred bore this inscription, written by Simonides (p. 164):—

"Go, stranger, and to Lacedæmon tell
That here, obeying her behests, we fell."

Battle of Sal'amis.—At first, however, the loss at Thermopylæ seemed in vain, and the Asiatic deluge poured south over the plains of Greece. Warned by the oracle that the safety of Athens lay in her "wooden walls," the inhabitants deserted the city, which Xerxes then burned. The ocean, however, seemed to "fight for Greece." In a storm the Persian fleet lost two hundred ships. But it was still so much superior, that the Greeks were fearful, and as usual quarreling,[1] when Themistocles determined to bring on the battle, and accordingly sent a spy to the enemy to say that his countrymen would escape if they were not attacked immediately. Thereupon the Persians blockaded the Hellenic fleet in the harbor of Salamis. Animated by the spirit of Thermopylæ, the Grecians silenced their disputes and rushed to the fray. They quickly defeated the Phœnician ships in the van, and then the very multitude of the vessels caused the ruin of the Persian fleet: for while some were

[1] "All the Thessalians, Locrians, and Bœotians, except the cities of Thespiæ and Platæa, sent earth and water to the Persian king at the first call to submit, although these tokens of subjection were attended by the curses of the rest of the Greeks, and the vow that a tithe of their estates should be devoted to the city of Delphi. Yet of the Greeks who did not favor Persia, some were willing to assist only on condition of being appointed to conduct and command the whole; others, if their country could be the first to be protected; others sent a squadron, which was ordered to wait till it was certain which side would gain the victory, and others pretended they were held back by the declarations of an oracle." An oft-told story, given in connection with this engagement, illustrates the jealousy of the Grecian generals. They were met to decide upon the prize for skill and wisdom displayed in the contest. When the votes were collected, it appeared that each commander had placed his own name first, and that of Themistocles second. While the Grecian leaders at Salamis were deliberating over the propriety of retreat, and Themistocles alone held firm, a knock was heard at the door, and Themistocles was called out to speak with a stranger. It was the banished Aristides. "Themistocles," said he, "let us be rivals still, but let our strife be which best may serve our country." He had crossed from Ægina in an open boat to inform his countrymen that they were surrounded by the enemy.

trying to escape, and some to come to the front, the Greeks, amid the confusion plying every weapon, sunk two hundred vessels, and put the rest to flight.

Xerxes, seated on a lofty throne erected on the beach, watched the contest. Terrified by the destruction of his fleet, he fled into Asia, leaving three hundred and fifty thousand picked troops under Mardonius to continue the war.

Battle of Himĕra.—While the hosts of Xerxes were pouring into Hellas on the northeast, she was assailed on the southwest by another formidable foe. An immense fleet, three thousand ships-of-war, sailing from Carthage to Sicily, landed an army under Hamilcar,[1] who laid siege to Himera. Gelo, tyrant of Syracuse, marched to the relief of Himera, and on the very day of Salamis utterly routed the Phœnician forces. The tyranny of the commercial oligarchy of Carthage might have been as fatal to the liberties of Europe as the despotism of Persia.

Battle of Platæa (479 B. C.).—Mardonius wintered in Thessaly, and the next summer invaded Attica. The half-rebuilt houses of Athens were again leveled to the ground. Finally the allies, over one hundred thousand strong, took the field under Pausanias, the Spartan. After the two armies had faced each other for ten days, want of water compelled Pausanias to move his camp. While *en route*, Mardonius attacked his scattered forces. The omens were unfavorable, and the Grecian leader dare not give the signal to engage. The Spartans protected themselves with their shields as best they could against the shower of arrows. Many Greeks were smitten, and fell, lamenting, not that they must fall, but that they could not strike a blow for their country. In his distress, Pausanias lifted up his streaming eyes toward the temple of Hera, beseeching the goddess, that,

---

[1] This was an ancestor of the Hamilcar of Punic fame (p. 230).

if the Fates forbade the Greeks to conquer, they might die like men. Suddenly the sacrifices became auspicious. The Spartans, charging in compact rank, shield touching shield, with their long spears swept all before them. The Athenians, coming up, stormed the intrenched camp. Scarcely forty thousand Persians escaped. The booty was immense. Wagons were piled up with vessels of gold and silver, jewels, and articles of luxury. One tenth of all the plunder was dedicated to the gods. The prize of valor was adjudged to the Platæans, and they were charged to preserve the graves of the slain, Pausanias promising with a solemn oath that the battle-field should be sacred forever.

That same day the Grecian fleet, having crossed the Ægean, destroyed the Persian fleet at MYCALE in Asia Minor.

The Effect of Marathon, Thermopylæ, Salamis, Platæa, and Mycăle was to give the death-blow to Persian rule in Europe. Grecian valor had saved a continent from eastern slavery and barbarism. More than that, the Persian wars gave rise to the real Hellenic civilization, and Marathon and Salamis may be looked upon as the birthplaces of Grecian glory.

Athenian Supremacy.—Greece was now, to paraphrase the language of Diodorus, at the head of the world, Athens at the head of Greece, and Themistocles at the head of Athens. The city of Athens was quickly rebuilt. During the recent war the Spartan soldiers had taken the lead, but Pausanias afterward proved a traitor, and, as Athens was so strong in ships, she became the acknowledged leader of all the Grecian states. A league, called the *Confederation of Delos* (477 B. C.), was formed to keep the Persians out of the Ægean. The different cities annually contributed to Athens a certain number of ships, or a fixed sum of money for the support of the navy. The ambition of Themistocles was to form a grand maritime empire, but, his share in the treason of Pausanias having been discovered, he was ostracized. Aristides, seeing the drift of affairs, had changed his views, and was already the popular commander of the fleet.

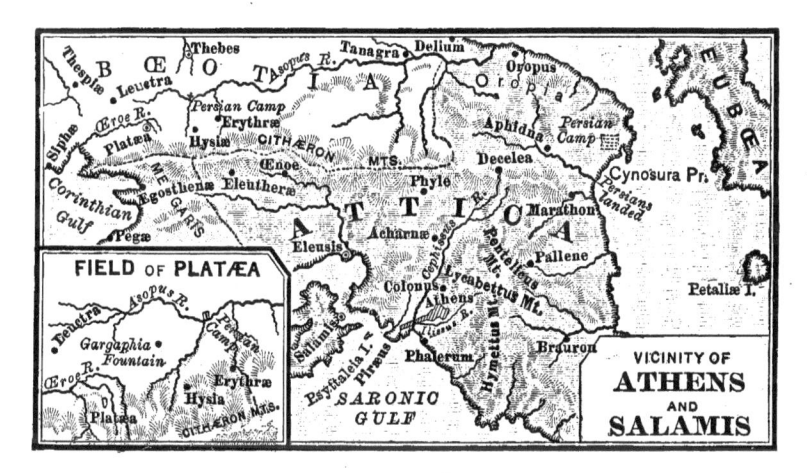

VICINITY OF ATHENS AND SALAMIS

Though the head of the party of the nobles, he secured a law abolishing the property qualification, and allowing any person to hold office.[1]

AGE OF PERICLES.
(479–429 B. C.)

The Leading Men at Athens, after the death of Aristides, were *Pericles* and *Cimon*. The heroes of the Persian invasions had passed from the stage, and new actors now appeared.

---

[1] The thoughtful student of history cannot but pause here to consider the fate of these three great contemporary men,—Pausanias, Themistocles, and Aristides. Pausanias fled to the temple of Minerva. The Spartans, not daring to violate this sanctuary, blocked the door (the traitor's mother laying the first stone), tore off the roof, guarded every avenue, and left the wretch to die of cold and hunger. Themistocles was welcomed by Artaxerxes, then King of Persia, and assigned the revenue of three cities. He lived like a prince, but finally ended his pitiable existence, it is said, with poison. Aristides the Just went down to his grave full of honors. The treasurer of the league, he had yet been so honest that tradition says he did not leave enough money to meet his funeral expenses. The grateful republic paid these rites, finished the education of his son, and portioned his daughters.

Cimon[1] renewed the glory of his father Miltiades, the victor at Marathon. He pushed on the war in Asia Minor against Persia with great vigor, finally routing her land and sea forces in the decisive battle of the *Eurymĕdon* (466 B. C.). As the head of the nobles, he was naturally friendly to aristocratic Sparta. The Helots and Messenians, taking advantage of an earthquake which nearly destroyed that city, revolted, and a ten-years' struggle (known in history as the Third Messenian War) ensued. The haughty Spartans were driven to ask aid from Athens. By the influence of Cimon, this was granted. But the Spartans became fearful of their allies, and sent the army home. All Athens rose in indignation, and Cimon was ostracized (461 B. C.) for exposing his city to such insult.

Pericles,[2] who was the leader of the democracy, now

---

[1] Cimon was the richest man in Athens. He kept open table for the public. A body of servants laden with cloaks followed him through the streets, and gave a garment to any needy person whom he met. His pleasure-garden was free for all to enter and pluck fruit or flowers. He planted oriental plane-trees in the market place; bequeathed to Athens the groves, afterward the Academy of Plato, with its beautiful fountains; built marble colonnades where the people were wont to promenade; and gave magnificent dramatic entertainments at his private expense.

[2] "To all students of Grecian literature, Pericles must always appear as the central figure of Grecian history. His form, manner, and outward appearance are well known. We can imagine that stern and almost forbidding aspect which repelled rather than invited intimacy; the majestic stature; the long head,—long to disproportion,—already, before his fiftieth year, silvered over with the marks of age; the sweet voice and rapid enunciation—recalling, though by an unwelcome association, the likeness of his ancestor Pisistratus. We knew the stately reserve which reigned through his whole life and manners. Those grave features were never seen to relax into laughter, twice only in his long career to melt into tears. For the whole forty years of his administration he never accepted an invitation to dinner but once, and that to his nephew's wedding, and then staid only till the libation [p. 199]. That princely courtesy could never be disturbed by the bitterest persecution of aristocratic enmity or popular irritation. To the man who had followed him all the way from the assembly to his own house, loading him with the abusive epithets with which, as we know from Aristophanes, the Athenian vocabulary was so richly stored, he paid no other heed than, on arriving at his own door, to turn to his torch-bearer with an order to light his reviler home. In public it was the same. Amidst the passionate gesticulations of Athenian oratory, amidst the tempest of an Athenian mob, his self-possession was never lost, his dress was never disordered, his language was ever studied and measured. Every speech that he delivered he wrote down previously. Every time that he spoke he offered up a prayer to Heaven that no word might escape his lips which he should wish unsaid. But when he did speak the effect was almost

had everything his own way. A mere private citizen, living plainly and unostentatiously, this great-hearted man, by his eloquence, genius, adroitness, and wisdom, shaped the policy of the state. Opposing foreign conquest, he sought home development. He was bent on keeping Athens all-powerful in Greece, and on making the people all-powerful in Athens. He had perfect confidence in a government by the people, if they were only properly educated. There were then no common schools or daily papers, and he was forced to use what the times supplied. He paid for all service in the army, on juries, at religious festivals and civil assemblies, so that the poorest man could take part in public affairs. He had the grand dramas of Æschylus, Euripides, and Sophocles performed free before the multitude. He erected magnificent public buildings, and adorned them with the noblest historical paintings. He enriched the temples of the gods with beautiful architecture and the exquisite sculptures of Phidias. He encouraged poets, artists, philosophers, and orators to do their best work. Under his fostering care, the Age of Pericles became the finest blossom and fruitage of Hellenic civilization.

Athens Ornamented and Fortified.—Matchless colonnades and temples were now erected, which are yet the wonder of the world. The Acropolis was so enriched with

awful. The 'fierce democracy' was struck down before it. It could be compared to nothing short of the thunders and lightnings of that Olympian Jove whom in majesty and dignity he resembled. It left the irresistible impression that he was always in the right. 'He not only throws me in the wrestle,' said one of his rivals, 'but when I have thrown him, he will make the people think that it is I and not he who has fallen.' What Themistocles, what Aristides, what Cimon, said, has perished from memory; but the condensed and vivid rhetorical images of Pericles were handed down from age to age as specimens of that eloquence which had held Athens and Greece in awe. 'The lowering of the storm of war' from Peloponnesus—'the spring taken out of the year' in the loss of the flower of Athenian youths—the comparison of Greece to 'a chariot drawn by two horses'—of Ægina to 'the eyesore of the Piræus'—of Athens to 'the school of Greece'—were traditionary phrases which later writers preserved, and which Thucydides either introduced or imitated in the 'Funeral Oration' which he has put in his mouth."

magnificent structures that it was called "the city of the gods." The Long Walls were built two hundred yards apart, and extended over four miles from Athens to Piræus —its harbor. Thus the capital was connected with the sea, and, while the Athenians held the command of the ocean, their ships could bring them supplies, even when the city should be surrounded by an enemy on land.

A SCENE IN ATHENS IN THE TIME OF PERICLES.

The Wonderful Spirit and enterprise of the Athenians are shown from the fact that, while they were thus erecting great public works at home, they were during a single year (458 B. C.) waging war in Cyprus, in Egypt, in Phœnicia, off

Ægina, and on the coast of Peloponnesus. The Corinthians, knowing that the Athenian troops were occupied so far from home, invaded Megara, then in alliance with Athens, but the "boys and old men" of Athens sallied out and routed them. So completely was the tide turned, that (450 B. C.) Artaxerxes I. made a treaty with Athens, agreeing to the independence of the Grecian cities in Asia Minor, and promising not to spread a sail on the Ægean Sea, nor bring a soldier within three days' march of its coast.

PELOPONNESIAN WAR.
(431–404 B. C.)

Causes of the War.—The meddling of Athens in the affairs of her allies, and the use of their contributions (p. 134) to erect her own public buildings, had aroused bitter hatred. Sparta, jealous of the glory and fame of her rival, watched every chance to interfere. At last an opportunity came. A quarrel arose between Corinth and her colony of Corcyra. Athens favored Corcyra; Sparta, Corinth. Nearly all Greece took sides in the dispute, according to race or political sympathy; the real question at issue being the broad one, whether the ruling power in Hellas should be Athens—Ionic, democratic and maritime; or Sparta—Doric, aristocratic and military. The Ionians and the democracy naturally aided Athens; the Dorians and the aristocracy, Sparta. Both parties were sometimes found within the same city, contending for the supremacy.

Allies of Athens.

All the islands of the Ægean (except Melos and Thera), Corcyra, Zacynthos, Chios, Lesbos, and Samos; the numerous Greek colonies on the coast of Asia Minor, Thrace, and Macedon; Naupactus, Platæa, and a part of Acarnania.

Allies of Sparta.

All the states of the Peloponnesus (except Argos and Achaia, which remained neutral); Locris, Phocis, and Megara; Ambracia, Anactorium, and the island of Leucas; and the strong Bœotian League, of which Thebes was the head.

Conduct of the War.—The Spartan plan was to invade Attica, destroy the crops, and persuade the Athenian allies to desert her. As Sparta was strong on land, and Athens on water, Pericles ordered the people of Attica to take refuge within the Long Walls of the city, while the fleet and army ravaged the coast of the Peloponnesus. When, therefore, Archida'mus, king of Sparta, invaded Attica, the people flocked into the city with all their movable possessions. Temporary buildings were erected in every vacant place in the public squares and streets, while the poorest of the populace were forced to seek protection in squalid huts beneath the shelter of the Long Walls. Pitiable indeed was the condition of the inhabitants during these hot summer days, as they saw the enemy, without hindrance, burning their homes and destroying their crops, while the Athenian fleet was off ravaging the coast of Peloponnesus. But it was worse the second year, when a fearful pestilence broke out in the crowded population. Many died, among them Pericles himself (429 B. C.).[1] This was the greatest loss of all, for there was no statesman left to guide the people.

[1] "When, at the opening of the Peloponnesian war, the long enjoyment of every comfort which peace and civilization could bring was interrupted by hostile invasion; when the whole population of Attica was crowded within the city of Athens; when, to the inflammable materials which the populace of a Grecian town would always afford, were added the discontented land-owners and peasants from the country, who were obliged to exchange the olive glades of Colonus, the thymy slopes of Hymettus, and the oak forests of Acharnæ, for the black shade of the Pelasgicum and the stifling huts along the dusty plain between the Long Walls; when without were seen the fire and smoke ascending from the ravage of their beloved orchards and gardens, and within the excitement was aggravated by the little knots which gathered at every corner, and by the predictions of impending evil which were handed about from mouth to mouth,—when all these feelings, awakened by a situation so wholly new in a population so irritable, turned against one man as the author of the present distress, then it was seen how their respect for that one man united with their inherent respect for law to save the state. Not only did Pericles restrain the more eager spirits from sallying forth to defend their burning property, not only did he calm and elevate their despondency by his speeches in the Pnyx and Ceramicus, not only did he refuse to call an assembly, but no attempt at an assembly was ever made. The groups in the streets never grew into a mob, and, even when to the horrors of a blockade were added those of a pestilence, public tranquillity was never for a moment disturbed, the order of the constitution was never for a moment infringed.

Demagogues now arose, chief among whom was *Cleon*, a cruel, arrogant boaster, who gained power by flattering the populace. About this time, also, the Spartans began to build ships to dispute the empire of the sea, on which Athens had so long triumphed.

The Memorable Siege of Platæa, which began in the third year of the war, illustrates the desperation and destruction that characterized this terrible struggle of twenty-seven years. In spite of Pausanias's oath (p. 134), Archida'mus with the Spartan army attacked this city, which was defended by only four hundred and eighty men. First the Spartan general closed every outlet by a wooden palisade, and constructed an inclined plane of earth and stone, up which his men could advance to hurl their weapons against the city. This work cost seventy days' labor of the whole army, but the garrison undermined the mound and destroyed it entirely. Next the Spartans built around the

And yet the man who thus swayed the minds of his fellow-citizens was the reverse of a demagogue. Unlike his aristocratic rival, Cimon, he never won their favor by indiscriminate bounty Unlike his democratic successor, Cleon, he never influenced their passions by coarse invectives. Unlike his kinsman, Alcibiades, he never sought to dazzle them by a display of his genius or his wealth. At the very moment when Pericles was preaching the necessity of manful devotion to the common country, he was himself the greatest of sufferers. The epidemic carried off his two sons, his sister, several other relatives, and his best and most useful political friends. Amidst this train of calamities he maintained his habitual self-command, until the death of his favorite son Paralus left his house without a legitimate representative to maintain the family and its hereditary sacred rites. On this final blow,—the greatest that, according to the Greek feeling, could befall any human being,—though he strove to command himself as before, yet at the obsequies of the young man, when it became his duty to place a garland on the dead body, his grief became uncontrollable, and he burst into tears. Every feeling of resentment seems to have passed away from the hearts of the Athenian people before the touching sight of the marble majesty of their great statesman yielding to the common emotion of their own excitable nature. Every measure was passed which could alleviate this deepest sorrow of his declining age. But it was too late, and he soon sank into the stupor from which he never recovered. As he lay apparently passive in the hands of the nurse, who had hung round his neck the amulets which in life and health he had scorned, whilst his friends were dwelling with pride on the nine trophies which on Bœotia and Samos, and on the shores of Peloponnesus, bore witness to his success during his forty years' career, the dying man suddenly broke in with the emphatic words, 'That of which I am most proud you have left unsaid: No Athenian, through my fault, was ever clothed in the black garb of mourning.' "—*Quarterly Review*

REGION OF OPERATIONS
IN THE
PELOPONNESIAN WAR.

J. WELLS DEL.

RUSSELL & STRUTHERS, ENG'S N.Y.

city two concentric walls, and roofed over the space between them so as to give shelter to the soldiers on guard. For two long years the Platæans endured all the horrors of a siege. Provisions ran low, and one stormy December night a part of the men stole out of the gate, placed ladders against the Spartan wall, climbed to the top, killed the sentinels, and escaped through the midst of the enemy with the loss of only one man. The rest of the garrison were thus enabled to hold out some time longer. But at length their food was exhausted, and they were forced to surrender. The cruel Spartans put every man to death, and then, to please the Thebans, razed the city to the ground. Heroic little Platæa was thus blotted out of the map of Greece.[1]

Alcibi′ades, a young nobleman, the nephew of Pericles and pupil of Socrates, by his wealth, beauty, and talent, next won the ear of the crowd. Reckless and dissolute, with no heart, conscience, or principle, he cared for nothing except his own ambitious schemes. Though peace had then come through the negotiations of Nicias, the favorite Athenian general, it was broken by the influence of this demagogue, and the bloody contest renewed.

Expedition to Sicily (415 B. C.).—The oppressions of the tyrants of Syracuse, a Dorian city in Sicily, gave an excuse for seizing that island, and Alcibiades advocated this brilliant scheme, which promised to make Athens irresistible. The largest fleet and army Hellas had yet sent forth were accordingly equipped. One morning, just before their departure, the busts of Hermes, that were placed along the roads of Attica to mark the distance, and in front of the Athenian houses as protectors of the people, were found to be mutilated. The populace, in dismay, lest a curse should fall on the city, demanded the punishment of those who had com-

[1] It was restored 387 B. C., again destroyed 374 B. C., and again rebuilt 338 B. C.

mitted this sacrilegious act. It was probable that some drunken revelers had done the mischief; but the enemies of Alcibiades made the people believe that he was the offender. After he sailed he was cleared of this charge, but a new one impended. This was that he had privately performed the Eleusinian mysteries (p. 184) for the amusement of his friends. To answer this heinous offense, Alcibiades was summoned home, but he escaped to Sparta, and gave the rival city the benefit of his powerful support. Meanwhile the exasperated Athenians condemned him to death, seized his property, and called upon the priests to pronounce him accursed.

The expedition had now lost the only man who could have made it a success. Nicias, the commander, was old and sluggish. Disasters followed apace. Finally Gylippus, a famous Spartan general, came to the help of Syracuse. Athens sent a new fleet and army, but she did not furnish a better leader, and the reënforcement served only to increase the final ruin. In a great sea-fight in the harbor of Syracuse the Athenian ships were defeated, and the troops attempting to flee by land were overtaken and forced to surrender (413 B. C.).

Fall of Athens.—The proud city was now doomed. Her best soldiers were dying in the dungeons of Syracuse. Her treasury was empty. Alcibiades was pressing on her destruction with all his revengeful genius. A Spartan garrison held Decelea, in the heart of Attica. The Athenian allies dropped off. The Ionic colonies revolted. Yet with the energy of despair Athens dragged out the unequal contest nine years longer. The recall of Alcibiades gave a gleam of success. But victory at the price of submission to such a master was too costly, and he was dismissed. Persian gold gave weight to the Lacedæmonian sword and equipped her fleet. The last ships of Athens were taken by Lysander, the Spartan, at Ægospŏtămi in the Hellespont (405 B. C.). Sparta now controlled the sea, and Athens, its harbor blockaded, suffered famine in addition to the horrors of war. The proud city surrendered at last (404 B. C.). Her ships were given up; and the Long Walls were torn down amid the playing of flutes and the rejoicings of dancers, crowned with garlands, as for a festival. "That day was deemed by the Peloponnesians," says Xenophon, "the commencement of liberty for Greece."

Thus ended the Peloponnesian war, twenty-seven years after its commencement, and seventy-six years after Salamis had laid the foundation of the Athenian power. Athens had fallen, but she possessed a kingdom of which Sparta could not deprive her. She still remained the mistress of Greece in literature and art.

The Thirty Tyrants.—A Spartan garrison was now placed on the Acropolis at Athens, and an oligarchy of thirty persons established. A reign of terror followed. The "Thirty Tyrants" put hundreds of citizens to death without form of trial. After they had ruled only eight months, the Athenian exiles returned in arms, overthrew the tyrants, and reëstablished a democratic government.

Retreat of the Ten Thousand (401 B. C.).—Now that peace had come at home, over ten thousand restless Greeks [1] went away to help Cyrus the Younger, satrap of Asia Minor, dethrone his elder brother, Artaxerxes. At *Cunaxa*, near Babylon, they routed the Persians. But Cyrus fell, and, to complete their misfortune, their chief officers were induced to visit the enemy's camp, where they were treacherously taken prisoners. Left thus in the heart of the Persian Em-

---

[1] Greece at this time was full of soldiers of fortune,—men who made war a trade, and served anybody who was able to pay them.

pire, the little army chose new captains, and decided to cut its way home again. All were ignorant alike of the route and the language of the people. Hostile troops swarmed on every side. Guides misled them. Famine threatened them. Snows overwhelmed them. Yet they struggled on for months. When one day ascending a mountain, there broke from the van the joyful shout of "The sea! The sea!" It was the Euxine,—a branch of that sea whose waters washed the shores of their beloved Greece.

About three-fourths of the original number survived to tell the story of that wonderful march (p. 172). Such an exploit, while it honored the endurance of the Greek soldier, revealed the weakness of the Persian Empire.

LACEDÆMON AND THEBAN DOMINION.

Lacedæmon Rule (405–371 B. C.).—Tempted by the glittering prospect of Eastern conquest, Sparta sent Agesila'us into Asia. His success there made Artaxerxes tremble for his throne. Again Persian gold was thrown into the scale. The Athenians were helped to rebuild the Long Walls, and soon their flag floated once more on the Ægean. Conon, the Athenian admiral, defeated the Spartan fleet off *Cnidus*, near Rhodes (394 B. C.). In Greece the Spartan rule, cruel and coarse, had already become unendurable. In every town Sparta sought to establish an oligarchy of ten citizens favorable to herself, and a *harmost*, or governor. Wherever popular liberty asserted itself, she endeavored to extinguish it by military force. But the cities of Corinth, Argos, Thebes, and Athens struck for freedom. Sparta was forced to recall Agesilaus. Strangely enough, she now made friends with the Persian king, who dictated the *Peace of Antalci-*

das[1] (387 B. C.). This ended the war, and gave Asia Minor to Persia. So low had Hellas fallen since the days of Salamis and Platæa!

Theban Rule (371-362 B. C.).—At the very height of Sparta's arrogance her humiliation came. The Bœotian League (p. 139) having been restored, and the oligarchical governments favorable to Sparta overthrown, a Spartan army invaded that state. At this juncture there arose in Thebes a great general, Epaminondas, who made the Theban army the best in the land. On the famous field of *Leuctra* (371 B. C.), by throwing heavy columns against the long lines of Spartan soldiers, he beat them for the first time in their history.[2] The charm of Lacedæmonian invincibility was broken. The stream of Persian gold now turned into Thebes. The tyrannical Spartan *harmosts* were expelled from all the cities. To curb the power of Sparta, the independence of Messenia, after three centuries of slavery, was reëstablished (p. 121). Arcadia was united in a league, having as its head Megalopŏlis, a new city now founded. A wise, pure-hearted statesman, Epaminondas sought to combine Hellas, and not, like the leaders of Athens or Sparta,

---

[1] So named from the Spartan envoy who managed it. This peace was a mournful incident in Grecian history. Its true character cannot be better described than by a brief remark and reply cited in Plutarch: "Alas, for Hellas!" observed some one to Agesilaus, "when we see our Laconians Medizing!"—"Nay," replied the Spartan king, "say rather the Medes (Persians) Laconizing."

[2] The Spartan lines were twelve ranks deep. Epaminondas (fighting *en échelon*) made his, at the point where he wished to break through, fifty ranks deep. At his side always fought his intimate friend Pelopidas, who commanded the Sacred Band. This consisted of three hundred brothers-in-arms,—men who had known one another from childhood, and were sworn to live and die together. In the crisis of the struggle Epaminondas cheered his men with the words, "One step forward!" While the bystanders after the battle were congratulating him over his victory, he replied that his greatest pleasure was in thinking how it would gratify his father and mother. Soon after Epaminondas returned from the battle of Leuctra, his enemies secured his election as public scavenger. The noble-spirited man immediately accepted the office, declaring that "the place did not confer dignity on the man, but the man on the place," and executed the duties of this unworthy post so efficiently as to baffle the malice of his foes.

selfishly to rule it. Athens at first aided him, and then, jealous of his success, sided with Lacedæmon. At *Mantinea* (362 B. C.), in Arcadia, Epaminondas fought his last battle, and died at the moment of victory.[1] As he alone had made Thebes great, she dropped at once to her former level.

Three states in succession—Athens, Sparta, and Thebes—had risen to take the lead in Greece. Each had failed. Hellas now lay a mass of quarreling, struggling states.

MACEDONIAN EMPIRE.

Rise of Macedonia.—The Macedonians were allied to the Greeks, and their kings took part in the Olympian games. They were, however, a very different people. Instead of living in a multitude of free cities, as in Greece, they dwelt in the country, and were all governed by one king. The polite and refined Athenian looked upon the coarse Macedonian as almost a barbarian. But about the time of the fall of Athens these rude northerners were fast taking on the Greek civilization.

Philip (359–336 B. C.) came to the throne of Macedonia well schooled for his career. A hostage for many years at the Theban court, he understood Grecian diplomacy and military art. He was now determined to be recognized not only as a Greek among Greeks, but as the head of all Greece. To this he bent every energy of his strong, wily nature. He extended his kingdom, and made it a compact empire. He thoroughly organized his army, and formed the famous

---

[1] He was pierced with a javelin, and to extract the weapon would cause his death by bleeding. Being carried out of the battle, like a true soldier he asked first about his shield, then waited to learn the issue of the contest. Hearing the cries of victory, he drew out the shaft with his own hand, and died a few moments after.

Macedonian phalanx,[1] that, for two centuries after, decided the day on every field on which it appeared. He craftily mixed in Grecian affairs, and took such an active part in the Sacred War [2] (355–346 B. C.), that he was admitted to the Amphictyonic Council (p. 115). Demosthenes, the great Athenian orator, seemed the only man clear-headed enough to detect Philip's scheme. His eloquent "Philippics" (p. 202) at last aroused his apathetic countrymen to a sense of their danger. The Second Sacred War, declared by the Amphictyons against the Locrians for alleged sacrilege, having been intrusted to Philip, that monarch marched through Thermopylæ, and his designs against the liberties of Greece became but too evident. Thebes and Athens now took the field. But at *Chærone'a* (338 B. C.) the Macedonian phalanx annihilated their armies, the Sacred Band perishing to a man.

PORTRAIT OF PHILIP OF MACEDON.

Greece was prostrate at Philip's feet. In a congress of

[1] The peculiar feature of this body was that the men were armed with huge lances twenty-one feet long. The lines were placed so that the front rank, composed of the strongest and most experienced soldiers, was protected by a bristling mass of five rows of lance-points, their own extending fifteen feet before them, and the rest twelve, nine, six, and three feet respectively. Formed in a solid mass, usually sixteen ranks deep, shield touching shield, and marching with the precision of a machine, the phalanx charge was irresistible. The Spartans, carrying spears only about half as long, could not reach the Macedonians.

[2] The pretext for the First Sacred War is said to have been that the Phocians had cultivated lands consecrated to Apollo. The Amphictyonic Council, led by Thebes, inflicted a heavy fine upon them. Thereupon they seized the Temple at Delphi, and finally, to furnish means for prolonging the struggle, sold the riches accumulated from the pious offerings of the men of a better day. The Grecians were first shocked and then demoralized by this impious act. The holiest objects circulated among the people, and were put to common uses. All reverence for the gods and sacred things was lost. The ancient patriotism went with the religion, and Hellas was forever fallen from her high estate. Everywhere her sons were ready to sell their swords to the highest bidder.

all the states except Sparta, he was appointed to lead their united forces against Persia. But while preparing to start he was assassinated (336 B. C.) at his daughter's marriage feast.

A TETRADRACHM OF ALEXANDER THE GREAT.

Alexander,[1] his son, succeeded to Philip's throne and ambitious projects. Though only twenty years old, he was

---

[1] On the day of Alexander's birth, Philip received news of the defeat of the Illyrians, and that his horses had won in the Olympian chariot-races. Overwhelmed by such fortune, the monarch exclaimed, "Great Jupiter, send me only some slight reverse in return for so many blessings!" That same day also the famous Temple of Diana, at Ephesus, was burned by an incendiary. Alexander was wont to consider this an omen that he should kindle a flame in Asia. On his father's side he was said to be descended from Hercules, and on his mother's from Achilles. He became a pupil of Aristotle (p. 176), to whom Philip wrote, announcing Alexander's birth, saying that he knew not which gave him the greater pleasure,—that he had a son, or that Aristotle could be his son's teacher. The young prince at fourteen tamed the noble horse Bucephalus, which no one at the Macedonian court dared to mount; at sixteen he saved his father in battle, and at eighteen defeated the Sacred Band upon the field at Chæronea. Before setting out upon his Persian expedition, he consulted the oracle at Delphi. The priestess refused to go to the shrine, as it was an unlucky day. Alexander thereupon grasped her arm. "Ah, my son," exclaimed she, "thou art irresistible!"—"Enough," shouted the delighted monarch, "I ask no other reply." He was equally happy of thought at Gordium. Here he was shown the famous Gordian knot, which, it was said, no one could untie except the one destined to be the conqueror of Asia. He tried to unravel the cord, but, failing, drew his sword and severed it at a blow. Alexander always retained a warm love for his mother, Olympias. She, however, was a violent woman. Antip'ater, who was left governor of Macedon during Alexander's absence, wrote, complaining of her conduct. "Ah," said the king, "Antipater does not know that one tear of a mother will blot out ten thousand of his letters." Unfortunately, the hero who subdued the known world had never conquered himself. In a moment of drunken passion he slew Clitus, his dearest friend, who had saved his life in battle. He shut himself up for days after this horrible deed, lamenting his crime, and refusing to eat or to transact any business. Yet in soberness and calmness he tortured and hanged Callisthenes, a Greek author, because he would not worship him as a god. Carried away by his success, he finally sent to Greece, ordering his name to be enrolled among the deities. Said the Spartans in reply, "If Alexander will be a god, let him."

more than his father's equal in statesmanship and military skill. Thebes having revolted, he sold its inhabitants as slaves, and razed the city, sparing only the temples and the house of Pindar the poet. This terrible example quieted all opposition. He was at once made captain-general of the Grecian forces to invade Persia, and, soon after, he set out upon that perilous expedition from which he never returned.

Alexander's Marches and Conquests.—In 334 B. C. Alexander crossed the Hellespont with thirty thousand infantry and four thousand five hundred cavalry. He was the first to leap on the Asiatic shore.[1] Pressing eastward, he defeated the Persians in two great battles,—one at the river *Granicus,* and the other at *Issus.*[2] Then he turned south and besieged Tyre. To reach the island on which the city stood, he built a stone pier two hundred feet wide and half a mile long, on which he rolled his ponderous machines, breached the wall, and carried the place by a desperate assault. Thence passing into Egypt, that country fell without a blow. Here he founded the famous city of Alexandria (p. 154). Resuming his eastern march, he routed the Persian host, a million strong, on the decisive field of *Arbéla.* Babylon was entered in triumph. Persepolis (p. 94) was burned to avenge the destruction of Athens one hundred and fifty years before (p. 132). Darius was pursued so closely, that, to prevent his falling into the conqueror's possession, he was slain by a noble.

[1] Alexander was a great lover of Homer (p. 162), and slept with a copy of the Iliad under his pillow. While his army was now landing, he visited the site of Troy, offered a sacrifice at the tomb of Achilles, hung up his own shield in the temple, and, taking down one said to have belonged to a hero of the Trojan war, ordered it to be henceforth carried before him in battle.

[2] Just before this engagement Alexander was attacked by a fever in consequence of bathing in the cold water of the Cydnus. While sick he was informed that his physician Philip had been bribed by Darius to poison him. As Philip came into the room, Alexander handed him the letter containing the warning, and then, before the doctor could speak, swallowed the medicine. His confidence was rewarded by a speedy recovery.

The mysterious East still alluring him on, Alexander, exploring, conquering,[1] founding cities, at last reached the river Hyph'asis, where his army refused to proceed further in the unknown regions. Instead of going directly back, he built vessels, and descended the Indus; thence the fleet cruised along the coast, while the troops returned through Gedro'sia (Beloochistan), suffering fearful hardships in its inhospitable deserts.[2] When he reached Babylon, ten years had elapsed since he crossed the Hellespont.

The next season, while just setting out from Babylon upon a new expedition into Arabia, he died (323 B. C.). With him perished his schemes and his empire.

Alexander's Plan was to mold the diverse nations which he had conquered into one vast empire, with the capital at Babylon. Having been the Cyrus, he desired to be the Darius of the Persians. He sought to break down the distinctions between the Greek and the Persian. He married the Princess Roxana, the "Pearl of the East," and induced many of his army to take Persian wives. He enlisted twenty thousand Persians into the Macedonian phalanx, and appointed natives to high office. He wore the Eastern dress, and adopted oriental ceremonies in his court. He respected the religion and the government of the various countries, restrained the satraps, and ruled more beneficently than their own monarchs.

The Results of the thirteen years of Alexander's reign have not yet disappeared. Great cities were founded by

---

[1] Porus, an Indian prince, held the banks of the Hydaspes with three hundred war-chariots and two hundred elephants. The Indians being defeated, Porus was brought into Alexander's presence. When asked what he wished, Porus replied, "Nothing except to be treated like a king." Alexander, struck by the answer, gave him his liberty, and enlarged his territory.

[2] One day while Alexander was parched with thirst, a drink of water was given him, but he threw it on the ground lest the sight of his pleasure should aggravate the suffering of his men.

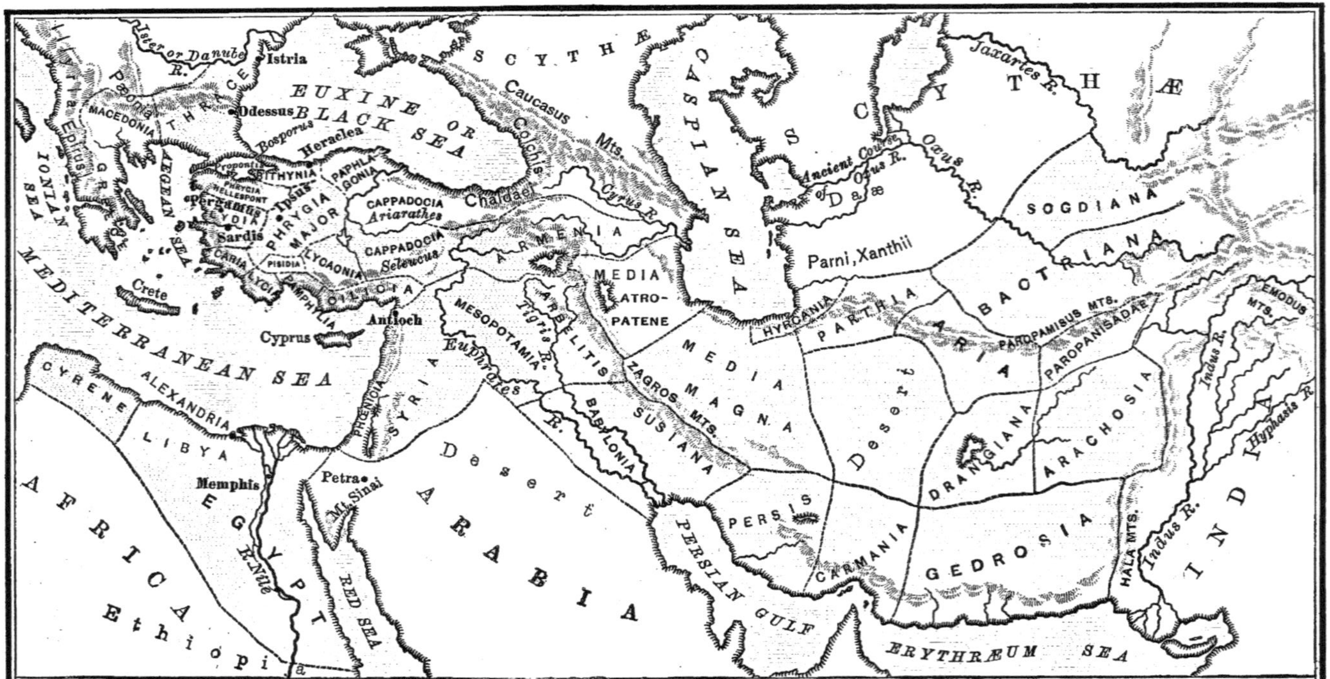

EMPIRE OF ALEXANDER THE GREAT *Boundary dark-red*

DISTRIBUTION OF THE TERRITORY AFTER THE BATTLE OF IPSUS 301 B. C.

Territory received by Ptolemy   *Territory received by Seleucus*

" " by Lysimachus   *" " by Cassander*

J. WELLS, DEL.   RUSSELL & STRUTHERS, ENG'S N.Y.

him, or his generals, which are still marts of trade. Commerce received new life. Greek culture and civilization spread over the Orient, and the Greek language became, if not the common speech, at least the medium of communication among educated people from the Adriatic to the Indus. So it came about, that, when Greece had lost her national liberty, she suddenly attained, through her conquerors, a world-wide empire over the minds of men.

But while Asia became thus Hellenized, the East exerted a reflex influence upon Hellas. As Rawlinson well remarks,—

"The Oriental habits of servility and adulation superseded the old free-spoken independence and manliness; patriotism and public spirit disappeared; luxury increased; literature lost its vigor; art deteriorated; and the people sank into a nation of pedants, parasites, and adventurers."

ALEXANDER'S SUCCESSORS.

Alexander's Principal Generals, soon after his death, divided his empire among themselves. A mortal struggle of twenty-two years followed, during which these officers, released from the strong hand of their master, "fought, quarreled, grasped, and wrangled like loosened tigers in an amphitheater." The greed and jealousy of the generals, or kings as they were called, were equaled only by the treachery of their men. Finally, by the decisive battle of *Ipsus* (301 B. C.), the conflict was ended, and the following distribution of the territory made:—

Ptolemy	Lysim'achus	Seleucus	Cassander
received Egypt, and conquered all of Palestine, Phœnicia, and Cyprus.	received Thrace and nearly all of Asia Minor.	received Syria and the East, and he afterward conquered Asia Minor, Lysimachus being slain.	received Macedon and Greece.

Ptolemy founded a flourishing Greek kingdom in Egypt. The Greeks, attracted by his benign rule, flocked thither in multitudes. The Egyptians were protected in their ancient religion, laws, and customs, so that these stiff-necked rebels against the Persian rule quietly submitted to the Macedonian. The Jews[1] in large numbers found safety under his paternal government. This threefold population gave to the second civilization which grew up on the banks of the Nile a peculiarly cosmopolitan character. The statues of the Greek gods were mingled with those of Osiris and Isis; the same hieroglyphic word was used to express a Greek and a lower Egyptian; and even the Jews forgot the language of Palestine, and talked Greek. Alexandria thus became, under the Ptolemies, a brilliant center of commerce and civilization. The building of a commodious harbor and a superb lighthouse, and the opening of a canal to the Red Sea, gave a great impetus to the trade with Arabia and India. Grecian architects made Alexandria, with its temples, obelisks, palaces, and theaters, the most beautiful city of the times. Its white marble lighthouse, called the Pharos, was one of the Seven Wonders of the World (p. 601). At the center of the city, where its two grand avenues crossed each other, in the midst of gardens and fountains, stood the Mausoleum, which contained the body of Alexander, embalmed in the Egyptian manner.

The Alexandrian Museum and Library founded by Ptolemy I. (Soter), but greatly extended by Ptolemy II. (Philadelphus), and enriched by Ptolemy III. (Euergetes), were the grandest monuments of this Greco-Egyptian kingdom. The Library comprised at one time, in all its collections, seven hundred thousand volumes. The Museum was a stately marble edifice surrounded by a portico, beneath which the philosophers walked and conversed. The pro-

---

[1] They had a temple at Alexandria similar to the one at Jerusalem, and for their use the Old Testament was translated into Greek (275-250 B. C.). From the fact that seventy scholars performed this work, it is termed the Septuagint.

fessors and teachers were all kept at the public expense. There were connected with this institution a botanical and a zoölogical garden, an astronomical observatory, and a chemical laboratory. To this grand university resorted the scholars of the world (see Steele's New Astronomy, p. 9). At one time in its history there were in attendance as many as fourteen thousand persons. While wars shook Europe and Asia, Archimedes and Hero the philosophers, Apelles the painter, Hipparchus and Ptolemy the astronomers, Euclid the geometer, Eratosthenes and Strabo the geographers, Manetho the historian, Aristophanes the rhetorician, and Apollonius the poet, labored in quiet upon the peaceful banks of the Nile. Probably no other school of learning has ever exerted so wide an influence. When Cæsar wished to revise the calendar, he sent for Sosigenes the Alexandrian. Even the early Christian church drew, from what the ancients loved to call "the divine school at Alexandria," some of its most eminent Fathers, as Origen and Athanasius. Modern science itself dates its rise from the study of nature that began under the shadow of the Pyramids.

Last of the Ptolemies.—The first three Ptolemies were able rulers. Then came ten weak or corrupt successors. The last Ptolemy married his sister,[1] the famous Cleopatra (p. 254), who shared his throne. At her death Egypt became a province of Rome (30 B. C.).

Seleucus was a conqueror, and his kingdom at one time stretched from the Ægean to India, comprising nearly all the former Persian empire. He was a famous founder of cities, nine of which were named for himself, and sixteen for his son Antiochus. One of the latter, Antioch in Syria (Acts xi. 26, etc.), became the capital instead of Babylon. The descendants of Seleucus (Seleucidæ) were unable to

[1] This kind of family intermarriage was common among the Pharaohs.

retain his vast conquests, and one province after another dropped away, until the wide empire finally shrank into Syria, which was grasped by the Romans (65 B. C.).

Several Independent States arose in Asia during this eventful period. *Pergamus* became an independent kingdom on the death of Seleucus I. (280 B. C.), and, mainly through the favor of Rome, absorbed Lydia, Phrygia, and other provinces. The city of Pergamus, with its school of literature and magnificent public buildings, rivaled the glories of Alexandria. The rapid growth of its library so aroused the jealousy of Ptolemy that he forbade the export of papyrus; whereupon Eumenes, king of Pergamus, resorted to parchment, which he used so extensively for writing that this material took the name of *pergamena*. By the will of the last king of Pergamus, the kingdom fell to Rome (p. 237). *Parthia* arose about 255 B. C. It gradually spread, until at one time it stretched from the Indus to the Euphrates. Never absorbed into the Roman dominion, it remained throughout the palmy days of that empire its dreaded foe. The twenty-ninth of the Arsacidæ, as its kings were called, was driven from the throne by Artaxerxes, a descendant of the ancient line of Persia, and, after an existence of about five centuries, the Parthian Empire came to an end. It was succeeded by the new Persian monarchy or kingdom of the Sassanidæ (226–652 A. D.). *Pontus*, a rich kingdom of Asia Minor, became famous through the long wars its great king Mithridates V. carried on with Rome (p. 243).

Greece and Macedonia, after Alexander's time, present little historic interest.[1] The chief feature was that nearly all the Grecian states, except Sparta, in order to make

---

[1] In 279 B. C. there was a fearful irruption of the Gauls under Brennus (see Brief Hist. France, p. 10). Greece was ravaged by the barbarians. They were finally expelled, and a remnant founded a province in Asia Minor named Galatia, to whose people in later times St. Paul directed one of his Epistles.

head against Macedonia, formed leagues similar to that of our government during the Revolution. The principal ones were the *Achæan* and the *Ætolian*. But the old feuds and petty strifes continued until all were swallowed up in the world-wide dominion of Rome, 146 B. C. (p. 236).

Athens under the Romans was prosperous. Other centers of learning existed,—Alexandria, Marseilles, Tarsus; but scholars from all parts of the extended empire of Rome still flocked to Athens to complete their education. True, war had laid waste the groves of Plato and the garden in which Epicurus lived, yet the charm of old associations continued to linger around these sacred places, and the Four Schools of Philosophy (p. 175) maintained their hold on public thought.[1] The Emperor Hadrian (p. 261) established a library, and built a pantheon and a gymnasium. The Antonines endowed university professorships. So late as the close of the 4th century A. D. a writer describes the airs put on by those who thought themselves "demigods, so proud are they of having looked on the Academy and Lyceum, and the Porch where Zeno reasoned." But with the fall of Paganism and the growth of legal studies—so peculiar to the Roman character—Athens lost her importance, and her schools were closed by Justinian (529 A. D.).

[1] It is strange to hear Cicero, in De Finibus, speak of these scenes as already classic ground: "After hearing Antiochus in the Ptolemæum, with Piso and my brother and Pomponius, . . . we agreed to take our evening walk in the Academy. So we all met at Piso's house, and, chatting as we went, walked the six stadia between the Gate Dipylum and the Academy. When we reached the scenes so justly famous, we found the quietude we craved. 'Is it a natural sentiment,' asked Piso, 'or a mere illusion, which makes us more affected when we see the spots frequented by men worth remembering than when we merely hear their deeds or read their works? It is thus that I feel touched at present, for I think of Plato, who, as we are told, was wont to lecture here. Not only do those gardens of his, close by, remind me of him, but I seem to fancy him before my eyes. Here stood Speusippus, here Xenocrates, here his hearer Polemon.' . . . 'Yes,' said Quintus, 'what you say, Piso, is quite true, for as I was coming hither, Colonus, yonder, called my thoughts away, and made me fancy that I saw its inmate Sophocles, for whom you know my passionate admiration.'—'And I, too,' said Pomponius, 'whom you often attack for my devotion to Epicurus, spend much time in his garden, which we passed lately in our walk.'"

2. THE CIVILIZATION.

"Athens is the school of Greece, and the Athenian is best fitted, by diversity of gifts, for the graceful performance of all life's duties."—Pericles.

Athens and Sparta.—Though the Greeks comprised many distinct tribes, inhabiting separate cities, countries, and islands, having different laws, dialects, manners, and customs, Athens and Sparta were the great centers of Hellenic life. These two cities differed widely from each other in thought, habits, and tastes. Sparta had no part in Grecian art or literature. "There was no Spartan sculptor, no Laconian painter, no Lacedæmonian poet." From Athens, on the contrary, came the world's masterpieces in poetry, oratory, sculpture, and architecture.

GREEK GALLEY WITH THREE BANKS OF OARS.

Society.—The ATHENIANS boasted that they were Autochthons,[1] *i. e.*, sprung from the soil where they lived; and that their descent was direct from the sons of the gods. The ancient Attic tribes were divided into *phratries*, or fraternities; the phratries into *gentes*, or clans; and the gentes into *hearths*, or families. The four tribes were bound together by the common worship of Apollo Patrôus, reputed father of their common ancestor, Ion. Each phratry had its particular sacred rites and civil compact, but all the phratries of the same tribe joined periodically in certain ceremonies. Each gens had also its own ancestral hero or god, its exclusive privilege

---

[1] In recognition of this belief, they wore in their hair, as an ornament, a golden grasshopper,—an insect hatched from eggs laid in the ground.

THE CIVILIZATION. 159

of priesthood, its compact of protection and defense, and its special burial-place. Last of all, every family had its private worship and exclusive ancestral rites. Thus their religion both unified and separated the Greeks; while the association of houses and brotherhoods powerfully influenced their early social and political life.

Athens in her golden days had, as we have already seen, neither king nor aristocracy. Every free citizen possessed a voice in the general government, and zealously maintained his rights and liberty as a member of the state. Although to belong to an old and noble house gave a certain position among all true-born Athenians, there was little of the usual exclusiveness attending great wealth or long pedigree. An Athenian might be forced from poverty to wear an old and tattered cloak, or be only the son of a humble imagemaker, as was Socrates, or of a cutler, as was Demosthenes, yet, if he had wit, bravery, and talent, he was as welcome to the brilliant private saloons of Athens as were the richest and noblest.

Trade and Merchandise were as unpopular in most parts of Greece as in Persia. The Greeks regarded arms, agriculture, music, and gymnastics as the only occupations worthy a freeman. To profit by retail trade was esteemed a sort of cheating, and handicrafts were despised because they tied men down to work, and gave no leisure for athletic exercises or social culture. In Sparta, where even agriculture was despised and all property was held in common, an artisan had neither public influence nor political rights; while in Thebes no one who had sold in the market within ten years was allowed part in the government. Even in democratic Athens, where extensive interests in shipbuilding and navigation produced a strong sentiment in favor of commerce, the poor man who lived on less than ten cents a day, earned by serving on juries[1] or in other public capacities, looked with disdain on the practical mechanic and tradesman. Consequently most of the Athenian stores and shops belonged to

[1] There were ten courts in Athens, employing, when all were open, six thousand jurymen. The Athenians had such a passion for hearing and deciding judicial and political questions, that they clamored for seats in the jury-box. Greek literature abounds with satires on this national peculiarity. In one of Lucian's dialogues, Menippus is represented as looking down from the moon and watching the characteristic pursuits of men. "The northern hordes were fighting, the Egyptians were plowing, the Phœnicians were carrying their merchandise over the sea, the Spartans were whipping their children, and the Athenians were *sitting in the jury-box.*" So also Aristophanes, in his satire called The Clouds, has his hero (Stropoiades) visit the School of Socrates, where he is shown a map of the world.
STUDENT.—"And here lies Athens."
STREP.—"Athens! nay, go to—— That cannot be. *I see no law courts sitting!*"

aliens, who paid heavy taxes and made large profits. Solon sought to encourage manufacturing industries, and engaged in commerce, for which he traveled; Aristotle kept a druggist's shop in Athens; and even Plato, who shared the national prejudice against artisans, speculated in oil during his Egyptian tour.

SPARTA, with her two kings, powerful ephors, and landed aristocracy, presents a marked contrast to Athens.

The Two Kings were supposed to have descended by different lines from the gods, and this belief preserved to them what little authority they retained under the supremacy of the ephors. They offered the monthly sacrifices to the gods, consulted the Delphian oracle, which always upheld their dignity, and had nominal command of the army. On the other hand, war and its details were decided by the ephors, two of whom accompanied one king on the march. The kings were obliged monthly to bind themselves by an oath not to exceed the laws, the ephors also swearing on that condition to uphold the royal authority. In case of default, the kings were tried and severely fined, or had their houses burned.

The population of Laconia, as we have seen, comprised Spartans, periœki, and helots (p. 119).

GRECIAN PEASANT.

The Spartans lived in the city, and were the only persons eligible to public office. So long as they submitted to the prescribed discipline and paid their quota to the public mess, they were *Equals*. Those who were unable to pay their assessment lost their franchise, and were called *Inferiors;* but by meeting their public obligation they could at any time regain their privileges.

The Periœki were native freemen. They inhabited the hundred townships of Laconia, having some liberty of local management, but subject always to orders from Sparta, the ephors having power to inflict the death penalty upon them without form of trial.

The Helot was a serf bound to the soil, and belonged not so much to the master as to the state. He was the pariah of the land. If he dared to wear a Spartan bonnet, or even to sing a Spartan song, he was put to death. The old Egyptian kings thinned the ranks of their surplus rabble by that merciless

THE CIVILIZATION. 161

system of forced labor which produced the pyramids; the Spartans did not put the blood of their helots to such useful account, but, when they became too powerful, used simply the knife and the dagger.[1] The helot served in war as a light-armed soldier attached to a Spartan or periœkian hoplite.[2] Sometimes he was clothed in heavy armor, and was given freedom for superior bravery. But a freed helot was by no means equal to a periœkus, and his known courage made him more than ever a man to be watched.

Literature.—In considering Egyptian, Assyrian, Babylonian, and Persian literature, we have had only fragments, possessing little value for the present age except as historical curiosities, or as a means of insight into the life and attainments of the people. Grecian literature, on the contrary, exists to-day as a model. From it poets continue to draw their highest inspiration; its first great historian is still known as the "Father of History;" its philosophy seems to touch every phase of thought and argument of which the human mind is capable; and its oratory has never been surpassed. So vast a subject should be studied by itself, and in this book we can merely furnish a nucleus about which the pupil may gather in his future reading the rich stores which await his industry. For convenience we shall classify it under the several heads of Poetry, History, Oratory, and Philosophy.

Poetry.—EPICS (Narrative Poems).—The earliest Grecian literature of which we have any knowledge is in verse. In the dawn of Hellas, hymns of praise to the gods were performed in choral dances about shrines and altars, and heroic legends woven into ballads were musically chanted to the sound of a four-stringed lyre. With this rhythmical story-telling, the Rhapsodists (*ode-stitchers*) used to delight the listening multitudes on festive occasions in

---

[1] The helots were once free Greeks like their masters, whom they hated so bitterly that there was a saying, "A helot could eat a Spartan raw." They wore a sheep-skin garment and dog-skin cap as the contemptuous badge of their slavery. There was constant danger of revolt, and from time to time the bravest of them were secretly killed by a band of detectives appointed by the government for that purpose. Sometimes a wholesale assassination was deemed necessary. During the Peloponnesian war the helots had shown so much gallantry in battle, that the Spartan authorities were alarmed. A notice was issued that two thousand of the bravest—selected by their fellows—should be made free. There was great rejoicing among the deluded slaves, and the happy candidates, garlanded with flowers, were marched proudly through the streets and around the temples of the gods. Then they mysteriously disappeared, and were never heard of more. At the same time seven hundred other helots were sent off to join the army, and the Spartans congratulated themselves on having done a wise and prudent deed.

[2] A hoplite was a heavy-armed infantryman. At Platæa every Spartan had seven helots, and every periœkus one helot to attend him.

aliens, who paid heavy taxes and made large profits. Solon sought to encourage manufacturing industries, and engaged in commerce, for which he traveled; Aristotle kept a druggist's shop in Athens; and even Plato, who shared the national prejudice against artisans, speculated in oil during his Egyptian tour.

SPARTA, with her two kings, powerful ephors, and landed aristocracy, presents a marked contrast to Athens.

The Two Kings were supposed to have descended by different lines from the gods, and this belief preserved to them what little authority they retained under the supremacy of the ephors. They offered the monthly sacrifices to the gods, consulted the Delphian oracle, which always upheld their dignity, and had nominal command of the army. On the other hand, war and its details were decided by the ephors, two of whom accompanied one king on the march. The kings were obliged monthly to bind themselves by an oath not to exceed the laws, the ephors also swearing on that condition to uphold the royal authority. In case of default, the kings were tried and severely fined, or had their houses burned.

The population of Laconia, as we have seen, comprised Spartans, periœki, and helots (p. 119).

The Spartans lived in the city, and were the only persons eligible to public office. So long as they submitted to the prescribed discipline and paid their quota to the public mess, they were *Equals*. Those who were unable to pay their assessment lost their franchise, and were called *Inferiors;* but by meeting their public obligation they could at any time regain their privileges.

The Periœki were native freemen. They inhabited the hundred townships of Laconia, having some liberty of local management, but subject always to orders from Sparta, the ephors having power to inflict the death penalty upon them without form of trial.

GRECIAN PEASANT.

The Helot was a serf bound to the soil, and belonged not so much to the master as to the state. He was the pariah of the land. If he dared to wear a Spartan bonnet, or even to sing a Spartan song, he was put to death. The old Egyptian kings thinned the ranks of their surplus rabble by that merciless system of forced labor which produced the pyramids; the Spartans did not put the blood of their helots to such useful account, but, when they became too powerful, used simply the knife and the dagger.[1] The helot served in war as a light-armed soldier attached to a Spartan or pericekian hoplite.[2] Sometimes he was clothed in heavy armor, and was given freedom for superior bravery. But a freed helot was by no means equal to a pericekus, and his known courage made him more than ever a man to be watched.

Literature.—In considering Egyptian, Assyrian, Babylonian, and Persian literature, we have had only fragments, possessing little value for the present age except as historical curiosities, or as a means of insight into the life and attainments of the people. Grecian literature, on the contrary, exists to-day as a model. From it poets continue to draw their highest inspiration; its first great historian is still known as the "Father of History;" its philosophy seems to touch every phase of thought and argument of which the human mind is capable; and its oratory has never been surpassed. So vast a subject should be studied by itself, and in this book we can merely furnish a nucleus about which the pupil may gather in his future reading the rich stores which await his industry. For convenience we shall classify it under the several heads of Poetry, History, Oratory, and Philosophy.

Poetry.—EPICS (Narrative Poems).—The earliest Grecian literature of which we have any knowledge is in verse. In the dawn of Hellas, hymns of praise to the gods were performed in choral dances about shrines and altars, and heroic legends woven into ballads were musically chanted to the sound of a four-stringed lyre. With this rhythmical story-telling, the Rhapsodists (*ode-stitchers*) used to delight the listening multitudes on festive occasions in

---

[1] The helots were once free Greeks like their masters, whom they hated so bitterly that there was a saying, "A helot could eat a Spartan raw." They wore a sheep-skin garment and dog-skin cap as the contemptuous badge of their slavery. There was constant danger of revolt, and from time to time the bravest of them were secretly killed by a band of detectives appointed by the government for that purpose. Sometimes a wholesale assassination was deemed necessary. During the Peloponnesian war the helots had shown so much gallantry in battle, that the Spartan authorities were alarmed. A notice was issued that two thousand of the bravest—selected by their fellows—should be made free. There was great rejoicing among the deluded slaves, and the happy candidates, garlanded with flowers, were marched proudly through the streets and around the temples of the gods. Then they mysteriously disappeared, and were never heard of more. At the same time seven hundred other helots were sent off to join the army, and the Spartans congratulated themselves on having done a wise and prudent deed.

[2] A hoplite was a heavy-armed infantryman. At Platæa every Spartan had seven helots, and every pericekus one helot to attend him.

princely halls, at Amphictyonic gatherings, and at religious assemblies. Among this troop of wandering minstrels there arose
Homer[1] (about 1000 B.C.), an Asiatic Greek, whose name has become immortal. The Iliad and Odyssey are the grandest epics ever written. The first contains the story of the Siege of Troy (p. 115); the second narrates the wanderings of Ulysses, king of Ithaca, on his return from the Trojan Conquest. Homer's style is simple, artistic, clear, and vivid. It abounds in sublime description, delicate pathos, pure domestic sentiment, and noble conceptions of character. His verse strangely stirred the Grecian heart. The rhapsodist Ion describes the emotion it produced:

HOMER.

"When that which I recite is pathetic, my eyes fill with tears; when it is awful or terrible, my hair stands on end, and my heart leaps. The spectators also weep in sympathy, and look aghast with terror."

Antiquity paid divine honors to Homer's name; the cities of Greece owned state copies of his works, which not even the treasuries of kings could buy; and his poems were then, as now, the standard classics in a literary education (p. 179).

---

[1] According to tradition, Homer was a schoolmaster, who, wearying of confinement, began to travel. Having become blind in the course of his wanderings, he returned to his native town, where he composed his two great poems. Afterward he roamed from town to town, singing his lays, and adding to them as his inspiration came. Somewhere on the coast of the Levant he died and was buried. His birthplace is unknown, and, according to an old Greek epigram,

"Seven rival towns contend for Homer dead,
Through which the living Homer begged his bread."

Many learned writers have doubted whether Homer ever existed, and regard the two great poems ascribed to him as a simple collection of heroic legends, recited by different bards, and finally woven into a continuous tale. The three oldest manuscripts we have of the Iliad came from Egypt, the last having been found under the head of a mummy excavated in 1887 at Hawara, in the Fayoom. Some critics assert that the story of the Siege of Troy is allegorical, a repetition of old Egyptian fancies, "founded on the daily siege of the east by the solar powers that every evening are robbed of their brightest treasures in the west." Dr. Schliemann, a German explorer, unearthed (1872-82) in Asia Minor what is believed to be the Homeric Ilium. His discoveries are said to refute all skepticism as to the historic reality of the Siege of Troy.

Hesiod, who lived after the time of Homer, wrote two long poems, "Works and Days"[1] and "Theogony." In the former he details his agricultural experiences, enriching them with fable, allegory, and moral reflections, and also furnishes a calendar of lucky and unlucky days for the use of farmers and sailors; the latter gives an account of the origin and history of the thirty thousand Grecian gods, and the creation of the world. The Spartans, who despised agriculture, called Hesiod the "poet of the helots," in contrast with Homer, "the delight of warriors." In Athens, however, his genius was recognized, and his poems took their place with Homer's in the school education of the day.

After Homer and Hesiod the poetic fire in Greece slumbered for over two hundred years. Then arose many lyric, elegiac, and epigrammatic poets, whose works exist only in fragments.

Tyrtæus, "the lame old schoolmaster," invented the trumpet, and gained the triumph for Sparta[2] in the Second Messenian War by his impassioned battle-songs.

Archil'ochus[3] was a satirical poet of great reputation among the ancients. His birthday was celebrated in one grand festival with that of Homer, and a single double-faced statue perpetuated their memory. He invented many rhythmical forms, and wrote with force and elegance. His satire was so venomous that he is said to have driven a whole family to suicide by his pen, used in

---

[1] The Works and Days was an earnest appeal to Hesiod's dissipated brother, whom he styles the "simple, foolish, good-for-naught Perses." It abounds with arguments for honest industry, gives numerous suggestions on the general conduct of society, and occasionally dilates on the vanity, frivolity, and gossip, which the author imputes to womankind.

[2] The story is that, in obedience to an oracle, the Spartans sent to Athens for a general who should insure them success. The jealous Athenians ironically answered their demand with the deformed Tyrtæus. Contrary to their design, the cripple poet proved to be just what was needed, and his wise advice and stirring war-hymns spurred the Spartans on to victory.

[3] One of the greatest of soldier poets, Archilochus proved himself a coward on the battle-field, afterward proclaiming the fact in a kind of apologetic bravado, thus:

"The foeman glories o'er my shield,
I left it on the battle-field.
I threw it down beside the wood,
Unscathed by scars, unstained with blood.
And let him glory; since from death
Escaped, I keep my forfeit breath.
I soon may find at little cost
As good a shield as that I lost"

When he afterward visited Sparta, the authorities, taking a different view of shield-dropping, ordered him to leave the city in an hour.

revenge for his rejection by one of the daughters. He likened himself to a porcupine bristling with quills, and declared,

> "One great thing I know,
> The man who wrongs me to requite with woe."

Sappho, "the Lesbian Nightingale," who sang of love, was put by Aristotle in the same rank with Homer and Archilochus. Plato called her the tenth muse, and it is asserted that Solon, on hearing one of her poems, prayed the gods that he might not die till he had found time to learn it by heart. Sappho's style was intense, brilliant, and full of beautiful imagery; her language was said to have a "marvelous suavity." She sought to elevate her countrywomen, and drew around her a circle of gifted poetesses whose fame spread with hers throughout Greece.

Alcæus, an unsuccessful lover of Sappho, was a polished, passionate lyrist. His political and war poems gained him high repute, but, like Archilochus, he dropped his shield in battle and ran from danger. His convivial songs were favorites with the classic topers. One of his best poems is the familiar one, beginning,

> "What constitutes a state?
> Not high-raised battlement or labored mound,
> Thick wall or moated gate."

Anacreon, a courtier of Hipparchus (p. 123), was a "society poet." Himself pleasure-loving and dissipated, his odes were devoted to "the muse, good humor, love, and wine." He lived to be eighty-five years old, and his memory was perpetuated on the Acropolis at Athens by a statue of a drunken old man.

Simonides was remarkable for his terse epigrams and choral hymns. He was the author of the famous inscription upon the pillar at Thermopylæ (p. 132), of which Christopher North says,

> "'Tis but two lines, and all Greece for centuries had them by heart. She forgot them, and Greece was living Greece no more."

Pindar, the "Theban Eagle," came from a long ancestry of poets and musicians. His fame began when he was twenty years old, and for sixty years he was the glory of his countrymen (p. 151). As Homer was the *poet*, and Sappho the *poetess*, so Pindar was the *lyrist*, of Greece. Of all his compositions, there remain entire only forty-five Triumphal Odes celebrating victories gained at the national games. His bold and majestic style abounds in striking metaphors, abrupt transitions, and complicated rhythms.

The Drama.—RISE OF TRAGEDY AND COMEDY.—In early times the wine-god Dionysus (Bacchus) was worshiped with hymns and dances around an open altar, a goat being the usual sacrifice.[1] During the Bacchic festivities, bands of revelers went about with their faces smeared with wine lees, shouting coarse and bantering songs to amuse the village-folk. Out of these rites and revels grew tragedy (goat-song) and comedy (village-song). The themes of the Tragic Chorus were the crimes, woes, and vengeance of the "fate-driven" heroes and gods, the murderous deeds being commonly enacted behind a curtain, or narrated by messengers. The great Greek poets esteemed fame above everything else, and to write for money was considered a degradation of genius. The prizes for which they so eagerly contended were simple crowns of wild olives.

Æschylus, Sophocles, and Euripides, the great tragic trio of antiquity, belong to the golden Age of Pericles. The first excelled in the sublime, the second in the beautiful, and the third in the pathetic.[2]

Æschylus (525–456 B. C.) belonged to a noble family in Eleusis, a village near Athens famous for its secret rites of Demeter (p. 184). Here, under the shadow of the sacred mysteries, a proud, earnest boy, he drank in from childhood a love of the awful and sublime. A true soldier poet, he did not, like Archilochus and Alcæus, vent all his courage in words, but won a prize for his bravery at Marathon, and shared in the glory of Salamis. In his old age he was publicly accused of sacrilege for having disclosed on the stage some details

---

[1] Grecian mythology represented Bacchus as a merry, rollicking god, whose attendants were fauns and satyrs,—beings half goat and half man. The early Tragic Chorus dressed in goat-skins. *Thespis*, a strolling player, introduced an actor or story-teller between the hymns of his satyr-chorus to fill up the pauses with a narrative. Æschylus added a second, and Sophocles a third actor; more than that never appeared together on the Athenian stage. Women were not allowed to act. A poet contesting for the prize generally offered three plays to be produced the same day in succession on the stage. This was called a *trilogy;* a farce or satyr-drama often followed, closing the series.

[2] " Oh, our Æschylus, the thunderous!
How he drove the bolted breath
Through the cloud, to wedge it ponderous
In the gnarled oak beneath.

" Oh, our Sophocles, the royal,
Who was born to monarch's place,
And who made the whole world loyal
Less by kingly power than grace.

" Our Euripides, the human,
With his droppings of warm tears,
And his touches of things common
Till they rose to touch the spheres."
Mrs. Browning, in " Wine of Cyprus."

of the Eleusinian mysteries. Becoming piqued at the rising success of Sophocles, who bore a prize away from him, he retired to Syracuse, where, at the court of Hiero, with Pindar, Simonides, and other literary friends, he passed his last years. Æschylus wrote over seventy tragedies, of which only seven are preserved.

"THE GREAT TRAGIC TRIO."

"Prometheus Bound" is perhaps his finest tragedy. In the old myth, Prometheus steals fire from heaven to give to man. For this crime Zeus sentences him to be bound upon Mount Caucasus, where for thirty thousand years an eagle should feed upon his vitals. The taunts and scoffs of the brutal sheriffs, "Strength" and "Force," who drag him to the spot; the reluctant riveting of his chains and bolts by the sympathizing Vulcan; the graceful pity of the ocean-nymphs who come to condole with him; the threats and expostulations of Mercury, who is sent by Zeus to force from the fettered god a secret he is withholding; the unflinching defiance of Prometheus, and the final opening of the dreadful abyss into which, amid fearful thunders, lightnings, and "gusts of all fierce winds," the rock and its sturdy prisoner drop suddenly and are swallowed up,—all these are portrayed in this drama with a force, majesty, and passion which in the whole range of literature is scarcely equaled.

FROM PROMETHEUS BOUND.—(*Prometheus to Mercury.*)
" Let the locks of the lightning, all bristling and whitening,
　　Flash, coiling me round,
While the ether goes surging 'neath thunder and scourging
　　Of wild winds unbound!
Let the blast of the firmament whirl from its place
　　The earth rooted below,
And the brine of the ocean, in rapid emotion,
　　Be it driven in the face
Of the stars up in heaven, as they walk to and fro!
Let him hurl me anon into Tartarus—on—
　　To the blackest degree, . . .
But he cannot join death to a fate meant for *me*."
　　　　　　　　　Mrs. Browning's Translation

Sophocles (495–406 B. C.), the sweetness and purity of whose style gained for him the title of the Attic Bee, was only twenty-seven years old when he won the prize away from Æschylus, then approaching sixty. Æschylus had been a gallant soldier; Sophocles was a polished gentleman. Less grand and impetuous, more graceful and artistic, than his great competitor, he came like sunshine after storm. The tragedies with which the elder poet had thrilled the Athenian heart were tinctured with the unearthly mysteries of his Eleusinian home; the polished creations of Sophocles reflected the gentle charm of his native Colo'nus,—a beautiful hill-village [1] near Athens, containing a sacred grove and temple. Sophocles improved the style of the Tragic Chorus, and attired his actors in "splendid robes, jeweled chaplets, and embroidered girdles." Of him, as of Æschylus, we have only seven tragedies remaining, though he is said to have composed over one hundred.

"Œdipus the King" was selected by Aristotle as the masterpiece of tragedy. Œdipus, so runs the plot, was son of Laius, king of Thebes. An oracle having foretold that he should "slay his father and marry his mother," Jocasta, the queen, exposes him to die in the forest. A shepherd rescues him. He grows up unconscious of his story, and journeys to Thebes. On the way he meets an old man, whose chariot jostles him. A quarrel ensues, and he slays the gray-haired stranger. Arrived at Thebes, he finds the whole city in commotion. A frightful monster, called the Sphinx, has propounded a riddle which no one can solve, and every failure costs a life. So terrible is the crisis that the hand of the widowed queen is offered to any one who will guess the riddle and so save the state. Œdipus guesses it, and weds Jocasta, his mother. After many years come fearful pestilences, which the oracle declares shall continue until the murderer of Laius is found and punished. The unconscious Œdipus pushes the search, and is confronted with the revelation of his unhappy destiny. Jocasta hangs herself in horror; Œdipus tears a golden buckle from her dress, thrusts its sharp point into both his eyes, and goes out to roam the earth.

In "Œdipus at Colonus" the blind old man, attended by his faithful daughter Antig'one, has wandered to Colonus, where he sits down to rest within the precincts of the sacred grove. The indignant citizens, discovering who the old man is, command him to depart from their borders. Meantime war is raging in Thebes between his two sons, and an oracle declares that only his body will decide success. Every means is used to obtain it, but the gods have willed that his sons shall slay each other. Œdipus, always "driven by fate," follows the Queen of Night, upon whose borders he has trespassed. The last moment comes; a sound of subterranean thunder is heard; his daughters, wailing and terrified, cling to him in wild embrace, a mysterious voice calls from beneath, "Œdipus! King Œdipus! come hither; thou art wanted!" The earth opens, and the old man disappears forever.

[1] Here, two years before the fall of Athens (p. 145), he closed his long, prosperous, luxurious life. "We can imagine Sophocles in his old age recounting the historic names and scenes with which he had been so familiar; how he had listened to the thunder of 'Olympian Pericles;' how he had been startled by the chorus of Furies in the play of Æschylus; how he had talked with the garrulous and open-hearted Herodotus; how he had followed Anaxagoras, the great skeptic, in the cool of the day among a throng of his disciples; how he had walked with Phidias and supped with Aspasia."—*Collins*.

168 GREECE.

The following is from a famous chorus in "Œdipus at Colonus," describing the beauties of the poet's home:—

> "Here ever and aye, through the greenest vale,
> Gush the wailing notes of the nightingale,
> From her home where the dark-hued ivy weaves
> With the grove of the god a night of leaves;
> And the vines blossom out from the lonely glade,
> And the suns of the summer are dim in the shade,
> And the storms of the winter have never a breeze
> That can shiver a leaf from the charmèd trees.
> . . . . . .
> And wandering there forever, the fountains are at play,
> And Cephissus feeds his river from their sweet urns, day by day;
> The river knows no dearth;
> Adown the vale the lapsing waters glide,
> And the pure rain of that pelucid tide
> Calls the rife beauty from the heart of earth."
>
> *Bulwer's Translation.*

Euripides[1] (480–406 B. C.), the "Scenic Philosopher," was born in Salamis on the day of the great sea-fight.[2] Twenty-five years afterward—the year after Æschylus died—his first trilogy was put upon the stage. Athens had changed in the half-century since the poet of Eleusis came before the public. A new element was steadily gaining ground. Doubts, reasonings, and disbeliefs in the marvelous stories told of the gods were creeping into society. Schools of rhetoric and philosophy were springing up, and already "to use discourse of reason" was accounted more important than to recite the Iliad and Odyssey entire. To Æschylus and to most of his hearers the Fates and the Furies had been dread realities, and the gods upon Olympus as undoubted personages as Miltiades or Themistocles; Sophocles, too, serenely accepted all the Homeric deities; but Euripides belonged to the party of "advanced thinkers," and

---

[1] Fragments of Antiope, one of the lost plays of Euripides, have recently come to light in a curious manner. At Gurob, in the Egyptian Fayoom, Prof. Petrie thought he detected writing on some of the papyrus scraps that were stuck together to form the paper-maché mummy-cases. Among these fragments, after they had been carefully separated, cleansed, and deciphered, were found portions of Plato's Phædo, and three pages of Antiope. The writing belongs to a period almost contemporary with Plato and Euripides themselves. Thus, in some of these Egyptian mummy-cases, made up of old waste paper, may yet be found the very autographs of the great masters of Greek literature. "If a bit of Euripides has leaped to light, why not some of the lost plays of Æschylus and Sophocles, or some songs of Sappho?" (For interesting account, see Biblia, September, 1891.)

[2] The three great tragic poets of Athens were singularly connected by the battle of Salamis. Æschylus, in the heroic vigor of his life, fought there; Euripides, whose parents had fled from Athens on the approach of the Persians, was born near the scene, probably on the battle-day; and Sophocles, a beautiful boy of fifteen, danced to the choral song of Simonides, celebrating the victory.

believed no more in the gods of the myths and legends than in the prophets and soothsayers of his own time. Discarding the ideal heroes and heroines of Sophocles, he modeled his characters after real men and women, endowing them with human passions and affections.[1] Of his eighty or ninety plays, seventeen remain.

"Mede'a" is his most celebrated tragedy. A Colchian princess skilled in sorcery becomes the wife of Jason, the hero of the Golden Fleece. Being afterward thrust aside for a new love, she finds her revenge by sending the bride an enchanted robe and crown, in which she is no sooner clothed than they burst into flame and consume her. To complete her vengeance, Medea murders her two young sons,—so deeply wronged by their father, so tenderly loved by herself,—and then, after hovering over the palace long enough to mock and jeer at the anguish of the frantic Jason, she is whirled away with the dead bodies of her children in a dragon-borne car, the chariot of her grandsire, the sun.

FROM MEDEA.—(*Medea to her sons.*)
"Why gaze you at me with your eyes, my children?
Why smile your last sweet smile? Ah me! ah me!
What shall I do? My heart dissolves within me,
Friends, when I see the glad eyes of my sons!
Yet whence this weakness? Do I wish to reap
The scorn that springs from enemies unpunished?
Die they must; this must be, and since it must,
I, I myself will slay them, I who bore them.
        O my sons!
Give, give your mother your dear hands to kiss.
O dearest hands, and mouths most dear to me,
And forms and noble faces of my sons!
O tender touch and sweet breath of my boys!"
                    Symonds's Translation.

COMEDY.—When *Aristophanes* appeared with the first of his sharp satires, Euripides had been for a quarter of a century before the public, and the Peloponnesian war was near at hand. The new poet whose genius was so full of mockery and mirth was a rich, aristocratic Athenian, the natural enemy of the ultra-democratic mob-orators of his day, whom he heartily hated and despised. In the bold and brilliant satires which now electrified all Athens,

---

[1] Aristophanes ridiculed his scenic art, denounced his theology, and accused him of corrupting society by the falsehood and deceit shown by his characters. The line in one of his plays,
    "Though the tongue swore, the heart remained unsworn,"
caused his arrest for seeming to justify perjury. When the people were violent in censure, Euripides would sometimes appear on the stage and beg them to sit the play through. On one occasion, when their displeasure was extreme, he tartly exclaimed, "Good people, it is my business to teach you, and not to be taught by you." Tradition relates that he was torn to pieces by dogs, set upon him by two rival poets, while he was walking in the garden of the Macedonian king, at Pella. The Athenians were eager to honor him after his death, and erected a statue in the theater where he had been so often hissed as well as applauded.

every prominent public man was liable to see his personal peculiarities paraded on the stage.[1] The facts and follies of the times were pictured so vividly, that when Dionysius, the Tyrant of Syracuse, wrote to Plato for information as to affairs in Athens, the great philosopher sent for answer a copy of "The Clouds."

Aristophanes wrote over fifty plays, of which eleven, in part or all, remain.

Of these, "The Frogs" and the "Woman's Festival" were direct satires on Euripides. "The Knights" was written, so the author declared, to "cut up Cleon the Tanner into shoe leather."[2] "The Clouds" ridiculed the new-school philosophers,[3] and "The Wasps," the Athenian passion for law-courts.

FROM THE CLOUDS.—(*Scene: Socrates, absorbed in thought, swinging in a basket, surrounded by his students. Enter Strepsiades, a visitor.*)

STR. Who hangs dangling in yonder basket?
STUD. HIMSELF. STR. And who's Himself? STUD. Why, Socrates.
STR. Ho, Socrates! Sweet, darling Socrates!
SOC. Why callest thou me, poor creature of a day?
STR. First tell me, pray, what *are* you doing up there?
SOC. I walk in air and contemplate the sun!
STR. Oh, *that's* the way that you despise the gods—
You get so near them on your perch there—eh?
SOC. I never could have found out things divine,
Had I not hung my mind up thus, and mixed
My subtle intellect with its kindred air.
Had I regarded such things from below,
I had learnt nothing. For the earth absorbs
Into itself the moisture of the brain.
It is the same with water-cresses.
STR. Dear me! So water-cresses grow by thinking!

The so-called *Old Comedy*, in which individuals were satirized, died with Aristophanes; and to it succeeded the *New Comedy*, portraying general types of human nature, and dealing with domestic life and manners.

Menander (342–291 B. C.), founder of this new school, was a

[1] Even the deities were burlesqued, and the devout Athenians, who denounced Euripides for venturing to doubt the gods and goddesses, were wild in applause when Aristophanes dragged them out as absurd cowards, or blustering braggarts, or as

"Baking peck-loaves and frying stacks of pancakes."

[2] The masks of the actors in Greek comedy were made to caricature the features of the persons represented. Cleon was at this time so powerful that no artist dared to make a mask for his character in the play, nor could any man be found bold enough to act the part. Aristophanes, therefore, took it himself, smearing his face with wine lees, which he declared "well represented the purple and bloated visage of the demagogue."

[3] It is said that Socrates, who was burlesqued in this play, was present at its performance, which he heartily enjoyed; and that he even mounted on a bench, that every one might see the admirable resemblance between himself and his counterfeit upon the stage.

THE CIVILIZATION.   171

warm friend of Epicurus (p. 177), whose philosophy he adopted. He admired, as heartily as Aristophanes had disliked, Euripides, and his style was manifestly influenced by that of the tragic poet. He excelled in delineation of character, and made his dramatic personages so real, that a century afterward it was written of him,

"O Life, and O Menander! Speak and say
Which copied which? Or Nature, or the play?"

Of his works only snatches remain, many of which were household proverbs among the Greeks and Romans. Such were: "He is well cleansed that hath his conscience clean," "The workman is greater than his work," and the memorable one quoted by St. Paul, "Evil communications corrupt good manners."

THE GREAT HISTORIANS OF GREECE.

History.—Here is another illustrious trio: Herodotus (484–420), Thucydides (471–400), and Xenophon (about 445–355). *Herodotus*, "Father of History," we recall as an old friend met in Egyptian study (p. 15). Having rank, wealth, and a passion for travel, he roamed over Egypt, Phœnicia, Babylon, Judea, and Persia, studying their history, geography, and national customs. In Athens, where he spent several years, he was the intimate friend of Sophocles. His history was divided into nine books, named after the nine Muses.[1] The principal subject is the Greek and Persian war; but, by way of episode, sketches of various nations are introduced. His style is artless, graphic, flowing, rich in description, and inter-

---

[1] Leonidas of Tarentum, a favorite writer of epigrams, who lived two hundred years after Herodotus, thus accounted for their names:—

"The Muses nine came one day to Herodotus and dined,
And in return, their host to pay, left each a book behind."

spersed with dialogue. He has been described as having "the head of a sage, the heart of a mother, and the simplicity of a child."

Thucydides is said to have been won to his vocation by hearing the history of Herodotus read at Olympia, which charmed him to tears. Rich, noble, and educated, he was in the prime of his manhood, when, at the opening of the Peloponnesian war, he received command of a squadron. Having failed to arrive with his ships in time to save a certain town from surrender, Cleon caused his disgrace, and he went into exile to escape a death penalty. During the next twenty years he prepared his "History of the Peloponnesian war." His style is terse, noble, and spirited; as an historian he is accurate, philosophic, and impartial. "His book," says Macaulay, "is that of a man and a statesman, and in this respect presents a remarkable contrast to the delightful childishness of Herodotus."

Xenophon's historical fame rests mostly on his Anabasis,[1] which relates the expedition of Cyrus and the Retreat of the Ten Thousand. He was one of the generals who conducted this memorable retreat, in which he displayed great firmness, courage, and military skill. A few years later the Athenians formed their alliance with Persia; and Xenophon, who still held command under his friend and patron, the Spartan king Agesilaus, was brought into the position of an enemy to his state. Having been banished from Athens, his Spartan friends gave him a beautiful country residence near Olympia, where he spent the best years of his long life. Next to the Anabasis ranks his Memorabilia (memoirs) of Socrates,[2] his friend and teacher. Xenophon was said by the ancients to be "the first man that ever took notes of conversation." The Memorabilia is a collection of these notes, in which the character and doctrines of Socrates are discussed. Xenophon was the author of fifteen works, all of which are extant. His style, simple, clear, racy, refined, and noted for colloquial vigor, is considered the model of classical Greek prose.

Oratory.—Eloquence was studied in Greece as an art. *Pericles,*

---

[1] This word means the "march up," viz., from the sea to Babylon. A more appropriate name would be Katabasis (march down), as most of the book is occupied with the details of the return journey.

[2] There is a story that Xenophon, when a boy, once met Socrates in a lane. The philosopher, barring the way with his cane, demanded, "Where is food sold?" Xenophon having replied, Socrates asked, "And where are men made good and noble?" The lad hesitated, whereupon Socrates answered himself by saying, "Follow me, and learn." Xenophon obeyed, and was henceforth his devoted disciple.

though he spoke only upon great occasions, Isoc'rates, and Æs'chines were all famed for powers of address, but

Demosthenes (385–322 B. C.) was the unrivaled orator of Greece, if not of the world. An awkward, sickly, stammering boy, by his determined energy and perseverance he "placed himself at the head of all the mighty masters of speech — unapproachable forever" (*Lord Brougham*). His first address before the public assembly was hissed and derided; but he was resolved to be an orator, and nothing daunted him. He used every means to overcome his natural defects,[1] and at last was rewarded by the palm of eloquence. He did not aim at display, but made every sentence subservient to his argument. "We never think of his words," said Fénelon; "we think only of the things he says." His oration "Upon the Crown"[2] is his masterpiece.

DEMOSTHENES.

Philosophy and Science.—THE SEVEN SAGES (Appendix), Cleobu'lus, Chi'lo, Perian'der, Pit'tacus, Solon, Bias, and Tha'lēs, lived about 600 B. C.[3] They were celebrated for their moral, social, and political wisdom.

[1] That he might study without hindrance, he shut himself up for months in a room under ground, and, it is said, copied the History of Thucydides eight times, that he might be infused with its concentrated thought and energy. Out on the seashore, with his mouth filled with pebbles, he exercised his voice until it sounded full and clear above the tumult of the waves; while in the privacy of his own room, before a full-length mirror, he disciplined his awkward gestures till he had schooled them into grace and aptness.

[2] It had been proposed that his public services should be rewarded by a golden crown, the custom being for an orator to wear a crown in token of his inviolability while speaking. Æschines, a fellow-orator, whom he had accused of favoring Philip, opposed the measure. The discussion lasted six years. When the two finally appeared before a vast and excited assembly for the closing argument, the impetuous eloquence of Demosthenes swept everything before it. In after years, though his whole life had proved him a zealous patriot, he was charged with having received bribes from Macedon. Exiled, and under sentence of death, he poisoned himself.

[3] About this time lived *Æsop*, who, though born a slave, gained his freedom and the friendship of kings and wise men by his peculiar wit. His fables, long preserved by oral tradition, were the delight of the Athenians, who read in them many a pithy

Thales founded a school of thinkers. He taught that all things were generated from water, into which they would all be ultimately resolved.

During the two following centuries many philosophers arose.—

Anaximan'der, the scientist, invented a sun-dial,—an instrument which had long been used in Egypt and Babylonia,—and wrote a geographical treatise, enriched with the first known map.

Anaxag'oras discovered the cause of eclipses, and the difference between the planets and fixed stars. He did not, like his predecessors, regard fire, air, or water as the origin of all things, but believed in a Supreme Intellect. He was accused of atheism,[1] tried, and condemned to death, but his friend Pericles succeeded in changing the sentence to exile. Contemporary with him was

Hippoc'rates, the father of physicians, who came from a family of priests devoted to Æsculapius, the god of medicine. He wrote many works on physiology, and referred diseases to natural causes, and not, as was the popular belief, to the displeasure of the gods.

Pythag'oras, the greatest of early philosophers, was the first to assert the movement of the earth in the heavens; he also made some important discoveries in geology and mathematics. At his school in Crotona, Italy, his disciples were initiated with secret rites; one of the tests of fitness being the power to keep silence under every circumstance. He based all creation upon the numerical rules of harmony, and asserted that the heavenly spheres roll in musical rhythm. Teaching the Egyptian doctrine of transmigration, he professed to remember what had happened to himself in a previous existence when he was a Trojan hero. His followers reverenced him as half divine, and their unquestioning faith passed into the proverb, *Ipse dixit* (He has said it).

Soc'rates (470–399 B. C.).—During the entire thirty years of the Peloponnesian war a grotesque-featured, ungainly, shabbily dressed, barefooted man might have been seen wandering the streets of Athens, in all weathers and at all hours, in the crowded market place, among the workshops, wherever men were gathered, incessantly asking and answering questions. This was Socrates,

---

public lesson. His statue, the work of Lysippus (p. 183), was placed opposite to those of the Seven Sages in Athens. Socrates greatly admired Æsop's Fables, and during his last days in prison amused himself by versifying them.

[1] The Greeks were especially angry because Anaxagoras taught that the sun is not a god. It is a curious fact that they condemned to death as an atheist the first man among them who advanced the idea of One Supreme Deity.

a self-taught philosopher, who believed that he had a special mission from the gods, and was attended by a "divine voice" which counseled and directed him. The questions he discussed pertained to life and morality, and were especially pointed against Sophists, who were the skeptics and quibblers of the day.[1] His earnest eloquence attracted all classes,[2] and among his friends were Alcibiades, Euripides, and Aristophanes. A man who, by his irony and argument, was continually "driving men to their wits' end," naturally made enemies. One morning there appeared in the portico where such notices were usually displayed the following indictment: "Socrates is guilty of crime; first, for not worshiping the gods whom the city worships, but introducing new divinities of his own; secondly, for corrupting the youth. The penalty due is death." Having been tried and convicted, he was sentenced to drink a cup of the poison-hemlock, which he took in his prison chamber, surrounded by friends, with whom he cheerfully conversed till the last. Socrates taught the unity of God, the immortality of the soul, the beauty and necessity of virtue, and the moral responsibility of man. He was a devout believer in oracles, which he often consulted. He left no writings, but his philosophy has been preserved by his faithful followers, Xenophon and Plato.

The Four Great Schools of Philosophy (4th century B. C.).—
1. THE ACADEMIC school was founded by that devoted disciple of Socrates, *Plato* (429-347), who delivered his lectures in the Academic Gardens. Plato[3] is perhaps best known from his argu-

---

[1] Their belief that "what I think is true *is* true; what seems right *is* right," colored state policy and individual action in the Peloponnesian war, and was responsible for much of its cruelty and baseness. The skeptic Pyrrho used to say: "It may be so, perhaps; I assert nothing, not even that I assert." Socrates taught his pupils by a series of logical questions which stimulated thought, cleared perception, and created in the learner a real hunger for knowledge. The "Socratic Method" of teaching is still in use. When addressed to braggarts and pretenders, the apparently innocent "Questions" of Socrates were a terror and a confusion.

[2] "Gradually the crowd gathered round him. At first he spoke of the tanners, and the smiths, and the drovers, who were plying their trades about him, and they shouted with laughter as he poured forth his homely jokes. But soon the magic charm of his voice made itself felt. The peculiar sweetness of its tone had an effect which even the thunder of Pericles failed to produce. The laughter ceased—the crowd thickened—the gay youth, whom nothing else could tame, stood transfixed and awe-struck . . . —the head swam—the heart leaped at the sound—tears rushed from their eyes, and they felt that, unless they tore themselves away from that fascinated circle, they should sit down at his feet and grow old in listening to the marvelous music of this second Marsyas."

[3] The Greeks had no family or clan names, a single appellation serving for an individual. To save confusion the father's name was frequently added. Attic wit

ments in regard to the immortality of the soul. He believed in one eternal God, without whose aid no man can attain wisdom or virtue, and in a previous as well as a future existence. All earthly knowledge, he averred, is but the recollection of ideas gained by the soul in its former disembodied state, and as the body is only a hindrance to perfect communion with the "eternal essences," it follows that death is to be desired rather than feared. His works are written in dialogue, Socrates being represented as the principal speaker. The abstruse topics of which he treats are enlivened by wit, fancy, humor, and picturesque illustration. His style was considered so perfect that an ancient writer exclaimed, "If Jupiter had spoken Greek, he would have spoken it like Plato." The fashionables of Athens thronged to the Academic Gardens to listen to "the sweet speech of the master, melodious as the song of the cicadas in the trees above his head." Even the Athenian women—shut out by custom from the intellectual groves—shared in the universal eagerness, and, disguised in male attire, stole in to hear the famous Plato.

2. THE PERIPATETIC school was founded by *Aristotle* (384-322), who delivered his lectures while walking up and down the shady porches of the Lyceum, surrounded by his pupils (hence called Peripatetics, *walkers*). An enthusiastic student under Plato, he remained at the academy until his master's death. A few years afterward he accepted the invitation of Philip of Macedon to become instructor to the young Alexander. Returning to Athens in 335 B.C., he brought the magnificent scientific collections given him by his royal patron, and opened his school in the Lyceum Gymnasium. Suspected of partisanship with Macedon, and accused of impiety, to avoid the fate of Socrates he fled to Euboea, where he died. Aristotle, more than any other philosopher, originated ideas whose influence is still felt. The "Father of Logic," the principles he laid down in this study have never been superseded. His books include works on metaphysics, psychology, zoölogy, ethics, politics, and rhetoric. His style is intricate and abstruse. He differed much from Plato, and, though he recognized an infinite, immaterial God, doubted the existence of a future life.

supplied abundant nicknames, suggested by some personal peculiarities or circumstance. Thus this philosopher, whose real name was Aris'tocles, was called Plato because of his broad brow. He was descended on his father's side from Codrus, the last hero-king of Attica, and on his mother's from Solon; but his admirers made him a son of the god Apollo, and told how in his infancy the bees had settled on his lips as a prophecy of the honeyed words which were to fall from them.

THE CIVILIZATION. 177

3. THE EPICURE'ANS were the followers of *Epicu'rus* (340–270), who taught that the chief end of life is enjoyment. Himself strictly moral, he lauded virtue as a road to happiness, but his followers so perverted this that "Epicurean" became a synonym for loose and luxurious living.—THE CYNICS (*kunikos*, dog-like) went to the other extreme, and, despising pleasure, gloried in pain and privation. They scoffed at social courtesies and family ties. The sect was founded by Antisthenes, a disciple of Socrates, but its chief exponent was *Diogenes*, who, it is said, ate and slept in a tub which he carried about on his head.[1]

4. THE STOICS were headed by *Zeno* (355–260), and took their name from the painted portico (*stoa*) under which he taught. Pain and pleasure were equally despised by them, and indifference to all external conditions was considered the highest virtue. For his example of integrity, Zeno was decreed a golden chaplet and a public tomb in the Ceramicus.

Grecian philosophy culminated in *Neo-Platonism*, a mixture of Paganism, mysticism, and Hebrew ethics, which exalted revelations and miracles, and gave to reason a subordinate place. In Alexandria it had a fierce struggle with Christianity, and died with its last great teacher, the beautiful and gifted Hypatia, who was killed by a mob.

LATER GREEK WRITERS.—*Plutarch* (50–120 A.D.) was the greatest of ancient biographers. His "Parallel Lives of Greeks and Romans" still delights hosts of readers by its admirable portraiture of celebrated men. *Lucian* (120–200 A.D.), in witty dialogues, ridiculed the absurdities of Greek mythology and the follies of false philosophers. His "Sale of the Philosophers" humorously pictures the founders of the different schools as auctioned off by Mercury.

LIBRARIES AND WRITING MATERIALS.—Few collections of books were made before the Peloponnesian war, but in later times it became fashionable to have private libraries,[2] and after the days of

---

[1] He was noted for his caustic wit and rude manners. Tradition says that Alexander the Great once visited him as he was seated in his tub, basking in the sun. "I am Alexander," said the monarch, astonished at the indifference with which he was received. "And I am Diogenes," returned the cynic. "Have you no favor to ask of me?" inquired the king. "Yes," growled Diogenes, "*to get out of my sunlight.*" He was vain of his disregard for social decencies. At a sumptuous banquet given by Plato he entered uninvited, and, rubbing his soiled feet on the rich carpets, cried out, "Thus I trample on your pride, O Plato!" The polite host, who knew his visitor's weakness, aptly retorted, "But with still greater pride, O Diogenes!"

[2] Aristotle had an immense library, which was sold after his death. Large

the tragic poets Athens not only abounded in book-stalls, but a place in the Agora was formally assigned to book-auctioneering. Manuscript copies were rapidly multiplied by means of slave labor, and became a regular article of export to the colonies. The Egyptian papyrus, and afterward the fine but expensive parchment, were used in copying books; the papyrus was written on only one side, the parchment on both sides.[1]

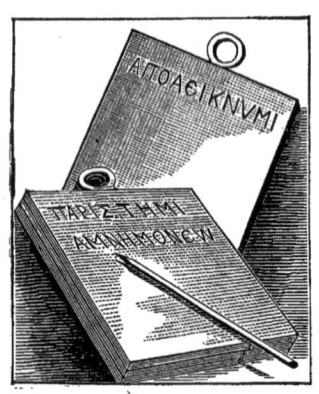

The reed pen was used as in Egypt, and double inkstands for black and red ink were invented, having a ring by which to fasten them to the girdle of the writer. Waxed tablets were employed for letters, note-books, and other requirements of daily life. These were written upon with a metal or ivory pencil (*stylus*), pointed at one end and broadly flattened at the other, so that in case of mistake the writing could be smoothed out and the tablet made as good as new. A large burnisher was sometimes used for the latter purpose. Several tablets joined together formed a book.

A GREEK TABLET.

Education.—A Greek father held the lives of his young children at his will, and the casting-out of infants to the chances of fate was authorized by law throughout Greece, except at Thebes. Girls were especially subject to this unnatural treatment. If a child were rescued, it became the property of its finder.

The Athenian Boy of good family was sent to school when seven years old, the school-hours being from sunrise to sunset. Until he was sixteen he was attended in his walks by a *pedagogue*,—usually

---

collections of books have been found in the remains of Pompeii and Herculaneum. Some of these volumes, although nearly reduced to coal, have by great care been unrolled, and have been published.

[1] The width of the manuscript (varying from six to fourteen inches) formed the length of the page, the size of the roll depending upon the number of pages in a book. When finished, the roll was coiled around a stick, and a ticket containing the title was appended to it. Documents were sealed by tying a string around them and affixing to the knot a bit of clay or wax, which was afterward stamped with a seal. In libraries the books were arranged in pigeon-holes or on shelves with the ends outward; sometimes several scrolls were put together in a cylindrical box with a cover. The reader unrolled the scroll as he advanced, rolling up the completed pages with his other hand (see illustration, p. 279).

some trusty, intelligent slave, too old for hard work,—who never entered the study room, no visitors, except near relatives of the master, being allowed therein on penalty of death. The boy was first taught grammar, arithmetic, and writing. His chief books were Hesiod and Homer, which he committed to memory. The moral lessons they contained were made prominent, for, says Plato, "Greek parents are more careful about the manner and habits of the youth than about his letters and music." Discipline was enforced with the rod. All the great lyric poems were set to music, which was universally taught. "Rhythms and harmonies," again says Plato, "are made familiar to the souls of the young, that they may become more gentle, and better men in speech and action." Symmetrical muscular development was considered so important that the young Athenian between sixteen and eighteen years of age spent most of his time in gymnastic exercises. During this period of probation the youth's behavior was carefully noted by his elders. At eighteen he was ceremoniously enrolled in the list of citizens. Two years were now given to public service, after which he was free to follow his own inclinations. If he were scholarly disposed, and had money and leisure,[1] he might spend his whole life in learning.

A GRECIAN YOUTH.

The little an Athenian girl was required to know was learned from her mother and nurses at home.

The Spartan Lad of seven years was placed under the control of the state. Henceforth he ate his coarse hard bread and black broth at the public table,[2] and slept in the public dormitory. Here he

---

[1] Our word "school" is derived from the Greek word for leisure. The education of the Greeks was obtained not so much from books as from the philosophical lectures, the public assembly, the theater, and the law courts, where much of their time was spent (p. 159).

[2] The public mess was so compulsory, that when, on his return from vanquishing the Athenians, King Agis ventured to send for his commons, that he might take his first meal at home with his wife, he was refused. The principal dish at the mess-table was a black broth, made from a traditional recipe. Wine mixed with water was drunk, but toasts were never given, for the Spartans thought it a sin to use two words when one would do. Intoxication and the Symposium (p. 199) were forbidden by law. Fat men were regarded with suspicion. Small boys sat on low stools near their fathers at meals, and were given half rations, which they ate in silence.

was taught to disdain all home affections as a weakness, and to think of himself as belonging only to Sparta. He was brought up to despise not only softness and luxury, but hunger, thirst, torture, and death. Always kept on small rations of food, he was sometimes allowed only what he could steal. If he escaped detection, his adroitness was applauded; if he were caught in the act, he was severely flogged; but though he were whipped to death, he must neither wince nor groan.[1]

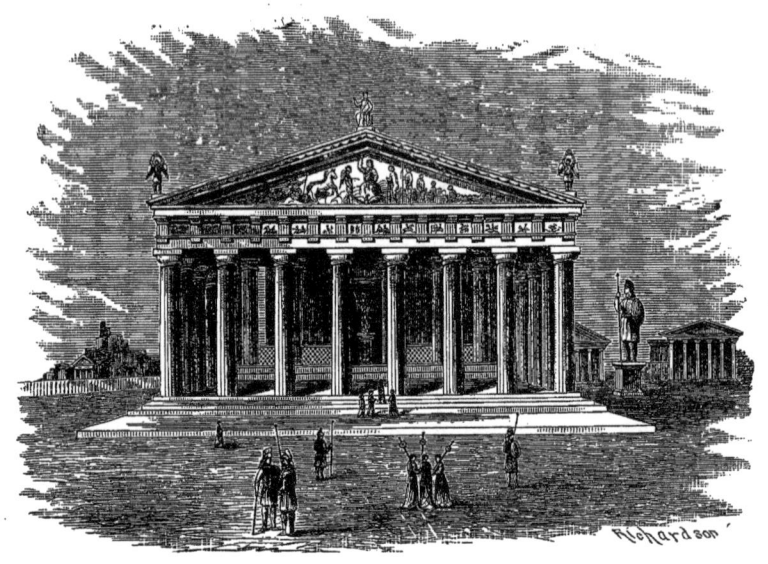

EAST END OF THE PARTHENON (AS RESTORED BY FERGUSSON).

Monuments and Art.—The three styles of Grecian architecture —Doric, Ionic, and Corinthian—are distinguished by the shape of their columns (see cut, p. 182).

The *Doric* was originally borrowed from Egypt (p. 40); the Parthenon at Athens, and the Temple of Zeus at Olympia, were among its most celebrated examples. The Parthenon, or House of the Maiden, situated on the Acropolis, was sacred to Pallas

[1] The Spartan lad had a model set before him. It was that of a boy who stole a fox and hid it under his short cloak. He must have been somewhat awkward,—no doubt the Spartan children were warned against this fault in his morals,—for he was suspected, and ordered to be flogged till he confessed. While the lashes fell, the fox struggled to escape. The boy, with his quivering back raw and bleeding, and his breast torn by savage claws and teeth, stood sturdily, and flinched not. At last the desperate fox reached his heart, and he dropped dead—but a hero!

Athena, the patron goddess of Attica. It was built throughout of fine marble from the quarry of Mount Pentelicus, near Athens, its glistening whiteness being here and there subdued by colors and gilding. The magnificent sculptures[1] which adorned it were designed by Phidias,—that inimitable artist whom Pliny designates as "before all, Phidias, the Athenian." The statue of the virgin goddess, within the temple, was forty feet high; her face, neck, arms, hands, and feet were ivory; her drapery was pure gold.[2] The temple at Olympia was built of porous stone, the roof being tiled with Pentelic marble. It stood on the banks of the Alpheus, in a sacred grove (Altis) of plane and olive trees. Not to have seen the Olympian statue of Zeus, by Phidias, was considered a calamity.[3]

The most celebrated *Ionic* temple was that of Artemis (Diana) at Ephesus, which was three times destroyed by fire, and as often rebuilt with increased magnificence.

Corinthian architecture was not generally used in Greece before the age of Alexander the Great.[4] The most beautiful example is the Choragic Monument of Lysicrates (pp. 188, 194), in Athens.

---

[1] These sculptures, illustrating events in the mythical life of the goddess, are among the finest in existence. Some of them were sent to England by Lord Elgin when he was British ambassador to Turkey, and are now in the British Museum, where, with various other sculptures from the Athenian Acropolis, all more or less mutilated, they are known as the Elgin Marbles.

[2] The Greeks accused Phidias of having purloined some of the gold provided him for this purpose; but as, by the advice of his shrewd friend Pericles, he had so attached the metal that it could be removed, he was able to disprove the charge. He was afterward accused of impiety for having placed the portraits of Pericles and himself in the group upon Athena's shield. He died in prison.

[3] The statue, sixty feet high, was seated on an elaborately sculptured throne of cedar, inlaid with gold, ivory, ebony, and precious stones; like the statue of Athena in the Parthenon, the face, feet, and body were of ivory; the eyes were brilliant jewels, and the hair and beard pure gold. The drapery was beaten gold, enameled with flowers. One hand grasped a scepter composed of precious metals, and surmounted by an eagle; in the other, like Athena, he held a golden statue of Nike (the winged goddess of victory). The statue was so high in proportion to the building, that the Greeks used to say, "If the god should rise, he would burst open the roof." The effect of its size, as Phidias had calculated, was to impress the beholder with the pent-up majesty of the greatest of gods. A copy of the head of this statue is in the Vatican. The statue itself, removed by Theodosius I. to Constantinople, was lost in the disastrous fire (A. D. 475) which destroyed the Library in that city. At the same time perished the Venus of Cnidus, by Praxiteles (p. 183), which the ancients ranked next to the Phidian Zeus and Athena.

[4] The invention of the Corinthian capital is ascribed to Callimachus, who, seeing a small basket covered with a tile placed in the center of an acanthus plant which grew on the grave of a young lady of Corinth, was so struck with its beauty that he executed a capital in imitation of it.—*Westropp's Hand-book of Architecture.*

182   GREECE.

The Propylæa, or entrance to the Athenian Acropolis, was a magnificent structure, which opened upon a group of temples, altars, and statues of surpassing beauty. All the splendor of Grecian art was concentrated on the state edifices, private architectural display being forbidden by law. After the Macedonian conquest, dwellings grew luxurious, and Demosthenes rebukes certain citizens for living in houses finer than the public buildings.

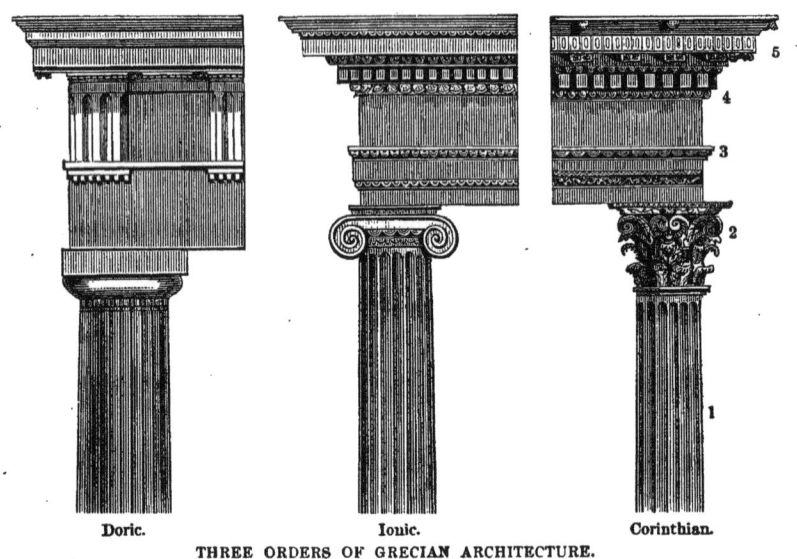

Doric.   Ionic.   Corinthian.
THREE ORDERS OF GRECIAN ARCHITECTURE.

(1, *shaft;* 2, *capital;* 3, *architrave;* 4, *frieze;* 5, *cornice.* *The entire part above the capital is the entablature. At the bottom of the shaft is the base, which rests upon the pedestal.*)

The Athenian Agora (market place), the fashionable morning resort, was surrounded with porticoes, one of which was decorated with paintings of glorious Grecian achievements. Within the inclosure were grouped temples, altars, and statues.

Not one ancient Greek edifice remains in a perfect state.

Paintings were usually on wood; wall-painting was a separate and inferior art. The most noted painters were *Apollodorus of Athens*, sometimes called the Greek Rembrandt; *Zeuxis* and *Parrhasius*, who contended for the prize—Parrhasius producing a picture representing a curtain, which his rival himself mistook for a real hanging, and Zeuxis offering a picture of grapes, which deceived even the birds; *Apelles*, the most renowned of all Greek artists, who painted with four colors, blended with a varnish of his own invention; his friend *Protogenes*, the careful painter, sculptor, and writer on art; *Nicias*, who, having refused a sum equal to seventy thousand dollars from Ptolemy I. for his masterpiece, bequeathed it to Athens; and *Pausias*, who excelled in wall-painting, and in delineating children, animals, flowers, and arabesques. The Greeks tinted the background and bas-reliefs of their sculptures, and even painted their inimitable statues, gilding the hair, and inserting glass or silver eyes.

In marble and bronze *statuary*, and in graceful *vase-painting*, the Greeks have never been surpassed. All the arts and ornamentation which we have seen in use among the previous nations were greatly improved upon by the Greeks, who added to other excellences an exquisite sense of beauty and a power of ideal expression peculiar to themselves. Besides *Phidias*, whose statues were distinguished for grandeur and sublimity, eminent among sculptors were *Praxiteles*, who excelled in tender grace and finish; *Scopas*, who delighted in marble allegory; and *Lysippus*, a worker in bronze, and the master of portraiture.[1]

3. THE MANNERS AND CUSTOMS.

Religion and Mythology.—Nothing marks more strongly the poetic imagination of the Greeks than the character of their religious worship. They learned their creed in a poem, and told it in marble sculpture. To them nature overflowed with deities. Every grove had its presiding genius, every stream and fountain its protecting nymph. Earth and air were filled with invisible spirits, and the sky was crowded with translated heroes,—their own half-divine ancestors. Their gods were intense personalities, endowed with human passions and instincts, and bound by domestic relations. Such deities appealed to the hearts of their worshipers, and the Greeks loved their favorite gods with the same fervor bestowed upon their earthly friends. On the summit of Mount Olympus, in Thessaly, beyond impenetrable mists, according to their mythology, the twelve[2] great gods held council.

---

[1] The masterpieces of Praxitéles were an undraped Venus sold to the people of Cnidus, and a satyr or faun, of which the best antique copy is preserved in the Capitoline Museum, Rome. This statue suggested Hawthorne's charming romance, The Marble Faun. The celebrated Niobe Group in the Uffizi Gallery, Florence, is the work of either Praxiteles or Scopas. The latter was one of the artists employed on the Mausoleum at Halicarnassus (Appendix). Lysippus and Apelles were favorites of Alexander the Great, who would allow only them to carve or paint his image.

[2] They were called the Twelve Gods, but the lists vary, increasing the actual number. Roman mythology was founded on Greek, and, as the Latin names are now in general use, they have been interpolated to assist the pupil's association.

GREECE.

Zeus (Jove or Jupiter) was supreme. He ruled with the thunderbolts, and was king over gods and men. His symbols were the eagle and the lightning, both associated with great height. His two brothers,

Poseidon (Neptune) and *Hades* (Pluto) held sway respectively over the sea and the depths under ground. As god of the sea, Poseidon had the dolphin for his symbol; as god over rivers, lakes, and springs, his symbols were the trident and the horse. Hades had a helmet which conferred invisibility upon the wearer. It was in much demand among the gods, and was his symbol. The shades of Hades, wherein the dead were received, were guarded by a three-headed dog, Cerberus.

Hera (Juno), the haughty wife of Zeus, was Queen of the Skies. Her jealousy was the source of much discord in celestial circles. The stars were her eyes. Her symbols were the cuckoo and the peacock.

Demeter (Ceres) was the bestower of bountiful harvests. Her worship was connected with the peculiarly sacred Eleusinian mysteries, whose secret rites have never been disclosed. Some think that ideas of the unity of God and the immortality of the soul were kept alive and handed down by them. Demeter's symbols were ears of corn, the pomegranate, and a car drawn by winged serpents.

Hestia (Vesta) was goddess of the domestic hearth. At her altar in every house were celebrated all important family events, even to the purchase of a new slave, or the undertaking of a short journey. The family slaves joined in this domestic worship, and Hestia's altar was an asylum whither they might flee to escape punishment, and where the stranger, even an enemy, could find protection. She was the personification of purity, and her symbol was an altar-flame.

Hephæstus (Vulcan) was the god of volcanic fires and skilled metal-work. Being lame and deformed, his parents, Zeus and Hera, threw him out of Olympus, but his genius finally brought about a reconciliation. Mount Etna was his forge, whence Prometheus stole the sacred fire to give to man. His brother,

Ares (Mars) was god of war. His symbols were the dog and the vulture.

Athena (Minerva) sprang full-armed from the imperial head of Zeus. She was the goddess of wisdom and of celestial wars, and the especial defender of citadels. Athena and Poseidon contested on the Athenian Acropolis for the supremacy over Attica. The one who gave the greatest boon to man was to win. Poseidon with his trident brought forth a spring of water from the barren rock; but Athena produced an olive-tree, and was declared victor. As a war-goddess she was called Pallas Athene. Her symbol was the owl.

Aphrodite (Venus) was goddess of love and beauty. She arose from the foam of the sea. In a contest of personal beauty between Hera, Athena, and Aphrodite, Paris decided for Aphrodite. She is often represented with a golden apple in her hand, the prize offered by Eris (strife), who originated the dispute. Her symbol was the dove.

Apollon (Apollo), the ideal of manly beauty, was the god of poetry and song. He led the Muses, and in this character his symbol was a lyre; as god of the fierce rays of the sun, which was his chariot, his symbol was a bow with arrows.

Artemis (Diana), twin-sister to Apollo, was goddess of the chase, and protector of the water-nymphs. All young girls were under her care. The moon was her chariot, and her symbol was a deer, or a bow with arrows.

Hermes (Mercury) was the god of cunning and eloquence. In the former capacity he was associated with mists, and accused of thieving. The winged-footed messenger of the gods, he was also the guide of souls to the realms of Hades, and of heroes in difficult expeditions. As god of persuasive speech and success in trade he was popular in Athens, where he was worshiped at the street-crossings.[1] His symbol was a cock or a ram.

---

[1] The "Hermes" placed at street-corners was a stone pillar, surmounted by a human head (p. 143).

THE MANNERS AND CUSTOMS.

Dionysus (Bacchus), god of wine, with his wife Ariadne, ruled the fruit season.
Hebe was a cup-bearer in Olympus.

There was a host of minor deities and personifications, often appearing in a group of three, such as the Three Graces,—beautiful women, who represented the brightness, color, and perfume of summer; the Three Fates,—stern sisters, upon whose spindle was spun the thread of every human life; the Three Hesperides,—daughters of Atlas (upon whose shoulders the sky rested), in whose western garden golden apples grew; the Three Harpies,—mischievous meddlers, who personated the effects of violent winds; Three Gorgons, whose terrible faces turned to stone all who beheld them; and Three Furies, whose mission was to pursue criminals.

There were nine Muses, daughters of Zeus and Mnemosyne (Memory), who dwelt on Mount Parnassus, and held all gifts of inspiration: Clio presided over history; Melpomene, tragedy; Thalia, comedy; Calliope, epic poetry; Urania, astronomy; Euterpe, music; Polyhymnia, song and oratory; Erato, love-songs; and Terpsichore, dancing.

PRESENTING OFFERINGS AT THE TEMPLE OF DELPHI.

Divination of all kinds was universal. Upon signs, dreams, and portents depended all the weighty decisions of life. Birds, especially crows and ravens, were watched as direct messengers from the gods, and so much meaning was attached to their voices, habits, manner of flight, and mode of alighting, that even in Homer's time the word "bird" was synonymous with "omen." The omens obtained by sacrifices were still more anxiously regarded. Upon the motions of the flame, the appearance of the ashes, and, above all, the shape and aspect of the victim's liver, hung such momentous human interests, that, as at Platæa, a great army was sometimes kept waiting for days till success should be assured through a sacrificial calf or chicken.

Oracles.—The temples of *Zeus* at *Dodona* (Epirus), and of *Apollo* at *Delphi* (Phocis), were the oldest and most venerated prophetic shrines. At Dodona three priestesses presided, to whom the gods spoke in the rustling leaves of a sacred oak, and the murmurs of a holy rill. But the favorite oracular god was Apollo, who, besides the Pythian temple at Delphi, had shrines in various parts of the land.[1] The Greeks had implicit faith in the Oracles, and consulted them for every important undertaking.

Priests and Priestesses shared in the reverence paid to the gods. Their temple duties were mainly prayer and sacrifice. They occupied the place of honor in the public festivities, and were supported by the temple revenues.

Grecian religion included in its observances nearly the whole range of social pleasures. Worship consisted of songs and dances, processions, libations, festivals, dramatic and athletic contests, and various sacrifices and purifications. The people generally were content with their gods and time-honored mythology, and left all difficult moral and religious problems to be settled by the philosophers and the serious-minded minority who followed them.

Religious Games and Festivals.—The *Olympian Games* were held once in four years in honor of Zeus, at Olympia. Here the Greeks gathered from all parts of the country, protected by a safe transit through hostile Hellenic states. The commencement of the Festival month having been formally announced by heralds sent to every state, a solemn truce suppressed all quarrels until its close. The competitive exercises consisted of running, leaping, wrestling, boxing, and chariot-racing. The prize was a wreath from the sacred olive-tree in Olympia. The celebration, at first confined to one day, came in time to last five days. Booths were scattered about the Altis (p. 181), where a gay traffic was carried on; while in the spacious council-room the ardent Greeks crowded to hear the newest works of poets, philosophers, and historians. All this excitement and enthusiasm were heightened by the belief that the pleasure enjoyed was an act of true religious worship. The *Pythian Games*, sacred to Apollo, occurred near Delphi, in the third year of each Olympiad, and in national dignity ranked next to the Olympic. The prize-wreath was laurel. The *Nemean* and the *Isthmian Games*, sacred respectively to Zeus and Poseidon, were held once in two years, and, like the Pythian, had prizes for music and poetry, as well as gymnastics, chariots, and horses. The Nemean

---

[1] A volcanic site, having a fissure through which gas escaped, was usually selected. The Delphian priestess, having spent three days in fasting and bathing, seated herself on a tripod over the chasm, where, under the real or imaginary effect of the vapors, she uttered her prophecies. Her ravings were recorded by the attending prophet, and afterward turned into hexameter verse by poets hired for the purpose. The shrewd priests, through their secret agents, kept well posted on all matters likely to be urged, and when their knowledge failed, as in predictions for the future, made the responses so ambiguous or unintelligible that they would seem to be verified by any result.

crown was of parsley, the Isthmian of pine. Sparta took interest only in the Olympic games, with which she had been connected from their beginning, and which, it is curious to note, were the only ones having no intellectual competition. Otherwise, Sparta had her own festivals, from which strangers were excluded.

The *Panathenæ'a*,[1] which took place once in four years at Athens, in honor of the patron goddess, consisted of similar exercises, terminating in a grand procession in which the whole Athenian population took part. Citizens in full military equipment; the victorious contestants with splendid chariots and horses; priests and attendants leading the sacrificial victims; dignified elders bearing olive-boughs; young men with valuable, artistic plate; and maidens, the purest and most beautiful in Athens, with baskets of holy utensils on their heads,—all contributed to the magnificent display. Matrons from the neighboring tribes carried oak-branches, while their daughters bore the chairs and sunshades of the Athenian maidens. In the center of the procession was a ship resting on wheels, having for a sail a richly embroidered mantle or *peplos*, portraying the victories of Zeus and Athena, wrought and woven by Attic maidens. The procession, having gone through all the principal streets round to the Acropolis, marched up through its magnificent Propylæa, past the majestic Parthenon, and at last reached the Erechtheion, or Temple of Athena Polias (p. 194). Here all arms were laid aside, and, amid the blaze of burnt-offerings and the ringing pæans of praise, the votive gifts were placed in the sanctuary of the goddess.

The Feast of Dionysus was celebrated twice during the spring season, the chief festival continuing for eight days. At this time those tragedies and comedies which had been selected by the archon— to whom all plays were first submitted—were brought out in the Dionysiac Theater [2] at Athens, in competition for prizes.

[1] The Panathenaic Procession formed the subject of the sculpture on the frieze around the Parthenon cella, in which stood the goddess sculptured by Phidias. Most of this frieze, much mutilated, is with the Elgin Marbles.

[2] This theater was built on the sloping side of the Acropolis, and consisted of a vast number of semicircular rows of seats cut out of the solid rock, accommodating thirty thousand persons. The front row, composed of white marble arm-chairs, was occupied by the priests, the judges, and the archons, each chair being engraved with the name of its occupant. Between the audience and the stage was the orchestra or place for the chorus, in the center of which stood the altar of Dionysus. Movable stairs led from the orchestra up to the stage, as the course of the drama frequently required the conjunction of the chorus with the actors. The stage itself extended the whole width of the theater, but was quite narrow, except at the center, where the representation took place. It was supported by a white marble wall, handsomely carved. There was a variety of machinery for change of scenes and for producing startling effects, such as the rolling of thunder, the descent of gods from heaven, the rising of ghosts and demons from below, etc. The theater

Each tribe furnished a chorus of dancers and musicians, and chose a *choragus*, whose business was not only to superintend the training and costumes of the performers, but also to bear all the expense of bringing out the play assigned to him. The office was one of high dignity, and immense sums were spent by the choragi in their efforts to eclipse each other; the one adjudged to have given the best entertainment received a tripod, which was formally consecrated in the temples, and placed upon its own properly inscribed monument in the Street of Tripods, near the theater.

The Actors, to increase their size and enable them the better to personate the gods and heroes of Greek tragedy, wore high-soled shoes, padded garments, and great masks which completely enveloped their heads, leaving only small apertures for the mouth and eyes. As their stilts and stage-attire impeded any free movements, their acting consisted of little more than a series of tableaux and recitations, while the stately musical apostrophes and narrations of the chorus filled up the gaps and supplied those parts of the story not acted on the stage.[1]

The Performance began early in the morning, and lasted all day, eating and drinking being allowed in the theater. The price of seats varied according to location, but the poorer classes were supplied free tickets by the government, so that no one was shut out by poverty from enjoying this peculiar worship.[2] Each play generally occupied from one and a half to two hours. The audience was exceedingly demonstrative; an unpopular actor could not deceive himself; his voice was drowned in an uproar of whistling, clucking, and hissing,

---

was open to the sky, but had an awning which might be drawn to shut out the direct rays of the sun, while little jets of perfumed water cooled and refreshed the air. To aid the vast assembly in hearing, brazen bell-shaped vases were placed in different parts of the theater.

[1] In comedy, the actors themselves often took the audience into their confidence, explaining the situation to them somewhat after the manner of some modern comic operas.

[2] Tragedy, which dealt with the national gods and heroes, was to the Greeks a true religious exercise, strengthening their faith, and quickening their sympathies for the woes of their beloved and fate-driven deities. When, as in rare instances, a subject was taken from contemporaneous history, no representation which would pain the audience was allowed, and on one occasion a poet was heavily fined for presenting a play which touched upon a recent Athenian defeat. Some great public lesson was usually hidden in the comedies, where the fashionable follies were mercilessly satirized; and many a useful hint took root in the hearts of the people when given from the stage, that would have fallen dead or unnoticed if put forth in the assembly. "Quick of thought and utterance, of hearing and apprehension, living together in open public intercourse, reading would have been to the Athenians a slow process for the interchange of ideas. But the many thousands of auditors in the Greek theater caught, as with an electric flash of intelligence, the noble thought, the withering sarcasm, the flash of wit, and the covert innuendo."—*Philip Smith.*

and he might esteem himself happy if he escaped from the boards without an actual beating. The favorite, whether on the stage or as a spectator, was as enthusiastically applauded.[1] In comedies, tumult was invited, and the people were urged to shout and laugh, the comic poet sometimes throwing nuts and figs to them, that their scrambling and screaming might add to the evidences of a complete success.

GRECIAN FEMALE HEADS.

Marriage.—Athenians could legally marry only among themselves. The ceremony did not require a priestly official, but was preceded by offerings to Zeus, Hera, Artemis, and other gods who presided over marriage.[2] Omens were carefully observed, and a bath in water from the sacred fountain, Kallirrhoë, was an indispensable preparation. On the evening of the wedding-day, after a merry dinner given at her

---

[1] At the Olympian games, when Themistocles entered, it is related that the whole assembly rose to honor him.

[2] In Homer's time the groom paid to the lady's father a certain sum for his bride. Afterward this custom was reversed, and the amount of the wife's dowry greatly affected her position as a married woman. At the formal betrothal preceding every marriage this important question was settled, and in case of separation the dowry was usually returned to the wife's parents.

father's house, the closely veiled bride was seated in a chariot between her husband and his "best man," all dressed in festive robes and garlanded with flowers. Her mother kindled the nuptial torch at the domestic hearth, a procession of friends and attendants was formed, and, amid the joyful strains of the marriage-song, the whistling of flutes, and the blinking of torches, the happy pair were escorted to their future home. Here they were saluted with a shower of sweetmeats, after which followed the nuptial banquet. At this feast, by privilege, the women were allowed to be present, though they sat at a separate table, and the bride continued veiled. The third day after marriage the veil was cast aside, and wedding-presents were received. The parties most concerned in marriage were seldom consulted, and it was not uncommon for a widow to find herself bequeathed by her deceased husband's will to one of his friends or relatives.

Death and Burial.—As a portal festooned with flowers announced a wedding, so a vessel of water placed before a door gave notice of a death within.[1] As soon as a Greek died, an obolus was inserted in his mouth to pay his fare on the boat across the River Styx to Hades. His body was then washed, anointed, dressed in white, garlanded with flowers, and placed on a couch with the feet toward the outer door. A formal lament[2] followed, made by the female friends and relatives, assisted by hired mourners. On the third day the body was carried to the spot where it was to be buried or burned. It was preceded by a hired chorus of musicians and the male mourners, who, dressed in black or gray, had their hair closely cut.[3] The female mourners walked behind the bier. If the body were burned, sacrifices were offered; then, after all was consumed, the fire was extinguished with wine, and the ashes, sprinkled with oil and wine, were collected in a clay or bronze cinerary. Various articles were stored with the dead, such as mirrors, trinkets, and elegantly painted vases. The burial was followed by a feast, which was considered as given by the deceased (compare p. 42). Sacrifices of milk, honey, wine, olives, and

---

[1] The water was always brought from some other dwelling, and was used for the purification of visitors, as everything within the house of mourning was polluted by the presence of the dead.

[2] Solon sought to restrain these ostentatious excesses by enacting that, except the nearest relatives, no women under sixty years of age should enter a house of mourning. In the heroic days of Greece the lament lasted several days (that of Achilles continued seventeen), but in later times an early burial was thought pleasing to the dead. The funeral pomp, which afterward became a common custom, was originally reserved for heroes alone. In the earlier Attic burials the grave was dug by the nearest relatives, and afterward sown with corn that the body might be recompensed for its own decay.

[3] When a great general died, the hair and manes of all the army horses were cropped.

THE MANNERS AND CUSTOMS. 191

flowers were periodically offered at the grave, where slaves kept watch. Sometimes a regular banquet was served, and a blood-sacrifice offered by the side of the tomb. The dead person was supposed to be conscious of all these attentions, and to be displeased when an enemy approached his ashes. Malefactors, traitors, and people struck by lightning,[1] were denied burial, which in Greece, as in Egypt, was the highest possible dishonor.

GRECIAN WARRIORS AND ATTENDANT.

Weapons of War and Defense.—The Greeks fought with long spears, swords, clubs, battle-axes, bows, and slings. In the heroic age, chariots were employed, and the warrior, standing by the side of the charioteer, was driven to the front, where he engaged in single combat. Afterward the chariot was used only in races. A soldier in full armor wore a leather or metal helmet, covering his head and face; a cuirass made of iron plates, or a leather coat of mail overlaid with iron scales; bronze greaves, reaching from above the knee

---

[1] Such a death was supposed to be a direct punishment from the gods for some great offense or hidden depravity.

down to the ankle; and a shield [1] made of ox-hides, covered with metal, and sometimes extending from head to foot. Thus equipped, they advanced slowly and steadily into action in a uniform phalanx of about eight spears deep, the warriors of each tribe arrayed together, so that individual or sectional bravery was easily distinguished. The light infantry wore no armor, but sometimes carried a shield of willow twigs, covered with leather. In Homer's time, bows six feet long were made of the horns of the antelope. Cavalry horses were protected by armor, and the rider sat upon a saddle-cloth, a luxury not indulged in on ordinary occasions. Stirrups and horseshoes were unknown. The ships of Greece, like those of Phœnicia and Carthage, were flat-bottomed barges or galleys, mainly propelled by oars. The oarsmen sat in rows or banks, one above the other, the number of banks determining the name of the vessel. Bows and arrows, javelins, ballistas, and catapults were the offensive weapons used at a distance; but the ordinary ship tactics were to run the sharp iron prow of the attacking vessel against the enemy's broadside to sink it, or else to steer alongside, board the enemy, and **make a hand-to-hand fight.**

SCENES IN REAL LIFE.

Retrospect.—We will suppose it to be about the close of the 5th century B. C., with the Peloponnesian war just ended. The world is two thousand years older than when we watched the building of the Great Pyramid at Gizeh, and fifteen centuries have passed since the Labyrinth began to show its marble colonnades. Those times are even now remote antiquities, and fifty years ago Herodotus delighted the wondering Greeks with his description of the ancient ruins in the Fayoom. It is nearly two hundred and fifty years since Asshurbanipal sat on the throne of tottering Nineveh, and one hundred and fifty since the fall of Babylon. Let us now visit Sparta.

Scene I.—*A Day in Sparta.*—A hilly, unwalled city on a river bank, with mountains in the distance. A great square or forum (Agora) with a few modest temples, statues, and porticoes. On the highest hill (Acropolis), in the midst of a grove, more temples and

---

[1] These shields were sometimes richly decorated with emblems and inscriptions. Thus Æschylus, in The Seven Chiefs against Thebes, describes one warrior's shield as bearing a flaming torch, with the motto, "I will burn the city;" and another as having an armed man climbing a scaling-ladder, and for an inscription, "Not Mars himself shall beat me from the towers."

[2] A ship with three banks of oars was called a trireme; with four, a quadrireme, etc. In the times of the Ptolemies galleys of twelve, fifteen, twenty, and even forty banks of oars were built. The precise arrangement of the oarsmen in these large ships is not known (see cut, p. 158).

statues, among them a brass statue of Zeus, the most ancient in Greece. In the suburbs the *hippodrome*, for foot and horse races, and the *platanistæ*,—a grove of beautiful palm-trees, partly inclosed by running streams,—where the Spartan youth gather for athletic sports. A scattered city, its small, mean houses grouped here and there; its streets narrow and dirty. This is Sparta.

If we wish to enter a house, we have simply to announce ourselves in a loud voice, and a slave will admit us. We shall hear no cry of puny infants within; the little boys, none of them over seven years old (p. 179), are strong and sturdy, and the girls are few; their weak or deformed brothers and surplus sisters have been cast out in their babyhood to perish, or to become the slaves of a chance rescuer.

The mother is at home,—a brawny, strong-minded, strong-fisted woman, whose chief pride is that she can fell an enemy with one blow. Her dress consists of two garments,—a *chiton;*[1] and over it a peplos, or short cloak, which clasps above her shoulders, leaving her arms bare. She appears in public when she pleases, and may even give her opinion on matters of state. When her husband or sons go forth to battle, she sheds no sentimental tears, but hands to each his shield, with the proud injunction, "Return with it, or upon it." No cowards, whatever their excuses, find favor with her. When the blind Eurytus was led by his slave into the foremost rank at Thermopylæ, she thought of him as having simply performed his duty; when Aristodemus made his blindness an excuse for staying away, she reviled his cowardice; and though he afterward died the most heroic of deaths at Platæa, it counted him nothing. She educates her daughters to the same unflinching defiance of womanly tenderness. They are trained in the palæstra or wrestling-school to run, wrestle, and fight like their brothers. They wear but one garment, a short sleeveless chiton, open upon one side, and often not reaching to the knee.

The Spartan gentleman, who sees little of his family (p. 120), is debarred by law from trade or agriculture, and, having no taste for art or literature, spends his time, when not in actual warfare, in daily military drill, and in governing his helots. He never appears in public without his attendant slaves, but prudence compels him to walk behind rather than before them. In the street his dress is a short, coarse cloak, with or without a chiton; perhaps a pair of thong-strapped sandals, a cane, and a seal-ring. He usually goes bare-headed, but when traveling in the hot sun wears a broad-brimmed hat or bonnet. His ideal character is one of relentless energy and brute force, and his

[1] The Doric chiton was a simple woolen shift, consisting of two short pieces of cloth, sewed or clasped together on one or both sides up to the breast; the parts covering the breast and back were fastened over each shoulder, leaving the open spaces at the side for arm-holes. It was confined about the waist with a girdle.

standard of excellence is a successful defiance of all pain, and an ability to conquer in every fight.

Scene II.—*A Day in Athens* (4th century B. C.).—To see Athens is, first of all, to admire the Acropolis,—a high, steep, rocky, but broad-crested hill, sloping toward the city and the distant sea; ascended by a marble road for chariots, and marble steps for pedestrians; entered through a magnificent gateway (the Propylæa); and crowned on its spacious summit—one hundred and fifty feet above the level at its base—with a grove of stately temples, statues,[1] and altars.

Standing on the Acropòlis, on a bright morning about the year 300 B. C., a magnificent view opens on every side. Away to the southwest for four miles stretch the Long Walls, five hundred and fifty feet apart, leading to the Piræan harbor; beyond them the sea, dotted with sails, glistens in the early sun. Between us and the harbors lie the porticoed and templed Agora, bustling with the morning commerce; the Pnyx,[2] with its stone bema, from which Demosthenes sixty or more years ago essayed his first speech amid hisses and laughter; the Areopagus, where from time immemorial the learned court of archons has held its sittings; the hill of the Museum, crowned by a fortress; the temples of Hercules, Demeter, and Artemis; the Gymnasium of Hermes; and, near the Piræan gate, a little grove of statues,—among them one of Socrates, who drank the hemlock and went to sleep a hundred years ago. At our feet, circling about the hill, are amphitheaters for musical and dramatic festivals; elegant temples and colonnades; and the famous Street of Tripods, more beautiful than ever since the recent erection of the monument of the choragus Lysicrates. Turning toward the east, we see the Lyceum, where Aristotle walked and talked within the last half century; and the Cynosarges, where Antisthenes, the father of the Cynics, had his school. Still further to the north rises the white top of Mount Lycabettus, beyond which is the plain of Marathon; and on the south the green and flowery ascent of Mount Hymettus, swarming with bees, and equally famous for its honey and

---

[1] Towering over all the other statues was the bronze Athena Promachus, by Phidias, cast out of spoils won at Marathon. It was sixty feet high, and represented the goddess with her spear and shield in the attitude of a combatant. The remains of the *Erechtheion*, a beautiful and peculiar temple sacred to two deities, stood near the Parthenon. It had been burned during the invasion of Xerxes, but was in process of restoration when the Peloponnesian war broke out. Part of it was dedicated to Athena Polias, whose olive-wood statue within its walls was reputed to have fallen from heaven. It was also said to contain the sacred olive-tree brought forth by Athena, the spring of water which followed the stroke of Poseidon's trident, and even the impression of the trident itself.

[2] The two hills, the Pnyx and the Areopagus, were famous localities. Upon the former the assemblies of the people were held. The stone pulpit (*bema*), from which the orators declaimed, and traces of the leveled arena where the people gathered to listen, are still seen on the Pnyx.

its marble. Through the city, to the southeast, flows the river Ilissus, sacred to the Muses. As we look about us, we are struck by the absence of spires or pinnacles. There are no high towers as in Babylon; no lofty obelisks as on the banks of the Nile; the tiled roofs are all flat or slightly gabled, and on them we detect many a favorite promenade.

GRECIAN LADIES AND ATTENDANT.

A Greek Home.—The Athenian gentleman usually arises at dawn, and after a slight repast of bread and wine goes out with his slaves [1] for a walk or ride, previous to his customary daily lounge in the market place. While he is absent, if we are ladies we may visit the household. We are quite sure to find the mistress at home, for, especially if she be young, she never ventures outside her dwelling without her husband's permission; nor does she receive within it any but her lady-friends and nearest male relatives. The exterior of the house is very plain. Built of common stone, brick, or wood, and coated with plaster, it abuts so closely upon the street that if the door has been made to open outward (a tax is paid for this privilege) the comer-out is obliged to knock before opening it, in order to warn the passers-by. The dead-wall before us has no lower windows, but a strong door furnished with

---

[1] No gentleman in Athens went out unless he was accompanied by his servants. To be unattended by at least one slave was a sign of extreme indigence, and no more to be thought of than to be seen without a cane. As to the latter, "a gentleman found going about without a walking-stick was presumed by the police to be disorderly, and was imprisoned for the night."

knocker and handle, and beside it a Hermes (p. 143) or an altar to Apollo. Over the door, as in Egypt, is an inscription, here reading, "To the good genius," followed by the name of the owner. In response to our knock, the porter, who is always in attendance, opens the door. Carefully placing our right foot on the threshold,—it would be an unlucky omen to touch it with the left,—we pass through a long corridor to a large court open to the sky, and surrounded by arcades or porticoes. This is the peristyle of the *andronitis*, or apartments belonging to the master of the house. Around the peristyle lie the banqueting, music, sitting, and sleeping rooms, the picture galleries and libraries. A second corridor, opening opposite the first, leads to another porticoed court, with rooms about and behind it. This is the *gynæconitis*, the domain of the mistress. Here the daughters and handmaidens always remain, occupied with their wool-carding, spinning, weaving, and embroidery, and hither the mother retires when her husband entertains guests in the andronitis. The floors are plastered and tastefully painted,[1] the walls are frescoed, and the cornices and ceilings are ornamented with stucco. The rooms are warmed from fireplaces, or braziers of hot coke or charcoal; they are lighted mostly from doors opening upon the porticoes. In the first court is an altar to Zeus, and in the second the never-forgotten one to Hestia. The furniture is simple, but remarkable for elegance of design. Along the walls are seats or sofas covered with skins or purple carpets, and heaped with cushions.

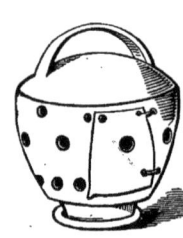

ANCIENT BRAZIER.

There are also light folding-stools[2] and richly carved arm-chairs, and scattered about the rooms are tripods supporting exquisitely painted vases. In the bedrooms of this luxurious home are couches of every degree of magnificence, made of olive-wood inlaid with gold and ivory or veneered with tortoise-shell, or of ivory richly embossed, or even of solid silver. On these are laid mattresses of sponge, feathers, or plucked wool; and over them soft, gorgeously colored blankets, or a coverlet made of peacock skins, dressed with the feathers on,[3] and perfumed with imported essences.

[1] In later times flagging and mosaics were used. Before the 4th century B. C. the plaster walls were simply whitewashed.

[2] The four-legged, backless stool was called a *diphros*; when an Athenian gentleman walked out, one of his slaves generally carried a diphros for the convenience of his master when wearied. To the diphros a curved back was sometimes added, and the legs made immovable. It was then called a *klismos*. A high, large chair, with straight back and low arms, was a *thronos*. The thronoi in the temples were for the gods, those in dwellings, for the master and his guests. A footstool was indispensable, and was sometimes attached to the front legs of the thronos.

[3] "One of the greatest improvements introduced by the Greeks into the art of

THE MANNERS AND CUSTOMS. 197

The mistress of the house, who is superintending the domestic labor, is dressed in a long chiton, doubled over at the top so as to form a kind of cape which hangs down loosely, clasped on the shoulders, girdled at the waist, and falling in many folds to her feet. When she ventures abroad, as she occasionally does to the funeral of a near relation, to the great religious festivals, and sometimes to hear a tragedy, she wears a cloak or *himation*.[1] The Athenian wife has not the privileges of the Spartan. The husband and father is the complete master of his household, and, so far from allowing his wife to transact any independent bargains, he may be legally absolved from any contract her request or counsel has induced him to make.—This is a busy morning in the home, for the master has gone to the market place to invite a few friends to an evening banquet. The foreign cooks, hired for the occasion, are already here, giving orders, and preparing choice dishes. At noon, all business in the market place having ceased, the Athenian gentleman returns to his home for his mid-day meal and his siesta.[2] As the cooler hours come on, he repairs to the crowded gymnasium, where he may enjoy the pleasures of the bath, listen to the learned lectures of philosophers and rhetoricians, or join in the racing, military, and gymnastic exercises.[3] Toward sunset he again seeks his home to await his invited guests.

The Banquet.—As each guest arrives, a slave[4] meets him in the court, and ushers him into the large triclinium or dining-room, where his host warmly greets him, and assigns to him a section of a couch. Before he reclines,[5] however, a slave unlooses his sandals and washes

sleeping was the practice of undressing before going to bed,—a thing unheard of until hit upon by their inventive genius."—*Felton.*

[1] The dress of both sexes was nearly the same. The himation was a large, square piece of cloth, so wrapped about the form as to leave only the right arm free. Much skill was required to drape it artistically, and the taste and elegance of the wearer were decided by his manner of carrying it. The same himation often served for both husband and wife, and it is related as among the unamiable traits of Xantippe, the shrewish wife of Socrates, that she refused to go out in her husband's himation. A gentleman usually wore a chiton also, though he was considered fully dressed in the himation alone. The lower classes wore only the chiton, or were clothed in tanned skins. Raiment was cheap in Greece. In the time of Socrates a chiton cost about a dollar; and an ordinary himation, two dollars.

[2] The poorer classes gathered together in groups along the porticoes for gossip or slumber, where indeed they not unfrequently spent their nights.

[3] Ball-playing, which was a favorite game with the Greeks, was taught scientifically in the gymnasium. The balls were made of colored leather, stuffed with feathers, wool, or fig-seeds, or, if very large, were hollow. Cock-and-quail fighting was another exciting amusement, and at Athens took place annually by law, as an instructive exhibition of bravery.

[4] A guest frequently brought his own slave to assist in personal attendance upon himself.

[5] The mode of reclining, which was similar to that in Assyria, is shown in the

his feet in perfumed wine. The time having arrived for dinner, water is passed around for hand ablutions, and small, low tables are brought in, one being placed before each couch. There are no knives and forks, no table-cloths or napkins. Some of the guests wear gloves to enable

A GREEK SYMPOSIUM.

them to take the food quite hot, others have hardened their fingers by handling hot pokers, and one, a noted gourmand, has prepared himself with metallic finger-guards. The slaves now hasten with the first course, which opens with sweetmeats, and includes many delicacies,

cut, "A Greek Symposium." The place of honor was next the host. The Greek wife and daughter never appeared at these banquets, and at their every-day meals the wife sat on the couch at the feet of her master. The sons were not permitted to recline till they were of age.

such as thrushes, hares, oysters, pungent herbs, and, best of all, Copaic eels, cooked crisp and brown, and wrapped in beet-leaves.[1] Bread is handed around in tiny baskets, woven of slips of ivory. Little talking is done, for it is good breeding to remain quiet until the substantial viands are honored. From time to time the guests wipe their fingers upon bits of bread, throwing the fragments under the table. This course being finished, the well-trained slaves sponge or remove the tables, brush up the dough, bones, and other remnants from the floor, and pass again the perfumed water for hand-washing. Garlands of myrtle and roses, gay ribbons, and sweet-scented ointments are distributed, a golden bowl of wine is brought, and the meal closes with a libation.

The *Symposium* is introduced by a second libation, accompanied by hymns and the solemn notes of a flute. The party, hitherto silent, rapidly grow merry, while the slaves bring in the dessert and the wine, which now for the first time appears at the feast. The dessert consists of fresh fruits, olives well ripened on the tree, dried figs, imported dates, curdled cream, honey, cheese, and the salt-sprinkled cakes for which Athens is renowned. A large crater or wine-bowl, ornamented with groups of dancing bacchanals, is placed before one of the guests, who has been chosen archon. He is to decide upon the proper mixture of the wine,[2] the nature of the forfeits in the games of the evening, and, in fact, is henceforth king of the feast. The sport begins with riddles. This is a favorite pastime; every failure in guessing requires a forfeit, and the penalty is to drink a certain quantity of wine. Music, charades, dancing and juggling performed by professionals, and a variety of entertainments, help the hours to fly, and the Symposium ends at last by the whole party inviting themselves to some other banqueting-place, where they spend the night in revel.[3]

[1] The Greeks were extravagantly fond of fish. Pork, the abhorred of the Egyptians, was their favorite meat. Bread, more than anything else, was the "staff of life," all other food, except sweetmeats—even meat—being called *relish*. Sweetmeats were superstitiously regarded, and scattering them about the house was an invitation to good luck.

[2] To drink wine clear was disreputable, and it was generally diluted with two thirds water.

[3] The fashionable Symposia were usually of the character described above, but sometimes they were more intellectual, affording an occasion for the brilliant display of Attic wit and learning. The drinking character of the party was always the same, and in Plato's dialogue, The Symposium, in which Aristophanes, Socrates, and other literary celebrities took part, the evening is broken in upon by two different bands of revelers, and daylight finds Socrates and Aristophanes still drinking with the host. "Parasites (a recognized class of people, who lived by sponging their dinners) and mountebanks always took the liberty to drop in wherever there was a feast, a fact which they ascertained by walking through the streets and snuffing at the kitchens."—*Felton*.

4. SUMMARY.

1. Political History.—The Pelasgians are the primitive inhabitants of Greece. In time the Hellenes descend from the north, and give their name to the land. It is the Heroic Age, the era of the sons of the gods,—Hercules, Theseus, and Jason,—of the Argonautic Expedition and the Siege of Troy. With the Dorian Migration ("Return of the Heraclidæ"), and their settlement in the Peloponnesus, the mythic stories end and real history begins. The kings disappear, and nearly all the cities become little republics. Hellenic colonies arise in Asia Minor, rivaling the glory of Greece itself. Lycurgus now enacts his rigid laws (850 B. C.). In the succeeding centuries the Spartans—pitiless, fearless, haughty warriors—conquer Messenia, become the head of the Peloponnesus, and threaten all Greece. Meanwhile—spite of Draco's Code, the Alcmæonidæ's curse, the factions of the men of the *plain*, the *coast*, and the *mountain*, and the tyranny of the Pisistratidæ—Athens, by the wise measures of Solon and Cleisthenes, becomes a powerful republic.

Athens now sends help to the Greeks of Asia Minor against the Persians, and the Asiatic deluge is precipitated upon Greece. Miltiades defeats Darius on the field of Marathon (490 B. C.). Ten years later Xerxes forces the Pass of Thermopylæ, slays Leonidas and his three hundred Spartans, and burns Athens; but his fleet is put to flight at Salamis, the next year his army is routed by Pausanias at Platæa, and his remaining ships are destroyed at Mycale. Thus Europe is saved from Persian despotism.

The Age of Pericles follows, and Athens, grown to be a great commercial city,—its streets thronged with traders and its harbor with ships,—is the head of Greece. Sparta is jealous, and the Peloponnesian war breaks out in 431 B. C. Its twenty-seven years of alternate victories and defeats end in the fatal expedition to Syracuse, the defeat of Ægospotami, and the fall of Athens.

Sparta is now supreme; but her cruel rule is broken by Epaminondas on the field of Leuctra. Thebes comes to the front, but Greece, rent by rivalries, is overwhelmed by Philip of Macedon in the battle of Chæronea. The conqueror dying soon after, his greater son, Alexander, leads the armies of united Greece into Asia. The battles of Granicus, Issus, and Arbela subdue the Persian Empire. Thence the conquering leader marches eastward to the Indus, and returns to Babylon only to die (323 B. C.). His generals divide his empire among themselves; while Greece, a prey to dissensions, at last drops into the all-absorbing Roman Empire (146 B. C.).

SUMMARY.

2. Civilization.—Athens and Sparta differ widely in thought, habits, and taste. *The Spartans* care little for art and literature, and glory only in war and patriotism. They are rigid in their self-discipline, and cruel to their slaves. They smother all tender home sentiment, eat at the public mess, give their seven-year-old boys to the state, and train their girls in the rough sports of the palæstra. They distrust and exclude strangers, and make no effort to adorn their capital with art or architecture.

The Athenians adore art, beauty, and intellect. Versatile and brilliant, they are fond of novelties and eager for discussions. Law courts abound, and the masses imbibe an education in the theater, along the busy streets, and on the Pnyx. In their democratic city, filled with magnificent temples, statues, and colonnades, wit and talent are the keys that unlock the doors of every saloon. Athens becomes the center of the world's history in all that pertains to the fine arts. Poetry and philosophy flourish alike in her classic atmosphere, and all the colonies feel the pulse of her artistic heart.

Grecian Art and Literature furnish models for all time. Infant Greece produces Homer and Hesiod, the patriarchs of epic poetry. Coming down the centuries, she brings out in song, and hymn, and ode, Sappho, Simonides, and Pindar; in tragedy, Æschylus, Sophocles, and Euripides; in comedy, Aristophanes and Menander; in history, Herodotus, Thucydides, and Xenophon; in oratory, Pericles and Demosthenes; in philosophy, Thales, Pythagoras, Socrates, Plato, and Aristotle; in painting, Apelles; in sculpture, Phidias, Praxiteles, and Lysippus.

Greek Mythology invests every stream, grove, and mountain with gods and goddesses, nymphs, and naiads. The beloved deities are worshiped with songs and dances, dramas and festivals, spirited contests and gorgeous processions. The Four Great National Games unite all Greece in a sacred bond. The Feasts of Dionysus give birth to the drama. The Four Great Schools of Philosophy flourish and decay, leaving their impress upon the generations to come. Finally Grecian civilization is transported to the Tiber, and becomes blended with the national peculiarities of the conquering Romans.

READING REFERENCES.

Grote's History of Greece.—Arnold's History of Greece.—Curtius's History of Greece.—Felton's Ancient and Modern Greece.—History Primers; Greece, and Greek Antiquities, edited by Green.—Smith's Student's History of Greece.—Becker's Charicles.—Guhl and Köner's Life of the Greeks and Romans.—Bryce's History of Greece, in Freeman's Series.—Freeman's General Sketch of European History.—Collier's History of Greece—Heeren's Historical Researches.—Putz's Hand-book of Ancient

GREECE.

History.—Bulwer's Rise and Fall of Athens.—Williams's Life of Alexander the Great.—Thirlwall's History of Greece.—Schliemann's Ilios, and Troja.—Niebuhr's Lectures on Ancient History.—Xenophon's Anabasis, Memorabilia, and Cyropædia. —St. John's The Hellenes.—Fergusson's History of Architecture.—Stuart's Antiquities of Athens.—Mahaffy's History of Greek Literature.—Murray's Hand-book of Greek Archæology.

CHRONOLOGY.

	B. C.
Dorian Migration, about	1100
Lycurgus, about	850
First Olympiad	776

[It is curious to notice how many important events cluster about this period, viz.: Rome was founded in 753; the Era of Nabonassar in Babylon began 747; and Tiglath-Pileser II., the great military king of Assyria, ascended the throne, 745.]

First Messenian War	743–724
Second Messenian War	685–668
Draco	621
Solon	594
Pisistratus	560
Battle of Marathon	490
Battles of Thermopylæ and Salamis	480
" " Platæa and Mycale	479
Age of Pericles	479–429
Peloponnesian War	431–404
Retreat of the Ten Thousand	400
Battle of Leuctra	371
Demosthenes delivered his "First Philippic" (Oration against Philip)	352
Battle of Chæronea	338
Alexander the Great	336–323
Battle of the Granicus	334
" " Issus	333
" " Arbela	331
Oration of Demosthenes on "The Crown"	330
Battle of Ipsus	301
Greece becomes a Roman Province	146

BAS-RELIEF OF THE NINE MUSES.

THE PROVINCES
OF THE
ROMAN EMPIRE,
at the time of its greatest extent.
SCALE OF ENGLISH MILES
100   500
On this Map Italia is divided into the 11 Regions of Augustus.

J. WELLS, DEL.

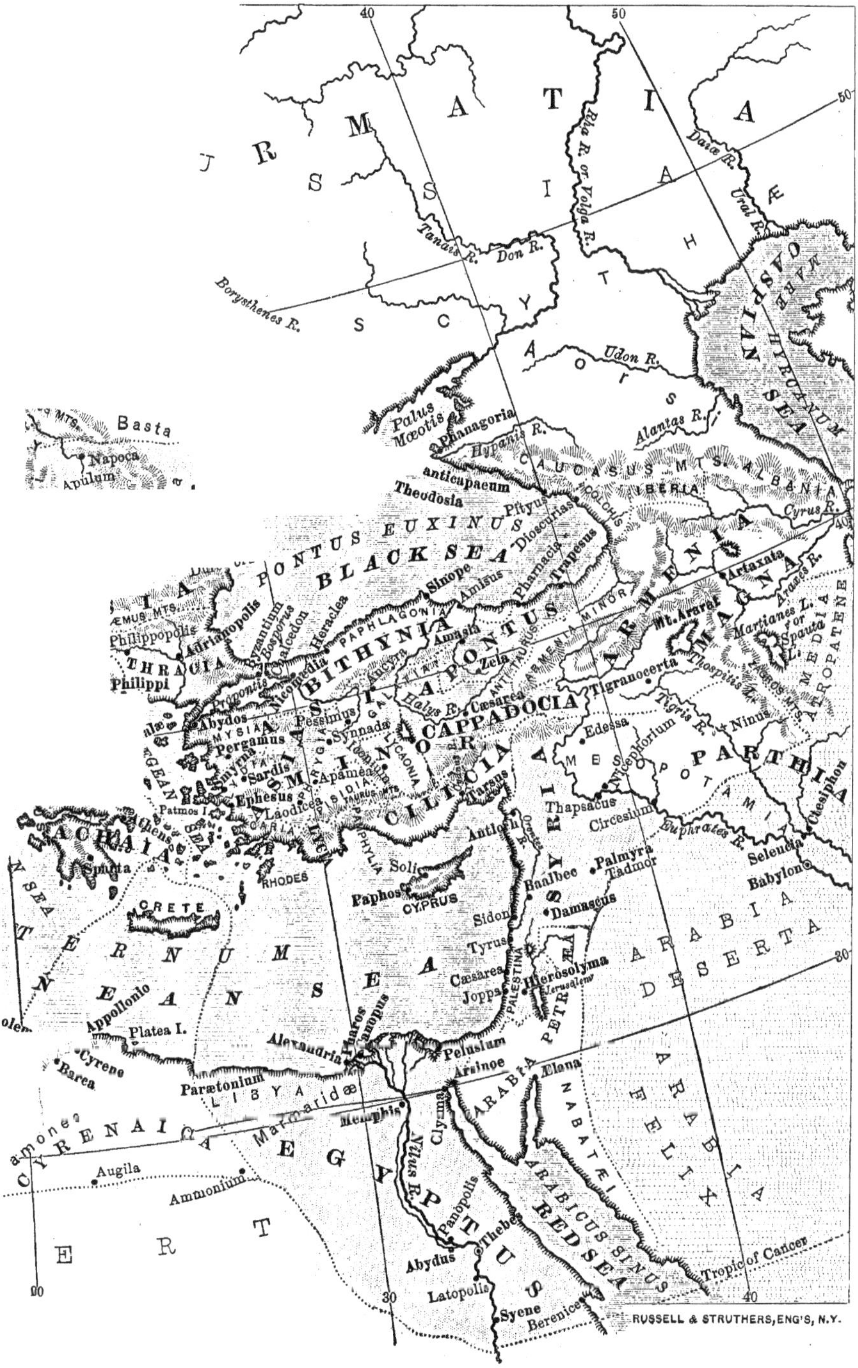

ROME.

1. THE POLITICAL HISTORY.

While Greece was winning her freedom on the fields of Marathon and Platæa, and building up the best civilization the world had then seen; while Alexander was carrying the Grecian arms and culture over the East; while the Conqueror's successors were wrangling over the prize he had won; while the Ptolemies were transplanting Grecian thought, but not Grecian freedom, to Egyptian soil,—there was slowly growing up on the banks of the Tiber a city that was to found an empire wider than Alexander's, and, molding Grecian civilization, art, and literature into new forms, preserve them long after Greece had fallen.

Contrasts between Greece and Italy.—*Duration.*—Greek history, from the First Olympiad (776 B. C.) to the Roman Conquest (146 B. C.), covers about six centuries, but the national strength lasted less than two centuries; Roman history, from the founding of Rome (753 B. C.) to its downfall (476 A. D.), stretches over twelve centuries.

Geographical Questions.—See maps, pp. 210 and 255. Describe the Tiber. Locate Rome; Ostia; Alba Longa; Veii (Veji); the Sabines; the Etruscans. Where was Carthage? New Carthage? Saguntum? Syracuse? Lake Trasimenus? Capua? Cannæ? Tarentum? Cisalpine Gaul? Iapygia (the "heel of Italy," reaching toward Greece)? Brutium (the "toe of Italy")? What were the limits of the empire at the time of its greatest extent? Name the principal countries which it then included. Locate Alexandria; Antioch; Smyrna; Philippi; Byzantium.

Manner of Growth.—Greece, cut up into small valleys, grew around many little centers, and no two leaves on her tree of liberty were exactly alike; Italy exhibited the unbroken advance of one imperial city to universal dominion. As a result, we find in Greece the fickleness and jealousies of petty states; in Italy, the power and resources of a mighty nation.

Direction of Growth.—Greece lay open to the East, whence she originally drew her inspiration, and whither she in time returned the fruits of her civilization; Italy lay open to the West, and westward sent the strength of her civilization to regenerate barbarian Europe.

Character of Influence.—The mission of Greece was to exhibit the triumphs of the mind, and to illustrate the principles of liberty; that of Rome, to subdue by irresistible force, to manifest the power of law, and to bind the nations together for the coming of a new religion.

Ultimate Results.—When Greece fell from her high estate, she left only her history and the achievements of her artists and statesmen; when the Roman Empire broke to pieces, the great nations of Europe sprang from the ruins, and their languages, civilization, laws, and religion took their form from the Mistress of the World.

The Early Inhabitants of Italy were mainly of the same Aryan swarm that settled Greece. But they had become very different from the Hellenes, and had split into various hostile tribes. Between the Arno and the Tiber lived the *Etruscans* or Tuscans,—a league of twelve cities. These people were great builders, and skilled in the arts. In northern Italy, Cisalpine Gaul was inhabited by *Celts*, akin to those upon the other side of the Alps. Southern Italy contained many prosperous *Greek* cities. The *Italians* occupied central Italy. They were divided into the *Latins*

THE POLITICAL HISTORY. 205

and *Oscans*. The former comprised a league of thirty towns (note, p. 117) south of the Tiber; the latter consisted of various tribes living eastward,—Samnites, Sabines, etc.[1]

Rome was founded[2] (753 B. C.) by the Latins, perhaps

---

[1] Some authorities group the Samnites, Sabines, Umbrians, Oscans, Sabellians, etc., as the *Umbrians;* and others call them the *Umbro Sabellians*. They were doubtless closely related.

[2] OF THE EARLY HISTORY OF ROME there is no reliable account, as the records were burned when the city was destroyed by the Gauls (390 B. C.), and it was five hundred years after the founding of the city (A. U. C., *anno urbis conditæ*) before the first rude attempt was made to write a continuous narrative of its origin. The names of the early monarchs are probably personifications, rather than the appellations of real persons. The word "Rome" itself means *border*, and probably had no relation to the fabled Romulus. The history which was accepted in later times by the Romans, and has come down to us, is a series of beautiful legends. In the text is given the real history as now received by the best critics, and in the notes the mythical stories.

ÆNEAS, favored by the god Mercury and led by his mother Venus, came, after the destruction of Troy, to Italy. There his son Ascanius built the Long White City (Alba Longa). His descendants reigned in peace for three hundred years. When it came time, according to the decree of the gods, that Rome should be founded,

ROMULUS AND REMUS were born. Their mother, Rhea Silvia, was a priestess of the goddess Vesta, and their father, Mars, the god of war. Amulius, who had usurped the Alban throne from their grandfather Numitor, ordered the babes to be thrown into the Tiber. They were, however, cast ashore at the foot of Mount Palatine. Here they were nursed by a wolf. One Faustulus, passing near, was struck by the sight, and, carrying the children home, brought them up as his own. Romulus and Remus, on coming to age, discovered their true rank, slew the usurper, and restored their grandfather Numitor to his throne.

ROMAN WOLF STATUE.

FOUNDING OF ROME.—The brothers then determined to found a city near the spot where they had been so wonderfully preserved, and agreed to watch the flight of birds in order to decide which should fix upon the site. Remus, on the Aventine Hill, saw six vultures, but Romulus, on the Palatine, saw twelve, and was declared victor. He accordingly began to mark out the boundaries with a brazen plow, **drawn by a bullock and a heifer.** As the mud wall rose, Remus in scorn jumped

a colony sent out from Alba Longa, as an outpost against the Etruscans, whom they greatly feared. At an early date it contained about one thousand miserable, thatched huts, surrounded by a wall. Most of the inhabitants were shepherds or farmers, who tilled the land upon the plain near by, but lived for protection within their fortifications on the Palatine Hill. It is probable that the other hills, afterward covered by Rome, were then occupied by Latins, and that the cities of Latium formed a confederacy, with Alba Longa at the head.

over it; whereupon Romulus slew him, exclaiming, "So perish every one who may try to leap over these ramparts!" The new city he called Rome after his own name, and became its first king. To secure inhabitants, he opened an asylum for refugees and criminals; but, lacking women, he resorted to a curious expedient. A great festival in honor of Neptune was appointed, and the neighboring people were invited to come with their families. In the midst of the games the young Romans rushed among the spectators, and each, seizing a maiden, carried her off to be his wife. The indignant parents returned home, but only to come back in arms, and thirsting for vengeance. The Sabines laid siege to the citadel on the Capitoline Hill. Tarpeia, the commandant's daughter, dazzled by the glitter of their golden bracelets and rings, promised to betray the fortress if the Sabines would give her "what they wore on their left arms." As they passed in through the gate, which she opened for them in the night, they crushed her beneath their heavy shields. Henceforth that part of the hill was called the Tarpeian Rock, and down its precipice traitors were hurled to death. The next day after Tarpeia's treachery, the battle raged in the valley between the Capitoline and Palatine Hills. In his distress, Romulus vowed a temple to Jupiter. The Romans thereupon turned, and drove back their foes. In the flight, Mettius Curtius, the leader of the Sabines, sunk with his horse into a marsh,

THE TARPEIAN ROCK (FROM AN OLD PRINT).

and nearly perished. Ere the contest could be renewed, the Sabine women, with disheveled hair, suddenly rushed between their kindred and new-found husbands, and implored peace. Their entreaties prevailed, the two people united, and their kings reigned jointly. As the Sabines came from Cures, the united people were called *Romans* and *Quirites*.

The Early Government was aristocratic. It had a king, a senate, and an assembly. The priest-king offered sacrifices, and presided over the senate. The senate had the right to discuss and vote; the assembly, to discuss only. Each original family or house (*gens*) was represented in the senate by its head. This body was therefore composed of the fathers (*patres*), and was from the beginning the soul of the rising city; while throughout its entire history the intelligence, experience, and wisdom gathered in the senate determined the policy and shaped the public life

ROMULUS, after the death of Tatius, became sole king. He divided the people into nobles and commons; the former he called *patricians*, and the latter *plebeians*. The patricians were separated into three tribes,—*Ramnes, Tities,* and *Luceres*. In each of these he made ten divisions, or *curiæ*. The thirty curiæ formed the assembly of the people. The plebeians, being apportioned as tenants and dependants among the patricians, were called *clients*. One hundred of the patricians were chosen for age and wisdom, and styled *fathers* (patres). After Romulus had reigned thirty-seven years, and done all these things according to the will of the gods, one day, during a violent thunder-storm, he disappeared from sight, and was henceforth worshiped as a god.

NUMA POMPILIUS, a pious Sabine, was the second king. Numa was wise from his youth, as a sign of which his hair was gray at birth. He was trained by Pythagoras (p. 174) in all the knowledge of the Greeks, and was wont, in a sacred grove near Rome, to meet the nymph Egeria, who taught him lessons of wisdom, and how men below should worship the gods above. By pouring wine into the spring whence Faunus and Picus, the gods of the wood, drank, he led them to tell him the secret charm to gain the will of Jupiter. Peace smiled on the land during his happy reign, and the doors of the temple of Janus remained closed.

TULLUS HOSTILIUS, the third king, loved war as Numa did peace. He soon got into a quarrel with Alba Longa. As the armies were about to fight, it was agreed to decide the contest by a combat between the Horatii (three brothers in the Roman ranks) and the Curatii (three brothers in the Alban). They were cousins, and one of the

TEMPLE OF JANUS.

Curatii was engaged to be married to a sister of one of the Horatii. In the fight two of the Horatii were killed, when the third pretended to run. The Curatii, because of their wounds, followed him slowly, and, becoming separated, he turned about and slew them one by one. As the victor returned laden with the spoils, he met his sister, who, catching sight of the robe which she had embroidered for her lover, burst into tears. Horatius, unable to bear her reproaches, struck her dead, saying, "So perish any Roman woman who laments a foe!" The murderer was condemned to die, but the people spared him because his valor had saved Rome. Alba submitted, but, the inhabitants proving treacherous, the city was razed, and the people were taken to Rome and located on the Cœlian Hill. The Albans and the Romans

that made Rome the Mistress of the World. The assembly (*comitia curiata*) consisted of the men belonging to these ancient families. Its members voted by *curiæ*; each curia contained the voters of ten houses (*gentes*).

Sabine Invasion and League.—The Sabines, coming down the valley of the Tiber, captured the Capitoline and Quirinal Hills. At first there were frequent conflicts between these near neighbors, but they soon came into alliance. Finally the two tribes formed one city, and the people were thereafter known as *Romans* and *Quirites*. Both had seats in

now became one nation, as the Sabines and the Romans had become in the days of Romulus. In his old age, Tullus sought to find out the will of Jupiter, using the spells of Numa, but angry Jove struck him with a thunderbolt.

ANCUS MARCIUS, the grandson of Numa, conquered many Latin cities, and, bringing the inhabitants to Rome, gave them homes on the Aventine Hill. He wrote Numa's laws on a white board in the Forum, built a bridge over the Tiber, and erected the Mamertine Prison, the first in the city.

TARQUINIUS PRISCUS, the fifth king, was an Etruscan, who came to Rome during the reign of Ancus. As he approached the city, an eagle flew, circling above his head, seized his cap, rose high in air, and then returning replaced it. His wife, Tanaquil, being learned in augury, foretold that he was coming to distinguished honor. Her prediction proved true, for he greatly pleased Ancus, who named him as his successor in place of his own children. The people ratified the choice, and the event proved its wisdom. Tarquin built the famous Drain (cloaca), which still remains, with scarce a stone displaced. He planned the Great Race-Course (Circus Maximus) and its games. He conquered Etruria, and the Etruscans sent him "a golden crown, a scepter, an ivory chair, a purple toga, an embroidered tunic, and an ax tied in a bundle of rods." So the Romans adopted these emblems of royal power as signs of their dominion.

Now, there was a boy named Servius Tullius brought up in the palace, who was a favorite of the king. One day while the child was asleep lambent flames were seen playing about his head. Tanaquil foresaw from this that he was destined to great things. He was henceforth in high favor; he married the king's daughter, and became his counselor. The sons of Ancus, fearing lest Servius should succeed to the throne, and being wroth with Tarquin because of the loss of their paternal inheritance, assassinated the king. But Tanaquil reported that Tarquin was only wounded, and wished that Servius might govern until he recovered. Before the deception was discovered,

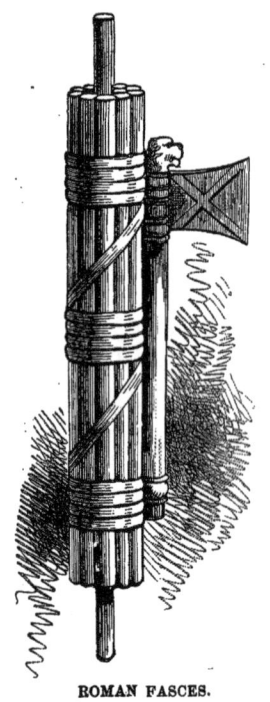

ROMAN FASCES.

the senate, and the king was taken alternately from each. This was henceforth the mode of Rome's growth; she admitted her allies and conquered enemies to citizenship, thus adding their strength to her own, and making her victories their victories.

Alba Longa, the chief town of the Latin League and the mother city of Rome, was herself, after a time, destroyed, and the inhabitants were transferred to Rome. The Alban nobles, now perhaps called *Luceres,* with the Sabines (*Tities*), already joined to the original Romans (*Ramnes*), made the

SERVIUS was firmly fixed in his seat. He made a league with the Latins, and, as a sign of the union, built to Diana a temple on the Aventine, where both peoples offered annual sacrifices for Rome and Latium. He enlarged Rome, inclosing the seven hills with a stone wall, and divided the city into four parts,—called *tribes,* after the old division of the people as instituted by Romulus,—and all the land about into twenty-six districts. The son of a bond-maid, Servius favored the common people. This was shown in his separation of all the Romans—patricians and plebeians—into five classes, according to their wealth. These classes were subdivided into centuries, and they were to assemble in this military order when the king wished to consult concerning peace or war, or laws. In the centuriate assembly the richest citizens had the chief influence, for they formed eighty centuries, and the knights (*equites*) eighteen centuries, each having a vote; while fewer votes were given to the lower classes. But this arrangement was not unjust, since the wealthy were to provide themselves with heavy armor, and fight in the front rank; while the poorest citizens, who formed but one century, were exempt from military service.

The two daughters of Servius were married to the two sons of Tarquinius the Elder. The couples were ill matched, in each case the good and gentle being mated with the cruel and haughty. Finally, Tullia murdered her husband, and Lucius killed his wife, and these two partners in crime, and of like evil instincts, were married. Lucius now conspired with the nobles against the king. His plans being ripe, one day he went into the senate and sat down on the throne. Servius, hearing the tumult which arose, hastened thither, whereupon Lucius hurled the king headlong down the steps. As the old man was tottering homeward, the usurper's attendants followed and murdered him. Tullia hastened to the senate to salute her husband as king; but he, somewhat less brutal than she, ordered her back. While returning, her driver came to the prostrate body of the king, and was about to turn aside, when she fiercely bade him go forward. The blood of her father spattered her dress as the chariot rolled over his lifeless remains. The place took its name from this horrible deed, and was thenceforth known as the Wicked Street.

LUCIUS TARQUINIUS, who thus became the seventh and last king, was surnamed Superbus (the Proud). He erected massive edifices, compelling the workmen to receive such pitiable wages that many in despair committed suicide. In digging the foundations of a temple to Jupiter, a bleeding head (*caput*) was discovered. This the king took to be an omen that the city was to become the head of the world, and so gave the name Capitoline to the temple, and the hill on which it stood. In the vaults of this temple were deposited the Sibylline books, concerning which a singular story was told. One day a sibyl from Cumæ came to the king, offering to sell him for a fabulous sum nine books of prophecies. Tarquin declined to buy, whereupon she burned

EARLY TRIBES
AND CITIES
OF THE
ITALIAN
PENINSULA,
before the
advent of the Gauls.
ADRIATIC SEA
TYRRHENIAN SEA
CYRNOS CORSICA
SARDO, SARDINIA
Ravenna
Ariminum
Ancon
Cupra
Pisæ
Arretium
Cortona
Clusium
Tarquinii
ROME
Ostia
Alalia
Olbia
Nora
Caralis
Sulcis
Minturnæ
Capua
Cumæ
Neapolis
Pompeii
Posidonia
Velia
Pyxus
Brundusium
Hyria
Tarentum
Hydruntum
Sybaris
Croton
Rhegium
Messana
Locri Epizephyrii
Liparææ or Æoliæ Is.
Panormus
Himera
Egesta
Motye
Selinus
Agrigentum
Camarina
Gela
Syracuse
Megara
Catana
Naxus
Magna Græcia
Mantua
Tridentum
Genua
Nicæa
VICINITY OF
ROME
Falerii
Sutrium
Feronia
Capena
Cures
Sabines
Eretum
Baccana
Veii
Fidenæ
Ficulea
Tibur (Tivoli)
Varia
Collatia
Gabii
L. Regillus
Præneste
Tusculum
Alba Longa
L. Albanus
Aricia
Carioli
Volcians
Laurentum
Ostia
Fregenæ
Janiculum
Appian Way
PLAN OF THE
ROMAN HILLS
1 Suburra
2 Roman Forum
3 Velabrum
4 Circus Maximus
5 Colosseum
6 Pantheon
7 Amphitheatre of Taurus
8 Mausoleum of Augustus
PINCIAN
QUIRINAL
VIMINAL
ESQUILINE
CAPITOLINE
PALATINE
CÆLIAN
AVENTINE
CAMPUS MARTIUS
Pons Sublicius
Tiber River
Wall of Servius
Appian Way

number of tribes three; of curiæ, thirty; and of houses, (probably) three hundred.

Etruscan Conquest.—The rising city was, in its turn, conquered by the Etruscans, who placed the Tarquins on the throne. This foreign dynasty were builders as well as warriors. They adorned Rome with elegant edifices of Etruscan architecture. They added the adjacent heights to the growing capital, and extended around the "seven-hilled city" a stone wall, which lasted eight centuries. Rome, within one hundred and fifty years after her founding, became the head of Latium.

three of the books, and demanded the same price for the remaining six. Tarquin laughed, thinking her mad; but when she burned three more, and still asked the original amount for the other volumes, the king began to reflect, and finally bought the books. They were thereafter jealously guarded, and consulted in all great state emergencies.

The Latin town of Gabii was taken by a stratagem. Sextus, the son of Tarquin, pretending to have fled from his father's ill usage, took refuge in that city. Having secured the confidence of the people, he secretly sent to his father, asking advice. Tarquin merely took the messenger into his garden, and, walking to and fro, knocked off with his cane the tallest poppies. Sextus read his father's meaning, and managed to get rid of the chief men of Gabii, when it was easy to give up the place to the Romans.

Tarquin was greatly troubled by a strange omen, a serpent having eaten the sacrifice on the royal altar. The two sons of the king were accordingly sent to consult the oracle at Delphi. They were accompanied by their cousin Junius, called Brutus because of his silliness; which, however, was only assumed, through fear of the tyrant who had already killed his brother. The king's sons made the Delphic god costly presents; Brutus brought only a simple staff, but, unknown to the rest, this was hollow and filled with gold. Having executed their commission, the young men asked the priestess which of them should be king. The reply was, "The one who first kisses his mother." On reaching Italy, Brutus, pretending to fall, kissed the ground, the common mother of us all.

As the royal princes and Tarquinius Collatinus were one day feasting in the camp a dispute arose concerning the industry of their wives. To decide it they at once hastened homeward through the darkness. They found the king's daughters at a festival, while Lucretia, the wife of Collatinus, was in the midst of her slaves, distaff in hand. Collatinus was exultant; but soon after, Lucretia, stung by the insults she received from Sextus, killed herself, calling upon her friends to avenge her fate. Brutus, casting off the mask of madness, drew forth the dagger she used, and vowed to kill Sextus and expel the detested race. The oath was repeated as the red blade passed from hand to hand. The people rose in indignation, and drove the Tarquins from the city. Henceforth the Romans hated the very name of king. Rome now became a free city after it had been governed by kings for two hundred and forty-five years. The people chose for rulers two consuls, elected yearly; and to offer sacrifices in place of the king, they selected a priest who should have no power in the state.

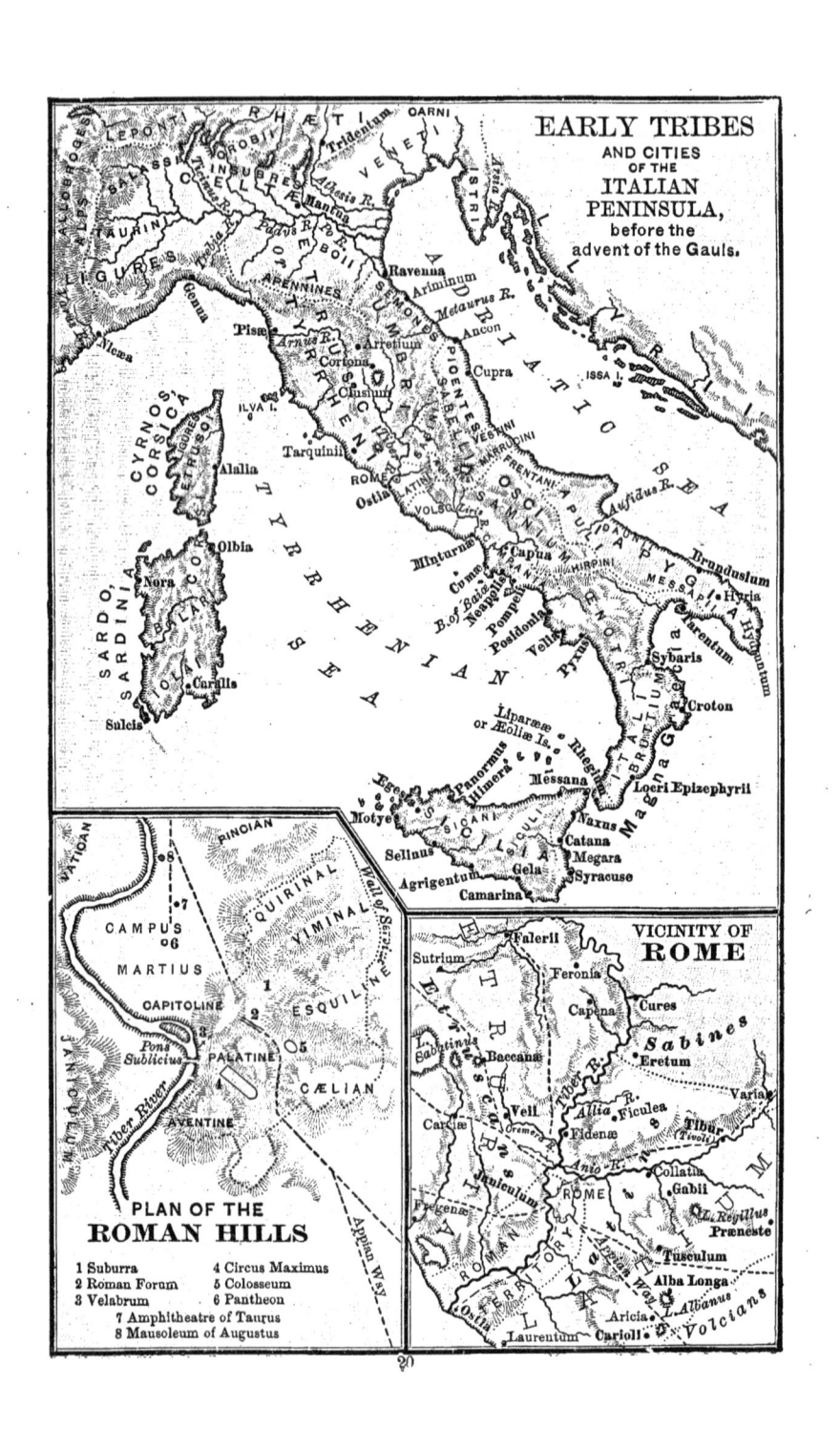

EARLY TRIBES
AND CITIES
OF THE
ITALIAN PENINSULA,
before the advent of the Gauls.

PLAN OF THE
ROMAN HILLS

1 Suburra
2 Roman Forum
3 Velabrum
4 Circus Maximus
5 Colosseum
6 Pantheon
7 Amphitheatre of Taurus
8 Mausoleum of Augustus

VICINITY OF
ROME

number of tribes three; of curiæ, thirty; and of houses, (probably) three hundred.

Etruscan Conquest.—The rising city was, in its turn, conquered by the Etruscans, who placed the Tarquins on the throne. This foreign dynasty were builders as well as warriors. They adorned Rome with elegant edifices of Etruscan architecture. They added the adjacent heights to the growing capital, and extended around the "seven-hilled city" a stone wall, which lasted eight centuries. Rome, within one hundred and fifty years after her founding, became the head of Latium.

three of the books, and demanded the same price for the remaining six. Tarquin laughed, thinking her mad; but when she burned three more, and still asked the original amount for the other volumes, the king began to reflect, and finally bought the books. They were thereafter jealously guarded, and consulted in all great state emergencies.

The Latin town of Gabii was taken by a stratagem. Sextus, the son of Tarquin, pretending to have fled from his father's ill usage, took refuge in that city. Having secured the confidence of the people, he secretly sent to his father, asking advice. Tarquin merely took the messenger into his garden, and, walking to and fro, knocked off with his cane the tallest poppies. Sextus read his father's meaning, and managed to get rid of the chief men of Gabii, when it was easy to give up the place to the Romans.

Tarquin was greatly troubled by a strange omen, a serpent having eaten the sacrifice on the royal altar. The two sons of the king were accordingly sent to consult the oracle at Delphi. They were accompanied by their cousin Junius, called Brutus because of his silliness; which, however, was only assumed, through fear of the tyrant who had already killed his brother. The king's sons made the Delphic god costly presents; Brutus brought only a simple staff, but, unknown to the rest, this was hollow and filled with gold. Having executed their commission, the young men asked the priestess which of them should be king. The reply was, "The one who first kisses his mother." On reaching Italy, Brutus, pretending to fall, kissed the ground, the common mother of us all.

As the royal princes and Tarquinius Collatinus were one day feasting in the camp a dispute arose concerning the industry of their wives. To decide it they at once hastened homeward through the darkness. They found the king's daughters at a festival, while Lucretia, the wife of Collatinus, was in the midst of her slaves, distaff in hand. Collatinus was exultant; but soon after, Lucretia, stung by the insults she received from Sextus, killed herself, calling upon her friends to avenge her fate. Brutus, casting off the mask of madness, drew forth the dagger she used, and vowed to kill Sextus and expel the detested race. The oath was repeated as the red blade passed from hand to hand. The people rose in indignation, and drove the Tarquins from the city. Henceforth the Romans hated the very name of king. Rome now became a free city after it had been governed by kings for two hundred and forty-five years. The people chose for rulers two consuls, elected yearly, and to offer sacrifices in place of the king, they selected a priest who should have no power in the state.

The Servian Constitution.—The Tarquins diminished patrician power and helped the plebs by a change in the constitution. Servius (p. 209) divided all the Romans into five classes, based on property instead of birth, and these into one hundred and ninety-three centuries or companies. The people were directed to assemble by centuries (*comitia centuriata*), either to fight or to vote. This body, in fact, constituted an army, and was called together on the field of Mars by the blast of the trumpet. To the new centuriate assembly was given the right of selecting the king and enacting the laws. The king was deprived of his power as

BRUTUS AND COLLATINUS were the first consuls. Soon after this the two sons of Brutus plotted to bring Tarquin back. Their father was sitting on the judgment-seat when they were brought in for trial. The stern old Roman, true to duty, sentenced both to death as traitors.

Tarquin now induced the Etruscans of the towns of Veii and Tarquinii to aid him, and they accordingly marched toward Rome. The Romans went forth to meet them. As the two armies drew near, Aruns, son of Tarquin, catching sight of Brutus, rushed forward, and the two enemies fell dead, each pierced by the other's spear. Night checked the terrible contest which ensued. During the darkness the voice of the god Silvanus was heard in the woods, saying that Rome had beaten, since the Etruscans had lost one man more than the Romans. The Etruscans fled in dismay. The matrons of Rome mourned Brutus for a whole year because he had so bravely avenged the wrongs of Lucretia.

Next came a powerful army of Etruscans under Porsenna, king of Clusium He captured Janiculum (a hill just aross the Tiber), and would have forced his way into the city with the fleeing Romans had not Horatius Cocles, with two brave men, held the bridge while it was cut down behind them. As the timbers tottered, his companions rushed across. But he kept the enemy at bay until the shouts of the Romans told him the bridge was gone, when, with a prayer to Father Tiber, he leaped into the stream, and, amid a shower of arrows, swam safely to the bank. The people never tired of praising this hero. They erected a statue in his honor, and gave him as much land as he could plow in a day.

> "And still his name sounds stirring
> Unto the men of Rome,
> As the trumpet-blast that cries to them
> To charge the Volscian home.
> And wives still pray to Juno
> For boys with hearts as bold
> As his who kept the bridge so well
> In the brave days of old."
> *Macaulay's Lays.*

Porsenna now laid siege to the city. Then Mucius, a young noble, went to the Etruscan camp to kill Porsenna. By mistake he slew the treasurer. Being dragged before the king, and threatened with death if he did not confess his accomplices, he thrust his right hand into an altar-fire, and held it there until it was burned to a

priest, this office being conferred on the chief pontiff. The higher classes, aggrieved by these changes, at last combined with other Latin cities to expel their Etruscan rulers. Kings now came to an end at Rome. This was in 509 B. C., —a year after Hippias was driven out of Athens (p. 124).

The Republic was then established. Two chief magistrates, *consuls* (at first called prætors), were chosen, it being thought that if one turned out badly the other would check him. The constitution of Servius was adopted, and the senate, which had dwindled in size, was restored to its ideal number, three hundred, by the addition of one hundred and sixty-four life-members (*conscripti*) chosen from the richest of the knights (*equites*), several of these being plebeians.

The Struggle between the Patricians and the Plebeians was the characteristic of the first two hundred years of the republic. The patricians were the descendants of the first settlers. They were rich, proud, exclusive, and demanded all the offices of the government. Each of these nobles was supported by a powerful body of *clients* or dependants. The plebeians were the newer families. They were generally poor, forbidden the rights of citizens,

---

crisp. Porsenna, amazed at his firmness, gave him his liberty. Mucius thereupon told the king that three hundred Roman youths had sworn to accomplish his death. Porsenna, alarmed for his life, made peace with Rome. Among the hostages given by Rome was Clœlia, a noble maiden, who, escaping from the Etruscan camp, swam the Tiber. The Romans sent her back, but Porsenna, admiring her courage, set her free.

Tarquin next secured a league of thirty Latin cities to aid in his restoration. In this emergency the Romans appointed a *dictator*, who should possess absolute power for six months. A great battle was fought at *Lake Regillus*. Like most ancient contests, it began with a series of single encounters. First, Tarquin and the Roman dictator fought; then the Latin dictator and the Roman master of horse. Finally the main armies came to blows. The Romans being worsted, their dictator vowed a temple to Castor and Pollux. Suddenly the Twin Brethren, taller and fairer than men, on snow-white horses and clad in rare armor, were seen fighting at his side. Everywhere the Latins broke and fled before them. Tarquin gave up his attempt in despair. That night two riders, their horses wet with foam and blood, rode up to a fountain before the Temple of Vesta at Rome, and, as they washed off in the cool water the traces of the battle, told how a great victory had been won over the Latin host (see Steele's New Astronomy, p. 227).

and not allowed to intermarry with the patricians. Obliged to serve in the army without pay, during their absence their farms remained untilled, and were often ravaged by the enemy. Forced, when they returned from war, to borrow money of the patricians for seed, tools, and food, if they failed in their payments they could be sold as slaves, or cut in pieces for distribution among their creditors. The prisons connected with the houses of the great patricians were full of plebeian debtors.

Secession to Mons Sacer.[1]—*Tribunes* (494 B. C.).— The condition of the plebs became so unbearable that they finally marched off in a body and encamped on the Sacred Mount, where they determined to build a new city, and let the patricians have the old one for themselves. The patricians,[2] in alarm, compromised by canceling the plebeian debts and appointing *tribunes of the people,* whose persons were sacred, and whose houses, standing open day and night, were places of refuge. To these new officers was afterward given the power of *veto* (I forbid) over any law passed by the senate and considered injurious to the plebs. Such was the exclusiveness of the senate, however, that the tribunes could not enter the senate-house, but were obliged to remain outside, and shout the "veto" through the open door.

There were now two distinct peoples in Rome, each with its own interests and officers. This is well illustrated in the fact that the agreement made on Mons Sacer was concluded in the form of an international treaty, with the usual oaths and sacrifices; and that the magistrates of the plebs were

---

[1] Piso mentions the Aventine as the probable "Mons Sacer," or Sacred Mount.

[2] Old Menenius Agrippa tried to teach the plebeians a lesson in a fable: Once upon a time the various human organs, tired of serving so seemingly idle a member as the stomach, "struck work;" accordingly the hands would carry no food to the mouth, and the teeth would not chew. Soon, however, all the organs began to fail, and then, to their surprise, they learned that they all depended on this very stomach.

declared to be inviolate, like the ambassadors of a foreign power.

The Three Popular Assemblies of Rome, with their peculiar organization and powers, marked so many stages of constitutional growth in the state.

The Assembly of Curies (comitia curiata), the oldest and long the only one, was based on the patrician separation into tribes (*Ramnes, Tities,* and *Luceres*). No plebeian had a voice in this gathering, and it early lost its influence, and became a relic of the past.

ROMAN PLEBEIANS.

The Assembly of Centuries (comitia centuriata), which came in with the Etruscan kings, was essentially a military organization. Based on the entire population, it gave the plebeians their first voice, though a weak one, in public affairs.

The Assembly of the Tribes (comitia tributa), introduced with the rising of the plebs, was based on the new separation into tribes, *i. e.*, wards and districts. The patricians were here excluded, as the plebeians had been at first; and Rome, which began with a purely aristocratic assembly, had now a purely democratic one.

The original number of the local tribes was twenty in all,—four city wards and sixteen country districts. With the growth of the republic and the acquisition of new territory, the number was increased to thirty-five (**241 B. C.**).

The Roman citizens were then so numerous and so scattered that it was impossible for them to meet at Rome to elect officers and make laws; but still the organization was kept up till the end of the republic.

An Agrarian Law (*ager*, a field) was the next measure of relief granted to the common people. It was customary for the Romans, when they conquered a territory, to leave the owners a part of the land, and to take the rest for themselves. Though this became public property, the patricians used it as their own. The plebeians, who bore the brunt of the fighting, naturally thought they had the best claim to the spoils of war, and with the assertion of their civil rights came now a claim for the rights of property.[1]

Spurius Cassius[2] (486 B. C.), though himself a patrician, secured a law ordaining that part of the public lands should be divided among the poor plebeians, and the patricians should pay rent for the rest. But the patricians were so strong that they made the law a dead letter, and finally, on the charge of wishing to be king, put Spurius to death, and leveled his house to the ground. The agitation, however, still continued.

The Decemvirs (451 B. C.).— The tribunes, through ignorance of the laws, which were jealously guarded as the exclusive property of the patricians, were often thwarted in their measures to aid the common people. The plebs of Rome, therefore, like the common people of Athens nearly two hundred years before (p. 121), demanded that the laws should be made public. After a long struggle the senate yielded. Ten men (*decemvirs*) were appointed

---

[1] Property at that early date consisted almost entirely of land and cattle. The Latin word for money, *pecunia* (cattle), indicates this ancient identity.

[2] Spurius was the author of the famous League of the Romans, Latins, and Hernicans, by means of which the Æquians and Volscians were long held in check. The men of the Latin League fought side by side until after the Gallic invasion.

to revise and publish the laws. Meanwhile the regular government of consuls and tribunes was suspended. The decemvirs did their work well, and compiled ten tables of laws that were acceptable. Their year of office having expired, a second body of decemvirs was chosen to write the rest of the laws. The senate, finding them favorable to the plebeians, forced the decemvirs to resign, introduced into the two remaining tables regulations obnoxious to the common people, and then endeavored to restore the consular government without the tribuneship. The plebs a second time seceded to the Sacred Mount, and the senate was forced to reinstate the tribunes.[1]

The Laws of the Twelve Tables remained as the grand result of the decemviral legislation. They were engraved on blocks of brass or ivory, and hung up in the

---

[1] The account of this transaction given in Livy's History is doubtless largely legendary. The story runs as follows: Three ambassadors were appointed to visit Athens (this was during the "Age of Pericles"), and examine the laws of Solon. On their return the decemvirs were chosen. They were to be supreme, and the consuls, tribunes, etc., resigned. The new rulers did admirably during one term, and completed ten tables of excellent laws that were adopted by the Assembly of Centuries. Decemvirs were therefore chosen for a second term. Appius Claudius was the most popular of the first body of decemvirs, and the only one reëlected. Now all was quickly changed; the ten men became at once odious tyrants, and Appius Claudius chief of all. Each of the decemvirs was attended by twelve lictors, bearing the fasces with the axes wherever he went in public. Two new tables of oppressive laws, confirming the patricians in their hated privileges, were added to the former tables. When the year expired the decemvirs called no new election, and held their office in defiance of the senate and the people. No man's life was safe, and many leading persons fled from Rome. The crisis soon came. One day, seeing a beautiful maiden, the daughter of a plebeian named Virginius, crossing the Forum, Claudius resolved to make her his own. So he directed a client to seize her on the charge that she was the child of one of his slaves, and then to bring the case before the decemvirs for trial. Claudius, of course, decided in favor of his client. Thereupon Virginius drew his daughter one side from the judgment-seat as if to bid her farewell. Suddenly catching up a butcher's knife from a block near by, he plunged it into his daughter's heart, crying, "Thus only can I make thee free!" Then brandishing the red blade, he hastened to the camp and roused the soldiers, who marched to the city, breathing vengeance. As over the body of the injured Lucretia, so again over the corpse of the spotless Virginia, the populace swore that Rome should be free. The plebeians flocked out once more to the Sacred Mount. The decemvirs were forced to resign. The tribunes and consuls were restored to power. Appius, in despair, committed suicide. (The version of this story given in the text above is that of Ihne, the great German critic, in his new work on Early Rome.)

Forum, where all could read them. Henceforth they constituted the foundation of the written law of Rome, and every schoolboy, as late as Cicero's time, learned them by heart.

Continued Triumph of the Plebs.—Step by step the plebeians pushed their demand for equal privileges with the patricians. First the *Valerian* and *Horatian decrees* (449 B. C.), so called from the consuls who prepared them, made the resolutions passed by the plebeians in the Assembly of the Tribes binding equally upon the patricians. Next the *Canuleian decree* (445 B. C.) abolished the law against intermarriage. The patricians, finding that the plebeians were likely to get hold of the consulship, compromised by abolishing that office, and by choosing, through the Assembly of Centuries, from patricians and plebeians alike, three *military tribunes* with consular powers. But the patricians did not act in good faith, and by innumerable arts managed to circumvent the plebs, so that during the next fifty years (until 400 B. C.) there were twenty elections of consuls instead of military tribunes, and when military tribunes were chosen they were always patricians. Meanwhile they also secured the appointment of *censors*, to be chosen from their ranks exclusively, who took the census, classified the people, and supervised public morals. Thus they constantly strove to offset the new plebeian power. So vindictive was the struggle that the nobles did not shrink from murder to remove promising plebeian candidates.[1] But the plebs held firm,

---

[1] Thus the Fabii, a powerful patrician house, having taken the side of the plebs, and finding that they could not thereafter live in peace at Rome, left the city, and founded an outpost on the Cremera, below Veii, where they could still serve their country. This little body of three hundred and six soldiers—including the Fabii, their clients and dependants—sustained for two years the full brunt of the Veientine war. At length they were enticed into an ambuscade, and all were slain except one little boy, the ancestor of the Fabius afterward so famous. During the massacre the consular army was near by, but patrician hate would not permit a rescue.

Again, during a severe famine at Rome (440 B. C.), a rich plebeian, named **Spurius**

and finally secured the famous *Licinian Rogation* (367 B. C.), which ordered,—

I. That, in case of debts on which interest had been met, the sum of the interest paid should be deducted from the principal, and the remainder become due in three successive years. (This bankrupt law was designed to aid the poor, now overwhelmed with debt, and so in the power of the rich creditor.)

II. That no citizen should hold more than five hundred jugera (about three hundred and twenty acres) of the public land, and should not feed on the public pastures more than a limited number of cattle, under penalty of fine.

III. That henceforth consuls, not consular tribunes, should be elected, and that one of the two consuls must be plebeian.

IV. That instead of two patricians being chosen to keep the Sibylline books (p. 209), there should be ten men, taken equally from both orders.

For years after its passage the patricians struggled to prevent the decree from going into effect. But the common people finally won. They never lost the ground they had gained, and secured, in rapid succession, the dictatorship, the censorship, the prætorship, and (300 B. C.) the right to be pontiff and augur. Rome at last, nearly two centuries after the republic began, possessed a democratic government. "Civil concord," says Weber, "to which a temple was dedicated at this time, brought with it a period of civic virtue and heroic greatness."

Wars with Neighboring Tribes.—While this long civil contest was raging within the walls of Rome, her armies were fighting without, striving to regain her lost supremacy over Latium, and sometimes for the very existence of the city. There was a constant succession of wars [1]

Mælius, sold grain to the poor at a very low rate. The patricians, finding that he was likely to be a successful candidate for office, accused him of wishing to be king, and as he refused to appear before his enemies for trial, Ahala, the master of horse, slew him in the Forum with his own hand.

[1] Various beautiful legends cluster around these eventful wars, and they have attained almost the dignity, though we cannot tell how much they contain of the truth, of history.

CORIOLANUS.—While the Romans were besieging Corioli, the Volscians made a sally, but were defeated. In the eagerness of the pursuit, Caius Marcius followed the enemy inside the gates, which were closed upon him. But with his good sword he hewed his way back, and let in the Romans. So the city was taken, and the hero

with the Latins, Æquians, Volscians, Etruscans, Veientes, and Samnites. Connected with these wars are the names, famous in Roman legend, of Coriolanus, Cincinnatus, and Camillus.

The Gallic Invasion.—In the midst of these contests a horde of Gauls crossed the Apennines, and spread like a devastating flood over central Italy. Rome was taken, and nearly all the city burned (390 B. C.). The invaders con-

received the name Coriolanus. Afterward there was a famine at Rome, and, grain arriving from Sicily, Caius would not sell any to the plebs unless they would submit to the patricians. Thereupon the tribunes sought to bring him to trial, but he fled, and took refuge among the Volsci. Soon after, he returned at the head of a great army, and laid siege to Rome. The city was in peril. As a final resort, his mother, wife, and children, with many of the chief women, clad in the deepest mourning, went forth and fell at his feet. Unable to resist their entreaties, Coriolanus exclaimed, "Mother, thou hast saved Rome, but lost thy son." Having given the order to retreat, he is said to have been slain by the angry Volsci.

CINCINNATUS RECEIVING THE DICTATORSHIP.

CINCINNATUS.—One day news came that the Æquians had surrounded the consul Minucius and his army in a deep valley, whence they could not escape. The only one in Rome deemed fit to meet this emergency was Titus Quinctius, surnamed Cincinnatus (the Curly-haired), who was now declared dictator. The officers who went to

sented to retire only on the payment of a heavy ransom. So deep an impression was made upon the Romans by the size, strength, courage, and enormous number of these barbarians, that they thenceforth called a war with the Gauls a *tumult*, and kept in the treasury a special fund for such a catastrophe.

The Final Effect of all these wars was beneficial to Rome. The plebeians, who formed the strength of her army, frequently carried their point against the patricians by refusing to fight until they got their rights. These long struggles, too, matured the Roman energy, and developed

announce his appointment found him plowing on his little farm of four acres, which he tilled himself. He called for his toga, that he might receive the commands of the senate with due respect, when he was at once hailed dictator. Repairing to the city, he assembled fresh troops, bidding each man carry twelve wooden stakes. That very night he surrounded the Æquians, dug a ditch, and made a palisade about their camp. Minucius, hearing the Roman war-cry, rushed up and fell upon the enemy with all his might. When day broke, the Æquians found themselves hemmed in, and were forced to surrender and to pass under the yoke. Cincinnatus, on his return, was awarded a golden crown. Having saved his country, he resigned his office and went back to his plow again, content with the quiet of his rustic home.

THE SIEGE OF VEII—the Troy of Roman legend—lasted ten years. Before that the Roman wars consisted mainly of mere forays into an enemy's country. Now the troops remained summer and winter, and for the first time received regular pay. In the seventh year of the siege, Lake Albanus, though in the heat of summer, overflowed its banks. The Delphic oracle declared that Veii would not fall until the lake was dried up, whereupon the Roman army cut a tunnel through the solid rock to convey the surplus water over the neighboring fields. Still the city did not yield. Camillus, having been appointed dictator, dug a passage under the wall. One day the king of Veii was about to offer a sacrifice, when the soothsayer told him that the city should belong to him who slew the victim. The Romans, who were beneath, heard these words, and, forcing their way through, hastened to the shrine, and Camillus completed the sacrifice. The gates were thrown open, and the Roman army, rushing in, overpowered all opposition.

THE CITY OF FALERII had aided the Veientes. When Camillus, bent on revenge, appeared before the place, a schoolmaster secretly brought into the Roman camp his pupils, the children of the chief men of Falerii. Camillus, scorning to receive the traitor, tied his hands behind his back, and, giving whips to the boys, bade them flog their master back into the city. The Falerians, moved by such magnanimity, surrendered to the Romans. Camillus entered Rome in a chariot drawn by white horses, and having his face colored with vermilion, as was the custom when the gods were borne in procession. Unfortunately, he offended the plebs by ordering each man to restore one tenth of his booty for an offering to Apollo. He was accused of pride, and of appropriating to his own use the bronze gates of Veii. Forced to leave the city, he went out praying that Rome might yet need his help. That time soon came. Five years after, the Gauls defeated the Romans at

THE RIVER ALLIA, where the slaughter was so great that the anniversary of the

the Roman character in all its stern, unfeeling, and yet heroic strength.

After the Gallic invasion Rome was soon rebuilt. The surrounding nations having suffered still more severely from the northern barbarians, and the Gauls being now looked upon as the common enemy of Italy, Rome came to be considered the common defender. The plebs, in rebuilding their ruined houses and buying tools, cattle, and seed, were reduced to greater straits than ever before (unless after the expulsion of the Etruscan kings); and to add to their burdens a double tribute was imposed by the government, in

---

battle became a black day in the Roman calendar. The wreck of the army took refuge in Veii. The people of Rome fled for their lives. The young patricians garrisoned the citadel; and the gray-haired senators, devoting themselves as an offering to the gods, put on their robes, and, sitting in their ivory chairs of magistracy, awaited death. The barbarians, hurrying through the deserted streets, at length came to the Forum. For a moment they stood amazed at the sight of those solemn figures. Then one of the Gauls put out his hand reverently to stroke the white beard of an aged senator, when the indignant Roman, revolting at the profanation, felled him with his staff. The spell was broken, and the senators were ruthlessly massacred.

The Siege of the Capitol lasted for months. One night a party of Gauls clambered up the steep ascent, and one of them reached the highest ledge of the rock. Just then some sacred geese in the Temple of Juno began to cry and flap their wings. Marcus Manlius, aroused by the noise, rushed out, saw the peril, and dashed the foremost Gaul over the precipice. Other Romans rallied to his aid, and the imminent peril was arrested. Finally the Gauls, weary of the siege, offered to accept a ransom of a thousand pounds of gold. This sum was raised from the temple treasures and the ornaments of the Roman women. As they were weighing the articles, the Romans complained of the scales being false, when Brennus, the Gallic chief, threw in his heavy sword, insolently exclaiming, "Woe to the vanquished!" At that moment Camillus strode in at the head of an army, crying, "Rome is to be bought with iron, not gold!" drove out the enemy, and not a man escaped to tell how low the city had fallen on that eventful day. When the Romans returned to their devastated homes, they were at first of a mind to leave Rome, and occupy the empty dwellings of Veii; but a lucky omen prevailed on them to remain. Just as a senator was rising to speak, a centurion relieving guard gave the command, "Plant your colors; this is the best place to stay in." The senators rushed forth, shouting, "The gods have spoken; we obey!" The people caught the enthusiasm, and cried out, "Rome forever!"

Marcus Manlius, who saved the Capitol, befriended the people in the distress which followed the Gallic invasion. One day, seeing a soldier dragged off to prison for debt, he paid the amount and released the man, at the same time swearing that while he had any property left, no Roman should be imprisoned for debt. The patricians, jealous of his influence among the plebs, accused him of wishing to become king. He was brought to trial in the Campus Martius; but the hero pointed to the spoils of thirty warriors whom he had slain; forty distinctions won in battle; his innumerable scars; and, above all, to the Capitol he had saved. His enemies, finding

order to replace the sacred gold used to buy off the Gauls. But this very misery soon led to the Licinian Rogations (p. 219), and so to the growth of liberty. Thus the plebs got a consul twenty-four years after the Gauls left, just as they got the tribunes fifteen years after the Etruscans left; the succeeding ruin both times being followed by a triumph of democracy.

The Capture of Veii (396 B. C.) gave the Romans a foothold beyond the Tiber; and, only three years after the Gallic invasion, four new tribes, carved out of the Veientine land, were added to the republic.

a conviction in that place impossible, adjourned to a grove where the Capitol could not be seen, and there the man who had saved Rome was sentenced to death, and at once hurled from the Tarpeian Rock.

QUINTUS CURTIUS.—Not long after the Licinian Rogations were passed, Rome was afflicted by a plague, in which Camillus died; by an overflow of the Tiber; and by an earthquake, which opened a great chasm in the Forum. The augurs declared that the gulf would not close until there were cast into it the most precious treasures; whereupon Quintus Curtius mounted his horse, and, riding at full speed, leaped into the abyss, declaring that Rome's best treasures were her brave men.

THE BATTLE OF MOUNT VESUVIUS (340 B. C.) was the chief event of the Latin war. Prior to this engagement the consul Manlius ordered that no one should quit his post under pain of death. But his own son, provoked by the taunts of a Tusculan officer, left the ranks, slew his opponent in single combat, and brought the bloody spoils to his father. The stern parent ordered him to be at once beheaded by the lictor, in the presence of the army. During the battle which followed, the Romans were on the point of yielding, when Decius, the plebeian consul, who had promised, in case of defeat, to offer himself to the infernal gods, fulfilled his vow. Calling the pontifex maximus, he repeated the form devoting the foe and himself to death, and then, wrapping his toga about him, leaped upon his horse, and dashed into the thickest of the fight. His death inspired the Romans with fresh hope, and scarce one fourth of the Latins escaped from that bloody field.

BATTLE OF THE CAUDINE FORKS.—During the second *Samnite war* there arose among the Samnites a famous captain named Caius Pontius. By a stratagem he enticed the Roman army into the Caudine Forks, in the neighborhood of Caudium. High mountains here inclose a little plain, having at each end a passage through a narrow defile. When the Romans were fairly in the basin, the Samnites suddenly appeared in both gorges, and forced the consuls to surrender with four legions. Pontius, having sent his prisoners under the yoke, furnished them with wagons for the wounded, and food for their journey, and then released them on certain conditions of peace. The senate refused to ratify the terms, and ordered the consuls to be delivered up to the Samnites, but did not send back the soldiers. Pontius replied that if the senate would not make peace, then it should place the army back in the Caudine Forks. The Romans, who rarely scrupled at any conduct that promised their advantage, continued the war. But when, twenty-nine years later, Pontius was captured by Fabius Maximus, that brave Samnite leader was disgracefully put to death as the triumphal chariot of the victor ascended to the Capitol.

The final result of the *Latin war* (340–338 B. C.) was to dissolve the old Latin League,[1] and to merge the cities of Latium, one by one, into the Roman state.

The three *Samnite wars* (343–290 B. C.) occupied half a century, with brief intervals, and were most obstinately contested. The long-doubtful struggle culminated at the great battle of Sentinum, in a victory over the combined Samnites, Gauls, and Greek colonists. Samnium became a subject-ally. *Rome was now mistress of central Italy.*

War with Pyrrhus (280–276 B. C.).—The rich city of Tarentum, in southern Italy, had not joined the Samnite coalition. Rome had therefore made a treaty with her, promising not to send ships of war past the Lacinian Promontory. But, having a garrison in the friendly city of Thurii, the senate ordered a fleet to that place; so one day, while the people of Tarentum were seated in their theater witnessing a play, they suddenly saw ten Roman galleys sailing upon the forbidden waters. The audience in a rage left their seats, rushed down to the shore, manned some ships, and, pushing out, sank four of the Roman squadron. The senate sent ambassadors to ask satisfaction. They reached Tarentum, so says the legend, during a feast of Bacchus. Postumius, the leader of the envoys, made so many mistakes in talking Greek, that the people laughed aloud, and, as he was leaving, a buffoon threw mud upon his white toga. The shouts only increased when Postumius, holding up his soiled robe, cried, "This shall be washed in torrents of your blood!" War was now inevitable. Tarentum,[2] unable to

---

[1] The Latin League (p. 216) was dissolved in the same year (338 B. C.) with the battle of Chæronea (p. 149).

[2] The Greek colonists retained the pride, though they had lost the simplicity, of their ancestors. They were effeminate to the last degree. "At Tarentum there were not enough days in the calendar on which to hold the festivals, and at Sybaris they killed all the cocks lest they should disturb the inhabitants in their sleep."

resist the "barbarians of the Tiber," appealed to the mother country for help. Pyrrhus, King of Epirus, came over with twenty-five thousand soldiers and twenty elephants. For the first time the Roman legion (p. 271) met the dreaded Macedonian phalanx. In vain the Roman soldiers sought to break through the bristling hedge, with their swords hewing off the pikes, and with their hands bearing them to the ground. To complete their discomfiture, Pyrrhus launched his elephants upon their weakened ranks. At the sight of that "new kind of oxen," the Roman cavalry fled in dismay.

Pyrrhus won a second battle in the same way. He then crossed over into Sicily to help the Greeks against the Carthaginians. When he returned, two years later, while attempting to surprise the Romans by a night attack, his troops lost their way, and the next morning, when weary with the march, they were assailed by the enemy. The once-dreaded elephants were frightened back by fire-brands, and driven through the Grecian lines. Pyrrhus was defeated, and, having lost nearly all his army, returned to Epirus.[1] The Greek colonies, deprived of his help, were subjugated in rapid succession.

[1] Many romantic incidents are told of this war. As Pyrrhus walked over the battle-field and saw the Romans lying all with wounds in front, and their countenances stern in death, he cried out, "With such soldiers I could conquer the world!"— Cineas, whom Pyrrhus sent to Rome as an ambassador, returned, saying, "The city is like a temple of the gods, and the senate an assembly of kings." Fabricius, who came to Pyrrhus's camp on a similar mission, was a sturdy Roman, who worked his own farm, and loved integrity and honor more than aught else, save his country. The Grecian leader was surprised to find in this haughty barbarian that same greatness of soul that had once made the Hellenic character so famous. He offered him "more gold than Rome had ever possessed" if he would enter his service, but Fabricius replied that "poverty, with a good name, is better than wealth." Afterward the physician of Pyrrhus offered to poison the king; but the indignant Roman sent back the traitor in irons. Pyrrhus, not to be outdone in generosity, set free all his captives, saying that "it was easier to turn the sun from its course than Fabricius from the path of honor."— Dentatus, the consul who defeated Pyrrhus, was offered by the grateful senate a tract of land. He replied that he already had seven acres, and that was sufficient for any citizen.

Rome was now mistress of peninsular Italy. She was ready to begin her grand career of foreign conquest.

The Roman Government in Italy was that of one city supreme over many cities. Rome retained the rights of declaring war, making peace, and coining money, but permitted her subjects to manage their local affairs. All were required to furnish soldiers to fight under the eagles of Rome. There were three classes of inhabitants,—*Roman citizens, Latins,* and *Italians.* The Roman citizens were those who occupied the territory of Rome proper, including others upon whom this franchise had been bestowed. They had the right to meet in the Forum to enact laws, elect consuls, etc. The Latins had only a few of the rights of citizenship, and the Italians or allies none. As the power of Rome grew, Roman citizenship acquired a might and a meaning (Acts xxii. 25; xxiii. 27; xxv. 11–21) which made it eagerly sought by every person and city; and the prize constantly held out, as a reward for special service and devotion, was that the Italian could be made a Latin, and the Latin a Roman.

The Romans were famous road-builders, and the great national highways which they constructed throughout their territories did much to tie them together (p. 282). By their use Rome kept up constant communication with all parts of her possessions, and could quickly send her legions wherever wanted.

A portion of the land in each conquered state was given to Roman colonists. They became the patricians in the new city, the old inhabitants counting only as plebs. Thus little Romes were built all over Italy. The natives looked up to these settlers, and, hoping to obtain similar rights, quickly adopted their customs, institutions, and language. So the entire peninsula rapidly assumed a uniform **national character**.

THE PUNIC[1] WARS.

Carthage (p. 76) was now the great naval and colonizing power of the western Mediterranean. She had established some settlements in western Sicily, and these were almost constantly at war with the Greeks on the eastern coast. As Sicily lay between Carthage and Italy, it was natural that two such aggressive powers as the Carthaginians and the Romans should come to blows on that island.

First Punic War (264–241 B. C.).—Some pirates seized Messana, the nearest city to Italy, and, being threatened by the Carthaginians and the Syracusans, asked help of Rome, in order to retain their ill-gotten possessions. On this wretched pretext an army was sent into Sicily. The Carthaginians were driven back, and Hiero, king of Syracuse, was forced to make a treaty with Rome. Agrigentum, an important naval depot belonging to Carthage, was then captured, in spite of a large army of mercenary soldiers which the Carthaginians sent to its defense.

Rome's First Fleet (260 B. C.).[2]—The Roman senate, not content with this success, was bent on contesting with Carthage the supremacy of the sea. One hundred and thirty vessels were accordingly built in sixty days, a stranded Phœnician galley being taken as a model. To compensate the lack of skilled seamen, the ships were provided with drawbridges, so that coming at once to close quarters their disciplined soldiers could rush upon the enemies' deck, and decide the contest by a hand-to-hand fight. They thus beat

---

[1] From *punicus*, an adjective derived from Pœni, the Latin form of the word Phœnicians.

[2] The Romans began to construct a fleet as early as 338 B. C., and in 267 we read of the questors of the navy; but the vessels were small, and Rome was a land-power until 260 B. C.

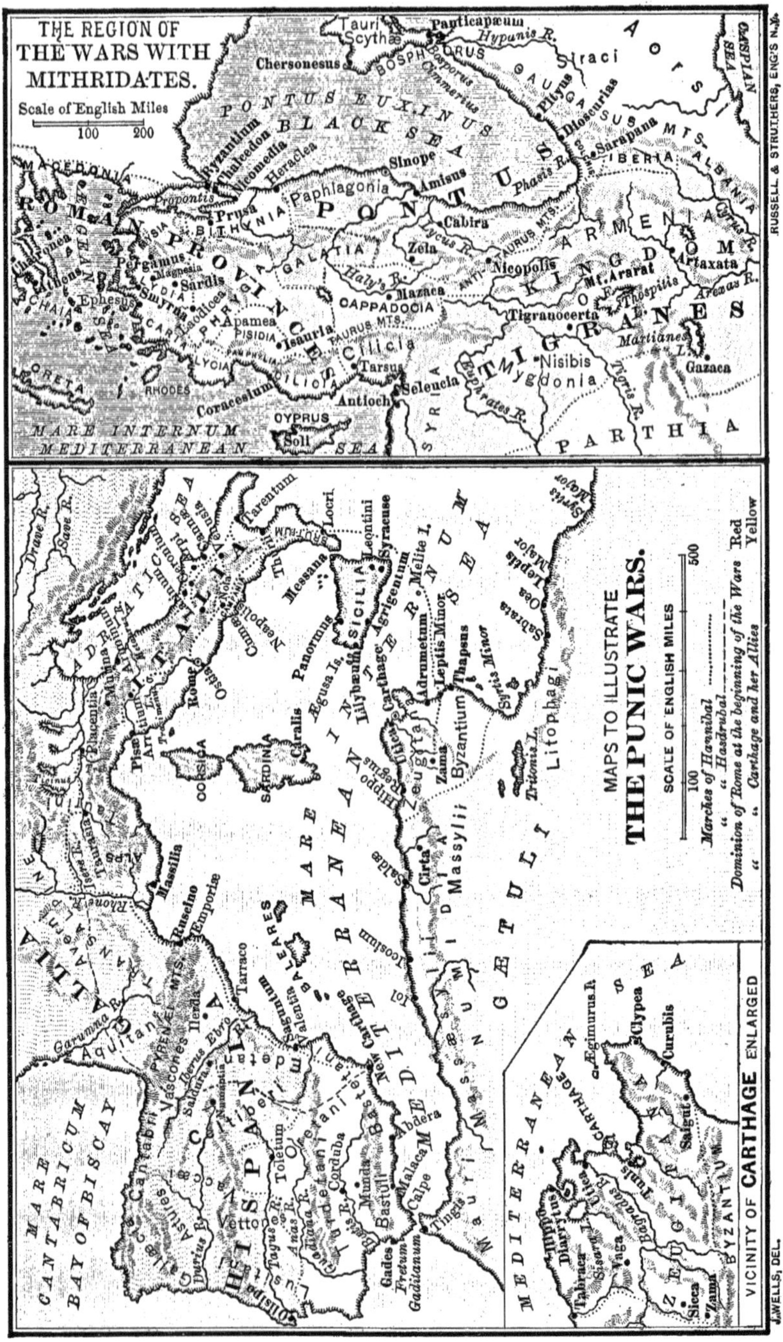
THE REGION OF THE WARS WITH MITHRIDATES.
Scale of English Miles
100 200
PONTUS EUXINUS
BLACK SEA
MARE INTERNUM
MEDITERRANEAN SEA
MAPS TO ILLUSTRATE
THE PUNIC WARS.
SCALE OF ENGLISH MILES
100 500
Marches of Hannibal
" Hasdrubal
Dominion of Rome at the beginning of the Wars Red
" " Carthage and her Allies Yellow
VICINITY OF CARTHAGE ENLARGED
MARE CANTABRICUM
BAY OF BISCAY
RUSSELL & STRUTHERS, ENG'S N.Y.
J.WELLS, DEL.

the Carthaginians in two great naval battles within four years.

Romans cross the Sea.—Under Regulus the Romans then crossed the Mediterranean, and "carried the war into Africa." The natives, weary of the oppressive rule of the Carthaginians, welcomed their deliverers. Carthage seemed about to fall, when the presence of one man turned the tide. Xanthippus, a Spartan general, led the Carthaginians to victory, destroyed the Roman army, and captured Regulus.[1]

After this the contest dragged on for several years; but a signal victory near *Panormus*, in Sicily, gave the Romans the ascendency in that island, and finally a great naval defeat off the Ægu'sæ Islands cost the Carthaginians the empire of the sea.

Effects.—Carthage was forced to give up Sicily, and pay thirty-two hundred talents of silver (about four million dollars) toward the war expenses. The Temple of Janus was shut for the first time since the days of Numa (p. 207).

Rome's First Province was Sicily. This was governed, like all the possessions which she afterward acquired outside of Italy, by magistrates sent each year from Rome. The people, being made not allies but subjects, were required to pay an annual tribute.

---

[1] It is said that Regulus, while at the height of his success, asked permission to return home to his little farm, as a slave had run away with the tools, and his family was likely to suffer with want during his absence. After his capture, the Carthaginians sent him to Rome with proposals of peace, making him swear to return in case the conditions were not accepted. On his arrival, he refused to enter the city, saying that he was no longer a Roman citizen, but only a Carthaginian slave. Having stated the terms of the proposed peace, to the amazement of all, he urged their rejection as unworthy of the glory and honor of Rome. Then, without visiting his home, he turned away from weeping wife and children, and went back to his prison again. The enraged Carthaginians cut off his eyelids, and exposed him to the burning rays of a tropic sun, and then thrust him into a barrel studded with sharp nails. So perished this martyr to his word and his country.—Historic research throws doubt on the truth of this instance of Punic cruelty, and asserts that the story was invented to excuse the barbarity with which the wife of Regulus treated some Carthaginian captives who fell into her hands; but the name of Regulus lives as the personification of sincerity and patriotic devotion.

Second Punic War (218–201 B. C.).—During the ensuing peace of twenty-three years, Hamilcar (surnamed Barca, lightning), the great statesman and general of Carthage, built up an empire in southern Spain, and trained an army for a new struggle with Rome. He hated that city with a perfect hatred. When he left home for Spain, he took with him his son Hannibal, a boy nine years old, having first made him swear at the altar of Baal always to be the enemy of the Romans. That youthful oath was never forgotten, and Hannibal, like his father, had but one purpose,—to humble his country's rival. When twenty-six years of age, he was made commander-in-chief of the Carthaginian army. Pushing the Punic power northward, he captured *Saguntum*. As that city was her ally, Rome promptly declared war against Carthage.[1] On the receipt of this welcome news, Hannibal, with the daring of genius, resolved to scale the Alps, and carry the contest into Italy.

Invasion of Italy.—In the spring of the year 218 B. C. he set out[2] from New Carthage. Through hostile tribes, over the swift Rhone, he pressed forward to the foot of the Alps. Here dangers multiplied. The mountaineers rolled down rocks upon his column, as it wearily toiled up the steep ascent. Snow blocked the way. At times the crack of a whip would bring down an avalanche from the impending heights. The men and horses slipped on the sloping ice-fields, and slid over the precipices into the awful crevasses. New roads had to be cut through the solid rock by hands benumbed with

---

[1] An embassy came to Carthage demanding that Hannibal should be surrendered. This being refused, M. Fabius, folding up his toga as if it contained something, exclaimed, "I bring you peace or war; take which you will!" The Carthaginians answered, "Give us which you wish!" Shaking open his toga, the Roman haughtily replied, "I give you war!"—"So let it be!" shouted the assembly.

[2] Before starting on this expedition, Hannibal went with his immediate attendants to Gades, and offered sacrifice in the temples for the success of the great work to which he had been dedicated eighteen years before, and to which he had been looking forward so long.

cold, and weakened by scanty rations. When at last he reached the smiling plains of Italy, only twenty-six thousand men were left of the one hundred and two thousand with whom he began the perilous march five months before.

HANNIBAL CROSSING THE ALPS.

Battles of Tre'bia, Trasime'nus, and Can- næ.—Arriving at the river *Trebia* in December, Hannibal found the Romans, under Sempronius, ready to dispute his progress. One stormy morning, he sent the light Numidian cavalry over to make a feigned attack on the enemy's camp. The Romans fell into the snare, and pursued the horsemen back across the river. When the legions, stiff with cold and faint with hunger, emerged from the icy waters, they found the Carthaginian army drawn up to receive them. Undismayed by the sight, they at once joined battle; but, in the midst of the struggle, Hannibal's brother Mago fell upon their rear with a body of men that had been hidden in a reedy ravine near by. The Romans, panic-stricken, broke and fled.

The fierce Gauls now flocked to Hannibal's camp, and remained his active allies during the rest of the war.

The next year Hannibal moved southward.[1] One day in June, the consul Flaminius was eagerly pursuing him along the banks of *Lake Trasimenus*. Suddenly, through the mist, the Carthaginians poured down from the heights, and put the Romans to rout.[2]

Fabius was now appointed dictator. Keeping on the heights where he could not be attacked, he followed Hannibal everywhere,[3] cutting off his supplies, but never hazarding a battle. The Romans became impatient at seeing their country ravaged while their army remained inactive, and Varro, the consul, offered battle on the plain of *Cannæ*. Hannibal drew up the Carthaginians in the shape of a half-moon having the convex side toward the enemy, and tipped

---

[1] In the low flooded grounds along the Arno the army suffered fearfully. Hannibal himself lost an eye by inflammation, and tradition says that his life was saved by the last remaining elephant, which carried him out of the swamp.

[2] So fierce was this struggle that none of the combatants noticed the shock of a severe earthquake which occurred in the midst of the battle.

[3] While Hannibal was ravaging the rich plains of Campania, the wary Fabius seized the passes of the Apennines, through which Hannibal must recross into Samnium with his booty. The Carthaginian was apparently caught in the trap. But his mind was fertile in devices. He fastened torches to the horns of two thousand oxen, and sent men to drive them up the neighboring heights. The Romans at the defiles, thinking the Carthaginians were trying to escape over the hills, ran to the defense. Hannibal quickly seized the passes, and marched through with his army.

the horns of the crescent with his veteran cavalry. The massive legions quickly broke through his weak center. But as they pressed forward in eager pursuit, his terrible horsemen fell upon their rear. Hemmed in on all sides, the Romans could neither fight nor flee. Twenty-one tribunes, eighty senators, and over seventy thousand men, fell in that horrible massacre. After the battle, Hannibal sent to Carthage over a peck of gold rings,—the ornaments of Roman knights. At Rome all was dismay. "One fifth of the citizens able to bear arms had fallen within eighteen months, and in every house there was mourning." All southern Italy, including Capua, the city next in importance to the capital, joined Hannibal.

Hannibal's Reverses.—The tide of Hannibal's victories, however, ebbed from this time. The Roman spirit rose in the hour of peril, and, while struggling at home for existence, the senate sent armies into Sicily, Greece, and Spain. The Latin cities remained true, not one revolting to the Carthaginians. The Roman generals had learned not to fight in the open field, where Hannibal's cavalry and genius were so fatal to them, but to keep behind walls, since Hannibal had no skill in sieges, and his army was too small to take their strongholds. Hannibal's brother Hasdrubal was busy fighting the Romans in Spain, and could send him no aid. The Carthaginians also were chary of Hannibal, and refused him help.

For thirteen years longer Hannibal remained in Italy, but he was at last driven into Brutium,—the toe of the Italian boot. Never did his genius shine more brightly. He continually sallied out to protect his allies, or to plunder and devastate. Once he went so near Rome that he hurled a javelin over its walls. Nevertheless, and in spite of his efforts, Capua was retaken. Syracuse promised aid, but was captured by the Roman army.[1] Hasdrubal finally managed to get out of Spain and cross the Alps, but at the *Metaurus*[2] (207 B. C.) he was routed and slain. The first notice Hannibal had of his brother's approach was when Hasdrubal's head was thrown into the Carthaginian camp. At the sight of this ghastly memorial, Hannibal exclaimed, "Ah, Carthage, I behold thy doom!"

Hannibal Recalled.—P. Scipio, who had already expelled the Carthaginians from Spain, now carried the war into Africa. Carthage was forced to summon her great general from Italy. He came to her defense, but met the first defeat of his life in the decisive battle of *Zama*. On that fatal field the veterans of the Italian wars fell, and Hannibal himself gave up the struggle. Peace was granted Carthage on her paying a crushing tribute, and agreeing not to go to war without the permission of Rome. Scipio received the name Africanus, in honor of his triumph.

Fate of Hannibal.—On the return of peace, Hannibal, with singular wisdom, began the reformation of his native city. But his enemies, by false representations at Rome, compelled him to quit Carthage, and take refuge at the court of Anti'ochus (p. 237). When at length his patron was at the feet of their common enemy, and no longer able to protect him, Hannibal fled to Bithynia, where, finding himself still pursued by the vindictive Romans, he ended his

---

[1] The siege of Syracuse (214-212 B. C.) is famous for the genius displayed in its defense by the mathematician Archimedes. He is said to have fired the Roman fleet by means of immense burning-glasses, and to have contrived machines that, reaching huge arms over the walls, grasped and overturned the galleys. The Romans became so timid that they would "flee at the sight of a stick thrust out at them." When the city was finally taken by storm, Marcellus gave orders to spare Archimedes. But a soldier, rushing into the philosopher's study, found an old man, who, ignoring his drawn sword, bade him "Noli turbare circulos meos" (Do not disturb my circles). Enraged by his indifference, the Roman slew him on the spot.

[2] This engagement, which decided the issue of Hannibal's invasion of Italy, is reckoned among the most important in the history of the world (see Creasy's Fifteen Decisive Battles, p. 96).

days by taking poison, which he had carried about with him in a hollow ring.

Third Punic War (149–146 B. C.).—Half a century passed, during which Carthage was slowly recovering her former prosperity. A strong party at Rome, however, was bent upon her destruction.[1] On a slight pretense war was again declared. The submission of the Carthaginians was abject. They gave up three hundred hostages, and surrendered their arms and armor. But when bidden to leave the city that it might be razed, they were driven to desperation. Old and young toiled at the forges to make new weapons. Vases of gold and silver, even the statues of the gods, were melted. The women braided their long hair into bow-strings. The Romans intrusted the siege to the younger Scipio.[2] He captured Carthage after a desperate struggle. Days of conflagration and plunder followed. The city, which had lasted over seven hundred years and numbered seven hundred thousand inhabitants, was utterly wasted. The Carthaginian territory was turned into the province of Africa.[3]

---

[1] Prominent among these was *Cato the Censor*. This rough, stern man, with his red hair, projecting teeth, and coarse robe, was the sworn foe to luxury, and the personification of the old Roman character. Cruel toward his slaves and revengeful toward his foes, he was yet rigid in morals, devoted to his country, and fearless in punishing crime. In the discharge of his duty as censor, rich furniture, jewels, and costly attire fell under his ban. He even removed, it is said, the cold-water pipes leading to the private houses. Jealous of any rival to Rome, he finished every speech with the words, "Delenda est Carthago!" (Carthage must be destroyed!) In Plutarch's *Lives* (p. 177), Cato is the counterpart of Aristides (p. 128).

[2] (1) *Publius Cornelius Scipio Africanus Major* (p. 234) was the conqueror of Hannibal. (2) *Publius Cornelius Scipio Æmilianus Africanus Minor*, the one spoken of in the text as the Destroyer of Carthage, was the son of *Lucius Æmilius Paullus*, the conqueror of Macedon (p. 236); he was adopted by P. Scipio, the son of Africanus Major. (3) *Lucius Cornelius Scipio Asiaticus*, who defeated Antiochus (p. 237), and hence received his last title, was the brother of Africanus Major.

[3] When Scipio beheld the ruin of Carthage, he is said to have burst into tears, and, turning to Polybius the historian, to have quoted the lines of Homer,—

"The day will come when Troy shall sink in fire,
And Priam's people with himself expire,"—

and, reflecting on the mutations of time, to have declared that Hector's words might yet prove true of Rome herself.

Rome was at last victor over her great rival. Events had decided that Europe was not to be given over to Punic civilization and the intellectual despotism of the East.

Wars in Macedon and Greece.—While Hannibal was hard-pressed in Italy he made a treaty with Philip, king of Macedon, and a descendant of Alexander. In the *First War* which ensued (214–207 B. C.), not much of importance occurred, but Rome had begun to mix in Grecian affairs, which, according to her wont, meant conquest by and by.

The Second War (200–197 B. C.) was brought about by Philip attacking the Roman allies. The consul Flaminius now entered Greece, proclaiming himself the champion of Hellenic liberty. Transported with this thought, nearly all Hellas ranged itself under the eagles (p. 257) of Rome. Philip was overthrown at the battle of *Cynoscephalæ* (197 B. C.), and forced to accept a most degrading peace.

After Philip's death, his son Perseus was indefatigable in his efforts to restore Macedon to its old-time glory.

The Third War (171–168 B. C.) culminated in the battle of *Pydna*, where the famous Roman general Paullus vanquished forever the cumbersome phalanx, and ended the Macedonian monarchy. One hundred and fifty-six years after Alexander's death, the last king of Macedon was led in triumph by a general belonging to a nation of which, probably, the Conqueror had scarcely heard.

The Results of these wars were reaped within a brief period. The Federal Unions of Greece were dissolved. Macedon was divided into four commonwealths, and finally, under pretense of a rebellion, made a Roman province (146 B. C.). In the same year that Carthage fell, Corinth,[1] the great seaport

---

[1] Mummius, the consul who took Corinth, which Cicero termed "The eye of Hellas," sent its wealth of statues and pictures to Rome. It is said, that, ignorant of the unique value of these works of art, he agreed with the captains of the vessels to furnish others in place of any they should lose on the voyage. One can but remem-

of the eastern Mediterranean, was sacked, and Greece herself, after being amused for a time with the semblance of freedom, was organized into the province of ACHAIA.

Syrian War (192-190 B. C.).—"Macedon and Greece proved easy stepping-stones for Rome to meddle in the affairs of Asia." At this time Antiochus the Great governed the kingdom of the Seleucidæ (p. 155), which extended from the Ægean beyond the Tigris. His capital, Antioch, on the Orontes, was the seat of Greek culture, and one of the chief cities of the world. He was not unwilling to measure swords with the Romans, and received Hannibal at his court with marked honor. During the interval between the second and third Macedonian wars the Ætolians, thinking themselves badly used by the Romans, invited Antiochus to come over to their help. He despised the wise counsel and military skill of Hannibal, and, appearing in Greece with only ten thousand men, was easily defeated by the Romans at *Thermopylæ*. The next year, L. Scipio (note, p. 235) followed him into Asia, and overthrew his power on the field of *Magnesia* (190 B. C.).

The great empire of the Seleucidæ now shrank to the kingdom of Syria. Though the Romans did not at present assume formal control of their conquest, yet, by a shrewd policy of weakening the powerful states, playing off small ones against one another, supporting one of the two rival factions, and favoring their allies, they taught the Greek cities in Asia Minor to look up to the great central power on the Tiber just as, by the same tortuous course, they had led Greece and Macedon to do. Thus the Romans aided Pergamus, and enlarged its territories, because its king helped them against Antiochus; and in return, when Attalus III.

ber, however, that this ignorant plebeian maintained his honesty, and kept none of the rich spoils for himself.

died, he bequeathed to them his kingdom. Rome thus acquired her first Asiatic province (133 B. C.).

War in Spain.—After the capture of Carthage and Corinth, Rome continued her efforts to subdue Spain. The rugged nature of the country, and the bravery of the inhabitants, made the struggle a doubtful one. The town of *Numantia* held out long against the younger Scipio (note, p. 235). Finally, in despair, the people set fire to the place, and threw themselves into the flames. When the Romans forced an entrance through the walls, they found silence and desolation within. Spain thus became a Roman province the same year that Attalus died, and thirteen years after the fall of Carthage and Corinth.

The Roman Empire (133 B. C.) now included southern Europe from the Atlantic to the Bosporus, and a part of northern Africa; while Syria, Egypt, and Asia Minor were practically its dependencies. The Mediterranean Sea was a "Roman lake," and *Rome was mistress of the civilized world.* Henceforth her wars were principally with barbarians.

Effect of these Conquests.—Italy had formerly been covered with little farms of a few acres each, which the industrious, frugal Romans cultivated with their own hands. When Hannibal swept the country with fire and sword, he destroyed these comfortable rural homes throughout entire districts. The people, unable to get a living, flocked to Rome. There, humored, flattered, and fed by every demagogue who wished their votes, they sank into a mere mob. The Roman race itself was fast becoming extinct.[1] It had

[1] "At the time when all the kings of the earth paid homage to the Romans, this people was becoming extinguished, consumed by the double action of eternal war, and of a devouring system of legislation; it was disappearing from Italy. The Roman, passing his life in camps, beyond the seas, rarely returned to visit his little field. He had in most cases, indeed, no land or shelter at all, nor any other domestic gods than the eagles of the legions. An exchange was becoming established between Italy and the provinces Italy sent her children to die in distant lands, and received in

perished on its hundred battle-fields. Rome was inhabited by a motley population from all lands, who poorly filled the place of her ancient heroes.

The captives in these various wars had been sold as slaves, and the nobles, who had secured most of the land, worked it by their unpaid labor. Everywhere in the fields were gangs of men whose only crime was that they had fought for their homes, tied together with chains; and tending the flocks were gaunt, shaggy wretches, carrying the goad in hands that had once wielded the sword.

The riches of Syracuse, Carthage, Macedonia, Greece, and Asia poured into Rome. Men who went to foreign wars as poor soldiers came back with enormous riches,—the spoils of sacked cities. The nobles were rich beyond every dream of republican Rome. But meanwhile the poor grew poorer yet, and the curse of poverty ate deeper into the state.

A few wealthy families governed the senate and filled all the offices. Thus a new nobility, founded on money alone, had grown up and become all-powerful. It was customary for a candidate to amuse the people with costly games, and none but the rich could afford the expense. The consul, at the end of his year of office, was usually appointed governor of a province, where, out of an oppressed people, he could recompense himself for all his losses. To keep the Roman populace in good humor, he would send back gifts of grain, and, if any complaint were made of his injustice and robbery, he could easily bribe the judges and senators, who were anxious only for the same chance which he had.

compensation millions of slaves. Thus a new people succeeded to the absent or destroyed Roman people. Slaves took the place of masters, proudly occupied the Forum, and in their fantastic saturnalia governed, by their decrees, the Latins and the Italians, who filled the legions. It was soon no longer a question where were the plebeians of Rome. They had left their bones on every shore. Camps, urns, and immortal roads,—these were all that remained of them."—*Michelet.*

240 ROME.

In the early days of the republic the soldier was a citizen who went forth to fight his country's battles, and, returning home, settled down again upon his little farm, contented and happy. Military life had now become a profession. Patriotism was almost a forgotten virtue, and the soldier fought for plunder and glory. In the wake of the army followed a crowd of venal traders, who bought up the booty; contractors, who "farmed" the revenues of the provinces; and usurers, who preyed on the necessities of all. These rich army-followers were known as knights (*equites*), since in the early days of Rome the richest men fought on horseback. They rarely took part in any war, but only reaped its advantages. The presents of foreign kings were no longer refused at Rome; her generals and statesmen demanded money wherever they went. Well might Scipio Africanus, instead of praying to the

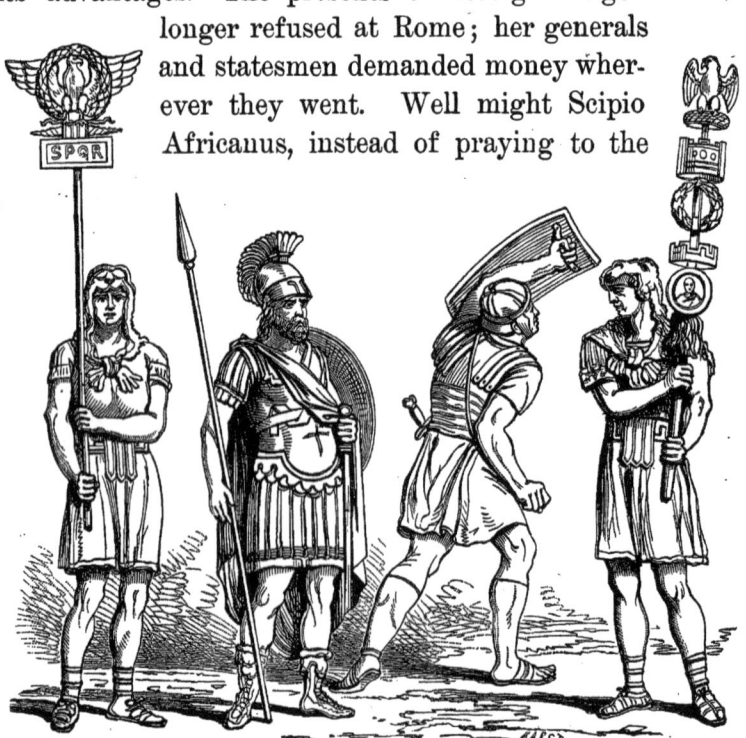

ROMAN SOLDIERS.

gods, as was the custom, to *increase* the state, implore them to *preserve* it.

In this general decadence the fine moral fiber of the nation lost its vigor. First the people left their own gods and took up foreign ones. As the ancients had no idea of one God for all nations, such a desertion of their patron deities was full of significance. It ended in a general skepticism and neglect of religious rites and worship. In addition, the Romans became cruel and unjust. Nothing showed this more clearly than their refusal to grant the Roman franchise to the Latin cities, which stood by them so faithfully during Hannibal's invasion. Yet there were great men in Rome, and the ensuing centuries were the palmiest of her history.

THE CIVIL WARS.

Now began a century of civil strife, during which the old respect for laws became weak, and parties obtained their end by bribery and bloodshed.

The Gracchi.—The tribune Tiberius Gracchus,[1] perceiving the peril of the state, secured a new agrarian law (p. 216), directing the public land to be assigned in small farms to the needy, so as to give every man a homestead; and, in addition, he proposed to divide the treasures of Attalus among those who received land, in order to enable them to build houses and buy cattle. But the oligarchs aroused a mob by which Gracchus was assassinated.

---

[1] Cornelia, the mother of Tiberius and Caius Gracchus, was the daughter of Scipio Africanus the Elder (note, p. 235). Left a widow, she was offered marriage with the king of Egypt, but preferred to devote herself to the education of her children. When a rich friend once exhibited to her a cabinet of rare gems, she called in her two sons, saying, "These are my jewels." Her statue bore the inscription by which she wished to be known, "The mother of the Gracchi."—Tiberius was the grandson of the Conqueror of Hannibal, the son-in-law of Appius Claudius, and the brother-in-law of the Destroyer of Carthage.

About ten years later his brother Caius tried to carry out the same reform by distributing grain to the poor at a nominal price (the "Roman poor-law"), by choosing juries from the knights instead of the senators, and by planting in conquered territories colonies of men who had no work at home. All went well until he sought to confer the Roman franchise upon the Latins. Then a riot was raised, and Caius was killed by a faithful slave to prevent his falling into the hands of his enemies.

With the Gracchi perished the freedom of the republic; henceforth the corrupt aristocracy was supreme.

Jugurtha (118–104 B. C.), having usurped the throne of Numidia, long maintained his place by conferring lavish bribes upon the senators. His gold conquered every army sent against him, and he declared that Rome itself could be had for money. He was finally overpowered by the consul Caius Marius,[1] and, after adorning the victor's triumph at Rome, was thrown into the Mamertine Prison to perish.[2]

The Cimbri and Teutones (113–101 B. C.), the vanguard of those northern hosts that were yet to overrun the empire, were now moving south, half a million strong, spreading dismay and ruin in their track. Six different Roman armies tried in vain to stay their advance. At Arausio alone eighty thousand Romans fell. In this emergency, the senate appealed to Marius, who, contrary to law, was again and again reinstated consul. He annihilated the Teutones at *Aquæ Sextiæ* (Aix); and, the next year, the Cimbri at *Vercellæ*, where the men composing the outer line of the

---

[1] Lucius Cornelius Sulla, the Roman questor (p. 243), captured Jugurtha by treachery. Claiming that he was the real hero of this war, he had a ring engraved which represented Jugurtha's surrender to him. Marius and Sulla were henceforth bitter rivals.

[2] This famous dungeon is still shown the traveler at Rome. It is an underground vault, built of rough stones. The only opening is by a hole at the top. As Jugurtha, accustomed to the heat of an African sun, was lowered into this dismal grave, he exclaimed, with chattering teeth, "Ah, what a cold bath they are giving me!"

barbarian army were fastened together with chains, the whole making a solid mass three miles square. The Roman broadsword mercilessly hewed its way through this struggling crowd. The Gallic women, in despair, strangled their children, and then threw themselves beneath the wheels of their wagons. The very dogs fought to the death.

Rome was saved in her second great peril from barbarians. Marius was hailed as the "third founder of the city."

Social War (90-88 B. C.).—Drusus, a tribune, having proposed that the Italians should be granted the coveted citizenship, was murdered the very day a vote was to be taken upon the measure. On hearing this, many of the Italian cities, headed by the Marsians, took up arms. The veteran legions, which had conquered the world, now faced each other on the battle-field. The struggle cost three hundred thousand lives. Houses were burned and plantations wasted as in Hannibal's time. In the end, Rome was forced to allow the Italians to become citizens.

First Mithridatic War (88-84 B. C.).—Just before the close of this bloody struggle, news came of the massacre of eighty thousand Romans and Italians residing in the towns of Asia Minor. Mithridates the Great, king of Pontus, and a man of remarkable energy and genius, had proclaimed himself the deliverer of Asia from the Roman yoke, and had kindled the fires of insurrection as far westward as Greece. The war against the Pontic monarch was confided to Sulla, who stood at the head of the Roman aristocracy. But Marius, the favorite leader of the people, by unscrupulous means wrested the command from his rival. Thereupon Sulla entered Rome at the head of the army. For the first time, civil war raged within the walls of the city. Marius was driven into exile.[1] Sulla then crossed into

---

[1] Marius, after many romantic adventures, was thrown into prison at Min

Greece. He carried on five campaigns, mainly at his private expense, and finally restored peace on the condition that Mithridates should give up his conquests and his fleet.

Return of Marius.—Meanwhile Cinna, one of the two consuls at Rome, recalled Marius, and together they entered the city with a body of men composed of the very dregs of Italy. The nobles and the friends of Sulla trembled at this triumph of the democracy. Marius now took a fearful vengeance for all he had suffered. He closed the gates, and went about with a body of slaves, who slaughtered every man at whom he pointed his finger. The principal senators were slain. The high priest of Jupiter was massacred at the altar. The consul Octavius was struck down in his curule-chair. The head of Antonius, the orator, was brought to Marius as he sat at supper; he received it with joy, and embraced the murderer. Finally the monster had himself declared consul, now the seventh time. Eighteen days after, he died, "drunk with blood and wine" (86 B. C.).

Sulla's Proscriptions.—Three years passed, when the hero of the Mithridatic war returned to Italy with his victorious army. His progress was disputed by the remains of the Marian party and the Samnites, who had not laid down their arms since the social war (p. 243). Sulla, however, swept aside their forces, and soon all Italy was prostrate before him. It was now the turn for the plebeians and the friends of Marius to fear. As Sulla met the senate, cries were heard in the neighboring circus. The senators sprang from their seats in alarm. Sulla bade them be quiet, remark-

turnæ. One day a Cimbrian slave entered his cell to put him to death. The old man turned upon him with flashing eye, and shouted, "Darest thou kill Caius Marius!" The Gaul, frightened at the voice of his nation's destroyer, dropped his sword and fled. Marius was soon set free by the sympathizing people, whereupon he crossed into Africa. Receiving there an order from the prætor to leave the province, he sent back the well-known reply, "Tell Sextilius that you have seen Caius Marius sitting in exile among the ruins of Carthage."

ing, "It is only some wretches undergoing the punishment they deserve." The "wretches" were six thousand of the Marian party, who were butchered in cold blood. "The porch of Sulla's house," says Collier, "was soon full of heads." Daily proscription-lists were made out of those doomed to die, and the assassins were rewarded from the property of their victims. Wealth became a crime when murder was gain. "Alas!" exclaimed one, "my villa is my destruction." In all the disaffected Italian cities the same bloody work went on. Whole districts were confiscated to make room for colonies of Sulla's legions. He had himself declared perpetual dictator,—an office idle since the Punic wars (p. 232). He deprived the tribunes of the right to propose laws, and sought to restore the "good old times" when the patricians held power, thus undoing the reforms of centuries. To the surprise of all, however, he suddenly retired to private life, and gave himself up to luxurious ease. The civil wars of Marius and Sulla had cost Italy the lives of one hundred and fifty thousand citizens.

Sertorius, one of the Marian party, betook himself to Spain, gained the respect and confidence of the Lusitanians, established among them a miniature Roman republic, and for seven years defeated every army sent against him. Even Pompey the Great was held in check. Treachery at last freed Rome from its enemy, Sertorius being slain at a banquet.

Gladiatorial War (73–71 B. C.).—A party of gladiators under Spartacus, having escaped from a training-school at Capua, took refuge in the crater of Vesuvius. Thither flocked slaves, peasants, and pirates. Soon they were strong enough to defeat consular armies, and for three years to ravage Italy from the Alps to the peninsula. Crassus finally, in a desperate battle, killed the rebel leader, and put his followers to flight. A body of five thousand, trying to escape into Gaul, fell in with Pompey the Great as he was returning from Spain, and were cut to pieces.[1]

Pirates in these troublous times infested the Mediterranean, so as to interfere with trade and stop the supply of provisions at Rome. The whole coast of Italy was in continual alarm. Parties of robbers landing dragged rich proprietors from their villas, and seized high officials, to hold them for ransom. Pompey, in a brilliant campaign of ninety days, cleared the seas of these buccaneers.

Great Mithridatic War (74-63 B. C.).—During Sulla's life the Roman governor in Asia causelessly attacked Mithridates, but being defeated, and Sulla peremptorily ordering him to desist, this *Second Mithridatic War* soon ceased. The *Third* or *Great War* broke out after the dictator's death. The king of Bithynia having bequeathed his possessions to the Romans, Mithridates justly dreaded this advance of his enemies toward his own boundaries, and took up arms to prevent it. The Roman consul, Lucullus, defeated the Pontic king, and drove him to the court of his son-in-law Tigranes, king of Armenia, who espoused his cause. Lucullus next overcame the allied monarchs. Meanwhile this wise general sought to reconcile the Asiatics to the Roman government by legislative reforms, by a mild and just rule, and especially by checking the oppressive taxation. The soldiers of his own army, intent on plunder, and the equites at Rome deprived of their profits, were incensed, and secured his recall.

Pompey was now granted the power of a dictator in the East.[2] He made an alliance with the king of Parthia, thus

---

[1] "Crassus," said Pompey, "defeated the enemy in battle, but I cut up the war by its roots."

[2] Cicero advocated this measure in the familiar oration, *Pro Lege Manilia.*

threatening Mithridates by an enemy in the rear. Then, forcing the Pontic monarch into a battle, he defeated him, and at last drove him beyond the Caucasus. Pompey, returning, reduced Syria, Phœnicia, and Palestine.

The spirit of Mithridates was unbroken, in spite of the loss of his kingdom. He was meditating a march around the Euxine, and an invasion of Italy from the northeast, when, alarmed at the treachery of his son, he took poison, and died a victim of ingratitude. By his genius and courage he had maintained the struggle with the Romans for twenty-five years.[1] On reaching Rome, Pompey received a two-days' triumph. Before his chariot walked three hundred and twenty-four captive princes; and twenty thousand talents were deposited in the treasury as the spoils of conquest. Pompey was now at the height of his popularity, and might have usurped supreme power, but he lacked the energy and determination.

Catiline's Conspiracy (63 B. C.).—During Pompey's absence at the East, Catiline, an abandoned young nobleman, had formed a widespread plot to murder the consuls, fire the city, and overthrow the government. Cicero, the orator, exposed the conspiracy;[2] whereupon Catiline fled, and was soon after slain, fighting at the head of a band of desperadoes.

The Chief Men of Rome now were Pompey, Crassus,

---

[1] The armor which fitted the gigantic frame of Mithridates excited the wonder alike of Asiatic and Italian. As a runner, he overtook the fleetest deer; as a rider, he broke the wildest steed; as a charioteer, he drove sixteen-in-hand; and as a hunter, he hit his game with his horse at full gallop. He kept Greek poets, historians, and philosophers at his court, and gave prizes not only to the greatest eater and drinker, but to the merriest jester and the best singer. He ruled the twenty-two nations of his realm without the aid of an interpreter. He experimented on poisons, and sought to harden his system to their effect. One day he disappeared from the palace and was absent for months. On his return, it appeared that he had wandered *incognito* through Asia Minor, studying the people and country.

[2] The orations which Cicero pronounced at this time against Catiline are masterpieces of impassioned rhetoric, and are still studied by every Latin scholar.

CAIUS JULIUS CÆSAR.

Cæsar,[1] Cicero, and Cato the Stoic,—a great-grandson of the Censor. The first three formed a league, known as the *Triumvirate* (60 B. C.). To cement this union, Pompey married Julia, Cæsar's only daughter. The triumvirs had everything their own way. Cæsar was head manager; he obtained the consulship, and afterward an appointment as governor of Gaul; Cicero was banished, and Cato sent to Cyprus.

---

[1] Cæsar was born 100 B. C. (according to Mommsen, 102 B. C.). A patrician, he was yet a friend of the people. His aunt was married to Marius; his wife Cornelia was the daughter of Cinna. During Sulla's proscription, he refused to divorce his wife at the bidding of the dictator, and only the intercession of powerful friends saved his life. Sulla detected the character of this youth of eighteen years, and declared, "There is more than one Marius hid in him." While on his way to Rhodes to study oratory, he was taken prisoner by pirates, but he acted more like their leader than captive, and, on being ransomed, headed a party which crucified them all. Having been elected pontiff during his absence at the East, he returned to Rome. He now became in succession quæstor, ædile, and pontifex maximus. His affable manners and boundless generosity won all hearts. As ædile, a part of his duty was to furnish amusement to the people, and he exhibited three hundred and twenty pairs of gladiators, clad in silver armor. His debts became enormous, the heaviest creditor being the rich Crassus, to whom half the senators are said to have owed money. Securing an appointment as prætor, at the termination of that office, according to the custom, he obtained a province. Selecting Spain, he there recruited his wasted fortune, and gained some military prominence. He then came back to Rome, relinquishing a triumph in order to enter the city and stand for the consulship. This gained, his next step was to secure a field where he could train an army, by whose help he might become master of Rome.

It is a strange sight, indeed, to witness this spendthrift, pale and worn with the excesses of the capital, fighting at the head of his legions, swimming rivers, plunging through morasses, and climbing mountains,—the hardiest of the hardy, and the bravest of the brave. But it is stranger still to think of this great general and statesman as a literary man. Even when riding in his litter or resting, he was still reading or writing, and often at the same time dictating to from four to seven amanuenses. Besides his famous Commentaries, published in the very midst of his eventful career, he composed works on rhetoric and grammar, as well as tragedies, lyrics, etc. His style is pure and natural, and the polished smoothness of his sentences gives no hint of the stormy scenes amid which they were formed.

CÆSAR remained in Gaul about nine years. He reduced the entire country; crossed the Rhine, carrying the Roman arms into Germany for the first time; and twice invaded Britain, —an island until then unknown in Italy except by name. Not only were the three hundred tribes of Transalpine Gaul thoroughly subdued, but they were made content with Cæsar's rule. He became their civilizer,—building roads and introducing Roman laws, institutions, manners, and customs. Moreover, he trained an army that knew no mind or will except that of its great general. Meanwhile, Cæsar's friends in Rome, with the Gallic spoils which he freely sent them, bribed and dazzled and intrigued to sustain their master's power, and secure him the next consulship.

CRASSUS was chosen joint consul with Pompey (56 B. C.); he secured the province of Syria. Eager to obtain the boundless treasures of the East, he set out upon an expedition against Parthia. On the way he plundered the temple at Jerusalem. While crossing the scorching plains beyond the Euphrates, not far from Carrhæ (the Harran of the Bible), he was suddenly surrounded by clouds of Parthian horsemen. Roman valor was of no avail in that ceaseless storm of arrows. During the retreat, Crassus was slain. His head was carried to the Parthian king, who, in derision, ordered it to be filled with molten gold. The death of Crassus ended the Triumvirate.

POMPEY, after a time, was elected joint consul with Crassus, and, later, sole consul; he obtained the province of Spain, which he governed by legates. He now ruled Rome, and was bent on ruling the empire. The death of his wife had severed the link which bound him to the conqueror of Gaul. He accordingly joined with the nobles, who were also alarmed by Cæsar's brilliant victories, and the strength his success gave the popular party. A law was therefore passed ordering Cæsar to resign his office and disband his army before he appeared to sue for the consulship. The tribunes,—Antony and Cassius,— who supported Cæsar, were driven from the senate. They fled to Cæsar's camp, and demanded protection.

Civil War between Cæsar and Pompey (49 B. C.).—

Cæsar at once marched upon Rome. Pompey had boasted that he had only to stamp his foot, and an army would spring from the ground; but he now fled to Greece without striking a blow. In sixty days Cæsar was master of Italy. The decisive struggle between the two rivals took place on the plain of *Pharsalia* (48 B. C.). Pompey was beaten. He sought refuge in Egypt, where he was treacherously slain. His head being brought to Cæsar, the conqueror wept at the fate of his former friend.

Cæsar now placed the beautiful Cleopatra on the throne of the Ptolemies, and, marching into Syria, humbled Pharnaces, the son of Mithridates, so quickly that he could write home this laconic dispatch, *Veni, Vidi, Vici* (I came, I saw, I conquered). Cato and other Pompeian leaders had assembled a great force in Africa, whereupon Cæsar hurried his conquering legions thither, and at *Thapsus* broke down all opposition (46 B. C.). Cato, in despair of the republic, fell upon his sword.

Cæsar now returned to Rome to celebrate his triumphs. The sands of the arena were reddened with the blood of wild beasts and gladiators; every citizen received a present, and a public banquet was spread on twenty-two thousand tables. The adulation of the senate surpassed all bounds. Cæsar was created dictator for ten years and censor for three, and his statue was placed in the Capitol, opposite to that of Jupiter. Meantime the sons of Pompey had rallied an army in Spain, whither Cæsar hastened, and, in a desperate conflict at *Munda* (45 B. C.), blotted their party out of existence. He then returned to new honors and a campaign of civil reforms.

Cæsar's Government.—At Cæsar's magic touch, order and justice sprang into new life. The provinces rejoiced in an honest administration. The Gauls obtained seats in the senate, and it was Cæsar's design to have all the provinces represented in that body by their chief men. The calendar was revised.[1] The distress among the poor was relieved by sending eighty thousand colonists to rebuild Corinth and Carthage. The number of claimants upon the public distribution of grain was reduced over one half. A plan was formed to dig a new channel for the Tiber and to drain the Pontine marshes. Nothing was too vast or too small for the comprehensive mind of this mighty statesman. He could guard the boundaries of his vast empire along the Rhine, Danube, and Euphrates; look after the paving of the

---

[1] The Roman year contained only three hundred and fifty-five days, and the midsummer and the mid-winter months then came in the spring and the fall. Julius Cæsar introduced the extra day of leap year, and July was named after him (see Steele's New Astronomy, p. 269).

Roman streets; and listen to the recitation of pieces for prizes at the theaters, bestowing the wreath upon the victor with extempore verse.

Cæsar's Assassination (44 B. C.).— Cæsar, now dictator for life, was desirous of being king in name, as in fact. While passing through the streets one day, he was hailed king; as the crowd murmured, he cried out, "I am not king, but Cæsar." Still, when Mark Antony, the consul and his intimate friend, at a festival, offered him a crown, Cæsar seemed to thrust it aside reluctantly. The ire of zealous republicans was excited, and, under the guise of a love of liberty and old Roman virtue, those who were jealous of Cæsar or who hated him formed a conspiracy for his assassination. Brutus and Cassius, the leaders, chose the fifteenth of the ensuing March for the execution of the deed. As the day approached, the air was thick with rumors of approaching disaster. A famous augur warned Cæsar to beware of the Ides[1] of March. The night before, his wife, Calpurnia, was disturbed by an ominous dream. On the way to the senate-house he was handed a scroll containing the details of the plot, but in the press he had no chance to read it. When the conspirators crowded about him, no alarm was caused, as they were men who owed their lives to his leniency, and their fortunes to his favor.

THE ROMAN EMBLEM.[2]

---

[1] In the Roman calendar the months were divided into three parts,—*Calends, Ides,* and *Nones*. The Calends commenced on the first of each month, and were reckoned backward into the preceding month to the Ides. The Nones fell on the seventh of March, May, July, and October, and on the fifth of the other months. The Ides came on the thirteenth of all months except these four, when they were the fifteenth.

[2] S. P. Q. R.,—Senatus Populusque Romanus (the Senate and Roman People).

Suddenly swords gleamed on every hand. For a moment the great soldier defended himself with the sharp point of his iron pen. Then, catching sight of the loved and trusted Brutus, he exclaimed, "Et tu, Brute!" (And thou, too, Brutus!) and, wrapping his mantle about his face, sank dead at the foot of Pompey's statue.[1]

The Result was very different from what the assassins had expected. The senate rushed out horror-stricken at the deed. The reading of Cæsar's will, in which he gave every citizen three hundred sesterces (over ten dollars), and threw open his splendid gardens across the Tiber as a public park, roused the popular fury. When Antony pronounced the funeral eulogy, and finally held up Cæsar's rent and bloody toga, the mob broke through every restraint, and ran with torches to burn the houses of the murderers. Brutus and Cassius fled to save their lives.

Second Triumvirate (43 B. C.).—Antony was fast getting power into his hand, when there arrived at Rome Octavius, Cæsar's great-nephew and heir. He received the support of the senate and of Cicero, who denounced Antony in fiery orations. Antony was forced into exile, and then, twice defeated in battle, took refuge with

---

[1] Cæsar's brief public life—for only five stirring years elapsed from his entrance into Italy to his assassination—was full of dramatic scenes. Before marching upon Rome, it is said (though research stamps it as doubtful) that he stopped at the Rubicon, the boundary between his province of Cisalpine Gaul and Italy, and hesitated long. To pass it was to make war upon the republic. At last he shouted, "The die is cast!" and plunged into the stream.—When he had crossed into Greece in pursuit of Pompey, he became impatient at Antony's delay in bringing over the rest of the army, and, disguising himself, attempted to return across the Adriatic in a small boat. The sea ran high, and the crew determined to put back, when Cæsar shouted, "Go on boldly, fear nothing, thou bearest Cæsar and his fortune!"—At the battle of Pharsalia, he ordered his men to aim at the faces of Pompey's cavalry. The Roman knights, dismayed at this attack on their beauty, quickly fled; after the victory Cæsar rode over the field, calling upon the men to spare the Roman citizens, and on reaching Pompey's tent put his letters in the fire unread.—When Cæsar learned of the death of Cato, he lamented the tragic fate of such high integrity and virtue, and exclaimed, "Cato, I envy thee thy death, since thou enviest me the glory of saving thy life!"

Lepidus, governor of a part of Spain and Gaul. Octavius returned to Rome, won the favor of the people, and, though a youth of only nineteen, was chosen consul. A triumvirate, similar to the one seventeen years before, was now formed between Antony, Octavius, and Lepidus. The bargain was sealed by a proscription more horrible than that of Sulla. Lepidus sacrificed his brother, Antony his uncle, and Octavius his warm supporter, Cicero. The orator's head having been brought to Rome, Fulvia thrust her golden bodkin through the tongue that had pronounced the Philippics against her husband Antony.

Battle of Philippi (42 B. C.).—Brutus and Cassius, who had gone to the East, raised an army to resist this new coalition. The triumvirs pursued them, and the issue was decided on the field of *Philippi*. Brutus[1] and Cassius were defeated, and in despair committed suicide. Octavius and Antony divided the empire between them, the former taking the West, and the latter the East. Lepidus received Africa, but was soon stripped of his share and sent back to Rome.

Antony and Cleopatra.—Antony now went to Tarsus to look after his new possessions. Here Cleopatra was summoned to answer for having supported Cassius against the triumvirs. She came, captivated Antony by her charms,[2]

---

[1] Brutus, before this battle, was disheartened. The triumvirs had proved worse tyrants than he could ever have feared Cæsar would become. He and Cassius quarreled bitterly. His wife, Portia, had died (according to some authorities) brokenhearted at the calamities which had befallen her country. One night, as he was sitting alone in his tent, musing over the troubled state of affairs, he suddenly perceived a gigantic figure standing before him. He was startled, but exclaimed, "What art thou, and for what purpose art thou come?"—"I am thine evil genius," replied the phantom; "we shall meet again at Philippi!"

[2] Cleopatra ascended the Cydnus in a galley with purple sails. The oars, inlaid with silver, moved to the soft music of flute and pipe. She reclined under a gold-spangled canopy, attired as Venus, and attended by nymphs, cupids, and graces. The air was redolent with perfumes. As she approached Tarsus, the whole city flocked to witness the magnificent sight, leaving Antony sitting alone in the tribunal.

and carried him to Egypt. They passed the winter in the wildest extravagance. Breaking away for a time from the silken chains of Cleopatra, Antony, upon the death of Fulvia, married the beautiful and noble Octavia, sister of Octavius. But at the first opportunity he went back again to Alexandria, where he laid aside the dignity of a Roman citizen and assumed the dress of an Egyptian monarch.[1] Cleopatra was presented with several provinces, and became the real ruler of the East.

Civil War between Octavius and Antony (31 B.C.). —The senate at last declared war against Cleopatra. Thereupon Antony divorced Octavia and prepared to invade Italy. The rival fleets met off the promontory of *Ac'tium*. Cleopatra fled with her ships early in the day. Antony, basely deserting those who were dying for his cause, followed her. When Octavius entered Egypt (30 B.C.), there was no resistance. Antony, in despair, stabbed himself. Cleopatra in vain tried her arts of fascination upon the conqueror. Finally, to avoid gracing his triumph at Rome, she put an end to her life, according to the common story, by the bite of an asp, brought her in a basket of figs. Thus died the last of the Ptolemies.

Result.—Egypt now became a province of Rome. With the battle of Actium ended the Roman republic. Cæsar Octavius was the undisputed master of the civilized world. After his return to Italy, he received the title of Augustus, by which name he is known in history. The civil wars were over.

---

[1] The follies and wasteful extravagance of their mad revels at Alexandria almost surpass belief. One day, in Antony's kitchen, there are said to have been eight wild boars roasting whole, so arranged as to be ready at different times, that his dinner might be served in perfection whenever he should see fit to order it. On another occasion he and the queen vied as to which could serve the more expensive banquet. Removing a magnificent pearl from her ear, she dissolved it in vinegar, and swallowed the priceless draught.

IMPERIAL ROME.

Establishment of the Empire.—After the clamor of a hundred years, a sweet silence seemed to fall upon the earth. The Temple of Janus was closed for the second time since the pious Numa. Warned by the fate of Julius, Augustus did not take the name of king, nor startle the Roman prejudices by any sudden seizure of authority. He kept up all the forms of the republic. Every ten years he went through the farce of laying down his rank as chief of the army, or *imperator*,—a word since contracted to emperor. He professed himself the humble servant of the senate, while he really exercised absolute power. Gradually all the offices of trust were centered in him. He became at once proconsul, consul, censor, tribune, and high priest.[1]

Massacre of Varus (9 A. D.).—Germany, under the vigorous rule of Drusus and Tiberius, step-sons of Augustus, now seemed likely to become as thoroughly Romanized as Gaul had been (Brief Hist. France, p. 11). Varus, governor of the province, thinking the conquest complete, attempted to introduce the Latin language and laws. Thereupon Arminius, a noble, freedom-loving German, aroused his countrymen, and in the wilds of the Teutoburg Forest took a terrible revenge for the wrongs they had suffered. Varus and his entire army perished.[2] Dire was the dismay at Rome when news came of this disaster. For days Augustus wandered through his palace, beating his head against the wall, and crying, "Varus, give me back my legions!" Six years later the whitened bones of these hapless warriors were buried by Germanicus, the gifted son of Drusus, who in vain endeavored to restore the Roman authority in Germany.

The Augustan Age (31 B. C.–14 A. D.) was, however, one of general peace and prosperity. The emperor lived unos-

---

[1] As consul, he became chief magistrate; as censor, he could decide who were to be senators; as tribune, he heard appeals, and his person was sacred; as imperator, he commanded the army; and as pontifex maximus, or chief priest, he was the head of the national religion. These were powers originally belonging to the king, but which, during the republic, from a fear of centralization, had been distributed among different persons. Now the emperor gathered them up again.

[2] Creasy reckons this among the fifteen decisive battles of the world. "Had Arminius been defeated," says Arnold, " our German ancestors would have been enslaved or exterminated, and the great English nation would have been struck out of existence."

tentatiously in his house, not in a palace, and his toga was woven by his wife Livia and her maidens. He revived the worship of the gods. His chosen friends were men of letters. He beautified Rome, so that he could truly boast that he "found the city of brick, and left it of marble." There was now no fear of pirates or hostile fleets, and grain came in plenty from Egypt. The people were amused and fed; hence they were contented. The provinces were well governed,[1] and many gained Roman citizenship. A single language became a universal bond of intercourse, and Rome began her work of civilization and education. Wars having so nearly ceased, and interest in politics having diminished, men turned their thoughts more toward literature, art, and religion.

The Birth of Christ, the central figure in all history, occurred during the widespread peace of this reign.

The Empire was, in general, bounded by the Euphrates on the east, the Danube and the Rhine on the north, the Atlantic Ocean on the west, and the deserts of Africa on the south. It comprised about a hundred millions of people, of perhaps a hundred different nations, each speaking its own language and worshiping its own gods. An army of three hundred and fifty thousand men held the provinces in check, while the Prætorian Guard of ten thousand protected the person of the emperor. The Mediterranean, which the Romans proudly called "our own sea," served as a natural highway between the widely sundered parts of this vast region, while the Roman roads, straight as an eagle's flight, bound every portion of the empire to its center. Everywhere the emperor's will was law. His smile or frown was

---

[1] One day when Augustus was sailing in the Bay of Baiæ, a Greek ship was passing. The sailors, perceiving the emperor, stopped their vessel, arrayed themselves in white robes, and, going on board his yacht, offered sacrifice to him as a god, saying, "You have given to us happiness. You have secured to us our lives and our goods."

the fortune or ruin of a man, a city, or a province. His character determined the prosperity of the empire.

He lived to be seventy-six years old, having reigned forty-four years. At his death [1] the senate decreed that divine honors should be given him, and temples were erected for his worship. From him the month August was named.

Henceforth the history of Rome is not that of the people, but of its emperors. Of these, forty-two were murdered, three committed suicide, and two were forced to abdicate the throne.[2] None of the early emperors was followed by his own son, but, according to the Roman law of adoption, they all counted as Cæsars. Nero was the last of them at all connected with Augustus, even by adoption, though the emperors called themselves Cæsar and Augustus to the last. After the death of Augustus,

COIN OF TIBERIUS CÆSAR.

Tiberius (14 A. D.), his step-son, secured the empire by a decree of the senate. The army on the Rhine would have

---

[1] The domestic life of Augustus was not altogether happy. He suffered greatly from the imperious disposition of Livia,—his fourth wife,—whom, however, he loved too dearly to coerce; from his step-son Tiberius, whose turbulence he was forced to check by sending him in exile to Rhodes; and still more keenly from the immoral conduct of his daughter Julia, whom, with her mother, Scribonia, he was also compelled to banish.

[2] In the following pages a brief account is given of the principal monarchs only; a full list of the emperors may be found on p. 311.

gladly given the throne to the noble Germanicus, but he declined the honor. Jealous of this kinsman, Tiberius, it is thought, afterward removed him by poison. The new emperor ruled for a time with much ability, yet soon proved to be a gloomy tyrant,[1] and finally retired to the Island of Capreæ, to practice in secret his infamous orgies. His favorite, the cruel and ambitious Sejā′nus, prefect of the Prætorian Guard, remained at Rome as the real ruler, but, having conspired against his master, he was thrown into the Mamertine Prison, and there strangled. Many of the best citizens fell victims to the emperor's suspicious disposition, and all, even the surviving members of his own family, breathed easier when news came of his sudden death.

The great event of this reign was the crucifixion of Christ[2] at Jerusalem, under Pilate, Roman procurator of Judea.

Caligula[3] (37 A. D.) inherited some of his father's virtues, but he was weak-minded, and his history records only a madman's freaks. He made his favorite horse a consul, and provided him a golden manger. Any one at whom the emperor nodded his head or pointed his finger was at once executed. "Would," said he, "that all the people at Rome had but one neck, so I could cut it off at a single blow."

Nero (54 A. D.) assassinated his mother and wife. In the midst of a great fire which destroyed a large part of Rome, he chanted a poem to the music of his lyre, while he watched the flames. To secure himself against the charge of having at least spread the fire, he ascribed the confla-

[1] His character resembled that of Louis XI. (see Brief Hist. France, p. 94).

[2] Over his cross was an inscription in three languages, significant of the three best developments then known of the human race,—ROMAN LAW, GREEK MIND, AND HEBREW FAITH.

[3] Caius, son of Germanicus, and great-grandson of Augustus, received from the soldiers the nickname of Caligula, by which he is always known, because he wore little boots (*caligulæ*) while with his father in camp on the Rhine.

gration to the Christians. These were cruelly persecuted,[1] St. Paul and St. Peter, according to tradition, being martyred at this time. In rebuilding the city, Nero substituted broad streets for the winding lanes in the hollow between the Seven Hills, and, in place of the unsightly piles of brick and wood, erected handsome stone buildings, each block surrounded by a colonnade.

COIN OF NERO.

Vespasian (69 A. D.) was made emperor by his army in Judea. An old-fashioned Roman, he sought to revive the ancient virtues of honesty and frugality. His son TITUS, after capturing Jerusalem (pp. 85, 284), shared the throne with his father, and finally succeeded to the empire. His generosity and kindness won him the name of the *Delight of Mankind*. He refused to sign a death-warrant, and pronounced any day lost in which he had not done some one a favor. During this happy period, Agricola conquered nearly all Britain, making it a Roman province; the famous Colosseum at Rome was finished; but Pompeii and

---

[1] Some were crucified. Some were covered with the skins of wild beasts, and worried to death by dogs. Some were thrown to the tigers and lions in the Amphitheater. Gray-haired men were forced to fight with trained gladiators. Worst of all, one night Nero's gardens were lighted by Christians, who, their clothes having been smeared with pitch and ignited, were placed as blazing torches along the course on which the emperor, heedless of their agony, drove his chariot in the races.

Herculaneum were destroyed by an eruption of Mount Vesuvius.[1]

Domitian[2] (81 A. D.) was a second Nero or Caligula. His chief amusement was in spearing flies with a pin; yet he styled himself "Lord and God," and received divine honors. He banished the philosophers, and renewed the persecution of the Christians. At this time St. John was exiled to the Isle of Patmos.

The Five Good Emperors (96–180 A. D.) now brought in the palmiest days of Rome. *Nerva*, a quiet, honest old man, distributed lands among the plebs, and taught them to work for a living. *Trajan*, a great Spanish general, conquered the Dacians and many Eastern peoples.; founded public libraries and schools in Italy; and tried to restore freedom of speech and simplicity of life.[3] *Hadrian* traveled almost incessantly over his vast empire, overseeing the government of the provinces, and erecting splendid buildings. *Antoninus Pius* was a second Numa; by his love of justice and religion, he diffused the blessings of peace and order over the civilized world. *Marcus Aurelius*[4] was a philosopher, and loved quiet. But the time of peace had passed. The Germans, pressed by Russian Slavs, fled before them, and crossed the Roman frontiers as in the time of Marius. The emperor was forced to take the field in person, and died during the eighth winter campaign.

Decline of the Empire.—The most virtuous of men was succeeded by a weak, vicious boy, his son Commodus.

---

[1] The forgotten site of Pompeii was accidentally discovered in 1748 (see p 300).

[2] Domitian is said to have once called together the senate to decide how a fish should be cooked for his dinner.

[3] Two centuries afterward, at the accession of each emperor, the senate wished that he might be "more fortunate than Augustus, more virtuous than Trajan."

[4] Marcus Aurelius took the name of his adoptive father, Antoninus so that this period is known as the *Age of the Antonines*.

An era of military despotism followed. Murder became domesticated in the palace of the Cæsars. The Prætorian Guards put up the imperial power at auction, and sold it to the highest bidder. The armies in the provinces declared for their favorite officers, and the throne became the stake of battle. Few of the long list of emperors who succeeded to the throne are worthy of mention.

Septim'ius Seve'rus (193 A. D.), a general in Germany, after defeating his rivals, ruled vigorously, though often cruelly. His triumphs in Parthia and Britain renewed the glory of the Roman arms.

Car'acal'lus (211 A. D.) would be remembered only for his ferocity, but that he gave the right of Roman citizenship to all the provinces, in order to tax them for the benefit of his soldiers. This event marked an era in the history of the empire, and greatly lessened the importance of Rome.

Alexander Seve'rus (222 A. D.) delighted in the society of the wise and good. He favored the Christians, and over the door of his palace were inscribed the words, "Do unto others that which you would they should do unto you." He won victories against the Germans and Persians (Sassanidæ, p. 156), but, attempting to establish discipline in the army, was slain by his mutinous troops in the bloom of youth.

The Barbarian Goths, Germans, and Persians, who had so long threatened the empire, invaded it on every side. The emperor Decius was killed in battle by the Goths. *Gallus* bought peace by an annual tribute. *Valerian* was taken prisoner by the Persian king, who carried him about in chains, and used him as a footstool in mounting his horse. The temple at Ephesus was burned at this time by the Goths.

During the general confusion, so many usurpers sprang up over the empire and established short-lived kingdoms, that this is known as the Era of the Thirty Tyrants.

The Illyrian Emperors (268–284 A. D.), however, rolled back the tide of invasion. *Claudius* vanquished the Goths in a contest which recalled the days of Marius and the Gauls. *Aurelian* drove the Germans into their native wilds, and defeated Zenobia, the beautiful and heroic queen of Palmyra, bringing her to Rome in chains of gold to grace his triumph. *Probus* triumphed at the East and the West, and, turning to the arts of peace, introduced the vine into Germany, and taught the legions to work in vineyard and field. *Diocle'tian* began a new method of government. To meet the swarming enemies of the empire, he associated with himself his comrade-in-arms, *Maximian;* each emperor took the title of Augustus, and appointed, under the name of Cæsar, a brave general as his successor. War raged at once in Persia, Egypt, Britain, and Germany, but the four rulers vigilantly watched over their respective provinces, and the Roman eagles conquered every foe.

In the year 303 A. D. the joint emperors celebrated the last triumph ever held at Rome. During the same year, also, began the last and most bitter persecution of the Christians,[1] so that this reign is called the Era of the Martyrs.

Spread of Christianity.—The religion founded by Jesus of Nazareth, and preached during the 1st century by Paul and the other Apostles (see Acts of the Apostles), had now spread over the Western Empire. It was largely, however, confined to the cities, as is curiously shown in the fact that the word "pagan" originally meant only a countryman. Though the Romans tolerated the religious belief of every nation which they conquered, they cruelly persecuted Christians. This was because the latter opposed the national

---

[1] In 305 A. D. both emperors resigned the purple. Diocletian amused himself by working in his garden, and when Maximian sought to draw him out of his retirement he wrote: "If you could see the cabbages I have planted with my own hand, you would never ask me to remount the throne."

religion of the empire, and refused to offer sacrifice to its gods, and to worship its emperors. Moreover, the Christians absented themselves from the games and feasts, and were accustomed to hold their meetings at night, and often in secret. They were therefore looked upon as enemies of the state, and were persecuted by even the best rulers, as Trajan and Diocletian. This opposition, however, served only to strengthen the rising faith. The heroism of the martyrs extorted the admiration of their enemies. Thus, when Polycarp was hurried before the tribunal and urged to curse Christ, he exclaimed, "Eighty-six years have I served Him, and He has done me nothing but good; how could I curse Him, my Lord and Saviour?" And when the flames rose around him he thanked God that he was deemed worthy of such a death. With the decaying empire, Heathenism grew weaker, while Christianity gained strength. As early as the reign of Septimius Severus, Tertullian declared that if the Christians were forced to emigrate, the empire would become a desert.

Loss of Roman Prestige.—Men no longer looked to Rome for their citizenship. The army consisted principally of Gauls, Germans, and Britons, who were now as good Romans as any. The emperors were of provincial birth. The wars kept them on the frontiers, and Diocletian, it is said, had never seen Rome until he came there in the twentieth year of his reign to celebrate his triumph. His gorgeous Asiatic court, with its pompous ceremonies and its king wearing the hated crown, was so ridiculed in Rome by song and lampoon that the monarch never returned. His headquarters were kept at Nicomedia (Bithynia) in Asia Minor, and Maximian's at Milan.

Constantine, the Cæsar in Britain, having been proclaimed Augustus by his troops, overthrew five rivals who contested the throne, and became sole ruler (324 A. D.). His reign marked an era in the world's history. It was characterized by three changes: 1. Christianity became, in a sense, the state religion.[1] 2. The capital was removed to Byzantium, a Greek city, afterward known as Constantinople (Constantine's city). 3. The monarchy was made an absolute despotism, the power of the army weakened, and a court established, whose nobles, receiving their honors directly from the emperor, took rank with, if not the place of, the former consul, senator, or patrician.

The First General (Œcumenical) **Council** of the Church was held at Nicæa (325 A. D.), to consider the teachings of *Arius*, a priest of Alexandria, who denied the divinity of Christ. Arianism was denounced, and the opposing doctrines of another Alexandrian priest, Athana'sius, were adopted as the *Nicene Creed*.

Christianity soon conquered the empire. The emperor *Julian*, the Apostate, an excellent man though a Pagan philosopher, sought to restore the old religion, but in vain. The best intellects, repelled from political discussion by the tyranny of the government, turned to the consideration of theological questions. This was especially true of the Eastern Church, where the Greek mind, so fond of metaphysical subtleties, was predominant.

Barbarian Invasions.—In the latter part of the 4th century, a host of savage Huns,[2] bursting into Europe, drove

---

[1] According to the legend, when Constantine was marching against Maxentius, the rival Augustus at Rome, he saw in the sky at mid-day a flaming cross, and beneath it the words, "IN THIS CONQUER!" Constantine accepted the new faith, and assumed the standard of the cross, which was henceforth borne by the Christian emperors.

[2] The Huns were a Turanian race from Asia. They were short, thick-set, with flat noses, deep-sunk eyes, and a yellow complexion. Their faces were hideously scarred with slashes to prevent the growth of the beard. An historian of the time compares their ugliness to the grinning heads carved on the posts of bridges. They dressed in skins, which were worn until they rotted off, and lived on horseback, carrying their families and all their possessions in huge wagons.

the Teutons in terror before them. The frightened Goths[1] obtained permission to cross the Danube for an asylum, and soon a million of these wild warriors stood, sword in hand, on the Roman territory. They were assigned lands in Thrace; but the ill treatment of the Roman officials drove them to arms. They defeated the emperor *Valens* in a terrible battle near Adrianople, the monarch himself being burned to death in a peasant's cottage, where he had been carried wounded. The victorious Goths pressed forward to the very gates of Constantinople.

Theodosius the Great, a Spaniard, raised from a farm to the throne, stayed for a few years the inevitable progress of events. He pacified the Goths, and enlisted forty thousand of their warriors under the eagles of Rome. He forbade the worship of the old gods, and tried to put down the Arian heresy, so prevalent at Constantinople. At his death (395 A. D.) the empire was divided between his two sons.

Henceforth the histories of the Eastern or Byzantine and the Western Empire are separate. The former is to go on at Constantinople for one thousand years, while Rome is soon to pass into the hands of the barbarians.

The 5th Century is known as the *Era of the Great Migrations.* During this period, Europe was turbulent with the movements of the restless Germans. Pressed by the Huns, the different tribes—the East and West Goths, Franks, Alans, Vandals, Burgundians, Longobards (Lombards), Allemanns, Angles, Saxons—poured south and west with irre-

---

[1] The Goths were already somewhat advanced in civilization through their intercourse with the Romans, and we read of Gothic leaders who were "judges of Homer, and carried well-chosen books with them on their travels." Under the teachings of their good bishop, Ul'philas, many accepted Christianity, and the Bible was translated into their language They, however, became Arians, and so a new element of discord was introduced, as they hated the Catholic Christians of Rome (see Brief Hist. France, p. 14).

sistible fury, arms in hand, seeking new homes in the crumbling Roman Empire. It was nearly two centuries before the turmoil subsided enough to note the changes which had taken place.

Three Great Barbaric Leaders, Al'aric the Goth, At'tila the Hun, and Gen'seric the Vandal, were conspicuous in the grand catastrophe.

1. *Alaric* having been chosen prince of the Goths, after the death of Theodosius, passed the defile of Thermopylæ, and devastated Greece, destroying the precious monuments of its former glory. Sparta and Athens, once so brave, made no defense. He was finally driven back by Stilicho, a Vandal, but the only great Roman general. Alaric next moved upon Italy, but was repeatedly repulsed by the watchful Stilicho. The Roman emperor Honorius, jealous of his successful general, ordered his execution. When Alaric came again, there was no one to oppose his progress. All the barbarian Germans, of every name, joined his victorious arms. Rome[1] bought a brief respite with a ransom of "gold, silver, silk, scarlet cloth, and pepper;" but The Eternal City, which had not seen an enemy before its walls since the day when it defied Hannibal, soon fell without a blow (410 A. D.). No Horatius was there to hold the bridge in this hour of peril. The gates were thrown open, and at midnight the Gothic trumpet awoke the inhabitants. For six days the barbarians held high revel, and then their clumsy

---

[1] "Rome, at this time, contained probably a million of inhabitants, and its wealth might well attract the cupidity of the barbarous invader. The palaces of the senators were filled with gold and silver ornaments,—the prize of many a bloody campaign. The churches were rich with the contributions of pious worshipers. On the entrance of the Goths, a fearful scene of pillage ensued. Houses were fired to light the streets. Great numbers of citizens were driven off to be sold as slaves; while others fled to Africa, or the islands of the Mediterranean. Alaric, being an Arian, tried to save the churches, as well as the city, from destruction. But now began that swift decay which soon reduced Rome to heaps of ruins, and rendered the title 'The Eternal City' a sad mockery."—*Smith.*

wagons, heaped high with priceless plunder, moved south along the Appian Way. Alaric died soon after.[1] His successor, Adolphus, triumphantly married the sister of the emperor,[2] and was styled an officer of Rome. Under his guidance, the Goths and Germans turned westward into Spain and southern Gaul. There they founded a powerful Visigothic kingdom, with Toulouse as its capital.

2. *Attila*, King of the hideous Huns, gathering half a million savages, set forth westward from his wooden palace in Hungary, vowing not to stop till he reached the sea. He called himself the Scourge of God, and boasted that where his horse set foot grass never grew again On the field of *Chalons* (451 A. D.), Æ'tius, the Roman general in Gaul, and Theodoric, King of the Goths, arrested this Turanian horde, and saved Europe to Christianity and Aryan civilization. Burning with revenge, Attila crossed the Alps and descended

ATTILA.

---

[1] The Goths, in order to hide his tomb, turned aside a stream, and, digging a grave in its bed, placed therein the body, clad in richest armor. They then let the water back, and slew the prisoners who had done the work.

[2] During this disgraceful campaign, Honorius lay hidden in the inaccessible morasses of Ravenna, where he amused himself with his pet chickens. When some one told him Rome was lost, he replied, "That cannot be, for I fed her out of my hand a moment ago," alluding to a hen which he called Rome.

into Italy. City after city was spoiled and burned.[1] Just as he was about to march upon Rome, Pope Leo came forth to meet him, and the barbarian, awed by his majestic mien and the glory which yet clung to that seat of empire, agreed to spare the city. Attila returned to the banks of the Danube, where he died shortly after, leaving behind him in history no mark save the ruin he had wrought.

3. *Genseric*, leading across into Africa the Vandals, who had already settled the province of *Vandal*usia in southern Spain, founded an empire at Carthage. Wishing to revive its former maritime greatness, he built a fleet and gained control of the Mediterranean. His ships cast anchor in the Tiber, and the intercessions of Leo were now fruitless to save Rome. For fourteen days the pirates plundered the city of the Cæsars. Works of art, bronzes, precious marbles, were ruthlessly destroyed, so that the word "vandalism" became synonymous with wanton devastation.

Fall of the Roman Empire (476 A. D.).—The commander of the barbarian troops in the pay of Rome now set up at pleasure one puppet emperor after another. The last of these phantom monarchs, Romulus Augustulus,[2] by a singular coincidence bore the names of the founder of the city and of the empire. Finally, at the command of Odo′acer, German chief of the mercenaries, he laid down his useless scepter. The senate sent the tiara and purple robe to Constantinople; and Zeno, the Eastern emperor, appointed Odoacer *Patrician of Italy*. So the Western Empire passed away, and only this once proud title remained to recall its former glory. Byzantium had displaced Rome.

---

[1] The inhabitants of Aquileia and other cities, seeking a refuge in the islands of the Adriatic, founded Venice, fitly named The Eldest Daughter of the Empire.

[2] Augustulus is the diminutive for Augustus.

270   ROME.

2. THE CIVILIZATION.

Society.—The early Roman social and political organization was similar to the Athenian (p. 158). The true Roman people comprised only the *patricians* and their *clients*. The patricians formed the ruling class, and, even in the time of the republic, gave to Roman history an aristocratic character. Several clients were attached to each patrician, serving his interests, and, in turn, being protected by him.

ROMAN CONSUL AND LICTORS.

The three original tribes of patricians (Ramnes, Tities, and Luceres) were each divided into ten *curiæ*, and each *curia* theoretically into ten *gentes* (houses or clans). The members of a Roman curia, or ward, like those of an Athenian *phratry*, possessed many interests in common, each curia having its own priest and lands. A gens comprised several families,[1] united usually by kinship and

---

[1] Contrary to the custom in Greece, where family names were seldom used, and a man was generally known by a single name having reference to some personal peculiarity or circumstance (p. 175), to every Roman three names were given: the *prænomen* or individual name, the *nomen* or clan name, and the *cognomen* or family name. Sometimes a fourth name was added to commemorate some exploit. Thus, in the case of Publius Cornelius Scipio Africanus, and his brother Lucius Cornelius Scipio Asiaticus (note, p. 235), we recognize all these titles.

intermarriage, and bearing the same name. Within the gens, each family formed its own little community, governed by the "paterfamilias," who owned all the property. The sons dwelt under the paternal roof, often long after they were married, and cultivated the family estate in common.

MAGISTRATES.—*The Consuls* commanded the army, and executed the decrees of the senate and the people. They were chosen annually. They wore a white robe with a purple border, and were attended by twelve lictors bearing the ax and rods (*fasces*, p. 208), emblems of the consular power. At the approach of a consul, all heads were uncovered, seated persons arose, and those on horseback dismounted. No one was eligible to the consulship until he was forty-three years of age, and had held the offices of quæstor, ædile, and prætor.

The Quæstors received and paid out the moneys of the state.

The Ædiles, two (and afterward four) in number, took charge of the public buildings, the cleaning and draining of the streets, and the superintendence of the police and the public games.

The Prætor was a sort of judge. At first there was only one, but finally, owing to the increase of Roman territory, there were sixteen, of these officers. In the later days of the republic it became customary for the consuls and the prætors, after serving a year in the city, to take command of provinces, and to assume the title of proconsul or proprætor.

The Two Censors were elected for five years. They took the census of the names and property of Roman citizens; arranged the different classes (p. 212); corrected the lists of senators and equites, striking out the unworthy, and filling vacancies; punished extravagance and immorality; levied the taxes; and repaired and constructed public works, roads, etc.

The Army.—Every citizen between the ages of seventeen and fifty was subject to military service, unless he was of the lowest class, or had served twenty campaigns in the infantry or ten in the cavalry. The drill was severe, and included running, jumping, swimming in full armor, and marching long distances at the rate of four miles per hour. There were four classes of foot-soldiers: viz., the *velites*, or light armed, who hovered in front; the *hastati*, so called because they anciently carried spears, and who formed the first line of battle; the *principes*, so named because in early times they were put in front, and who formed the second line; and the *triarii*, veterans who composed the third line. Each legion

272   ROME.

contained from three to six thousand men. The legions were divided and subdivided into cohorts, companies (*manipuli*), and centuries.

ARMS AND MODE OF WARFARE.—The national arm of the Romans was the *pilum*, a heavy iron-pointed spear, six feet long, and weighing ten or eleven pounds. This was thrown at a distance of ten to fifteen paces, after which the legionary came to blows with his stout, short sword. The velites began the battle with light javelins, and then retired behind the rest. The hastati, the principes, and the triarii, each, in turn, bore the brunt of the fight, and, if defeated, passed through intervals between the manipuli of the other lines, and rallied in the rear.

SIEGE OF A CITY.

[1] Later in Roman history the soldier ceased to be a citizen, and remained constantly with the eagles until discharged. Marius arranged his troops in two lines,

The Romans learned from the Greeks the use of military engines, and finally became experts in the art of sieges. Their principal machines were the *ballista* for throwing stones; the *catapult* for hurling darts; the *battering-ram* (so called from the shape of the metal head) for breaching walls; and the *movable tower*, which could be pushed close to the fortifications, and so overlook them.

On the march each soldier had to carry, besides his arms, grain enough to last from seventeen to thirty days, one or more wooden stakes, and often intrenching tools. When the army halted, even for a single night, a ditch was dug about the site for the camp, and a stout palisade made of the wooden stakes, to guard against a sudden attack. The exact size of the camp, and the location of every tent, street, etc., were fixed by a regular plan common to all the armies.

Literature.—For about five centuries after the founding of Rome, there was not a Latin author. When a regard for letters at last arose, the tide of imitation set irresistibly toward Greece. Over two centuries after Æschylus and Sophocles contended for the Athenian prize, *Livius Andronicus*, a Greek slave, made the first Latin translation of Greek classics (about 240 B. C.), and himself wrote and acted[1] plays whose inspiration was caught from the same source. His works soon became text-books in Roman schools, and were used till the time of Virgil. *Nævius*, a soldier-poet, "the last of the native minstrels," patterned after Euripides in tragedy, and Aristophanes in comedy. The Romans resented the exposure of their national and personal weaknesses on the stage, sent the bold satirist to prison, and finally banished him. *Ennius*, the father of Latin song, called himself the "Roman Homer." He unblushingly borrowed from his great model, decried the native fashion of ballad-writing, introduced hexameter verse, and built up a new style of literature, closely

---

and Cæsar generally in three; but the terms *hastati*, *principes*, and *triarii* lost their significance. The place of the velites was taken by Cretan archers, Balearic slingers, and Gallic and German mercenaries. In time, the army was filled with foreigners; the heavy pilum and breastplate were thrown aside; all trace of Roman equipment and discipline disappeared, and the legion became a thing of the past.

[1] For a long time he was the only performer in these dramas. He recited the dialogues and speeches, and sang the lyrics to the accompaniment of a flute. So favorably was the new entertainment received by Roman audiences, and so often was the successful actor *encored*, that he lost his voice, and was obliged to hire a boy, who, hidden behind a curtain, sang the canticas, while Livius, in front, made the appropriate gestures. This custom afterward became common on the Roman stage.

founded on the Grecian.[1] His "Annals," a poetical Roman history, was for two centuries the national poem of Rome. Ennius, unlike Nævius, flattered the ruling powers, and was rewarded by having his bust placed in the tomb of the Scipios. *Plautus* (254–184 B. C.), who pictured with his coarse, vigorous, and brilliant wit the manners of his day, and *Ter'ence* (195–159 B. C.), a learned and graceful humorist, were the two great comic poets of Rome.[2] They were succeeded by *Lucil'ius* (148–103 B. C.), a brave soldier and famous knight, whose sharp, fierce satire was poured relentlessly on Roman vice and folly.

Among the early prose writers was *Cato the Censor* (234–149 B. C.), son of a Sabine farmer, who was famous as lawyer, orator, soldier, and politician (p. 235). His hand-book on agriculture, "De Re Rustica," is still studied by farmers, and over one hundred and fifty of his strong, rugged orations find a place among the classics. His chief work, "The Origines," a history of Rome, is lost.

Varro (116–28 B. C.), "the most learned of the Romans," first soldier, then farmer and author, wrote on theology, philosophy, history, agriculture, etc. He founded large libraries and a museum of sculpture, cultivated the fine arts, and sought to awaken literary tastes among his countrymen.

To the last century B. C. belong the illustrious names of Virgil and Horace, Cicero, Livy, and Sallust. First in order of birth was *Cicero*,[3] orator, essayist, and delightful letter-writer. Most elo-

---

[1] Ennius claimed that the soul of the old Greek bard had in its transmigration entered his body from its preceding home in a peacock. He so impressed his intellectual personality upon the Romans that they were sometimes called the "Ennian People." Cicero greatly admired his works, and Virgil borrowed as unscrupulously from Ennius, as Ennius had filched from Homer.

[2] It is noticeable that of all the poets we have mentioned, not one was born at Rome. Livius was a slave from Magna Græcia; Nævius was a native of Campania; Ennius was a Calabrian, who came to Rome as a teacher of Greek; Plautus (meaning flat-foot—his name being, like Plato, a sobriquet) was an Umbrian, the son of a slave, and served in various menial employments before he began play-writing; and Terence was the slave of a Roman senator. To be a Roman slave, however, was not incompatible with the possession of talents and education, since, by the pitiless rules of ancient warfare, the richest and most learned citizen of a captured town might become a drudge in a Roman household, or be sent to labor in the mines.

[3] Marcus Tullius Cicero (106–43 B. C.), son of a book-loving, country gentleman, was educated at Rome, studied law and philosophy at Athens, traveled two years in Asia Minor, and then settled in Rome as an advocate. Plunging into the politics of his time, he soon became famous for his thrilling oratory, and was made, in succession, quæstor, ædile, prætor, and consul. For his detection of Catiline's conspiracy, he received the title of Pater Patriæ. His subsequent banishment, recall, and tragic death are historical (p. 248). Cicero was accused of being vain, vacillating, unamiable, and extravagant. He had an elegant mansion on the Palatine Hill, and

quent of all the Romans, his brilliant genius was not exhausted in the rude contests of the Forum and Basilica, but expanded in thoughtful political essays and gossipy letters. Cicero studied Greek models, and his four orations on the "Conspiracy of Catiline" rank not unfavorably with the Philippics of Demosthenes. His orations, used for lessons in Roman schools before he died, are, with his essays, "De Republica," "De Officiis," and "De Senectute," familiar Latin text-books of to-day.

Sallust,[1] a polished historian after the style of Thucydides, holds his literary renown by two short works,—"The Conspiracy of Catiline" and "The Jugurthine War," which are remarkable for their condensed vigor and vivid portrayal of character.

Virgil[2] and Horace, poet-friends of the Augustan age, are well known to us. Virgil left ten "Eclogues," or "Bucolics," in which he patterned after Theocritus, a celebrated Sicilian poet of the Alexandrian age; "The Georgics," a work on Roman agriculture and stock-breeding, in confessed imitation of Hesiod's "Works and Days;" and the "Æneid," modeled upon the Homeric poems.

---

numerous country villas, his favorite one at Tusculum being built on the plan of the Academy at Athens. Here he walked and talked with his friends in a pleasant imitation of Aristotle, and here he had a magnificent library of handsomely bound volumes, to which he continually added rare works, copied by his skillful Greek slaves. His favorite poet was Euripides, whose Medea (p. 169), it is said, he was reading when he was overtaken by his assassinators.

[1] *Caius Sallustius Crispus* (86-34 B. C.), who was expelled from the senate for immorality, served afterward in the civil war, and was made governor of Numidia by Julius Cæsar. He grew enormously rich on his provincial plunderings, and returned to Rome to build a magnificent palace on the edge of the Campus Martius, where, in the midst of beautiful gardens, groves, and flowers, he devoted his remaining years to study and friendship.

[2] The small paternal estate of *Publius Virgilius Maro* (70-19 B. C.), which was confiscated after the fall of the republic, was restored to him by Augustus. The young country poet, who had been educated in Cremona, Milan, and Naples, expressed his gratitude for the imperial favor in a Bucolic (shepherd-poem), one of several addressed to various friends. Their merit and novelty—for they were the first Latin pastorals—attracted the notice of Mæcenas, the confidential adviser of the emperor; and presently "the tall, slouching, somewhat plebeian figure of Virgil was seen among the brilliant crowd of statesmen, artists, poets, and historians who thronged the audience-chamber of the popular minister," in his sumptuous palace on the Esquiline Hill. Mæcenas, whose wealth equaled his luxurious tastes, took great delight in encouraging men of letters, being himself well versed in Greek and Roman literature, the fine arts, and natural history. Acting upon his advice, Virgil wrote the Georgics, upon which he spent seven years. The Æneid was written to please Augustus, whose ancestry it traces back to the "pious Æneas" of Troy, the hero of the poem. In his last illness, Virgil, who had not yet polished his great work to suit his fastidious tastes, would have destroyed it but for the entreaties of his friends. In accordance with his dying request, he was buried near Naples, where his tomb is still shown above the Posilippo Grotto.

His tender, brilliant, graceful, musical lines are on the tongue of every Latin student. The "Æneid" became a text-book for the little Romans within fifty years after its author's death, and has never lost its place in the schoolroom.

CICERO, VIRGIL, HORACE, AND SALLUST.

Horace,[1] in his early writings, imitated Archilochus and Lucilius, and himself says:—

"The shafts of my passion at random I flung,
And, dashing headlong into petulant rhyme,
I recked neither where nor how fiercely I stung."
Ode I. 15.

---

[1] *Quintus Horatius Flaccus* (65–8 B. C.), "the wit who never wounded, the poet who ever charmed, the friend who never failed," was the son of a freedman, who gave his boy a thorough Roman education, and afterward sent him to Athens,—still the school of the world. Here he joined the army of Brutus, but after the defeat at Philippi,—where his bravery resembled that of Archilochus and Alcæus (p. 164),—he returned to Rome to find his father dead, and all his little fortune confiscated. Of this time he afterward wrote:—

"Want stared me in the face; so then and there
I took to scribbling verse in sheer despair"

The proceeds of his poems and the gifts of friends bought him a clerkship in the quæstor's department, and made him modestly independent. Virgil introduced him

But his kind, genial nature soon tempered this "petulant rhyme." His "Satires" are rambling, sometimes ironical, and always witty. Like Virgil, he loved to sing of country life. He wrote laboriously, and carefully studied all his metaphors and phrases. His "Odes" have a consummate grace and finish.

Livy,[1] who outlived Horace by a quarter of a century, wrote one hundred and forty-two volumes of "Roman History," beginning with the fabulous landing of Æneas, and closing with the death of Drusus (8 B. C.). Thirty-five volumes remain. His grace, enthusiasm, and eloquence make his pages delightful to read, though he is no longer accepted as an accurate historian.

The 1st century A. D. produced the two Plinys, Tacitus, Juvenal, and Seneca.

Pliny the Elder[2] is remembered for his "Natural History," a work of thirty-seven volumes, covering the whole range of the scientific knowledge of his time.

Pliny the Younger, the charming letter-writer, and *Tacitus*, the orator and historian, two rich, eloquent, and distinguished noblemen, were among the most famous intellectual men of their time.[3]

to Mæcenas, who took him into an almost romantic friendship, lasting through life. From this generous patron he received the gift of the "Sabine Farm," to which he retired, and which he has immortalized by his descriptions. He died a few months after his "dear knight Mæcenas," to whom he had declared nearly a score of years before,

"Ah, if untimely Fate should snatch thee hence,
Thee, of my soul a part,"
"Think not that I have sworn a bootless oath,
For we shall go, shall go,
Hand linked in hand, where'er thou leadest, both
The last sad road below."

He was buried on the Esquiline Hill, by the side of his princely friend.

[1] *Titus Livius* (59 B. C.-17 A. D.). Little is known of his private life except that he was the friend of the Cæsars. So great was his renown in his own time, that, according to legend, a Spaniard traveled from Cadiz to Rome to see him, looked upon him, and contentedly retraced his journey.

[2] Of this Pliny's incessant research, his nephew (Pliny the Younger) writes: "From the twenty-third of August he began to study at midnight, and through the winter he rose at one or two in the morning. During his meals a book was read to him, he taking notes while it went on, for he read nothing without making extracts. In fact he thought all time lost which was not given to study." Besides his Natural History, Pliny the Elder wrote over sixty books on History, Rhetoric, Education, and Military Tactics: he also left "one hundred and sixty volumes of Extracts, written on both sides of the leaf, and in the minutest hand." His eagerness to learn cost him his life, for he perished in approaching too near Vesuvius, in the great eruption which buried Pompeii and Herculaneum (79 A. D.).

[3] Tacitus was sitting one day in the circus, watching the games, when a stranger entered into a learned disquisition with him, and after a while inquired, "Are you

They scanned and criticised each other's manuscript, and became by their intimacy so linked with each other that they were jointly mentioned in people's wills, legacies to friends being a fashion of the day. Of the writings of Tacitus, there remain a part of the "Annals" and the "History of Rome," a treatise on "Germany," and a "Life of Agricola." Of Pliny, we have only the "Epistles" and a "Eulogium upon Trajan." The style of Tacitus was grave and stately, sometimes sarcastic or ironical; that of Pliny was vivid, graceful, and circumstantial.

Seneca (7 B. C.–65 A. D.), student, poet, orator, and stoic philosopher, employed his restless intellect in brilliant ethical essays, tragedies, and instructive letters written for the public eye.[1] His teachings were remarkable for their moral purity, and the Christian Fathers called him "The Divine Pagan."

Juvenal, the mocking, eloquent, cynical satirist, belongs to the close of the century. His writings are unsurpassed in scathing denunciations of vice.[2]

Libraries and Writing Materials.—The Roman stationery differed little from the Grecian (p. 178). The passion for collecting books was so great that private libraries sometimes contained over sixty thousand volumes.[3] The *scribæ* and *librarii*, slaves who were attached to library service, were an important part of a Roman gentleman's household. Fifty or a hundred copies of a book were often made at the same time, one scribe reading while the others

of Italy or from the provinces?"—"You know me from your reading," replied the historian. "Then," rejoined the other, "you must be either Tacitus or Pliny."

[1] Seneca was the tutor and guardian of the young Nero, and in later days carried his friendship so far as to write a defense of the murder of Agrippina. But Nero was poor and in debt; Seneca was immensely rich. To charge him with conspiracy, sentence him to death, and seize his vast estates, was a policy characteristic of Nero. Seneca, then an old man, met his fate bravely and cheerfully. His young wife resolved to die with him, and opened a vein in her arm with the same weapon with which he had punctured his own, but Nero ordered her wound to be ligatured. As Seneca suffered greatly in dying, his slaves, to shorten his pain, suffocated him in a vapor bath.

[2] Juvenal's style is aptly characterized in his description of another noted satirist:

"But when Lucilius, fired with virtuous rage,
Waves his keen falchion o'er a guilty age,
The conscious villain shudders at his sin,
And burning blushes speak the pangs within;
Cold drops of sweat from every member roll,
And growing terrors harrow up his soul."

[3] Seneca ridiculed the fashionable pretensions of illiterate men who "adorn their rooms with thousands of books, the titles of which are the delight of the yawning owner."

THE CIVILIZATION. 279

wrote.[1] Papyrus, as it was less expensive than parchment, was a favorite material. The thick black ink used in writing was made from soot and gum; red ink was employed for ruling the columns. The Egyptian reed-pen (*calamus*) was still in vogue.

ROMAN LIBRARY.

[1] A book was written upon separate strips of papyrus. When the work was completed, the strips were glued together; the last page was fastened to a hollow reed, over which the whole was wound; the bases of the roll were carefully cut, smoothed, and dyed; a small stick was passed through the reed, the ends of which were adorned with ivory, golden, or painted knobs (*umbilici*), the roll was wrapped in parchment, to protect it from the ravages of worms, and the title-label was affixed:— the book was then ready for the library shelf or circular case (*scrinium*). The portrait of the author usually appeared on the first page, and the title of the book was written both at the beginning and the end. Sheets of parchment were folded and sewed in different sizes, like modern books.—An author read the first manuscript of his new work before as large an audience as he could command, and judged from its reception whether it would pay to publish. "If you want to recite," says Juvenal, "Maculonus will lend you his house, will range his freedmen on the furthest benches, and will put in the proper places his strong-lunged friends (these corresponded to our modern *claqueurs* or hired applauders); but he will not give what it costs to hire the benches, set up the galleries, and fill the stage with chairs." These readings often became a bore, and Pliny writes: "This year has brought us a great crop of poets. Audiences come slowly and reluctantly; even then they do not stop, but go away before the end; some indeed by stealth, others with perfect openness."

There were twenty-nine public libraries at Rome. The most important was founded by the emperor Trajan, and called—from his *nomen* (p. 270), Ulpius—the Ulpian Library.

Education.—As early as 450 B. C. Rome had elementary schools, where boys and girls were taught reading, writing, arithmetic, and music. The Roman boy mastered his alphabet at home by playing with lettered blocks. At school he chanted the letters, syllables, and words in class, after the teacher's dictation. Arithmetic was learned by the aid of his fingers, or with stone counters and a tablet ruled in columns; the counters expressing certain values, according to the columns on which they were placed. He learned to write on wax tablets (p. 178), his little fingers being guided by the firm hand of the master; afterward he used pen and ink, and the blank side of secondhand slips of papyrus.[1] Boys of wealthy parents were accompanied to school by a slave, who carried their books, writing tablets, and counting boards, and also by a Greek pedagogue, who, among other duties, practiced them in his native language. Girls were attended by female slaves.

Livius Andronicus opened a new era in school education. Ennius, Nævius, and Plautus added to the Livian text-books, and the study of Greek became general. In later times there were excellent higher schools where the masterpieces of Greek and Latin literature were carefully analyzed. State jurisprudence was not neglected, and every schoolboy was expected to repeat the Twelve Tables from memory. Rhetoric and declamation were given great importance, and boys twelve years old made set harangues on the most solemn occasions.[2] As at Athens, the boy of sixteen years

---

[1] The copies set for him were usually some moral maxim, and, doubtless, many a Roman schoolboy labored over that trite proverb quoted from Menander by Paul, and which still graces many a writing-book: "Evil communications corrupt good manners."—Roman schoolmasters were very severe in the use of the *ferula*. Plautus says that for missing a single letter in his reading, a boy was "striped like his nurse's cloak" with the black and blue spots left by the rod. Horace, two centuries later, anathematized his teacher as *Orbilius plagosus* (Orbilius of the birch); and Martial, the witty epigrammatist and friend of Juvenal, declares that in his time "the morning air resounded with the noise of floggings and the cries of suffering urchins."

[2] Julius Cæsar pronounced in his twelfth year the funeral oration of his aunt, and Augustus performed a similar feat. The technical rules of rhetoric and declamation were so minute, that, while they gave no play for genius, they took away the risk of failure. Not only the form, the turns of thought, the cadences, everything except the actual words, were modeled to a pattern, but the manner, the movements, the arrangement of the dress, and the tones of the voice, were subject to rigid rules. The hair was to be sedulously coifed; explicit directions governed the use of the handkerchief; the orator's steps in advance or retreat, to right or to left, were all numbered. He might rest only so many minutes on each foot, and place one only so

formally entered into manhood, the event being celebrated with certain ceremonies at home and in the Forum and by the assumption of a new style of toga, or robe (p. 295). He could now attend the instruction of any philosopher or rhetorician he chose, and visit the Forum and Tribunals, being generally escorted by some man of note selected by his father. He finished his education by a course in Athens.

Monuments and Art.—The early *Italian temples* were copied from the Etruscans; the later ones were modifications of the Grecian. Round temples (Etruscan) were commonly dedicated to Vesta or Diana; sometimes a dome [1] and portico were added, as in the Pantheon.

ROMAN TOGA.

The Basilica,[2] or Hall of Justice, was usually rectangular, and divided into three or five aisles by rows of columns, the middle aisle being widest. At the extremity was a semicircular, arched recess (*apse*) for the tribunal, in front of which was an altar, all important public business being preceded by sacrifice.

Magnificent Palaces were built by the Cæsars, of which the Golden House of Nero, begun on the Palatine and extending by means of intermediate structures to the Esquiline, is a familiar example.[3] At Tibur (the modern Tivoli), Hadrian had a variety

---

many inches before the other; the elbow must not rise above a certain angle; the fingers should be set off with rings, but not too many or too large; and in raising the hand to exhibit them, care must be taken not to disturb the head-dress. Every emotion had its prescribed gesture, and the heartiest applause of the audience was for the perfection of the pantomime. This required incessant practice, and Augustus, it is said, never allowed a day to pass without spending an hour in declamation.

[1] Vaulted domes and large porticoes are characteristic of Roman architecture. The favorite column was the Corinthian, for which a new composite capital was invented. The foundation stone of a temple was laid on the day consecrated to the god to whom it was erected, and the building was made to face the point of the sun's rising on that morning. The finest specimens of Roman temple architecture are at Palmyra and Baalbec in Syria.

[2] The early Christian churches were all modeled after the Basilica.

[3] A court in front, surrounded by a triple colonnade a mile long, contained the em-

of structures, imitating and named after the most celebrated buildings of different provinces, such as the Temple of Serapis at Canopus in Egypt, and the Lyceum and Academy at Athens. Even the Valley of Tempe, and Hades itself, were here typified in a labyrinth of subterranean chambers.

In Military Roads, Bridges, Aqueducts, and Harbors, the Romans displayed great genius. Even the splendors of Nero's golden house dwindle into nothing compared with the harbor of Ostia, the drainage works of the Fucinine Lake, and the two large aqueducts, Aqua Claudia and Anio Nova.[1]

Military Roads.—Unlike the Greeks, who generally left their roads where chance or custom led, the Romans sent out their highways in straight lines from the capital, overcoming all natural difficulties as they went; filling in hollows and marshes, or spanning them with viaducts; tunneling rocks and mountains; bridging streams and valleys; sparing neither labor nor money to make them perfect.[2] Along the principal ones were placed temples,

peror's statue, one hundred and twenty feet high. In other courts were gardens, vineyards, meadows, artificial ponds with rows of houses on their banks, and woods inhabited by tame and ferocious animals. The walls of the rooms were covered with gold and jewels; and the ivory with which the ceiling of the dining-halls was inlaid was made to slide back, so as to admit a rain of roses or fragrant waters on the heads of the carousers. Under Otho, this gigantic building was continued at an expense of over $2,500,000, but only to be pulled down for the greater part by Vespasian. Titus erected his Baths on the Esquiline foundation of the Golden Palace, and the Colosseum covers the site of one of the ponds.

[1] The Lacus Fucinus in the country of the Marsi was the cause of dangerous inundations. To prevent this, and to gain the bed of the lake for agricultural pursuits, a shaft was cut through the solid rock from the lake down to the river Liris, whence the water was discharged into the Mediterranean. The work occupied thirty thousand men for eleven years. The Aqua Claudia was fed by two springs in the Sabine mountain, and was forty-five Roman miles in length; the Anio Nova, fed from the river Anio, was sixty-two miles long. These aqueducts extended partly above and partly under ground, until about six miles from Rome, where they joined, and were carried one above the other on a common structure of arches—in some places one hundred and nine feet high—into the city.

[2] In building a road, the line of direction was first laid out, and the breadth, which was usually from thirteen to fifteen feet, marked by trenches. The loose earth between the trenches having been excavated till a firm base was reached, the space was filled up to the proposed height of the road, which was sometimes twenty feet above the solid ground. First was placed a layer of small stones; next broken stones cemented with lime; then a mixture of lime, clay, and beaten fragments of brick and pottery; and finally a mixture of pounded gravel and lime, or a pavement of hard, flat stones, cut into rectangular slabs or irregular polygons. All along the roads milestones were erected. Near the Arch of Septimius Severus in the Roman Forum may still be seen the remains of the "Golden Milestone" (erected by Augustus),—a gilded marble pillar on which were recorded the names of the roads, and their length from the metropolis.

triumphal arches, and sepulchral monuments. The Appian Way —called also *Regina Viarum* (Queen of Roads)—was famous for the number, beauty, and richness of its tombs. Its foundations were laid 312 B. C. by the censor Appius Claudius, from whom it was named.

BRIDGE OF ST. ANGELO, AND HADRIAN'S TOMB (RESTORED).

The Roman *Bridges* and *Viaducts* are among the most remarkable monuments of antiquity. In Greece, where streams were narrow, little attention was paid to bridges, which were usually of wood, resting at each extremity upon stone piers. The Romans applied *the arch*, of which the Greeks knew little or nothing, to the construction of massive stone bridges [1] crossing the wide rivers of their various provinces. In like manner, marshy places or valleys liable to inundation were spanned by viaducts resting on solid arches. Of these bridges, which may still be seen in nearly every corner of the old Roman Empire, one of the most interesting is the Pons

---

[1] In early times the bridges across the Tiber were regarded as sacred, and their care was confided to a special body of priests, called *pontifices* (bridge-makers). The name of *Pontifex Maximus* remained attached to the high priest, and was worn by the Roman emperor. It is now given to the Pope. Bridges were sometimes made of wood-work and masonry combined.

Ælius, now called the Bridge of St. Angelo, built by Hadrian across the Tiber in Rome.

Aqueducts were constructed on the most stupendous scale, and at one time no less than twenty stretched their long lines of arches[1] across the Campagna, bringing into the heart of the city as many streams of water from scores of miles away.

In their stately *Harbors* the Romans showed the same defiance of natural difficulties. The lack of bays and promontories was supplied by dams and walls built far out into the sea; and even artificial islands were constructed to protect the equally artificial harbor. Thus, at Ostia, three enormous pillars, made of chalk, mortar, and Pozzuolan clay, were placed upright on the deck of a colossal ship, which was then sunk; the action of the salt water hardening the clay, rendered it indestructible, and formed an island foundation.[1] Other islands were made by sinking flat vessels loaded with huge blocks of stone. Less imposing, but no less useful, were the *canals* and *ditches*, by means of which swamps and bogs were transformed into arable land; and the subterranean *sewers* in Rome, which, built twenty-five hundred years ago, still serve their original purpose.

Triumphal Arches,[2] erected at the entrance of cities, and across streets, bridges, and public roads, in honor of victorious generals or emperors, or in commemoration of some great event, were peculiar to the Romans; as were also the

Amphitheaters,[3] the Flavian, better known as the Colosse′um, being the most famous. This structure was built mostly of blocks

---

[1] Their remains, striking across the desolate Campagna in various directions, and covered with ivy, maiden-hair, wild flowers, and fig-trees, form one of the most picturesque features in the landscape about Rome. "Wherever you go, these arches are visible; and toward nightfall, glowing in the splendor of a Roman sunset, and printing their lengthening sun-looped shadows upon the illuminated slopes, they look as if the hand of Midas had touched them, and changed their massive blocks of cork-like travertine into crusty courses of molten gold."—*Story's Roba di Roma*.

[2] Many of these arches still remain. The principal ones in Rome are those of Titus and Constantine, near the Colosseum, and that of Septimius Severus in the Roman Forum. The Arch of Titus, built of white marble, commemorates the destruction of Jerusalem. On the bas-reliefs of the interior are represented the golden table, the seven-branched candlestick, and other precious spoils from the Jewish Temple, carried in triumphal procession by the victors. To this day no Jew will walk under this arch.

[3] The Roman theater differed little from the Grecian (p. 187, note). The first amphitheater, made in the time of Julius Cæsar, consisted of two wooden theaters, so placed upon pivots that they could be wheeled around, spectators and all, and either set back to back, for two separate dramatic performances, or face to face, making a closed arena for gladiatorial shows.

of travertine, clamped with iron and faced with marble; it covered about five acres, and seated eighty thousand persons. At its dedication by Titus (A. D. 80), which lasted a hundred days, five thousand wild animals were thrown into the arena. It continued to be used for gladiatorial and wild-beast fights for nearly four hundred years. On various public occasions it was splendidly fitted up with gold, silver, or amber furniture.

THE RUINS OF THE COLOSSEUM.

The Thermæ (public baths, literally *warm waters*) were constructed on the grandest scale of refinement and luxury. The Baths of Caracalla, at Rome, contained sixteen hundred rooms, adorned with precious marbles. Here were painting and sculpture galleries, libraries and museums, porticoed halls, open groves, and an imperial palace.

The arts of *Painting*, *Sculpture*, and *Pottery* were borrowed first from the Etruscans, and then from the Greeks;[1] in *mosaics* the

---

[1] "Roman art," says Zerffi, "is a misnomer; it is Etruscan, Greek, Assyrian, and Egyptian art, dressed in an eclectic Roman garb by foreign artists. The Pantheon contained a Greek statue of Venus, which, it is said, had in one ear the half of the pearl left by Cleopatra. To ornament a Greek marble statue representing a goddess with part of the earring of an Egyptian princess is highly characteristic of Roman taste in matters of art."

Romans excelled.[1] In later times Rome was filled with the magnificent spoils taken from conquered provinces, especially Greece. Greek artists flooded the capital, bringing their native ideality to serve the ambitious desires of the more practical Romans, whose dwellings grew more and more luxurious, until exquisitely frescoed walls, mosaic pavements, rich paintings, and marble statues became common ornaments in hundreds of elegant villas.

3. THE MANNERS AND CUSTOMS.

General Character.—However much they might come in contact, the Roman and the Greek character never assimilated. We have seen the Athenian quick at intuition, polished in manner, art-loving, beauty-worshiping; fond of long discussions and philosophical discourses, and listening all day to sublime tragedies. We find the Roman grave, steadfast, practical, stern, unsympathizing;[2] too loyal and sedate to indulge in much discussion; too unmetaphysical to relish philosophy; and too unideal to enjoy tragedy. The Spartan deified endurance; the Athenian worshiped beauty; the Roman was embodied dignity. The Greeks were proud and exclusive, but not uncourteous to other nations; the Rómans had but one word (*hostis*) for strangers and enemies. Ambitious, determined, unflinching, they pushed their armies in every direction of the known world, and, appropriating every valuable achievement of the peoples they conquered, made all

---

[1] The mosaic floors, composed of bits of marble, glass, and valuable stones, were often of most elaborate designs. One discovered in the so-called House of the Faun, at Pompeii, is a remarkable battle scene, supposed to represent Alexander at Issus. It is preserved, somewhat mutilated, in the museum at Naples.

[2] What we call *sentiment* was almost unknown to the Romans. The Greeks had a word to express affectionate family love; the Romans had none. Cicero, whom his countrymen could not understand, was laughed at for his grief at the death of his daughter. The exposure of infants was sanctioned as in Greece,—girls, especially, suffering from this unnatural custom,—and the power of the Roman father over the life of his children was paramount. Yet Roman fathers took much pains with their boys, sharing in their games and pleasures, directing their habits, and taking them about town. Horace writes gratefully of his father, who remained with him at Rome during his school-days and was his constant attendant.—*Satire* I. 4.

It is not strange, considering their indifference to their kindred, that the Romans were cruel and heartless to their slaves. In Greece, even the helot was granted some little consideration as a human being, but in Rome the unhappy captive—who may have been a prince in his own land—was but a chattel. The lamprey eels in a certain nobleman's fish-pond were fattened on the flesh of his bondmen; and, if a Roman died suspiciously, all his slaves—who sometimes were numbered by thousands—were put to the torture. The women are accused of being more pitiless than the men, and the faces of the ladies' maids bore perpetual marks of the blows, scratches, and pin-stabs of their petulant mistresses.

the borrowed arts their own, lavishing the precious spoils upon their beloved Rome. Their pride in Roman citizenship amounted to a passion, and for the prosperity of their capital they were ready to renounce the dearest personal hope, and to cast aside all mercy or justice toward every other nation.

Religion.—The Romans, like the Greeks, worshiped the powers of nature. But the Grecian gods and goddesses were living, loving, hating. quarrelsome beings, with a history full of romantic incident and personal adventure; the Roman deities were solemn abstractions mysteriously governing every human action,[1] and requiring constant propitiation with vows, prayers, gifts, and sacrifices. A regular system of bargaining existed between the Roman worshiper and his gods. If he performed all the stipulated religious duties, the gods were bound to confer a reward; if he failed in the least, the divine vengeance was sure. At the same time, if he could detect a flaw in the letter of the law, or shield himself behind some doubtful technicality, he might cheat the gods with impunity.[2] There was no room for faith, or hope, or love—only the binding nature of legal forms. Virtue, in our modern sense, was unknown, and piety consisted, as Cicero declares, in " justice toward the gods."

In religion, as in everything else, the Romans were always ready to borrow from other nations. Their image-worship came from the Etruscans; their only sacred volumes [3] were the purchased "Sibylline Books;" they drew upon the gods of Greece, until in time they had transferred and adopted nearly the entire Greek Pantheon;[4] Phœnicia

---

[1] The farmer had to satisfy "the spirit of breaking up the land and the spirit of plowing it crosswise, the spirit of furrowing and the spirit of harrowing, the spirit of weeding and the spirit of reaping, the spirit of carrying the grain to the barn and the spirit of bringing it out again." The little child was attended by over forty gods. Vaticanus taught him to cry; Fabulinus, to speak; Edusa, to eat; Potina, to drink; Abeona conducted him out of the house; Interduca guided him on his way; Domidúca led him home, and Adeona brought him in.

[2] "If a man offered wine to Father Jupiter, and did not mention very precisely that it was only the cup-full which he held in his hand, the god might claim the whole year's vintage. On the other hand, if the god required so many heads in sacrifice, by the letter of the bond he would be bound to accept garlic-heads; if he claimed an animal, it might be made out of dough or wax."—*Wilkins's Roman Antiquities.*

[3] The Egyptians had their Ritual; the Hindoos, their Vedas; the Chinese, their Laws of Confucius; the Hebrews, the Psalms and prayers of David; but neither Greeks nor Romans had books such as these. They had poetry of the highest order, but no psalms or hymns, litanies or prayers.

[4] Jupiter (Zeus) and Vesta (Hestia) were derived by Greeks and Romans from their common ancestors. Among the other early Italian gods were Mars (afterward identified with the Greek Ares), Hercules (Herakles), Juno (Hera), Minerva (Athena), and Neptune (Poseidon). The union of the Palatine Romans with the Quirinal Sabines was celebrated by the mutual worship of Quirinus, and a gate called the Janus was erected in the valley, afterward the site of the Forum. This gate was

and Phrygia lent their deities to swell the list; and finally our old Egyptian friends, Isis, Osiris, and Serapis, became as much at home upon the Tiber as they had been for ages on the Nile. The original religious ideas of the Romans can only be inferred from a few peculiar rites which characterized their worship. The Chaldeans had astrologers; the Persians had magi; the Greeks had sibyls and oracles; the Romans had

Augurs. Practical and unimaginative, the Latins would never have been content to learn the divine will through the ambiguous phrases of a human prophet; they demanded a direct yes or no from the gods themselves. Augurs existed from the time of Romulus. Without their assistance no public act or ceremony could be performed. Lightning and the flight of birds were the principal signs by which the gods were supposed to make known their will;[1] some birds of omen communicated by their cry, others by their manner of flight.

ROMAN AUGUR.

The *Haruspices*, who also expounded lightnings and natural phenomena, made a specialty of divination by inspecting the internal organs of sacrificed animals, a custom we have seen in Greece (p. 185).

always open in time of war, and closed in time of peace. All gates and doors were sacred to the old Latin god Janus, whose key fitted every lock. He wore two faces, one before and one behind, and was the god of all beginnings and endings, all openings and shuttings.—With the adoption of the Greek gods, the Greek ideas of personality and mythology were introduced, the Romans being too unimaginative to originate any myths for themselves. But, out of the hardness of their own character, they disfigured the original conception of every borrowed god, and made him more jealous, threatening, merciless, revengeful, and inexorable than before. "Among the thirty thousand deities with which they peopled the visible and invisible worlds, there was not one divinity of kindness, mercy, or comfort."

[1] In taking the auspices, the augur stood in the center of a consecrated square, and divided the sky with his staff into quarters (cut); he then offered his prayers, and, turning to the south, scanned the heavens for a reply. Coming from the left, the signs were favorable; from the right, unfavorable. If the first signs were not desirable, the augurs had only to wait until the right ones came. They thus compelled the gods to sanction their decisions, from which there was afterward no appeal. In the absence of an augur, the "Sacred Chickens," which were carried about in coops during campaigns, were consulted. If they ate their food greedily, especially if they scattered it, the omen was favorable; if they refused to eat, or moped in the coop, evil was anticipated.

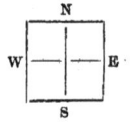

Their art was never much esteemed by the more enlightened classes; and Cato, who detested their hypocrisy, wondered "how one haruspex could look at another in the streets without laughing."

The Family Worship of Vesta, goddess of the hearth, was more exclusive in Rome than in Greece, where slaves joined in the home devotions. A Roman father, himself the priest at this ceremony, would have been shocked at allowing any but a kinsman to be present, for it included the worship of the *Lares and Penates*, the spirits of his ancestors and the guardians of his house. So, also, in the public service at the Temple of Vesta, the national hearth-stone, the patricians felt it a sacrilege for any but themselves to join. The worship of Vesta, Saturnus (the god of seed-sowing), and Opo (the harvest goddess) was under the direction of the

College of Pontifices, of which, in regal times, the king was high priest. Attached to this priestly college—the highest in Rome—were the *Flamens*[1] (*flare*, to blow the fire), who were priests of Jupiter, Mars, and Quirinus; and the *Vestal Virgins*, who watched the eternal fire in the Temple of Vesta.[2]

The Salii, or "leaping priests," receive their name from the warlike dance which, in full armor, they performed every March before all the temples. They had the care of the Sacred Shields, which they carried about in their annual processions, beating them to the

[1] The *Flamen Dialis* (Priest of Jupiter) was forbidden to take an oath, mount a horse, or glance at an army. His hand could touch nothing unclean, and he never approached a corpse or a tomb. As he must not look at a fetter, the ring on his finger was a broken one, and, as he could not wear a knot, his thick woolen toga, woven by his wife, was fastened with buckles. (In Egypt, we remember, priests were forbidden to wear woolen, p. 20.) If his head-dress (a sort of circular pillow, on the top of which an olive-branch was fastened by a white woolen thread) chanced to fall off, he was obliged to resign his office. In his belt he carried the sacrificial knife, and in his hand he held a rod to keep off the people on his way to sacrifice. As he might not look on any secular employment, he was preceded by a lictor, who compelled every one to lay down his work till the Flamen had passed. His duties were continuous, and he could not remain for a night away from his house on the Palatine. His wife was subject to an equally rigid code. She wore long woolen robes, and shoes made of the leather of sacrificed animals. Her hair was tied with a purple woolen ribbon, over which was a kerchief, fastened with a twig from a lucky tree. She also carried a sacrificial knife.

[2] *The Vestal* always dressed in white, with a broad band, like a diadem, round her forehead. During sacrifice or in processions she was covered with a white veil. She was chosen for the service when from six to ten years old, and her vows held for thirty years, after which time, if she chose, she was released and might marry. Any offense offered her was punished with death. In public, every one, even the consul, made way for the lictor preceding the maiden, and she had the seat of honor at all public games and priestly banquets. If, however, she accidentally suffered the sacred fire to go out, she was liable to corporeal punishment by the pontifex maximus; if she broke her vows, she was carried on a bier to the Campus Sceleratus, beaten with rods, and buried alive. The number of vestal virgins never exceeded six at any one time.

time of an old song in praise of Janus, Jupiter, Juno, Minerva, and Mars. One of the shields was believed to have fallen from heaven. To mislead a possible pillager of so precious a treasure, eleven more were made exactly like it, and twelve priests were appointed to watch them all.

The Fetiales had charge of the sacred rites accompanying declarations of war, or treaties of peace. War was declared by throwing a bloody spear across the enemy's frontier. A treaty was concluded by the killing of a pig with a sacred pebble.

Altars were erected to the emperors, where vows and prayers were daily offered.[1] In the times of Roman degeneracy the city was flooded with quack Chaldean astrologers, Syrian seers, and Jewish fortune-tellers. The women, especially, were ruled by these corrupt impostors, whom they consulted in secret and by night, and on whom they squandered immense sums. Under these debasing influences, profligacies and enormities of every kind grew and multiplied. The old Roman law which commanded that the parricide should be "sewn up in a sack with a viper, an ape, a dog, and a cock, and then cast into the sea," was not likely to be rigidly enforced when a parricide sat on the throne, and poisonings were common in the palace. That the pure principles of Christianity, which were introduced at this time, should meet with contempt, and its disciples with bitter persecution, was inevitable.

Games and Festivals.—The Roman public games were a degraded imitation of the Grecian, and, like them, connected with religion. When a divine favor was desired, a vow of certain games was made, and, as the gods regarded promises with suspicion, the expenses were at once raised. Each of the great gods had his own festival month and day.

The Saturnalia, which occurred in December, and which in later times lasted seven days, was the most remarkable. It was a time of general mirth and feasting; schools were closed; the senate adjourned; presents were made; wars were forgotten; criminals had certain privileges; and the slaves, whose lives were ordinarily at the mercy of their masters, were permitted to jest with them, and were even waited upon by them at table;—all this in memory of the free and happy rule of ancient Saturn.

The gymnastic and musical exercises of the Greeks never found much favor in Rome; tragedies were tolerated only for the splendor of the costumes and the scenic wonders; and even comedies failed to

---

[1] "Not even the Egyptians, crouching in grateful admiration before a crocodile, so outraged humanity as did those polite Romans, rendering divine honors to an emperor like Aurelius Commodus, who fought seven hundred and thirty-five times as a common gladiator in the arena before his enervated people."—*Zerffi.*

THE MANNERS AND CUSTOMS. 291

satisfy a Roman audience. Farces and pantomimes won great applause; horse and chariot races were exciting pleasures from the time of the kings; but, of all delights, nothing could stir Rome like a gladiatorial or wild-beast fight. At first connected with the Saturnalia, the sports of the arena soon became too popular to be restricted, and mourning sons in high life paid honors to a deceased father by furnishing a public fight, in which from twenty-five to seventy-five gladiators were hired to take part, the contest often lasting for days.

THE GLADIATORS ("POLLICE VERSO," PAINTING BY GÉRÔME).

Gladiatorial Shows were advertised by private circulars or public announcements. On the day of the performance, the gladiators marched in solemn procession to the arena, where they were matched in pairs,[1]

[1] The gladiators fought in pairs or in matched numbers. A favorite duel was between a man without arms, but who carried a net in which to insnare his opponent, and a three-pronged fork with which to spear him when caught, and another man in full armor, whose safety lay in evading his enemy while he pursued and killed him. "It is impossible to describe the aspect of an amphitheater when gladiators fought. The audience became frantic with excitement; they rose from their seats; they yelled; they shouted their applause as a ghastly blow was dealt which sent the life-blood spouting forth. '*Hoc habet*'—'he has it'—'he has it,' burst from ten thousand throats, and was re-echoed, not only by a brutalized populace, but by

and their weapons formally examined. "An awning gorgeous with purple and gold excluded the rays of the mid-day sun; sweet strains of music floated in the air, drowning the cries of death; the odor of Syrian perfumes overpowered the scent of blood; the eye was feasted by the most brilliant scenic decorations, and amused by elaborate machinery." At the sound of a bugle and the shout of command, the battle opened. When a gladiator was severely wounded, he dropped his weapons, and held up his forefinger as a plea for his life. This was sometimes in the gift of the people; often the privilege of the vestal virgins; in imperial times, the prerogative of the emperor. A close-pressed thumb or the waving of a handkerchief meant mercy; an extended thumb and clinched upright fist forbade hope. Cowards had nothing to expect, and were whipped or branded with hot irons till they resumed the fight. The killed and mortally wounded were dragged out of the arena with a hook.

The Wild-beast Fights were still more revolting, especially when untrained captives or criminals were forced to the encounter. Many Christian martyrs, some of whom were delicate women, perished in the Colosseum. We read of twenty maddened elephants turned in upon six hundred war captives; and in Trajan's games, which lasted over one hundred and twenty days, ten thousand gladiators fought, and over that number of wild beasts were slain. Sometimes the animals, made furious by hunger or fire, were let loose at one another. Great numbers of the most ferocious beasts were imported from distant countries for these combats. Strange animals were sought after, and camelopards, white elephants, the rhinoceros, and the hippopotamus, goaded to fury, delighted the assembled multitudes. Noble game became scarce, and at last it was forbidden by law to kill a Getulian lion out of the arena, even in self-defense.

Naval Fights, in flooded arenas, were also popular. The Colosseum was sometimes used for this purpose, as many as thirty vessels taking part. At an entertainment given by Augustus in the flooded arena of the Flaminian Circus, thirty-six crocodiles were pursued and killed.

Marriage was of two kinds. In one the bride passed from the control of her father into that of her husband; in the other the

---

imperial lips, by purple-clad senators and knights, by noble matrons and consecrated maids."—*Sheppard's Fall of Rome.* So frenzied with the sight of blood did the spectators become, that they would rush into the arena and slay on every side; and so sweet was the applause of the mob, that captives, slaves, and criminals were envied the monopoly of the gladiatorial contest, and laws were required to restrict knights and senators from entering the lists. Some of the emperors fought publicly in the arena, and even women thus debased themselves. Finally, such was the mania, that no wealthy or patrician family was without its gladiators, and no festival was complete without a contest. Even at banquets, blood was the only stimulant that roused the jaded appetite of a Roman.

parental power was retained. The former kind of marriage could be contracted in any one of three different ways. Of these, the religious form was confined to the patricians; the presence of the pontifex maximus, the priest of Jupiter, and ten citizens, was necessary as witnesses; a sacred cake (*far*) was broken and solemnly tasted by the nuptial pair, whence this ceremony was termed *confarreatio*. A second manner was by purchase (*coemptio*), in which the father formally sold his daughter to the groom, she signifying her consent before witnesses. The third form, by prescription (*usus*), consisted simply in the parties having lived together for a year without being separated for three days at any time.

The marriage ceremony proper differed little in the various forms. The betrothal consisted of the exchange of the words *spondesne* (Do you promise?) and *spondeo* (I promise), followed by the gift of a ring from the groom. On the wedding-morning, the guests assembled at the house of the bride's father, where the auspices—which had been taken before sunrise by an augur or a haruspex—were declared, and the solemn marriage contract was spoken. The bride's attendant then laid her hands upon the shoulders of the newly married pair, and led them to the family altar, around which they walked hand in hand, while a cow, a pig, and a sheep were offered in sacrifice—the gall having been first extracted and thrown away, to signify the removal of all bitterness from the occasion. The guests having made their congratulations, the feast began. At nightfall the bride was torn with a show of force from her mother's arms (in memory of the seizure of the Sabine women, p. 206); two boys, whose parents were both alive, supported her by the arms; torches were lighted, and a gay procession, as in Greece, accompanied the party to the house of the groom. Here the bride, having repeated to her spouse the formula, "*Ubi tu Caius, ibi ego Caia*" (Where thou art Caius, I am Caia), anointed the door-posts and wound them with wool, and was lifted over the threshold. She was then formally welcomed into the *atrium* by her husband with the ceremony of touching fire and water, in which both participated. The next day, at the second marriage feast, the wife brought her offerings to the gods of her husband's family, of which she was now a member, and a Roman matron.

DRESSING A ROMAN BRIDE.

Burial.[1]—When a Roman died it was the duty of his nearest relative to receive his last breath with a kiss, and then to close his eyes and mouth (compare Æneid, iv. 684). His name was now called several times by all present, and, there being no response, the last farewell (*vale*) was said. The necessary utensils and slaves having been hired at the temple where the death registry was kept, the body was laid on the ground, washed in hot water, anointed with rich perfumes, clad in its best garments, placed on an ivory bedstead, and covered with blankets of purple, embroidered with gold.[2] The couch was decorated with flowers and foliage, but upon the body itself were placed only the crowns of honor fairly earned during its lifetime; these accompanied it into the tomb. By the side of the funereal bed, which stood in the *atrium* facing the door, as in Greece, was placed a pan of incense. The body was thus exhibited for seven days, branches of cypress and fir fastened in front of the house announcing a mourning household to all the passers-by. On the eighth morning, while the streets were alive with bustle, the funeral took place. Behind the hired female mourners, who sang wailing dirges, walked a band of actors, who recited scraps of tragedy applicable to the deceased, or acted comic scenes in which were sometimes mimicked his personal peculiarities.[3] In front of the bier marched those who personated the prominent ancestors of the dead person. They wore waxen masks (p. 303), in which and in their dress were reproduced the exact features and historic garb of these long-defunct personages.[4] The bier, carried by the nearest relatives, or by slaves freed by the will of the deceased, and surrounded by the family friends dressed in black (or, in imperial times, in white), was thus escorted to the Forum. Here the mask-wearers seated themselves about it, and one of the relatives mounted the rostrum to eulogize the deceased and his ancestors. After the eulogy, the procession re-formed, and the body was taken to

---

[1] The Romans, like the Greeks, attached great importance to the interment of their dead, as they believed that the spirit of an unburied body was forced to wander for a hundred years. Hence it was deemed a religious duty to scatter earth over any corpse found uncovered by the wayside, a handful of dust being sufficient to appease the infernal gods. If the body of a friend could not be found, as in shipwreck, an empty tomb was erected, over which the usual rites were performed.

[2] We are supposing the case of a rich man. The body of a poor person was, after the usual ablutions, carried at night to the common burial-ground outside the Esquiline gate, and interred without ceremony.

[3] At Vespasian's obsequies an actor ludicrously satirized his parsimony. "How much will this ceremony cost?" he asked in the assumed voice of the deceased emperor. A large sum having been named in reply, the actor extended his hand, and greedily cried out, "Give me the money and throw my body into the Tiber."

[4] Frequently the masks belonging to the collateral branches of the family were borrowed, that a brilliant show might be made. Parvenus, who belong to all time, were wont to parade images of fictitious ancestors.

the spot where it was to be buried or burned, both forms being used, as in Greece. If it were burned, the nearest relative, with averted face, lighted the pile. After the burning, the hot ashes were drenched with wine, and the friends collected the bones in the folds of their robes, amid acclamations to the *manes* of the departed. The remains, sprinkled with wine and milk, were then—with sometimes a small glass vial filled with tears—placed in the funeral urn; a last farewell was spoken, the lustrations were performed, and the mourners separated. When the body was not burned, it was buried with all its ornaments in a coffin, usually of stone.[1] The friends, on returning home from the funeral, were sprinkled with water, and then they stepped over fire, as a purification. The house also was ceremoniously purified. An offering and banquet took place on the ninth day after burial, in accordance with Greek custom.

Dress.—The *toga*, worn by a Roman gentleman, was a piece of white woolen cloth about five yards long and three and a half wide, folded lengthways, so that one edge fell below the other. It was thrown over the left shoulder, brought around the back and under the right arm, then, leaving a loose fold in front, thrown again over the left shoulder, leaving the end to fall behind. Much pains was taken to drape it gracefully, according to the exact style required by fashion. A tunic, with or without sleeves, and in cold weather a vest, or one or more extra tunics, were worn under the toga. Boys under seventeen years of age wore a toga with a purple hem; the toga of a senator had a broad purple stripe, and that of a knight had two narrow stripes. The use of the toga was forbidden to slaves, strangers, and, in imperial times, to banished Romans.

The *pœnula*, a heavy, sleeveless cloak, with sometimes a hood attached, and the *lacerna*, a thinner, bright-colored one arranged in folds, were worn out of doors over the toga. The *paludamentum*, a rich, red cloak draped in picturesque folds, was permitted only to the military general-in-chief, who, in imperial times, was the emperor himself. The *sagum* was a short military cloak. The *synthesis*, a gay-colored easy robe, was worn over the tunic at banquets, and by the nobility during the Saturnalia. Poor people had only the tunic, and in cold weather a tight-fitting wool or leather cloak. When not on a journey, the Roman, like the Greek, left his head uncovered, or protected it with his toga. Rank decided the style of shoe; a consul used a red one, a senator a black one with a silver crescent, ordinary folk a plain black, slaves and poorest people wooden clogs. In the house, sandals only were worn, and at dinner even these were laid aside.

[1] That from Assos in Lycia was said to consume the entire body, except the teeth, in forty days: hence it was called *sarcophagus* (flesh-eating), a name which came to stand for any coffin.

A Roman matron dressed in a linen under-tunic, a vest, and the *stola*, a long, short-sleeved garment, girdled at the waist and flounced or hemmed at the bottom. Over this, when she went out, she threw a *palla*, cut and draped like her husband's toga or like the Greek himation. Girls and foreign women, who were not permitted the stola, wore over the tunic a palla, arranged like the Doric chiton (p. 193). Women—who, like the men, went hatless—protected their heads with the palla, and wore veils, nets, and various light head-coverings. This led to elaborate fashions in hair-dressing. A caustic soap imported from Gaul was used for hair-dyeing, and wigs were not uncommon. Bright colors, such as blue, scarlet, violet, and especially yellow,—the favorite tint for bridal veils,—enlivened the feminine wardrobe. Finger-rings were worn in profusion by both sexes, and a Roman lady of fashion luxuriated in bracelets, necklaces, and various ornaments set with diamonds, pearls, emeralds, and other jewels, whose purchase frequently cost her husband his fortune.

SCENES IN REAL LIFE.

Scene I.—*A Day in Rome.*—Let us imagine ourselves on some bright, clear morning, about eighteen hundred years ago, looking down from the summit of the Capitoline Hill upon the "Mistress of the World." As we face the rising sun, we see clustered about us a group of hills crowned with a vast assemblage of temples, colonnades, palaces, and sacred groves. Densely packed in the valleys between are towering tenements,[1] shops with extending booths, and here and there a templed forum, amphitheater, or circus. In the valley at our feet, between the Via Sacra and the Via Nova,—the only paved roads in the whole city fit for the transit of heavy carriages,—is the Forum Romanum, so near us that we can watch the storks that stalk along the roof of the Temple of Concord.[2] This Forum is the great civil and legislative heart of the city. Here are the Regia or palace of the chief pontiff, with its two adjoining basilicas; the Temple of Vesta, on whose altar burns the sacred flame; the Senate House, fronted by the Rostra, from which Roman orators address assembled multitudes; various temples, including the famous one of Castor and Pollux; and

---

[1] Ancient authors frequently mention the extreme height of Roman houses, which Augustus finally limited to seventy feet. Cicero says of Rome that "it is suspended in the air;" and Aristides, comparing the successive stories to the strata of the earth's crust, affirms that if they were laid out on one level they "would cover Italy from sea to sea." To economize lateral space, the exterior walls were forbidden to exceed a foot and a half in thickness.

[2] Storks were encouraged to build in the roof of this temple, as peculiar social instincts were attributed to them (see Steele's Popular Zoölogy, p. 146).

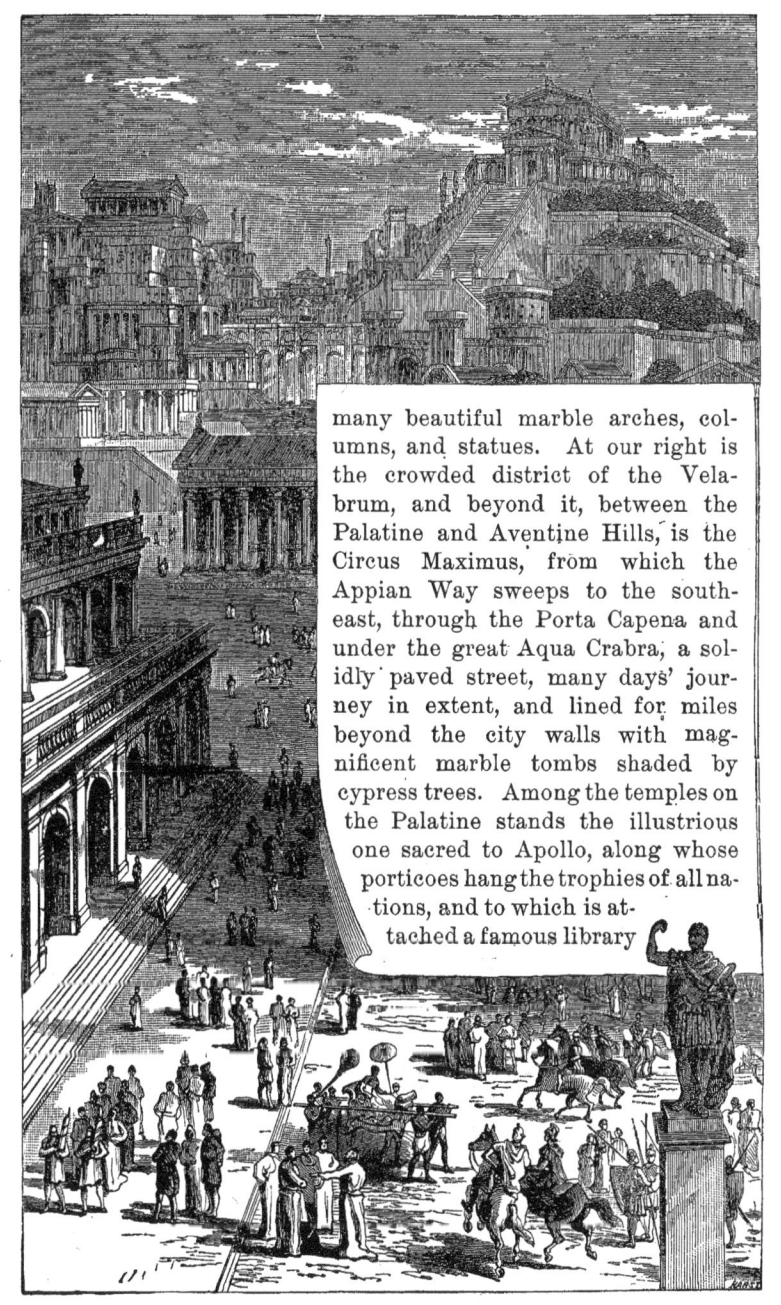

many beautiful marble arches, columns, and statues. At our right is the crowded district of the Velabrum, and beyond it, between the Palatine and Aventine Hills, is the Circus Maximus, from which the Appian Way sweeps to the southeast, through the Porta Capena and under the great Aqua Crabra, a solidly paved street, many days' journey in extent, and lined for miles beyond the city walls with magnificent marble tombs shaded by cypress trees. Among the temples on the Palatine stands the illustrious one sacred to Apollo, along whose porticoes hang the trophies of all nations, and to which is attached a famous library

ROME IN THE TIME OF AUGUSTUS CÆSAR.

of Greek and Roman books; near it is the Quadrata, a square mass of masonry, believed to be mysteriously connected with the fortunes of the city, and beneath which certain precious amulets are deposited. Interspersed among these public buildings on the Palatine are many isolated mansions surrounded by beautiful gardens fragrant with the odors of roses and violets, in which the Romans especially delight. There is no arrangement of streets upon the hills; that is a system confined to the crowded Suburra, which adjoins the Roman Forum at our front, and lies at the foot of the Quirinal, Viminal, and Esquiline Hills. This district, which was once a swampy jungle and afterward a fashionable place for residences (Julius Cæsar was born in the Suburra), is now the crowded abode of artificers of all kinds, and is the most profligate as well as most densely populated part of Rome.

Turning about and facing the west, we see, toward the north, the Campus Martius, devoted from the earliest period to military exercises and the sports of running, leaping, and bathing. On this side of the open meadows stand some of the principal temples, the great Flaminian Circus, and the theaters of Pompeius and Marcellus, with their groves, porticoes, and halls. Precisely in the center of the plain rises the Pantheon of Agrippa, and further on we see the Amphitheater of Taurus,[1] and the Mausoleum of Augustus. At our front, beyond the curving, southward-flowing Tiber, is a succession of terraces, upon whose heights are many handsome residences. This quarter, the Janiculum, is noted for its salubrity, and here are the Gardens of Cæsar, and the Naumachia (a basin for exhibiting naval engagements) of Augustus, fed by a special aqueduct, and surrounded by walks and groves. Glancing down the river, we see the great wharf called the Emporium, with its immense store-houses, in which grain, spices, candles, paper, and other commodities are stored; and just beyond it, the Marmorata, a special dock for landing building-stone and foreign marbles. It is yet early morning, and the streets of Rome are mainly filled with clients and their slaves hurrying to the *atria* (p. 303) of their wealthy patrons to receive the customary morning dole.[2] Here and

[1] The whole of this northern district comprehends the chief part of modern Rome, and is now thronged with houses.

[2] In early times the clients were invited to feast with their patron in the *atrium* of his mansion, but in later days it became customary, instead, for stewards to distribute small sums of money or an allowance of food, which the slaves of the clients carried away in baskets or in small portable ovens, to keep the cooked meats hot.

> "Wedged in thick ranks before the donor's gates,
> A phalanx firm of chairs and litters waits.
> *Once*, plain and open was the feast,
> And every client was a bidden guest;
> *Now*, at the gate a paltry largess lies,
> And eager hands and tongues dispute the prize."—*Juvenal.*

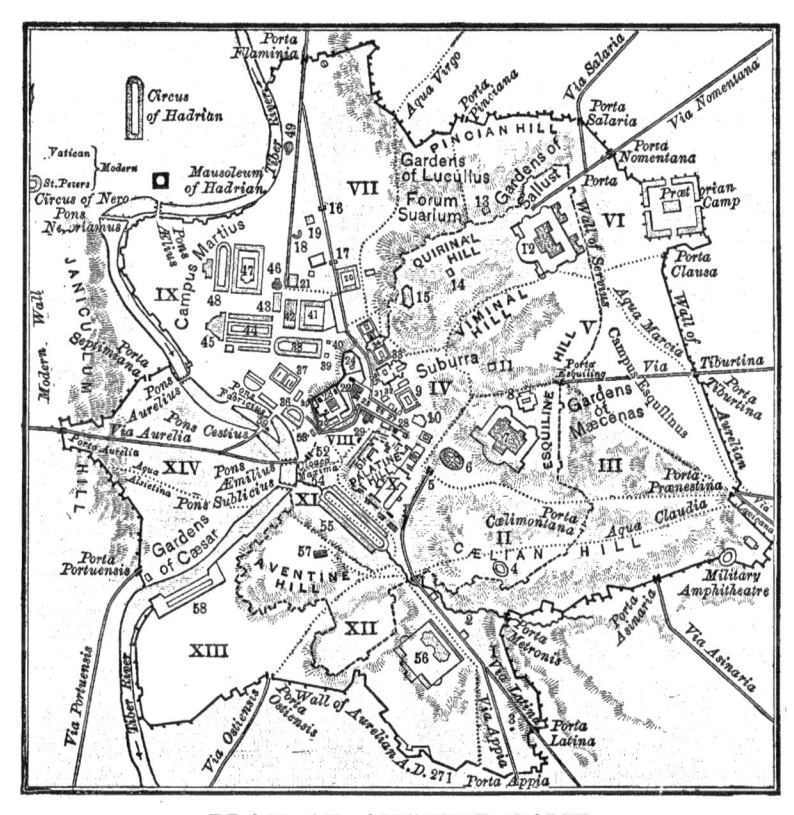

PLAN OF ANCIENT ROME,
SHOWING THE DIVISION INTO
THE XIV REGIONS OF AUGUSTUS
AND THE POSITION OF THE PRINCIPAL BUILDINGS.

I. PORTA CAPENA.
1. Porta Capena.
2. Valley of Egeria.
3. Tomb of Scipio.

II. CÆLIMONTIUM.
4. Temple of Divus Claudius.
5. Arch of Constantine.

III. ISIS ET SERAPIS.
6. Colosseum.
7. Baths of Titus.
8. Baths of Trajan.

IV. VIA SACRA.
9. Forum of Vespasian.
10. Basilica of Constantine.

V. ESQUILINA CUM VIMINALI.
11. Temple of Juno.

VI. ALTA SEMITA.
12. Baths of Diocletian.
13. Temple of Flora.
14. Temple of Quirinus.
15. Baths of Constantine.

VII. VIA LATA.
16. Arch of Aurelius.
17. Arch of Claudius.

18. Amphitheater of Taurus.
19. Column of Antoninus.
20. Camp of Agrippa.
21. Temple of Isis and Serapis.

VIII. FORUM ROMANUM.
22. Capitoline Hill.
23. Temple of Jupiter Tonans.
24. Arx.
25. Golden Milestone.
26. Roman Forum.
27. Temple of Vesta.
28. Via Sacra.
29. Lupercal.
30. Tarpeian Rock.
31. Arch of Severus.
32. Curia (Senate House).
33. Forum of Augustus.
34. Basilica Ulpia.
35. Temple of Janus.

IX. CIRCUS FLAMINIUS.
36. Theater of Marcellus.
37. Port. of Octavius and Philippa.
38. Circus Flaminius.
39. Temple of Apollo.

40. Temple of Bellona.
41. Septa Julia.
42. Diribitorium.
43. Baths of Agrippa.
44. Port. of Pompey.
45. Theater of Pompey.
46. Pantheon.
47. Bath[s] of Nero.
48. Race-course.
49. Mausoleum of Augustus.

X. PALATIUM.
50. Palace of Nero.
51. Palace of Augustus.

XI. CIRCUS MAXIMUS.
52. Velabrum.
53. Forum Olitorium.
54. Forum Boarium.
55. Circus Maximus.

XII. PISCINA PUBLICA.
56. Baths of Antoninus.

XIII. AVENTINUS.
57. Balnea Suræ.
58. Emporium.

XIV. TRANS TIBERIM.
59. Temple of Æsculapius.

there a teacher hastens to his school, and in the Suburra the workers in metal and in leather, the clothiers and perfume sellers, the book-dealers, the general retailers, and the jobbers of all sorts, are already beginning their daily routine. We miss the carts laden with merchandise which so obstruct our modern city streets; they are forbidden by law to appear within the walls during ten hours between sunrise and sunset. But, as the city wakes to life, long trains of builders' wagons, weighted with huge blocks of stone or logs of timber, bar the road, and mules, with country produce piled in baskets suspended on either side, urge their way along the constantly increasing crowd. Here is a mule with a dead-boar thrown across its back, the proud hunter stalking in front, with a strong force of retainers to carry his spears and nets. There comes a load drawn by oxen, upon whose horns a wisp of hay is tied; it is a sign that they are vicious, and passers-by must be on guard. Now a passage is cleared for some dignified patrician, who, wrapped in his toga, reclining in his luxurious litter, and borne on the broad shoulders of six stalwart slaves, makes his way to the Forum attended by a train of clients and retainers. In his rear, stepping from stone to stone [1] across the slippery street wet by the recent rains, we spy some popular personage on foot, whose advance is constantly retarded by his demonstrative acquaintances, who throng about him, seize his hand, and cover his lips with kisses.[2]

The open cook-shops swarm with slaves who hover over steaming kettles, preparing breakfast for their wonted customers; and the tables of the vintners, reaching far out upon the wayside, are covered with bottles, protected from passing pilferers by chains. The restaurants are hung with festoons of greens and flowers; the image of a goat,[3] carved on a wooden tablet, betokens a milk depot; five hams, ranged

[1] In Pompeii, the sidewalks are elevated a foot or more above the street level, and protected by curb-stones. Remains of the stucco or the coarse brick-work mosaic which covered them are still seen. In many places the streets are so narrow that they may be crossed at one stride; where they are wider, a raised stepping-stone, and sometimes two or three, have been placed in the center of the crossing. Though these stones were in the middle of the carriage-way, the wheels of the *biga*, or two-horsed chariot, could roll in the spaces between, while the loosely harnessed horses might step over them or pass by the side. Among the suggestive objects in the exhumed city are the hollows worn in these stepping-stones by feet which were forever stilled more than eighteen hundred years ago.

[2] "At every meeting in the street a person was exposed to a number of kisses, not only from near acquaintance, but from every one who desired to show his attachment, among whom there were often mouths not so clean as they might be. Tiberius, who wished himself not to be humbled by this custom, issued an edict against it, but it does not appear to have done much good. In winter only it was considered improper to annoy another with one's cold lips."—*Becker's Gallus*.

[3] A goat driven about from door to door, to be milked for customers, is a common sight in Rome to-day, where children come out with gill or half-pint cups to get their morning ration.

in a row, proclaim a provision store; and a mill, driven by a mule, advertises a miller's and baker's shop, both in one. About the street corners are groups of loungers collected for their morning gossip, while gymnasts and gladiators, clowns, conjurers, snake-charmers, and a crowd of strolling swine,—who roam at will about the imperial city,— help to obstruct the narrow, tortuous highways. The professional street-beggars are out in force; squatting upon little squares of matting, they piteously implore a dole, or, feigning epilepsy, fall at the feet of some rich passer-by. Strangers, too, are here; men of foreign costume and bearing come from afar to see the wonders of the world-conquering city, and, as they gaze distractedly about, dazed by the din of rumbling wagons, shouting drivers, shrill-voiced hucksters, braying asses, and surging multitudes, suddenly there comes a lull. The slaves, whose task it is to watch the sun-dials and report the expiration of each hour, have announced that the sun has passed the mid-day line upon the pavement. Soon all tumult ceases, and for one hour the city is wrapped in silence.

The luxurious *siesta* over, Rome awakes to new enjoyment. Now come the pleasures and excitement of the circus and the theater, or the sports upon the Campus Martius, whither the young fashionables repair in crowds, to swim, run, ride, or throw the javelin, watched by an admiring assembly of seniors and women, who, clustered in porticoes, are sheltered from the burning sun. Then follows the luxury of the warm and vapor baths, with perfuming and anointing, and every refinement of physical refreshment as a preparation for the coming *cœna* or dinner (p. 306). But wherever one may seek enjoyment for the early evening, it is well to be housed before night comes on, for the streets of Rome swarm with nocturnal highwaymen, marauders, and high-blooded rowdies, who set the police at open defiance, and keep whole districts in terror. There are other dangers, too, for night is the time chosen by the careful housewife to dump the slops and *débris* from her upper windows into the open drain of the street below. Fires, also, are frequent, and, though the night-watch is provided with hatchets and buckets to resist its progress, a conflagration, once started in the crowded Suburra or Velabrum, spreads with fearful rapidity, and will soon render hundreds of families homeless.[1] Meanwhile the carts, shut out by law during the daytime, crowd and jostle one another in the eagerness of their noisy drivers to finish their duties

---

[1] The tenements of the lower classes in Rome were so crowded that often whole families were huddled together in one small room. The different stories were reached by stairways placed on the outside of the buildings.—There were no fire-insurance companies, but the sufferers were munificently recompensed by generous citizens, their loss being not only made good in money, but followed by presents of books, pictures, statues, and choice mosaics, from their zealous friends. Martial insinuates that on this account parties were sometimes tempted to fire their own premises.

and be at liberty for the night, while here and there groups of smoking flambeaux mark the well-armed trains of the patricians on their return from evening banquets. As the night advances, the sights and sounds gradually fade and die away, till in the first hours of the new day the glimmering lantern of the last wandering pedestrian has disappeared, and the great city lies under the stars asleep.

Scene II.—*A Roman Home.*[1]—We will not visit one of the tall lodging-houses which crowd the Suburra, though in passing we may glance at the plain, bare outside wall, with its few small windows[2] placed in the upper stories and graced with pots of flowers; and at the outside stairs by which the inmates mount to those dizzy heights, and under which the midnight robber and assassin often lurk. Sometimes we see a gabled front or end with a sloping roof, or feel the shade of projecting balconies which stretch far over the narrow street. On many a flat roof, paved with stucco, stone, or metal, and covered with earth, grow fragrant shrubs and flowers. Coming into more aristocratic neighborhoods, we yet see little domestic architecture to attract us. It is only when a spacious vestibule, adorned with statues and mosaic pillars, lies open to the street, that we have any intimation of the luxury within a Roman dwelling. If, entering such a vestibule, we rap with the bronze knocker, the unfastened folding-doors are pushed aside by the waiting janitor (who first peeps at us through the large open spaces in the door-posts),[3] and we find ourselves in the little ostium or entrance hall leading to the atrium. Here we are greeted, not only by the "*salve*" (welcome) on the mosaic pavement, but by the same cheerful word chattered by a trained parrot hanging above the door. We linger to notice the curiously carved door-posts, inlaid with tortoise-shell, and the door itself, which, instead of hinges, is provided

A ROMAN LAMP.

---

[1] No traces of ancient private dwellings exist in Rome, except in the ruins of the Palace of the Cæsars on the Palatine, where the so-called "House of Livia" (wife of Augustus), remains tolerably perfect. It is similar in dimensions and arrangement to the best Pompeian dwellings, though far superior in paintings and decorations. The "House of Pansa" in Pompeii, the plan of which is described in the text, is considered a good representative example of a wealthy Roman's home.

[2] Panes of glass have been found in Pompeii, though it was more usual to close the window-holes with movable wooden shutters, clay tablets, talc, or nets.

[3] In ancient times the janitor, accompanied by a dog, was confined to his proper station by a chain. As it was not customary to keep the door locked, such a protection was necessary. In the "House of the Tragic Poet," exhumed at Pompeii, a fierce black and white dog is depicted in the mosaic pavement, and underneath it is the inscription, "CAVE CANEM" (Beware of the Dog).

with wedge-shaped pins, fitting into sockets or rings, and then we pass into the atrium, the room about which cluster the most sacred memories of Roman domestic life. Here in ancient times all the simple meals were taken beside the hearth on which they were prepared, and by which the sacrifices were daily offered up to the beloved Lares and Penates.[1] Here was welcomed the master's chosen bride, and here, a happy matron,[2] she afterward sat enthroned in the midst of her industrious maids, spinning and weaving the household garments. From their niches upon these walls, by the side of glistening weapons captured in many a bloody contest, the waxen masks of honored ancestors have looked down for generations, watching the bodies of the family descendants, as one by one they have lain in state upon the funeral bier. — But increase of luxury has banished the stewing-pans, the busy looms, and the hospitable table to other apartments in the growing house. The Lares and Penates have left their primitive little closets by the atrium cooking-hearth for a larger and separate sacrarium, and spacious kitchens now send forth savory odors from turbot, pheasant, wild boar, and sausages, to be served up in summer or winter tricliniums by a host of well-trained slaves.[3] The household dead are still laid here, but the waxen masks of olden times are gradually giving place to brazen shield-shaped plates on which are dimly imaged

[1] At every meal the first act was to cast a portion of each article of food into the fire that burned upon the hearth, in honor of the household gods.

[2] The Roman matron, unlike the Greek, enjoyed great freedom of action, both within and without her house, and was always treated with attention and respect.

[3] The Romans were fond of amazing their guests with costly dainties, such as nightingales, peacocks, and the tongues and brains of flamingoes. Caligula dissolved pearls in powerful acids, in imitation of Cleopatra, and spent $400,000 on a single repast. A dramatic friend of Cicero paid over $4,000 for a dish of singing birds; and one famous epicure, after having exhausted the sum of four million dollars in his good living, poisoned himself because he had not quite half a million left! Fish was a favorite food, and the mansions of the rich were fitted up with fish-ponds (*piscinæ*) for the culture of rare varieties, which were sometimes caught and cooked on silver gridirons before invited guests, who enjoyed the changing colors of the slowly dying fish, and the tempting odor of the coming treat. Turbots, mackerels, eels, and oysters were popular delicacies, and a fine mullet brought sometimes as much as $240. In game the fatted hare and the wild boar, served whole, were ranked first. Pork, as in Greece, was the favorite meat, beef and mutton being regarded with little favor. Great display was made in serving, and Juvenal ridicules the airs of the professional carver of his time, who, he says,—

"Skips like a harlequin from place to place,
And waves his knife with pantomimic grace—
For different gestures by our curious men
Are used for different dishes, hare and hen."

In vegetables the Romans had lettuce, cabbage, turnips, and asparagus. Mushrooms were highly prized. The poorer classes lived on cheap fish, boiled chick-peas, beans, lentils, barley bread, and *puls* or gruel.

features, or to bronze and marble busts.[1] The little aperture in the center of the ceiling, which served the double purpose of escape for smoke and the admission of sunlight, has been enlarged, and is supported by costly marble pillars, alternating with statues; directly underneath it, the open cistern reflects each passing cloud, and mirrors the now-unused altar, which, for tradition's sake, is still left standing by its side. When the rain, wind, or heat becomes severe, a tapestry curtain, hung horizontally, is drawn over the aperture, and sometimes a pretty fountain, surrounded by flowering plants, embellishes the pool of water. Tapestries, sliding by rings on bars, conceal or open to view the apartments which adjoin the atrium. As we stand at the entrance-door of this spacious room,[2] with the curtains all drawn aside,

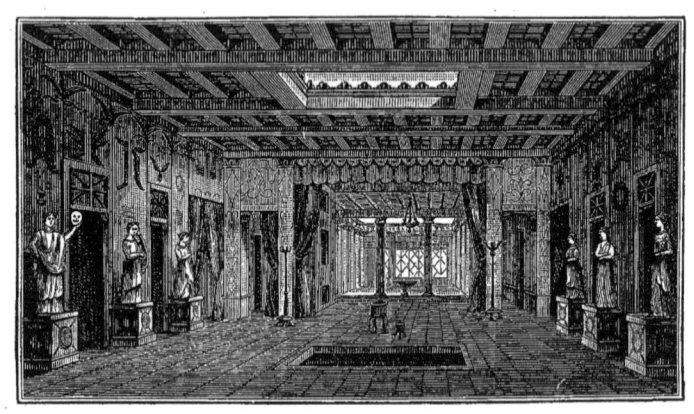

THE HOUSE OF PANSA (VIEW FROM THE ENTRANCE-DOOR OF THE ATRIUM).

we look down a long and beautiful vista; past the central fountain and altar; through the open tablinum, paved with marbles and devoted to the master's use; into the peristyle, a handsome open court surrounded by pillared arcades, paved with mosaics, and beautified, like the atrium, with central fountain and flowers; and still on, through the large banqueting hall, or family state-room (*œcus*), beyond the transverse corridor, and into the garden which stretches across the rear of the mansion. If we stop to glance into the library which adjoins the tablinum, we shall find its walls lined with cupboards stored

---

[1] Pliny speaks of the craving for portrait statues, which induced obscure persons, suddenly grown rich, to buy a fictitious ancestry, there being ready antiquarians then, as now, who made it a business to furnish satisfactory pedigrees.

[2] The atrium in the House of Pansa was nearly fifty feet long, and over thirty wide. As this was only a moderate-sized house in a provincial town, it is reasonable to suppose that the city houses of the rich were much more spacious.

with parchment rolls and adorned with busts and pictures of illustrious men, crowned by the presiding statues of Minerva and the Muses. In general furniture, we notice beautiful tripod-stands holding graceful vases, chairs after Greek patterns, and *lecti* [1] on which to recline when reading or writing. Occasionally there is a small wall-mirror, made of polished metal, and the walls themselves are brilliantly painted in panels, bearing graceful floating figures and scenes of mythological design. The floors are paved with bricks, marbles, or mosaics, and the rooms are warmed or cooled by pipes through which flows hot or cold water. In extreme weather there are portable stoves. There is a profusion of quaintly shaped bronze and even golden lamps, whose simple oil-fed wicks give forth at night a feeble glimmer.[2] As we pass through the fauces into the peristyle, a serpent slowly uncoils itself from its nest in one of the alæ, which has been made the household sanctuary,[3] and glides toward the triclinium in search of a crumb from the mid-day meal.

The large triclinium at the right of the peristyle is furnished with elegantly inlaid sofas, which form three sides of a square about a costly cedar or citrus-wood table.[4] At banquets the sofas are

[1] A *lectus* was neither bed nor sofa, but a simple frame with a low ledge at one end, and strung with girth on which a mattress and coverings were laid. Lecti were made of brass, or of cedar inlaid with ivory, tortoise-shell, and precious metals, and were provided with ivory, gold, or silver feet. Writing-desks with stools were unknown; the Roman reclined on the lectus when he wrote, resting his tablet upon his knee.

[2] The Romans were in the habit of making New-Year's gifts, such as dried figs, dates, and honeycomb, as emblems of sweetness, or a little piece of money as a hope for good luck. But the favorite gift was a lamp, and great genius was displayed in the variety of elegant designs which were invented in search of the novel and unique.

[3] Serpents were the emblems of the Lares, and were not only figured upon the altars, but, to insure family prosperity, a certain kind was kept as pets in the houses, where they nestled about the altars and came out like dogs or cats to be noticed by visitors, and to beg for something to eat. These sacred reptiles, which were of considerable size, but harmless except to rats and mice, bore such a charmed life that their numbers became an intolerable nuisance. Pliny intimates that many of the fires in Rome were kindled purposely to destroy their eggs.

[4] The citrus-wood tables, so prized among the Romans, cost from $40,000 to $50,000 apiece. Seneca is said to have owned five hundred citrus-wood tables. Vases of murrha—a substance identified by modern scientists with glass, Chinese porcelain, agate, and fluor-spar—were fashionable, and fabulous sums were paid for them. An ex-consul under Nero had a murrha wine-ladle which cost him $300,000, and which on his death-bed he deliberately dashed to pieces, to prevent its falling into the hands of the grasping tyrant. Bronze and marble statues were abundant in the houses and gardens of the rich, and cost from $150 for the work of an ordinary sculptor, to $30,000 for a genuine Phidias, Scopas, or Praxiteles. To gratify such expensive tastes, large fortunes were necessary, and the Romans—in early times averse to anything but arms and agriculture—developed shrewd, sharp business qualities. They roamed over foreign countries in search of speculations, and turned out swarms of bankers and merchants, who amassed enormous sums to

decked with white hangings embroidered with gold, and the soft wool-stuffed pillows upon which the guests recline are covered with gorgeous purple. Here, after his daily warm and vapor bath, the perfumed and enervated Roman gathers a few friends—in number not more than the Muses nor less than the Graces—for the evening supper (*cœna*). The courses follow one another as at a Grecian banquet. Slaves[1] relieve the master and his guests from the most trifling effort,

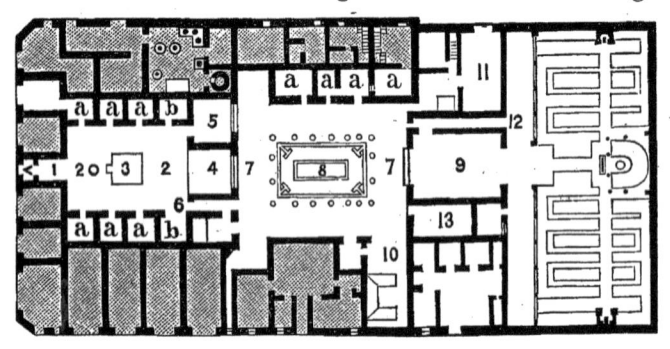

PLAN OF THE HOUSE OF PANSA.

(v) The *Vestibulum*, or hall; (1) The *Ostium*; (2) The *Atrium*, off which are six cubicula or sleeping-rooms; (3) The *Impluvium*, before which stands the pedestal or altar of the household gods; (4) The *Tablinum*, or chief room; (5) The *Pinacotheca*, or library and picture gallery; (6) The *Fauces*, or corridor; (7) The *Peristylium*, or court, with (8) its central fountain; (9) The *Æcus*, or state-room; (10) The *Triclinium*; (11) The kitchen; (12) The transverse corridor, with garden beyond; and (13) The *Lararium*, a receptacle for the more favorite gods, and for statues of illustrious personages.

carving each person's food or breaking it into fragments which he can raise to his mouth with his fingers,—forks being unknown,—and pouring water on his hands at every remove. The strictest etiquette prevails; long-time usages and traditions are followed; libations are offered to the protecting gods; spirited conversation, which is undignified and Greekish, is banished; and only solemn or caustic aphorisms on life and manners are heard. "People at supper," says Varro, "should be neither mute nor loquacious: eloquence is for the forum; silence for the bed-chamber." On high days, rules are banished; the host becomes the "Father of the supper," convivial excesses grow coarse and absurd, and all the follies and vices of the Greek symposium are exaggerated.

be spent on fashionable whims (see "Business Life in Ancient Rome," Harper's Half-hour Series).

[1] There were slaves for every species of service in a Roman household, and their number and versatility of handicraft remind one of the retinue of an Egyptian lord. Even the defective memory or limited talent of an indolent or over-taxed Roman was supplemented by a slave at his side, whose business it was to recall forgotten incidents and duties, to tell him the names of the persons he met, or to suggest appropriate literary allusions in his conversation.

Scene III.—*A Triumphal Procession.*—Rome is in her holiday attire. Streets and squares are festively adorned, and incense burns on the altars of the open temples. From steps and stands, improvised along the streets for the eager crowd, grow loud and louder shouts of "Io triumphe!" for the procession has started from the triumphal gate on its way through the city up to the Capitol. First come the lictors, opening a passage for the senate, the city magistrates, and important citizens. Pipers and flute-players follow. Then appear the spoils and booty; art-treasures, gold and silver coins, valuable plate, products of the conquered soil, armor, standards, models of captured cities and ships, pictures of battles, tablets inscribed with the victor's deeds, and statues personifying the towns and rivers of the newly subjected land,—all carried by crowned soldiers on the points of long lances or on portable stands. Chained kings, princes, and nobles, doomed to the Mamertine Prison, walk sullenly behind their lost treasures. In their wake are the sacrificial oxen with gilt horns, accompanied by priests; and then—preceded by singers, musicians, and jesters, the central object of all this grand parade—the VICTORIOUS GENERAL.[1] Clad in a tunic borrowed from the statue of the Capitoline Jupiter, with the eagle-topped ivory scepter in his hand and the triumphal crown held above his head, the conqueror proudly stands in his four-horse chariot, followed by his equally proud, victorious army. Through the Flaminian Circus, along the crowded Velabrum and the Circus Máximus, by the Via Sacra and the Forum, surges the vast procession up to the majestic Capitol. Here the triumphator lays his golden crown in the lap of Jupiter, and makes the imposing sacrifice. A feast of unusual sumptuousness ends the eventful day.

Scene IV.—*The Last of a Roman Emperor.*—"It is the Roman habit to consecrate the emperors who leave heirs. The mortal remains are buried, according to custom, in a splendid manner; but the wax image of the emperor is placed on an ivory bed, covered with gold-embroidered carpets, in front of the palace. The expression of the face is that of one dangerously ill. To the left side of the bed stand, during a greater part of the day, the members of the senate; to the right, the ladies entitled by birth or marriage to appear at court, in the usual simple white mourning-dresses without gold ornaments or necklaces. This ceremony lasts seven days, during which time the imperial physicians daily approach the bed as if to examine the patient, who, of course, is declining rapidly. At last they declare the emperor dead. The bier is now transported by the highest born knights and the

---

[1] Only dictators, consuls, prætors, and occasionally legatos, were permitted the triumphal entrance. Sometimes the train of spoils and captives was so great that two, three, and even four days were required for the parade. In later times the triumphal procession was exclusively reserved for the emperor.

younger senators through the Via Sacra to the old Forum, and there deposited on a scaffolding built in the manner of a terrace. On one side stand young patricians, on the other noble ladies, intoning hymns and pæans in honor of the deceased to a solemn, sad tune; after which the bier is taken up again, and carried to the Campus Martius. A wooden structure in the form of a house has been erected on large blocks of wood on a square base; the inside has been filled with dry sticks; the outside is adorned with gold-embroidered carpets, ivory statues, and various sculptures. The bottom story, a little lower than the second, shows the same form and ornamentation as this; it has open doors and windows; above these two stories rise others, growing narrow toward the top, like a pyramid. The whole structure might be compared to the lighthouses erected in harbors. The bier is placed in the second story; spices, incense, odoriferous fruits and herbs being heaped round it. After the whole room has been filled with incense, the knights move in procession round the entire structure, and perform some military evolutions; they are followed by chariots filled with persons wearing masks and clad in purple robes, who represent historic characters, such as celebrated generals and kings. After these ceremonies are over, the heir to the throne throws a torch into the house, into which, at the same time, flames are dashed from all sides, which, fed by the combustible materials and the incense, soon begin to devour the building. At this juncture an eagle rises into the air from the highest story as from a lofty battlement, and carries, according to the idea of the Romans, the soul of the dead emperor to heaven; from that moment he partakes of the honors of the gods."—*Herodian.*

4. SUMMARY.

1. **Political History.**—Rome began as a single city. The growth of her power was slow but steady. She became head, *first*, of the neighboring settlements; *second*, of Latium; *third*, of Italy; and, *fourth*, of the lands around the Mediterranean. In her early history, there was a fabulous period during which she was ruled by kings. The last of the seven monarchs belonged to a foreign dynasty, and upon his expulsion a republic was established. Two centuries of conflict ensued between the patricians and the plebs; but the latter, going ofttimes to Mount Sacer, gained their end and established a democracy.

Meanwhile, wars with powerful neighbors and with the awe-inspiring Gauls had developed the Roman character in all its sternness, integrity, and patriotism. Rome next came in contact with Pyrrhus, and learned how to fortify her military camps; then with Carthage, and she found out the value of a navy. An apt pupil, she gained the mastery of the sea, invaded Africa, and in the end razed Carthage to the ground. Turning to the west, she secured Spain—the silver-producing country of that age—and Gaul, whose fiery sons filled the depleted ranks of her legions. At the east she intrigued where she could, and fought where she must, and by disorganizing states made them first her dependencies, and then her provinces. Greece, Macedon, Asia Minor, Syria, Egypt, Babylon, were but stepping-stones in her progress until Parthia alone remained to bar her advance to the Indus and the ocean.

But within her gates the struggle between the rich and the poor still went on. Crowds of slaves—captives of her many wars—thronged her streets, kept her shops, waited in her homes, tilled her land, and tended her flocks. The plebeians, shut out from honest toil, struggled for the patrician's dole. The civil wars of Sulla and Marius drenched her pavements with the blood of her citizens. The triumphs of Cæsar shed a gleam of glory over the fading republic, but the mis-aimed daggers of Brutus and Cassius that slew the dictator struck at the heart of liberty as well.

Augustus brought in the empire and an era of peace. Now the army gained control of the state. Weak and wicked emperors, the luxury of wealth, the influx of oriental profligacy, the growth of atheism, and the greed of conquest, undermined the fabric of Roman greatness. The inhabitants of the provinces were made Romans, and, Rome itself being lost in the empire it had created, other cities became the seats of government. Amid the ruins of the decaying monarchy a new religion supplanted the old, and finally Teutonic hordes from the north overwhelmed the city that for centuries their own soldiers had alone upheld.

2. Civilization.—As in Greece the four ancient Attic tribes were subdivided into phratries, gentes, and hearths, so in Rome the three original patrician tribes branched into curiæ, gentes, and families, the paterfamilias owning all the property, and holding the life of his children at will.

The *civil magistrates* comprised consuls, quæstors, ædiles, and prætors.

The *army* was organized in legions, cohorts, companies, and centuries, with four classes of foot-soldiers, who fought with the pilum and the javelin, protected themselves with heavy breastplates, and carried on sieges by the aid of ballistas, battering-rams, catapults, and movable towers. In later times the ranks were filled by foreigners and mercenaries.

Roman *literature*, child of the Grecian, is rich with memorable names. Ushered in by Livius Andronicus, a Greek slave, it grew with Nævius, Ennius, Plautus, Terence, Cato, and Lucilius. The learned

Varro, the florid Cicero, the graceful Virgil, the genial Horace, the eloquent Livy, and the polished Sallust, ennobled the last century before Christ. The next hundred years produced the studious Pliny the Elder, the two inseparable friends Pliny the Younger and Tacitus, the sarcastic Juvenal, and the wise Seneca.

The *monuments* of the Romans comprise splendid aqueducts, triumphal arches, military roads, bridges, harbors, and tombs. Their magnificent palaces and luxurious thermæ were fitted up with reckless extravagance and dazzling display. All the spoils of conquered nations enriched their capital, and all the foreign arts and inventions were impressed into their service.

The proud, dignified, ambitious Roman had no love or tenderness for aught but his national supremacy. Seldom indulging in sentiment toward family or kindred, he recognized no law of humanity toward his slaves. His *religion* was a commercial bargain with the gods, in which each was at liberty to outwit the other. His *worship* was mostly confined to the public ceremonies at the shrine of Vesta, and the constant household offerings to the Lares and Penates. His *public games* were a degraded imitation of the Grecian, and he took his chief delight in bloody gladiatorial shows and wild-beast fights.

A *race of borrowers*, the Romans assimilated into their nationality most of the excellences as well as many of the vices of other peoples, for centuries stamping the whole civilized world with their character, and dominating it by their successes. "As to Rome all ancient history converges, so from Rome all modern history begins."

Finally, as a central point in the history of all time, in the midst of the brilliancy of the Augustan age, while Cicero, Sallust, Virgil, and Horace were fresh in the memory of their still living friends, with Seneca in his childhood and Livy in his prime, the empire at its best, and Rome radiant in its growing transformation from brick to marble under the guiding rule of the great Augustus Cæsar, there was born in an obscure Roman province the humble Babe whose name far outranks all these, and from whose nativity are dated all the centuries which have succeeded.

READING REFERENCES.

Merivale's History of the Romans.—Ihne's History of Rome, and Early Rome.— History Primers; Rome, and Roman Antiquities, edited by Green.—Arnold's History of Rome.—Niebuhr's History of Rome.—Smith's smaller History of Rome.— Gibbon's Decline and Fall of the Roman Empire.—Guhl and Köner's Life of the Greeks and Romans.—Knight's Social Life of the Romans. Plutarch's Lives.—Milman's History of Christianity.—Mommsen's History of Rome.—Froude's Life of Cæsar. —Becker's Charicles, and Gallus.—Macaulay's Lays of Ancient Rome.—Shakspere's

Julius Cæsar, Coriolanus, and *Antony and Cleopatra.—Forsyth's Life of Cicero.—Napoleon's (III.) Life of Cæsar.—Canina's Edifices of Ancient Rome.—Fergusson's History of Architecture.—Bulwer's Last Days of Pompeii,* and *Rienzi the Last of the Tribunes.—Michelet's Roman Republic.—Heeren's Historical Researches.—Putz's Hand-book of Ancient History.—Hare's Walks in Rome.—Kingsley's Hypatia.—Lord's Old Roman World.—Mann's Ancient and Mediæval Republics.—Lawrence's Primer of Roman Literature.—Collins's Ancient Classics for English Readers (a series giving striking passages from the Greek and Roman classics, with excellent explanatory notes, lives of the authors, etc.).—Dyer's Pompeii.—Herbermann's Business Life in Ancient Rome.—Lanciani's Ancient Rome in the Light of Recent Discoveries.*

CHRONOLOGY.

	B. C.
Rome founded	753
Republic established	509
The Decemvirs	451
Rome taken by Gauls	390
First Samnite War	343–341
Great Latin War	340–338
Second Samnite War	326–304
Third " "	298–290
Wars with Pyrrhus	280–276
First Punic War	264–241
Second " "	218–201
Battle of the Trebia	218
" " Lake Trasimenus	217
" " Cannæ	216
Siege of Capua	214–211
Battle of the Metaurus	207
" " Zama	202
Second Macedonian War	200–197
Battle of Magnesia	190
Death of Hannibal and Scipio Africanus	183
Third Macedonian War	171–168
Battle of Pydna	168
Third Punic War	149–146
Fall of Carthage and Corinth	146
Death of Tiberius Gracchus	133
Jugurthine War	111–104
Marius defeated Teutones at Aquæ Sextiæ (Aix)	102
Marius defeated Cimbri	101
Social War	90–88
First Mithridatic War	88–84
Massacre by Marius	87
Second Mithridatic War	83–81
Sulla's Proscriptions	83
Third Mithridatic War	74–63
War of Spartacus	73–71
Mediterranean Pirates	67
Conspiracy of Catiline	63

	B. C.
First Triumvirate	60
Cæsar in Gaul	58–49
" invades Britain	55
" crosses the Rubicon	49
Battle of Pharsalia—death of Pompey	48
Suicide of Cato	46
Cæsar assassinated	44
Second Triumvirate, death of Cicero	43
Battle of Philippi, suicide of Brutus and Cassius	42
Battle of Actium	31
Augustus	31

	A. D.
Tiberius	14
Caligula	37
Claudius	41
Nero	54
Galba	68
Otho	69
Vitellius	69
Vespasian	69
Titus	79
Domitian	81
Nerva	96
Trajan	98
Hadrian	117
Antoninus Pius	138
M. Aurelius Antoninus	161–180
L. Verus	161–169
Commodus	180
Pertinax	193
Didius Julianus	193
Septimius Severus	193
Caracallus	211–217
Geta	211–212
Macrinus	217
Elagabalus (the sun-priest)	218
Alexander Severus	222

(The Twelve Cæsars (with Julius))

	A.D.
Maximinus	235
Gordian I. } Gordian II. }	238
Pupienus Maximus } Balbinus }	238
Gordian III	238–244
Philip the Arabian	244
Decius	249
Gallus	251
Æmilian	253
Valerian	253
Gallienus	260
Claudius II	268
Aurelian	270
Tacitus	275
Florian	276
Probus	276
Carus	282
Carinus and Numerian	283
Diocletian, with Maximian	284
Constantius, with Galerius	305
Constantine I. (the Great), with Galerius, Severus, and Maxentius	306

	A.D.
Constantine, with Licinius	307
Constantine, with Maximinus	308
Constantine, alone	323
Constantine II., Constantius II., Constans I.	337
Julian the Apostate	361
Jovian	363
Valentinian I	364
Gratian and Valentinian II	375
Valentinian II	383
Theodosius (East and West)	392
Honorius	395
Theodosius II. (East and West)	423
Valentinian III	425
Petronius Maximus	455
Avitus	455
Majorian	457
Libius Severus	461
Anthemius	467
Olybrius	472
Glycerius	473
Julius Nepos	474
Romulus Augustulus	475–476

TOMBS ALONG THE APPIAN WAY.

APPENDIX.

THE SEVEN WONDERS OF THE WORLD, as reckoned by the Greeks, were The Egyptian Pyramids; The Temple, Walls, and Hanging Gardens of Babylon; The Greek Statue of Jupiter at Olympia; The Temple of Diana at Ephesus; The Mausoleum at Halicarnassus; The Pharos at Alexandria; and The Colossus of Rhodes. All but the last three have already been described.

The Mausoleum was a monument erected by Artemisia, Queen of Caria (B. C. 353), to her deceased husband Mausolus. It was built of the most precious marbles, and decorated in the highest style of Grecian art. Its cost was so immense that the philosopher Anaxagoras on seeing it exclaimed, "How much money is changed into stone!" Not a vestige of it now remains.

The Pharos was a lighthouse built by the first two Ptolemies on the Isle of Pharos. The wrought stone of which it was constructed was adorned with columns, balustrades, etc., of the finest marble. The tower, protected by a sea-wall, stood about four hundred feet high, and its light could be seen over forty miles.

The Colossus of Rhodes was a hollow bronze statue of Apollo, one hundred and five feet high, near the Rhodian harbor. An inner winding staircase led up to the head. It was overthrown by an earthquake (224 B. C.). The Delphic oracle having forbade its reërection, it lay in ruins for over nine centuries, when it was sold by the Saracens to a Jew, who, it is said, loaded nine hundred camels with the metal.

THE SEVEN WISE MEN were variously named even in Greece. The following translation of a Grecian doggerel gives one version:—

> "I'll tell the names and sayings and the places of their birth
> Of the Seven great ancient Sages, so renowned on Grecian earth.
> The Lindian *Cleobulus* said, 'The man was still the best;'
> The Spartan *Chilo*, 'Know thyself,' a heaven-born phrase confessed;
> Corinthian *Periander* taught 'Our anger to command;'
> 'Too much of nothing,' *Pittacus*, from Mitylene's strand;
> Athenian *Solon* this advised, 'Look to the end of life;'
> And *Bias* from Prienè showed 'Bad men are the most rife;'
> Milesian *Thales* urged that 'None should e'er a surety be;'
> Few were these words, but, if you look, you'll much in little see."
> *Collins's Ancient Classics.*

HISTORICAL RECREATIONS.
ANCIENT PEOPLES.

1. How did a workman's scribble, made thousands of years ago, preserve a royal name, and link it to a monument?
2. What king ordered the sea to be whipped because the waves had injured his bridges?
3. Who among the ancients were the greatest sailors? Who had a religious horror of the sea?
4. What kings took a pet lion when they went to war? Who once took cats and dogs? Who used elephants in battle? Camels? Scythed chariots?
5. What is the oldest book in the world?
6. Compare the character of an Egyptian and an Assyrian; an Egyptian and a Chinaman; a Babylonian and a Persian.
7. What king was so overwhelmed by his successes that he prayed for a reverse?
8. What Roman emperor gave up his throne to enjoy his cabbage-garden?
9. What emperor once convened the senate to decide how to cook a fish?
10. Who gained a kingdom by the neighing of a horse?
11. Who is the oldest literary critic on record?
12. What was the "Dispensary of the Soul"?
13. Who was the "Egyptian Alexander the Great"?
14. What statue was reported to sing at sunrise?
15. Which of the earliest races is noted for intellectual vigor? For religious fervor? For massive architecture?
16. What is the "Book of the Dead"? The Zend-Avesta? The Epic of Pentaur? The Rig-Veda?
17. Who had a palace at Nimroud? At Koyunjik? At Khorsabad? At Persepolis? At Luxor? At Karnak? At Susa?
18. Compare the character of a Spartan and an Athenian; a Roman and a Greek.
19. What people made the intoxication of their king an annual display?
20. What city was called the "Daughter of Sidon and the Mother of Carthage"? What was the "School of Greece"? The "Eye of Greece"? The "Seven-hilled City"?
21. What king had a servant remind him three times a day of a proposed vengeance?
22. Who fought and who won the battle of Marathon? Platæa? Thermopylæ? Salamis? Himera? Mycale?
23. Who were the Cyclops?

24. Where and when were iron coins used as currency? Gold and silver rings? Engraved gems?

25. Who was Asshurbanipal? Tiglath-Pileser? Khufu? Seti? Asshur-izir-pal? Sennacherib? Cyrus? Cambyses?

26. Which do you think was the most religious nation? The most warlike? The most patient? The most intellectual? The most artistic?

27. Where were animals worshiped? The sun? The planets? The elements? Vegetables? The Evil Spirit?

28. Who built the Great Wall of China? The Great Pyramid? The Labyrinth?

29. How were women treated in Egypt? In Assyria? In Persia? In Athens? In Sparta? In Rome?

30. Who was Buddha? Sebak? Pasht? Thoth? Bel? Ishtar? Moloch? Asshur? Ormazd? Nin? Nergal? Baal?

31. How many Assyrian and Babylonian kings can you mention who bore the names of gods?

32. How did a Babylonian gentleman compliment the gods?

33. What does the word *Pharaoh* or *Phrah* mean? *Ans.* According to some authorities it means *the sun*, from the Egyptian "ph-Ra;" by others it is derived from "pe-raa," *grand house*, a title corresponding to our "Sublime Porte."

34. Who was the "Religious Conqueror"?

35. What were the Pools of Peace? The realms of Hades?

36. Who was Che Hwang-te? Nebuchadnezzar? Darius? The Last of the Ptolemies?

37. Who was the "False Smerdis"?

38. Who were the Accadians, and where did they live?

39. What city was captured during a royal revelry?

40. What nations believed in the transmigration of souls?

41. When was the Era of Nabonassar? The First Olympiad? The age of Pericles?

42. What famous story is related of Cornelia, the mother of the Gracchi?

43. Mention the ornaments worn by gentlemen in ancient times.

44. Who was the real Sardanapalus? Sesostris?

45. What religion teaches that the vilest insects and even the seeds of plants have souls?

46. What poem is called the "Egyptian Iliad"?

47. What Roman emperor resembled Louis XI. of France in character?

48. Who was Herodotus? Manetho? Thucydides? Livy? Xenophon? Tacitus? Sallust? Cæsar?

49. What is meant by "seceding to the Sacred Mount"?

50. What great war was begun through helping some pirates?
51. What nation considered theft a virtue?
52. What Greek was called by Solon "a bad imitation of Ulysses"?
53. What was the original meaning of *slave?* Of *tyrant?*
54. Who sculptured the famous Niobe Group?
55. What are the "Elgin Marbles"?
56. Who were the "Lost Tribes"?
57. A great king married the "Pearl of the East." Who was he? Who was she? Why did he marry her?
58. Who were the Pericœki? The Helots? The Spartans? The Dorians? The Ionians? The Hellenes?
59. What is meant by "taking Egerean counsel"?
60. What was the Amphictyonic Council? The Council of the Elders? The Court of Areopagus?
61. Name the principal battles of the Persian wars; the Punic wars.
62. Who engaged in the Messenian wars?
63. What were the Seven Wonders of the World?
64. Name the Seven Wise Men, with their mottoes.
65. What Roman emperor amused himself by spearing flies?
66. Who were the "Five Good Emperors" of Rome?
67. Name the most important Egyptian kings. What can you tell about them?
68. Describe the ceremonies of the Magi.
69. How many relics found in tombs can you mention?
70. What is the Rosetta stone? The Behistun Inscription?
71. Describe the Homa ceremony.
72. What was the Apis? "The Lights"?
73. Tell what you can of the Memnonium; the Colosseum; the Ramesseum; the Colossus of Rhodes; the Hanging Gardens of Babylon; the Great Sphinx.
74. Who was the greatest builder among the Pharaohs?
75. What country forbade its priests to wear woolen undergarments?
76. Compare the dress and ceremonies of an Egyptian priest and a Roman flamen.
77. Where was the Parthenon? The Palace of the Cæsars? The Erechtheium? The "Temple of the Sphinx"?
78. What people had no sacred books?
79. Who were the greatest borrowers among the ancients?
80. What is the difference between hieroglyphics and cuneiform writing? What peoples used them?
81. What people used to write on the shoulder-bones of animals?
82. Mention all the writing implements you can remember, and the peoples who used them.

83. Who was Pindar? Simonides? Horace? Sappho? Hesiod? Anacreon?

84. When was an army driven with whips to an assault?

85. Who was "Little Boot"?

86. Give the origin of the word *Vandal*.

87. How did a ray from the setting sun once save a city?

88. What king sat on a marble throne while reviewing his army?

89. What emperor once lighted his grounds with burning Christians?

90. What people wore a golden grasshopper as a head-ornament? What did it signify?

91. Describe the Alexandrian Museum and Library.

92. What was the Athenian Lyceum? The Academy?

93. What Greek philosopher kept a drug-store in Athens?

94. Describe the building of a pyramid.

95. What is the oldest account of the Creation? Of the Deluge? In what language were they written?

96. How many great men can you name who died in prison? Who were assassinated? Who voluntarily committed suicide? Who were sentenced by law to kill themselves?

97. What Greek poem was found under the head of a mummy?

98. What king began his reign by glorifying his father, and ended it by erasing his father's name from the Temple walls and substituting his own?

99. Mention the twelve great Grecian gods, with their attributes.

100. What was the kinship of Isis, Osiris, and Horus, according to Egyptian mythology?

101. Where did people ride on a seat strapped between two donkeys?

102. What great Greek philosopher was an oil speculator?

103. Who were the Cynics?

104. Describe a Chaldean home.

105. What people buried their dead in stone jars? Who embalmed their dead? Who buried them in honey? Who exposed them to wild beasts? Who burned them? Who covered them with wax before burial? Who made feasts for them? Give the post mortem travels of Rameses II.

106. Describe the education of an Egyptian boy. A Persian boy.

107. Who were the "Ten Thousand Immortals"?

108. Describe a Persian military march.

109. Who invented the alphabet?

110. What happened in Egypt when a cat died? A dog?

111. Describe an Assyrian lion-hunt.

112. What nation excelled in sculptured bas-relief? In brick-enameling? In bronze and marble statuary? In gem-cutting?

113. Compare Egyptian and Assyrian art; religion; literature.

114. Describe an Assyrian royal banquet; a Persian banquet of wine.

115. What national architecture was distinguished by pyramids and obelisks? By tall, slender pillars and elaborate staircases?

116. What nations built their houses on high platforms?

117. Describe the education of a Spartan boy; an Athenian; a Roman.

118. How did the Assyrians go to war?

119. Who was called the "Third Founder of Rome"?

120. How many times in Roman history was the Temple of Janus closed? *Ans.* Eight.

121. What city was entitled "The Eldest Daughter of the Empire"?

122. Who boasted that grass never grew where his horse had trodden?

123. What did Europe gain by the battle of Chalons?

124. Describe a Macedonian phalanx.

125. Who were the "Tragic Trio" of Greece? The Historical Trio?

126. What people covered the mouth of their dead with gold-leaf? Who provided their dead with money to pay their fare across the river Styx? Who furnished them with dates for refreshment in the spirit-world? Tell what you can of the Egyptian *Ka*.

127. Describe the stationery of the Egyptians; the Assyrians and Babylonians; the Persians; the Greeks and Romans.

128. Who made the first discovery of an Assyrian monument?

129. What people used second-hand coffins?

130. What nation cased the beams of their palaces with bronze? Who overlaid them with silver and gold?

131. What modern archæologist discovered the remains of ancient Troy? Describe Cesnola's discoveries; Flinders Petrie's.

132. How did Rameses II. and Asshurbanipal resemble each other?

133. Describe the contents and one of the regulations of Asshurbanipal's library.

134. Who is your favorite Greek? Your favorite Roman?

135. What people loaded the roofs of their houses with earth as a protection from sun and rain? Who had roof-gardens? [In Italy and in the East roof-gardens are still common.]

136. When and where were bronze and iron used for jewelry?

137. In what country was it considered disreputable for a gentleman to walk the streets without a cane?

138. In what country did gentlemen wear cylinders on their wrists? For what did they use them?

HISTORICAL RECREATIONS.

139. How did the views of the Greeks and the Persians differ in regard to fire and cremation?

140. Describe an Egyptian funeral; a Greek; a Roman.

141. Who sowed corn over newly-made graves?

142. Describe an Egyptian nobleman's home.

143. Compare Æschylus, Sophocles, and Euripides.

144. Who was Aristophanes? Menander? Plautus? Terence? Lucian?

145. What people entertained a mummy as a guest at parties?

146. Who were the Sargonidæ? Sassanidæ? Seleucidæ? Alcmæonidæ? Heraclidæ?

147. Name the great men of the age of Pericles; of the Augustan age.

148. Describe a Theban dinner-party; a Greek symposium; a Roman banquet.

149. How did an Egyptian fight? An Assyrian? A Babylonian? A Persian? A Greek? A Roman?

150. Name ten great battles before the time of Christ.

151. Describe a Spartan home; an Athenian; a Roman.

152. What Egyptian king changed the course of a river in order to found a city?

153. Describe the Magian rites.

154. Tell what you can of a Roman Vestal.

155. Who were the Three Graces? Three Fates? Three Hesperides? Three Harpies? Three Gorgons? Three Furies?

156. Describe the Nine Muses.

157. For what was the Pnyx celebrated? The Areopagus?

158. In what country was it considered unamiable for a wife to refuse to wear her husband's clothes?

159. What philosopher is said to have lived in a tub?

160. What kind of table-napkins did the Greeks use?

161. Who was the "Blind Bard"? The "Poet of the Helots"? The "Lame old Schoolmaster"? The "Lesbian Nightingale"? The "Theban Eagle"? The "Attic Bee"? The "Mantuan Bard"?

162. Who was called the "Light of Mankind"?

163. What poets dropped their shield in battle and ran from danger?

164. How many Greek poets can you name? Latin poets?

165. What were the "Four Great Schools of Philosophy"?

166. A great philosopher, when burlesqued in a famous play, mounted a bench that the audience might compare him with his ridiculous counterpart. Who was he? Who wrote the play? Were they friends?

167. In what city was cock-and-quail fighting enjoined by law as an instructive exhibition?

168. What Greek poet likened himself to a porcupine?
169. Who was Confucius? Lycurgus? Draco? Æsop? Solon?
170. Describe the peculiar tactics that decided the battle of Marathon; Leuctra; Chæronea; Cannæ.
171. What were the Philippics?
172. What great poets were linked with the battle of Salamis?
173. Where, and as a reward for what, was a wreath of olive conferred? Of parsley? Of laurel? Of pine?
174. What great orator received a golden crown for his public services?
175. What were the Eleusinian mysteries? What great poet is connected with them? Who was accursed for revealing them?
176. What was a Greek trilogy?
177. Who wrote a history named after the Nine Muses?
178. Who was Eucles? Cleisthenes? Leonidas? Pausanias?
179. Compare the style of Xenophon and of Thucydides.
180. Who was the first authenticated "reporter"?
181. What philosopher was tried for atheism because he believed in one great God?
182. Tell what you can of Pythagoras; Socrates; Plato; Aristotle; Zeno.
183. Who was Cimon? Pericles? Aristides? Themistocles?
184. Who was Mardonius? Xerxes? Miltiades?
185. Describe a Babylonian wedding; a Greek wedding; a Roman wedding.
186. Describe the Panathenæa; the Feast of Dionysus.
187. Compare the Babylonian Sacees and the Roman Saturnalia.
188. Who were Hippias and Hipparchus? Who was Pisistratus?
189. Who was Cleopatra? Mark Antony? Brutus? Pompey?
190. What great philosopher was born the year that Pericles died?
191. What great historian died in the year of the "Retreat of the Ten Thousand"?
192. Who formed the "First Triumvirate?" The Second?
193. In what siege did the women braid their long hair into bowstrings?
194. Who were the Seven Sages?
195. How did Hannibal lose an eye?
196. On what field did the Macedonian phalanx fight its last battle?
197. What was the characteristic of the first two centuries of the Roman republic?
198. How did the phrase "Romans and Quirites" arise?
199. Describe a triumphal entrance into Rome.
200. What were the Laws of the Twelve Tables?
201. Tell the story of the "Rape of the Sabines."

202. Who refused a gift of land because he already possessed seven acres?
203. How did Hannibal once outwit Fabius?
204. Tell the story of the capture of Rome by the Gauls.
205. In what battle were gold rings a part of the spoils?
206. In what year did Nineveh fall? Babylon?
207. During what battle did an earthquake occur without being noticed by the combatants?
208. What province was left to the Romans by will?
209. What mathematician was killed in the midst of a problem?
210. Who was Pliny the Younger's dearest friend?
211. What famous general sat amid the ruins of a great city and quoted Homer?
212. What warriors trimmed their hair on the eve of a battle?
213. Distinguish between the different Scipios; the two Catos; the two Plinys.
214. What poet was commemorated by the statue of a drunken old man?
215. What general declared that the greatest joy he had in a victory was the pleasure his success would give to his parents?
216. What emperor boasted that he found his capital of brick, and left it of marble?
217. What emperor wore a toga woven by his wife and daughters?
218. Who were Alexander's favorite artists? Who was his tutor?
219. What was the Roman Poor Law?
220. How many Roman emperors were murdered? How many committed suicide? How many died a natural death?
221. In what country were fat men suspected?
222. What battle ended the Roman republic?
223. What great philosopher died the same year with Demosthenes? Which was the elder?
224. Describe "A Day in Rome;" a Roman home.
225. Describe the different modes of publishing books in ancient times. Name the royal founders of ancient libraries.
226. When was the Era of Martyrs? Of the Thirty Tyrants?
227. What king had the title "Conqueror of Babylon" inscribed upon his signet-ring?
228. Describe a morning in Nineveh.
229. Tell something connected with Mount Olympus; Mount Parnassus; Mount Hymettus; Mount Sinai; Mount Pentelicus.
230. How did his Roman citizenship help St. Paul?
231. When did elephants win a battle?
232. When did the Grecians fight in Italy?
233. Who were the road-builders of antiquity?

234. Show how the struggle of each petty Grecian state for *autonomy* prevented the unity and prosperity of Greece.

*235. Compare the personal rights of man among the ancients with those that he enjoys among the Christian nations of to-day.

236. Describe the mode of Rome's growth as a nation.

237. What was the character of Rome's government over her provinces?

238. Under what emperor did all the provincials acquire Roman citizenship?

239. Explain the expression, "Chæronea was the coffin, as Marathon was the cradle, of Hellenic liberty."

240. What was the origin of the word *politics? Pagan?*

241. Who first used the expression, "*Delenda est Carthago*"?

242. Narrate the circumstances of the death of Archimedes.

243. Describe the three popular assemblies of Rome.

244. How did the Romans procure a model for the ships of their first fleet?

245. What hostile general once threw a javelin over the walls of Rome?

246. Who said, "It is easier to turn the sun from its course than Fabricius from the path of honor"?

247. Tell the story of Lucretia; Virginia; Horatius Cocles; Mucius; Romulus and Remus; Coriolanus; Cincinnatus; Camillus; Marcus Manlius; Quintus Curtius; Decius; Caius Pontius.

248. Name the twelve Cæsars.

249. For what is the date 146 B. C. noted?

250. Describe the funeral of a Roman emperor.

INDEX
AND PRONOUNCING VOCABULARY.

_**_* The figures refer to the page number.

NOTE. — Diacritical marks are as follows: ā, ē, ī, ō, ū, are long; ă, ĕ, ĭ, ŏ, ŭ, short, as in ăm, mĕt, ĭn, ŏn, ŭp; â, ä, à, ạ, as in câre, ärm, àsk, ạll; u as in full; ē as in tẽrm; ė as in there; ҫ like s; ġ like j; ҽh like k; ş like z; th as in thine.

Abram in Canaan, 80; in Egypt, 39.
Aby'dus, temple of, 18.
Academy at Athens, the, 175, 282.
Ac'cad, 45, 46.
Accā'dian, the, 45.
Achæ'an League, the, 157.
Achæans, conquest of, by Dorians, 117.
Achaia (å-kā'ya), province of, 237.
Achilles (ă-kĭl'leez), 116, 190.
Acrŏp'olis, 123, 128, 145, 180–182, 187, 194.
Actium (ăk'shē-ŭm), battle of, 254.
Æ'diles, Roman, 271.
Ægŏspŏt'ămĭ, battle of, 145.
Æne'as, 117, 205.
Æne'id, the, 117, 275.
Æ-ō'li-an War, the, 116.
Æ-ŏl'ic Colonies, 118.
Æ'quians, the, 220.
Æschines (ĕs'kĭ-neez), 173.
Æschylus (ĕs'kĭ-lŭs), 127, 165, 168, 192.
Æsop (ē'sŏp), 173, 174.
Aetius (a-ē'shĭ-ŭs) at Châlons, 268.
Ætō'li-an League, 157.
Ætolians, the, at Thermopylæ, 237.
Africa, 19.
Agamem'non captures Troy, 116.
Agăth'o-clēs, tyrant of Sicily, 79.
Agĕsilā'us, King of Sparta, 146.
A'ġis, King of Sparta, 179.
Ag'ora, the Athenian, 182.
Agrarian Law, 216.
Agric'ola conquers Britain, 260.
Agrigen'tum, capture of, 227.
Agrip'pa, 214, 298.
Agrippina (à-grĭp-pī'na), 259.
A'hab, 48.
A'haz, 49.
Ahrĭman (äh'rĭ-man), Persian god, 98.
Aix (ăks), battle of, 242.
Al'aric the Goth, 267.
Al'ba Lon'ga, 205, 209.
Alçæ'us, Greek poet, 164.
Alçĭbī'a-dēṣ, 141, 143, 144, 175.
Alc-mæ-ŏn'ĭdæ, the, 123, 124.
Alexander the Great, 150–152, 177.
Alexander Sevē'rus, 262.
Alexandria, 151, 154.
Allia, 221.
Alphabet, 77, 113.
Al'tis, the Greek, 181, 186.
Am'brōse. See Christian Fathers.

Amenemhe (ä-men-em'ĕ) III., 39.
Amphĭctyŏn'ic Council, 115, 149.
Amphitheater, Flavian (Colosseum), 284.
Am'unoph III., 17.
Anăb'asis, the, 172.
Anăc'reon, 164.
Anaxăġ'oras, 167, 174.
Anaximan'der, 174.
Androni'cus, Livius, 273.
Antăl'çidas, Peace of, 146.
An'ti-ŏeh, 155, 237.
Antī'o-ehus the Great, 234, 237.
Antip'ater, 150.
Antĭs'thenēṣ, 177, 194.
An'tonīnes, age of the, 261.
Antoni'nus, Marcus, 261.
Antoninus, Pius, 261.
An'tony, Mark, 251–254.
Apĕl'lēṣ, 155, 183.
Ape'pi II., 80.
Aphrodī'te, 184.
A'pis, 31.
Apŏl'lo (Apollon), 184.
Apollodō'rus, Greek painter, 182.
Apollō'nius, Greek poet, 155.
Ap'pian Way, the, 283.
Ap'pius Clau'dius, 217, 283.
Aqueducts of Rome, 282.
Arbe'la, battle of, 151.
Arch of Constantine, 284; of Severus, 284; of Titus, 284.
Arehĭdā'mus, 140, 141.
Arehĭl'oehus, 163.
Archimedes (är-kĭ-mē'deez), 155, 234.
Architecture. See Art.
Ar'ehons, Athenian, 121.
A-re-ŏp'agus, court of, 122, 194.
A'rēṣ (Mars), god of war, 184, 192.
Argonautic Expedition, 115.
Ar'gŏs, 117, 146.
Aria or Iran, 10.
Ariad'ne, 185.
A'rianism, 265, 266.
Aristī'dēṣ, 128, 129, 132, 135.
Aristodē'mus, 193.
Aristŏph'anēṣ, 155, 169, 175, 199.
Aristŏt'le, 150, 176, 177, 194.
A'rius, 265.
Arminius, 256.
Armor. See Military customs.
Arsă'çĭdæ, the, 150.

(xi)

INDEX.

Art, Assyrian and Babylonian, 55, 71, 72, 113, 413; Chaldean, 64, 65, 71; Chinese, 110; Egyptian, 26, 44; Greek, 137, 145, 154, 158, 180, 193, 194, 201; Hebrew, 85; Hindoo, 105; Persian, 96, 104; Phœnician, 77; Roman, 281, 285, 305, 310.
Artaxerxes (är-taks-ĕrks'eez), 135, 145.
Artaxerxes (Babegan), 156.
Ar'temis, 184, 189, 194.
Arts and Inventions, Assyrian and Babylonian, 48, 59, 71, 72; Chaldean, 64; Chinese, 111; Egyptian, 28, 44; Greek, 183; Hebrew, 85; Hindoo, 105; Persian, 97, 104; Phœnician, 77; Roman, 282, 310.
Ar'yan race, 10-13, 51, 88, 89, 105, 114, 204.
Ascā'nius, son of Æneas, 205.
Aspā'sia, 167.
Assemblies, Congregation of Israel, 86; Greek, 116, 194; Roman, 208, 212, 215 (see *Comitia*).
As'shur, Assyrian god, 62; emblem of, 98.
Asshurbăn'ipal, 49, 54, 67, 69, 70.
Asshur-e-med'i-lin (Saracus), 47, 50, 55.
Asshur-ī'zir-pal, 48.
Assyria, 17, 46-70, 88, 89.
Astar'te (Ash'ta-rŏth), 79.
Astrologers, 52, 56, 288, 290.
Asty'agĕs, 88.
Athē'na, 180, 181, 184, 187, 194.
Athenian art, 123, 181-183; constitution (of Solon), 122; democracy, 119, 124, 139, 159; education, 178; homes, 195; kings, 121; literature, 123, 161-172; Panathenaic procession, 187; respect for Pericles, 140, 141; schools closed, 157; schools of philosophy, 175-177; senate, 123; supremacy, 134; symposia, 197-199; theaters, 170, 187-189; tyrants, 128.
Athenians, the, 134, 137, 138, 159, 170, 179, 194, 197, 201.
Athens, 119, 121-140, 144, 146, 157, 158, 194.
At'talus, 237.
Attic wit, 199.
At'tica, 121, 124, 143, 176.
At'tila, 267, 268.
Augurs, Roman, 205, 208, 251, 293.
Augustan age, the, 256, 310.
Augŭs'tulus Rŏm'ulus, 269.
Augustus Cæsar, 252-258, 296, 298.
Aurē'lian, 263.
Av'entīne Hill, 205, 208, 209, 214, 217.
Bā'al, 78.
Baalbec (bäl-bĕk'), 75, 281.
Babel, Tower of, 55.
Babylon, 46, 50, 51, 58, 89.
Babylonian art, 55; curious customs, 63; empire, 45, 46, 50; literature, 54, 55, 71; religion, 61; scene, 63; writing, 52.
Bac'chus (Diony'sus), 185, 187.
Bac'tria, 10, 93.
Basil'icas, Roman, 281.
Behĭs'tun Inscription, 53, 90.
Belshăz'zar, 51.
Beni Hassan, tombs of, 40.
Berŏ'sus, 46.
Bethho'ron, Joshua at, 82.
Bias. See *Seven Sages*.
Bible, the, 85, 154, 226.

Bœ-ō'tian League, 139, 147.
Book of the Dead, Egyptian, 24.
Borsip'pa, Temple of Nebo at, 55.
Brahma and the Brahmans, 105-107.
Bren'nus, Gallic leader, 156.
Britain, 249.
British Empire, 587; museum, 52, 55, 60, 181.
Brutium, 203, 233.
Brutus, L. Junius, 211, 212.
Brutus, M. Junius, 251-253.
Bubas'tis, 26.
Buddha (bood'dä), 107, 111.
Burial customs, 32-35, 43, 63, 65, 71, 99, 104, 190, 191, 294, 307.
Byzan'tine Empire, the, 266, 269.
Cæsar, Caius (kā'yus). See *Caligula*.
Cæsar, Julius, 248-252, 280, 298, 302.
Cairo (kī'rō), 21.
Calendar, 155, 222, 250, 251.
Calends, Ides, and Nones, 251.
Calig'ula, 259, 303.
Callim'achus, 181.
Calli'o-pe. See *Muses*.
Calpur'nia, 251.
Calydō'nian Boar, hunt of the, 116.
Camby'sēs, King of Persia, 15, 90.
Camil'lus, 221-223.
Campus Mar'tius, 222, 299, 301, 308.
Can'næ, battle of, 232.
Canulē'ian Decree, 218.
Capitoline Hill, 206, 208, 222, 296, 307; museum, 183.
Capua, 203, 233.
Caracal'la, or Caracallus, 262, 285.
Carchemish (kär'kee-mish), 87.
Carthage, 73, 76, 227-235, 244, 250, 269.
Carthagin'ians, the, 133, 227-235.
Cassius (kăsh'e-us), Caius Longī'nus, 251-253.
Cassius, Spurius, 216.
Castes, Chaldean, 52; Hindoo, 105.
Castor and Pollux, 213, 296.
Catiline's Conspiracy, 247, 275.
Cato the Censor, 235, 274, 289.
Caudine Forks, battle of, 223.
Cauca'sian race, the, 10.
Ce'crops, 121.
Celts, the, 12.
Censors, Roman, 218, 256, 271. See *Cato*.
Centuries. See *Assemblies*.
Cerami'cus, the, 140, 177.
Cer'berus, 184.
Cĕ'reṣ. See *Demeter*.
Cesnō'la, Luigi Palma di, 77, 87.
Chæronē'a, battle of, 149.
Ehaldē'a. See *Babylon*.
Châlons (shä-lŏn'), battle of, 268.
Chompollion (sham-pŏl'e-on), François, 22.
Che Hwang-te, 109.
Cheops (kē'ops), 16, 36, 37.
Chilo (kī'lo). See *Seven Sages*.
China, 109-112.
Chios (kī'ŏs), 139.
Chivalry, 410-412, 439.
Ehorăgic Monument, 181, 194.
Ehorā'gus, Greek, 188.

INDEX. xiii

Christ, 257, 259, 310.
Christian Church, the, 265; Fathers, 155.
Christianity, 263, 265.
Christians, the, 260, 262-264.
Cicero, 157, 236, 247, 248, 253, 274, 296, 303, 310.
Cimbri, 242, 244.
Cī'mon, 136, 141.
Cincinnā'tus, 220.
Cin'eas, ambassador to Rome, 225.
Cinna, 244.
Circus Flaminius, 299.
Circus Maximus, 208, 297.
Cisal'pine Gaul, 204.
Cities, Christianized, 263; free, 383, 392.
Civilization, Aryan, 12; Assyrian and Babylonian, 51, 71; Chinese, 110; Egyptian, 19, 43; Greek, 119, 158, 201; Hebrew, 85; Hindoo, 105; Persian, 92, 103; Phœnician, 77; Roman, 270, 309.
Clau'dius, Emperor, 263.
Cleīs'thenēs, or Clīs'thenēs, 124.
Cleobu'lus. See *Seven Sages.*
Clē'on, 141, 170, 172.
Cleopā'tra, 155, 249, 253, 254, 285, 303.
Clients, Roman, 207, 213, 270, 298.
Cli'o. See *Muses.*
Cloā'ca, Roman, 208.
Cloe'lia, 213.
Clyde, Lord. See *Campbell.*
Cnidus (nī'dus), 146, 181, 183.
Cō'clēs, Horatius, 212.
Code, Buddhist, 107, 108; Draco's, 121, 122; Laws of the Twelve Tables, 217, 280; Mosaic, 85, 86; Servian Constitution, 212; Solon's Constitution, 122, 123; Zoroastrian, 93.
Cō'drus, 121, 176.
Cœ'lian Hill, 207.
Collatī'nus, husband of Lucretia, 211.
Colleges. See *Universities* and *Education.*
Colossē'um, the, 260, 284, 292.
Comitia Centuriata, 212, 215.
Comita Curiata, 208, 215.
Comita Tributa, 215.
Commerce, Assyrian and Babylonian, 59, 60; Chinese, 110; Greek, 118, 154, 159, 200; Hebrew, 85; Hindoo, 105; Persian, 92, 97; Phœnician, 73-77, 118; Roman, 298, 305.
Com'modus, 261.
Commonwealth, Hebrew, 85.
Confederations, 134, 206.
Confucius (kon-fū'she-us), 111.
Cō'non, Greek admiral, 146.
Con'stantine the Great, 264, 265.
Constantinople, 181, 265, 266, 269.
Consulship, Roman, 213, 218, 256, 265, 307.
Corcy'ra, 139.
Corinth, 117, 236, 237, 250.
Corinthian capital, 181, 182, 281.
Coriolā'nus (Caius Marcius), 219.
Cornelia, 241.
Councils, Amphictyonic, 115, 149; ecclesiastical, 265; of Elders, 116; of Nice, 265.
Crassus, 245-249.
Crœsus (kree'sus), 89.
Cumæ'an sibyl, 209.

Cunax'a, battle of, 145.
Cuneiform writing, 53, 65, 92.
Curatii, 207.
Cu'rēs, 206.
Cu'riæ, Roman, 211, 270.
Cu'riēs. See *Assemblies.*
Cur'ti-us, Mettius, 206.
Cyax'arēs, 50, 88.
Cy'clops, 114.
Cy'lon, 123.
Cȳn'ics, the, 177.
Cȳnosar'gēs, the, 194.
Cynoscephʹalæ, battle of, 236.
Cyprus, Di Cesnola at, 77, 87; settlement of, 73.
Cyrus the Great, 51, 84, 88, 89, 125.
Cyrus the Younger, 145, 172.
Dacians, the, 261.
Damascus, 49.
Daniel, 84.
Dardanelles (där-dă-nĕlz'), 115.
Darius (da-rī'us) I.; 91, 125, 126, 129.
Darius III., 151.
David, Hebrew King, 83.
Dē'bir, 77.
Deb'orah, 82.
Decem'virs, the, 216, 217.
Dēcius, 262.
Dē'los, 134.
Delphi, temple at, 115, 124, 186.
Demagogues, 141, 143, 170.
Demē'ter, 184.
Demŏs'thenēs, 149, 173.
Denta'tus, 225.
Diā'na. See *Artemis.*
Dictatorship, Roman, 213, 219, 245, 246, 250, 307.
Dido founds Carthage, 76.
Dioclē'tian, 263, 264.
Diodō'rus Sic'ulus, 15.
Diŏg'enēs, 177.
Diony'sus, god of wine, 185, 187.
Dodō'na, temple of Zeus at, 185.
Domitian, Roman Emperor, 261.
Dorians, migration of, 117, 119.
Doric Colonies, 118.
Draco, Laws of, 121, 122.
Drusus, 256.
Education, Assyrian and Babylonian, 55, 71; Chinese, 111; Egyptian, 26, 44, 155; Greek, 137, 155, 157, 162, 163, 178, 201; Hebrew, 86; Persian, 94, 103; Phœnician, 77; Roman, 257, 280, 286.
Egeria, the nymph, 207.
Egypt, 15-44, 50, 151, 154, 254.
E'hud, 82.
Elba, 570.
Eleusin'ian Mysteries, 144, 165, 184.
Eleusis, 165.
Elgin marbles, 181, 187.
Embalming. See *Burial customs.*
En'nius, 273.
Epaminon'das, 147, 148.
Eph'esus, 117.
Eph'ors, 120.
Ep'ics, 25, 163, 273, 275.
Epicure'ans, 177.
Epicu'rus, 177.
Epī'rus, 225.

INDEX.

Equites (ĕk'wĭ-teez), 213, 240.
Er'ato, 185.
Eratos'thenēṣ, 155.
Erechthe'ium, 194.
Esarhád'don, 49.
Esquiline Hill, 277, 281, 298.
Ethiopia conquered by Egypt, 17.
Etrus'cans, the, 204, 206, 208, 211.
Eu'clēṣ, 127.
Eumenes (ṵ'mĕ-ṉeez), 23.
Eumen'idēṣ (Furies), the, 185.
Euphrā'tēṣ, the, 13, 45, 50, 58.
Eurip'idēṣ, 168, 275.
Eurym'edon, battle of, 136.
Euter'pe. See *Muses*.
Exig'uus, 10.
Exodus of the Jews, 82.
Fabii (fā'bĭ-ī), the, 218.
Fā'bius, M., Roman dictator, 230, 232.
Fabri'cius, 225.
Famine in Athens, 145; in Canaan, 39; in Egypt, 39; in Rome, 218, 220; in Russia, 599.
Fates, the three, 185.
Fayoom (fī-oom'), the, 32, 39, 162, 168, 192.
Festivals, 30, 38, 62, 63, 92, 115, 150, 165, 186, 201, 239, 290, 307.
Fire, Great, in London, 507; in Rome, 259.
Fire-worship, 99.
Flamin'ius, 236.
Fleece, the Golden, 115.
Forum, Roman, 296, 298, 299; monuments in, 282, 284; uses of, 239, 281, 300, 308.
Fucinine, Lake, 282.
Ful'via, wife of Mark Antony, 253.
Furies, the, 185.
Gā'bĭ-ī, capture of, 211.
Gā'dēṣ (Cadiz), 73, 230.
Galā'tia, 156.
Galleys, Greek and Roman, 192, 224.
Gallus, Roman Emperor, 262.
Games and Sports, 38, 67, 186, 197, 250, 285, 290, 310.
Gauls, the, 220, 232, 250, 264.
Genghis Khan (jĕn'gĭs kän), 109, 403.
Genseric (jĕn'sĕr-ĭk), 269.
German migrations, 266–269.
German'icus, 256.
Gid'eon, 82.
Gizeh (gē'zĕ), 16, 18, 35.
Gladiatorial games, 291; war, 245.
Glaṣṣ, 28, 44, 59, 71, 78, 302.
Good Hope, Cape of, 19.
Gorgons, the, 185.
Goths, the, 262, 263, 266.
Grac'chī, the, 241.
Gracchus, Caius, 241.
Graçchus, Tiberius, 241.
Graces, the three, 185.
Granī'cus, battle of, 151.
Greece, 113–203. See *Athens* and *Sparta*.
Gunpowder, 111.
Gȳlippus (jī-lip'us), Spartan general, 144.
Hā'dēṣ, 184.
Hā'drian, Roman Emperor, 261.
Halicarnas'sus, 183, appendix, i.
Hā'lys, the river, 88.
Hamil'car, father of Hannibal, 133, 230.

Hamit'ic race, 10, 13.
Hannibal, 230–235, 237.
Harpies, the, 185.
Has'drubal, 233, 234.
Hebe, 185.
Hebrews, the, 18, 80–87.
Hector, son of Priam, 116.
Helen, wife of Menelā'us, 116.
Hel'las and the Helle'nes, 114, 115, 117.
Hellespont, Alexander crosses the, 151.
Hē'lots, Spartan, 119, 136, 160, 161.
Hephæs'tus, 184.
Hera, 184, 189.
Heracleī'dæ, return of the, 117.
Herculā'neum destroyed, 261.
Her'culēṣ, Twelve Labors of, 115.
Her'mēṣ, 143, 184, 196.
Hē'ro, Greek mathematician, 155.
Heród'otus, 15, 110, 167, 171, 192.
Hesiod (hee'sĭ-ŏd), 163.
Hes'tia, 184, 196, 310.
Hī'ero, King of Syracuse, 227.
Hieroglyphics, Egyptian, 22.
Hills, plan of Roman, 210, 299.
Him'era, battle of, 133.
Hindoos, the, 105–108.
Hippar'chus, 123, 155.
Hip'pias, 123.
Hippoc'ratēṣ, 174.
Hiram, King of Tyre, 78.
Hit'tites, the, 86.
Homer, 116, 151, 162, 189, 192.
Homes and home life, Athenian, 195 Chaldean, 63; Egyptian, 38, 40; Roman 302; Spartan, 193.
Honō'rius, Roman Emperor, 267.
Horace, Roman poet, 276, 310.
Horatian Decree, 218.
Horatii and Curatii, 207.
Horus, Egyptian god, 30, 31.
Huns, the, 109, 265.
Hyksos, 17.
Hypatia, 177.
Hystas'pēṣ, Darius, 53.
Iliad, Homer's, 116, 151, 162.
Iliad, the Egyptian, 26.
Immortals, the Persian, 129, 130.
India, 105–108, 152.
Indo-European. See *Aryan*.
Inscriptions, famous, 18, 22, 53, 90, 259.
Institutes of Vishnu and Gautama, 108.
Inventions. See *Arts and Inventions*.
Ionians, the, 117, 118, 119, 139.
Ionic colonies, 117, 144.
Ipsus, battle of, 153.
Iran or Aria, 10.
Israel, kingdom of, 82–84.
Issus, battle of, 151.
Isthmian games, 186. See *Games*.
Italy, 203–312.
Janiculum, 212, 298.
Janus, Temple of, 207, 287, 288.
Jason, 115, 169.
Jehu, 48.
Jericho, capture of, 82.
Jerome. See *Christian Fathers*.
Jerusalem, 50, 83, 84, 85.
Jews, the. See *Hebrews*.
Jordan River, 81, 82.

INDEX. xv

Joseph, 80.
Joshua, 82.
Jove. See *Zeus.*
Judah, kingdom of, 84.
Judea, 80–86.
Judges, the, 82.
Jugur'tha, 242–244.
Julian, the Apostate, 265.
Juno. See *Hera.*
Jupiter. See *Zeus.*
Ju'venal, 278.
Ka, the Egyptian, 24, 38.
Kär'näk, Great Temple of, 9, 17, 26.
Khu-en-A'ten, King of Egypt, 17.
Khu'fu. See *Cheops.*
Kshatriyas (kshá'trē-yás), 105.
Labyrinth, Egyptian, 17, 39, 65.
Lacedæ'mon, 119, 132, 146.
Laconia, 121, 158, 160.
Lā'rēş and Penā'tēş, 289, 310.
Latin League, 205, 213, 216, 224.
Latium, 206.
Lāy'ard, Austen Henry, 55.
Leo I., Pope, saves Rome, 269.
Leon'idas at Thermopylæ, 129.
Leonidas of Tarentum, 171.
Lep'idus, 253.
Leuc'tra, battle of, 147.
Libraries, 18, 45, 54, 55, 71, 106, 154, 156, 157, 162, 177, 178, 274, 275, 278–280, 297, 304.
Licin'ian Rogation, 219.
Linnæ'us, 55.
Livy, 277, 310.
Lō'crians, the, 149.
Long Walls, the, 138, 140, 145, 146, 194.
Lost Tribes of Israel, the, 84.
Lotus flower, 62.
Lucil'ius, 274.
Lu'cius Tarquin'ius, 209.
Lucretia, 211.
Lucul'lus, 246.
Lux'or, 26.
Lyce'um, 157, 194, 282.
Lycur'gus, 120.
Lydia, 89, 125.
Lysan'der, 145.
Lysim'achus, 153.
Lysip'pus, 174, 183.
Macedonia, 46, 148, 157, 236.
Mæce'nas, 275, 277.
Mā'ġi, mā'ġianism, 97, 99.
Magna Græcia, 118.
Magnesia, battle of, 237.
Mā'ġo, 232.
Magyars, the, 374.
Mamertine Prison, 208, 242, 259, 307.
Măn'etho, 15, 155.
Man'lius, Marcus, 222.
Mäntinē'a, 148.
Man'tua, 550.
Mar'athon, battle of, 126.
Marcius, Ancus, 208.
Marcius, Caius (Coriolanus), 219.
Marco Polo, 109.
Marcus Aurē'lius, 261.
Mardō'nius, 126, 133.
Mariette (mä-re-ĕt), 27.
Mā'rius Ca'ius, 242, 243, 244, 248.

Marriage customs, 63, 189, 292.
Mars. See *Ares.*
Marseilles (mär-sālz), 118.
Martyrs, era of, 263.
Massilia (Marseilles), 118.
Maxim'ian, Roman Emperor, 263.
Max'imus Fā'bius, 223.
Medē'a, 169, 275.
Mē'dia, 88.
Meg'aclēş, 123.
Megalop'olis, 147.
Meleā'ger, 116.
Melpom'e-ne. See *Muses.*
Mem'non, the vocal, 14, 17.
Memnō'nium, the, 26.
Memphis, 15, 16, 27, 30, 31, 39, 40, 43, 90.
Menan'der, 170.
Menelā'us, 116.
Mē'nēş, 15.
Mercury. See *Hermes.*
Mesopotā'mia, 17, 45.
Messā'na, capture of, 227.
Messē'nia, 121, 147.
Messenian wars, 121, 136, 163.
Metau'rus, battle of, 234.
Met'tius Cur'tius, 206.
Migrations, Era of Great, 266.
Mil'an, 264.
Milē'tus, 117.
Military customs, 21, 60, 69, 101–103, 126, 149, 191, 225, 271, 307, 309; roads, Roman, 282.
Minep'tah, 17, 82.
Miner'va. See *Athens.*
Minu'cius, 221.
Mithridā'tēş the Great, 243, 246, 247.
Mithridat'ic wars, 243, 246.
Mnemosyne (nĕ-mōs'e-nee), 185.
Mœris (mē'ris), Lake, 17, 32, 39.
Moloch, 78, 79.
Mons Sacer, 214, 217.
Monuments. See *Art.*
Mortgage-pillars, Greek, 123.
Moses, 80, 82, 86.
Mount Ath'os, 126.
Mount Etna (Vulcan's Forge), 184.
Mount Vesuvius, battle of, 223.
Mounts Ossa and Pelion, 113.
Mummies, 32, 33, 34, 35, 42.
Mum'mius takes Corinth, 236.
Mun'da, battle of, 250.
Muses, the, 164, 171, 185, 195.
Museums, Alexandrian, 154; British (London), 52, 55, 60, 181; Capitoline (Rome), 182; Gizeh, 18; Louvre (Paris), 55; Turin, 41; Uffizi (Florence), 183; Vatican (Rome), 181.
Myc'ă-le, battle of, 134.
Nabonā'dius, 51.
Nabonas'sar, era of, 46.
Nabopolas'sar, 50, 70.
Næ'vius, 273.
Nebuchadnez'zar, 50, 84.
Nē'cho, 19.
Nē'mean games, 186.
Neo-Platonism, 177.
Neptune. See *Poseidon.*
Nē'ro, 259, 278, 305.
Ner'va, 261.

Nice (nees), or Niçæ'a (in Asia Minor), 265.
Ni'çias, Greek painter, 183.
Nicias, Greek general, 143.
Nile Valley, the, 13, 15.
Nimroud, 48, 55, 59.
Nin'eveh, 47, 50, 58.
Nirvana (neer-vä'nä), 107.
Nu'ma, Pompil'ius, 207.
Numan'tia, siege of, 238.
Nu'mitor, 205.
Octā'via, 254.
Octavius. See *Augustus Cæsar*.
Odoā'çer, Patrician of Italy, 269.
Odyssey, the, 117, 162.
Œdipus Trilogy, the, 167.
Oligarchy, 117, 120, 146.
Olym'pia, 115. .
Olympian games, 186; gods, 183.
Omens, 185, 189, 196, 251.
O'phir, 74.
Oppert (op'ĕrt), M., 53.
Oracles, 167, 185.
Or'mazd, 79, 93, 98.
Osī'ris, 24, 31, 34, 42, 154.
Os'tia, harbor of, 282, 284.
Ostracism, 124, 129.
Pactō'lus, the river, 89.
Pal'atine Hill, 205, 206, 274, 281, 297, 302.
Palestine, 46, 50, 82, 83, 153, 259. See *Jerusalem*.
Palmyra, 75, 281.
Panathenæ'a, the, 187.
Pansa, house of, 304, 306.
Pantheism, 106.
Pantheon, 298.
Papy'rus, 23.
Parchment, 23, 156.
Pariahs, Hindoo, 106.
Paris, son of Priam, 116.
Parnas'sus, Mount, 185.
Par'thenon, the, 180.
Par'thia, 156, 249, 262, 309.
Pasar'gadæ, 96.
Patricians, Roman, 213.
Patrō'clēs, 77.
Paul'lus, Roman general, 235, 236.
Pausā'nias, 133-135.
Pau'sias, Greek painter, 183.
Pedagogues, 178, 194, 197, 280.
Pelas'gians, the, 114.
Pelop'idas, 147.
Peloponnesian war, 139-145.
Peloponnesus, 117, 121.
Penā'tēs. See *Lares*.
Penel'opē, 117.
Per'gamus, 23, 156, 237.
Pĕrian'der. See *Seven Sages*.
Pĕr'īclēs, 136, 140; events of age of, 135, 137, 200.
Pericæ'ki, 119, 160.
Peripatet'ics, the, 176.
Persep'olis, 94, 151.
Per'seus, 236.
Persian Empire, 46, 88-104; wars, 125-134.
Pe'trie, Flinders, Egyptologist, 39, 168.
Phalanx, Macedonian, 149.
Pharaohs, the. See *Egypt*.

Phar'naçēs, 249.
Phid'ias, Greek sculptor, 137, 181, 183, 305.
Philip II. of Macedon, 148-150.
Philip III., 236.
Philip'pi, battle of, 253.
Philip'pics of Demosthenes, 149, 173, 202.
Philis'tines, 82.
Philosophy and philosophers, 25, 155, 157, 175, 201, 274, 278.
Phocians, the, 149.
Phœnicia, 73-79; Greeks in, 138.
Phtah-hō'tep, 25.
Pilate, Pontius, 259.
Pin'dar, Greek poet, 151, 164.
Pirates, 246.
Pisis'tratus, 123, 136.
Pit'tacus. See *Seven Sages*.
Platæ'a, 127, 133, 141, 143.
Plato, 160, 168, 175, 199.
Plau'tus, 274.
Plebe'ians, definition of, 213.
Plin'y the Elder, 277.
Pliny the Younger, 277.
Plu'tarch, 177.
Pluto. See *Hades*.
Pnyx, the, 140, 194.
Politics, derivation of name, 117.
Pol'ycarp, 264.
Polyhym'nia. See *Muses*.
Pompeii (pŏm-pā'yee), 260, 286, 300, 302.
Pompey the Great, 245-249.
Pontifex Maximus, 283.
Pontifices (Pontiffs), College of, 289.
Pontius, Caius, 223.
Pontus, kingdom of, 156.
Popes, power of the. See *Papal Power*.
Porsen'na besieges Rome, 212.
Portia, wife of Brutus, 253.
Poseï'don, god of the sea, 184.
Postu'mius, 224.
Praxit'elēs, 183, 305.
Prī'am, King of Troy, 116.
Pris'cus, Tarquin'ius, 208.
Pro'bus, 263.
Propon'tis (Sea of Marmora), 118.
Propylæ'a, 182.
Protog'enēs, Greek painter, 183.
Psammet'ichus, 18.
Ptol'emies, the, 153-155, 192.
Punic wars, 227, 230, 235.
Punishments, 52, 60, 86, 88, 91, 92, 101, 191, 242, 245, 259, 260, 280, 286.
Pydna, battle of, 236.
Pyrrhus (pir'us), 224.
Pythag'oras, 174.
Pythian games, 186.
Quakers. See *Friends*.
Quintus Curtius, 223.
Quirinal Hill, 208, 298.
Quirī'tēs, 208.
Races, historic, 10, 13.
Ram'esēs II., King of Egypt, 18, 80.
Ramessē'um, the, 26.
Ram'nēs, 209.
Rawlinson, Sir Henry, 53.
Reġil'lus, Lake, battle of, 213.
Reg'ulus, 229.
Rē'mus, 205.

INDEX.

Republic, Athenian, 124; Greek cities, 118; Hebrew, 85; Roman, 213, 215, 223, 308, 309.
Rhapsodists, the Greek, 161.
Rig-Veda, the Hindoo, 106.
Ritual, the Egyptian. See *Book of the Dead.*
Roads, Roman, 226, 282.
Roman Empire, 46, 255, 257, 261, 269.
Rome, 205-312.
Rom'ulus, 205.
Rosetta stone, 22.
Roxan'a ("Pearl of the East"), 152.
Sabines, the, 206, 209.
Sacred Band, 147; wars, Grecian, 149.
Sacrifices, human, 79.
Sagun'tum, capture of, 230.
St. Paul, 260.
St. Peter, 260.
Sal'amis, battle of, 132.
Sal'lust, 275, 310.
Samā'ria, 49, 84.
Sammur'amit, 48.
Samson, 82.
Samuel, 83.
Sanskrit literature, 106.
Sappho (săf'fo), 164.
Sar'acus, 47, 50.
Sardanapā'lus I., 48.
Sardanapalus II., 49.
Sardinia, 73.
Sar'dis, 89, 125.
Sar'gon, and the Sargon'idæ, 46, 49.
Sassan'idæ, 93, 156.
Sā'traps of Persia, 91.
Sat-ur-nā'lia, 239, 290, 295.
Saul, 83.
Scarabæ'i, Egyptian, 30, 33, 41.
Scenes in real life, 35, 63, 192, 296.
Schliemann (shlee'män), 162.
School, name derived, 179.
Science, 28, 93, 111, 113, 173.
Scipio Africanus Major, 234, 235.
Scipio Africanus Minor, 235, 238.
Scipio Asiaticus, 235, 237.
Scō'pas, 183, 305.
Seleucidæ (se-lū'si-dee), the, 155, 237.
Seleū'cus, 155.
Semīr'amis, 49.
Semit'ic race, 10.
Semprō'nius, 231.
Sen'eca, 278, 305, 310.
Sennăeh'erĭb, 49, 57, 67.
Sentī'num, battle of, 224.
Sep'tuagint, 154.
Sertō'rius, 245.
Ser'vius Tul'lius, 208.
Sesorta'sens, the, 17.
Sesŏs'trĭs, 18.
Se'ti (Minep'tah), 17.
Seven Sages, 173, appendix i.
Seven Wonders of the World, appendix i.
Sevē'rus, Alexander, 262.
Severus, Septim'ius, 262, 282, 284.
Sextil'ius, 244.
Sex'tus, Tarquin'ius, 211.
Shălmanē'ṣer II., 48.
Shalmaneser IV., 49.
Shepherd kings, the, 17.

Ships and boats, 38, 192, 227, 253.
Sĭb'yllĭne books, 209.
Sicily, 73, 118, 133.
Sī'don, 73, 78.
Silk, 105.
Simŏn'ĭdēṣ, 168.
Slaves and slavery, 18, 36, 37, 49, 60, 63, 80, 86, 119, 160, 161, 179, 195, 197-199, 214, 229, 239, 267, 274, 275, 280, 286, 290, 292, 295, 298, 300, 301, 303, 306.
Slavs, the, 12, 13.
Smerdis, son of Cyrus, 91.
Smerdis the False, 90, 91.
Sŏc'ratēṣ, 159, 170, 172, 174, 197, 199.
Solomon, 83.
Solon, 89, 122, 123, 160, 190. See *Seven Sages.*
Sŏph'ists, the, 175.
Sŏph'oclēṣ, 165, 166, 167.
Sosig'enēṣ revises calendar, 155.
Spain, 238.
Sparta, 117, 119, 126, 139, 160, 192.
Spar'tacus, 245.
Spartans, 119, 129, 139, 141, 143, 160, 193.
Spu'rius Mæ'lius, 219.
Statues, famous: Æsop, 174; Anacreon, 164; Athena Polias, 194; Athena Promachus, 194; Bel, Beltis, and Ishtar, 59; Cæsar, 250; Faun of Praxiteles, 183; Jupiter, the Capitoline, 250, 307; Memnon, 14, 17; Niobe group, 183; Pallas Athena, 181; Pompey, 252; Rameses, 26; Romulus and Remus, 205; Seven Sages, the, 174; Shafra, 37; Sheikhel-Beled, 27; Venus of Cnidus, 181, 183; Zeus, 181.
Stĭl'ieho, 267.
Stoics, the, 177.
Strā'bo, 155.
Sudra (soo'drā), the Hindoo, 106.
Sulla, 242-245.
Sympō'sium, 198, 199.
Syr'ąguse, 118, 143, 144, 227, 233, 234.
Syria, 46, 49, 50.
Syrian war (Rome), 237.
Tac'itus, 277.
Tā'o-iṣm, 111.
Taren'tum, attack on, 224.
Tarpē'ia, treachery of, 206.
Tarpē'ian Rock, 206, 223.
Tarquin, 208-213.
Tarquinii (quin'i-ī), 212.
Tar'shish, 74.
Tarsus, Cleopatra at, 253.
Tartars, the, 109.
Templars. See *Knights Hospitallers and Templars.*
Ten Thousand, retreat of the, 145.
Ter'ence, 274.
Terpsich'o-re. See *Muses.*
Tertul'lian, 264.
Teutons, 12, 13; defeated by Marius, 242.
Thăl'ēṣ. See *Seven Sages.*
Thap'sus, battle of, 250.
The'aters, 170, 187-189, 284, 298, 336, 472.
Thebes (theebz), Egypt, 16, 17; Greece, 147, 149, 151.
Themis'toclēṣ, 128, 129, 132, 135, 189.
Theŏd'oric, 268, 318.
Theodō'sius I. (the Great), 266.

INDEX.

Ther'mæ, Roman, 285.
Thermŏp'ylæ, 129, 237.
Thĕ'se-us, 116.
Thes'pis, 165.
Thothmes (tŏt'meez) I., of Egypt, 17.
Thothmes III., 17.
Thrace, Persians defeated at, 126.
Thucydides (thu-sĭd'ĭ-deez), 172.
Tī'ber, the, 204, 205, 212, 250, 283.
Tĭbē'rius, 256, 300.
Tī'bur (Tivoli), 281.
Tĭg'lathinin, 47.
Tĭg'lăth-Pĭlĕ'ser I., 47.
Tiglath-Pileser III., 49.
Tigranes (ti-grä'neez), 246.
Tigris-Euphrates basin, 13, 45.
Tī'tus, Roman Emperor, 85, 260, 285.
Trä'jan, Roman Emperor, 261, 292.
Transmigration of souls, 24, 106, 174.
Trasimē'nus, battle of, 232.
Trĕ'bia, battle of, 231.
Tribunes, 214, 217, 218, 256.
Tril'ogy, definition of, 165.
Trī'o, historical, 171; tragic, 165.
Trī'reme, 192.
Trium'virate, First, 248; Second, 252.
Trojan war, 116.
Troy, 115, 116, 162.
Tul'lus Hostil'ius, 207.
Turanian peoples, 10, 46, 109.
Twelve Tables, Laws of the, 217.
Tyrants, 123, 133, 145, 170, 262.
Tyre, 50, 73, 151.
Tyrian dyes, 78.
Tyrtæus (tir-tee'us), Greek poet, 163.
Ulm (oolm), battle of, 562.
Ul'philas, 266.
Ulys'sĕs, 117.
Universities, Colleges, and Schools: Chinese, 111; Egyptian, 26, 44; Greek, 137, 155, 157, 163, 178; Hebrew, 86; Roman, 273, 275, 276, 280, 300.

Urā'nia, muse of astronomy, 185.
Uruch, the earliest Chaldean king, 64.
U'tica founded, 73.
Vaisya, the Hindoo, 106.
Vā'lens, defeat of, 266.
Valerian Decree, 218.
Vandals, 269.
Var'ro, 232.
Vā'rus, massacre of, 256.
Vedas (vă'dăs), the, 106.
Ve-i-en'tine war, 218.
Veii (vĕ'yī), 212, 218, 221.
Vendidad, the Hindoo, 93.
Venice, 269.
Venus. See *Aphrodite*.
Vercel'læ (vĕr-chĕl'lee), battle of, 242.
Vespā'sian, 260, 294.
Vesta, 310. See *Hestia*.
Vestal virgins, 289.
Vesu'vius, battle of, 223.
Viminal Hill, 298.
Virgil, 275, 310.
Virginia, Roman maiden, 217.
Vishnu, 106, 108.
Vulcan. See *Hephæstus*.
Vullush III., 48.
World-Empires, the, 46.
Writing materials, 23, 43, 44, 52-54, 71, 92, 104, 177, 279, 280, 305.
Xanthip'pus, Spartan general, 229.
Xantippe (xan-tip'pe), 197.
Xenocrates (ze-nŏk'ra-teez), 157.
Xenophon (zĕn'o-fon), 47, 172.
Xerxes (zêrks'eez), 129, 130, 132, 133.
Za'ma, battle of, 234.
Zend-Avesta, 93.
Zĕ'no, 157, 177.
Zenō'bia, 263.
Zeus (zūs), 166, 180, 181, 184, 185, 186, 187, 189, 196.
Zeuxis (zūks'is), 182.
Zoroas'ter, 93.

ESSENTIALS IN MEDIÆVAL AND MODERN HISTORY

From Charlemagne to the Present Day. By SAMUEL BANNISTER HARDING, Ph.D., Professor of European History, Indiana University. In consultation with ALBERT BUSHNELL HART, LL.D., Professor of History, Harvard University

$1.50

THIS book is distinguished by the same vital pedagogical features which characterize the other volumes of the Essentials in History Series. It is intended for a year's work in secondary schools, and meets the requirements of the College Entrance Examination Board, and of the New York State Education Department.

¶ The difficulties usually encountered in treating mediæval and modern history are here overcome by an easy and satisfactory method. By this plan Italy, France, Germany, and England are taken up in turn as each becomes the central figure on the world's stage. About a third of the book is devoted to the period previous to the Reformation; another third to modern history from the Reformation to the French Revolution; and the remainder to the century and a quarter since the occurrence of that great event. These proportions give an opportunity to discuss the greatness of England, the unification of Italy, and of Germany, and the present organization of Europe under the control of the concert of powers, on the same plane as the Crusades, or the Thirty Years' War, or the age of Louis XIV.

¶ The three most difficult problems in mediæval history — the feudal state, the church, and the rivalry between the empire and the church — are here discussed with great clearness and brevity. The central idea of the book is the development of the principle of national independence in both politics and religion from the earlier condition of a world empire.

AMERICAN BOOK COMPANY

ESSENTIALS IN ENGLISH HISTORY

From the Earliest Records to the Present Day. By ALBERT PERRY WALKER, A.M., Master in History, English High School, Boston. In consultation with ALBERT BUSHNELL HART, LL.D., Professor of History, Harvard University

$1.50

LIKE the other volumes of the Essentials in History Series, this text-book is intended to form a year's work in secondary schools, following out the recommendation of the Committee of Seven, and meeting the requirements of the College Entrance Examination Board, and of the New York State Education Department. It contains the same general features, the same pedagogic apparatus, and the same topical method of treatment. The text is continuous, the sectional headings being placed in the margin. The maps and illustrations are worthy of special mention.

¶ The book is a model of good historical exposition, unusually clear in expression, logical and coherent in arrangement, and accurate in statement. The essential facts in the development of the British Empire are vividly described, and the relation of cause and effect is clearly brought out.

¶ The treatment begins with a brief survey of the whole course of English history, deducing therefrom three general movements: (1) the fusing of several races into the English people; (2) the solution by that people of two great problems: free and democratic home government, and practical, enlightened government of foreign dependencies; and (3) the extreme development of two great fields of industry, commerce and manufacture. The narrative follows the chronological order, and is full of matter which is as interesting as it is significant, ending with a masterly summary of England's contribution to civilization.

AMERICAN BOOK COMPANY

ESSENTIALS IN AMERICAN HISTORY

From the Discovery to the Present Day. By ALBERT BUSHNELL HART, LL.D., Professor of History, Harvard University

$1.50

PROFESSOR HART was a member of the Committee of Seven, and consequently is exceptionally qualified to supervise the preparation of a series of text-books which carry out the ideas of that Committee. The needs of secondary schools, and the entrance requirements to all colleges, are fully met by the Essentials in History Series.

¶ This volume reflects in an impressive manner the writer's broad grasp of the subject, his intimate knowledge of the relative importance of events, his keen insight into the cause and effect of each noteworthy occurrence, and his thorough familiarity with the most helpful pedagogical features — all of which make the work unusually well suited to students.

¶ The purpose of the book is to present an adequate description of all essential things in the upbuilding of the country, and to supplement this by good illustrations and maps. Political geography, being the background of all historical knowledge, is made a special topic, while the development of government, foreign relations, the diplomatic adjustment of controversies, and social and economic conditions have been duly emphasized.

¶ All sections of the Union, North, East, South, West, and Far West, have received fair treatment. Much attention is paid to the causes and results of our various wars, but only the most significant battles and campaigns have been described. The book aims to make distinct the character and public services of some great Americans, brief accounts of whose lives are given in special sections of the text. Towards the end a chapter sums up the services of America to mankind.

AMERICAN BOOK COMPANY

OUTLINES OF GENERAL HISTORY

By FRANK MOORE COLBY, M.A., recently Professor
of Economics, New York University

$1.50

THIS volume provides at once a general foundation for historical knowledge and a stimulus for further reading.
It gives each period and subject its proper historical perspective, and provides a narrative which is clear, connected, and attractive. From first to last only information that is really useful has been included.

¶ The history is intended to be suggestive and not exhaustive. Although the field covered is as wide as possible, the limitations of space have obliged the writer to restrict the scope at some points; this he has done in the belief that it is preferable to giving a mere catalogue of events. For example, the history of the United States has not been included, while that of the non-Aryan peoples, especially since the beginning of the mediaeval period, has not received the attention that has been given to the races to which the leading nations of the world belong. The chief object of attention in the chapters on mediaeval and modern history is the European nations, and in treating them an effort has been made to trace their development as far as possible in a connected narrative, indicating the causal relations of events. Special emphasis is given to the great events of recent times.

¶ The book is plentifully supplied with useful pedagogical features. The narrative follows the topical manner of treatment, and is not over-crowded with names and dates. The various historical phases and periods are clearly shown by a series of striking progressive maps, many of which are printed in colors. The illustrations are numerous and finely executed. Each chapter closes with a summary and synopsis for review, covering all matters of importance.

AMERICAN BOOK COMPANY

A HISTORY OF ENGLISH LITERATURE

By REUBEN POST HALLECK, M.A. (Yale), Louisville Male High School

$1.25

HALLECK'S HISTORY OF ENGLISH LITERATURE traces the development of that literature from the earliest times to the present in a concise, interesting, and stimulating manner. Although the subject is presented so clearly that it can be readily comprehended by high school pupils, the treatment is sufficiently philosophic and suggestive for any student beginning the study.

¶ The book is a history of literature, and not a mere collection of biographical sketches. Only enough of the facts of an author's life are given to make students interested in him as a personality, and to show how his environment affected his work. Each author's productions, their relation to the age, and the reasons why they hold a position in literature, receive treatment commensurate with their importance.

¶ One of the most striking features of the work consists in the way in which literary movements are clearly outlined at the beginning of each chapter. Special attention is given to the essential qualities which differentiate one period from another, and to the animating spirit of each age. The author shows that each period has contributed something definite to the literature of England, either in laying characteristic foundations, in presenting new ideals, in improving literary form, or in widening the circle of human thought.

¶ At the end of each chapter a carefully prepared list of books is given to direct the student in studying the original works of the authors treated. He is told not only what to read, but also where to find it at the least cost. The book contains a special literary map of England in colors.

AMERICAN BOOK COMPANY

INTRODUCTION TO AMERICAN LITERATURE

$1.00

By BRANDER MATTHEWS, A.M., LL.B., Professor of Literature, Columbia University

PRESIDENT ROOSEVELT, in an extended and appreciative review in *The Bookman* says: "The book is a piece of work as good of its kind as any American scholar has ever had in his hands. It is just the kind of book that should be given to a beginner, because it will give him a clear idea of what to read, and of the relative importance of the authors he is to read; yet it is much more than merely a book for beginners. Any student of the subject who wishes to do good work hereafter must not only read Mr. Matthews's book, but must largely adopt Mr. Matthews's way of looking at things, for these simply written, unpretentious chapters are worth many times as much as the ponderous tomes which contain what usually passes for criticism; and the principles upon which Mr. Matthews insists with such quiet force and good taste are those which must be adopted, not only by every student of American writings, but by every American writer, if he is going to do what is really worth doing. There is little room for division of opinion as to the excellence of Mr. Matthews's arrangement as a whole, and as to the soundness of his judgments. He preserves always the difficult balance between sympathy and justice. . . . In short, Mr. Matthews has produced an admirable book, both in manner and matter, and has made a distinct addition to the very literature of which he writes."

¶ The book is amply provided with pedagogical features. Each chapter includes questions for review, bibliographical notes, facsimiles of manuscripts, and portraits, while at the end of the volume is a brief chronology of American literature.

AMERICAN BOOK COMPANY

COMPOSITION-RHETORIC
$1.00

By STRATTON D. BROOKS, Superintendent of Schools, Boston, Mass., and MARIETTA HUBBARD, formerly English Department, High School, La Salle, Ill.

THE fundamental aim of this volume is to enable pupils to express their thoughts freely, clearly, and forcibly. At the same time it is designed to cultivate literary appreciation, and to develop some knowledge of rhetorical theory. The work follows closely the requirements of the College Entrance Examination Board, and of the New York State Education Department.

¶ In Part One are given the elements of description, narration, exposition, and argument; also special chapters on letter-writing and poetry. A more complete and comprehensive treatment of the four forms of discourse already discussed is furnished in Part Two. In each part is presented a series of themes covering these subjects, the purpose being to give the pupil inspiration, and that confidence in himself which comes from the frequent repetition of an act. A single new principle is introduced into each theme, and this is developed in the text, and illustrated by carefully selected examples. These principles are referred to again and again as the subject grows.

¶ The pupils are taught how to correct their own errors, and also how to get the main thought in preparing their lessons. Careful coördination with the study of literature and with other school studies is made throughout the book.

¶ The modern character of the illustrative extracts can not fail to interest every boy and girl. Concise summaries are given following the treatment of the various forms of discourse, and toward the end of the book there is a very comprehensive and compact summary of grammatical principles. More than usual attention is devoted to the treatment of argument. The appendix contains the elements of form, the figures of speech, etc.

AMERICAN BOOK COMPANY

THE GATEWAY SERIES
HENRY VAN DYKE, General Editor

SHAKESPEARE'S MERCHANT OF VENICE. Felix E. Schelling, University of Pennsylvania. $0.35.
SHAKESPEARE'S JULIUS CAESAR. Hamilton W. Mabie, "The Outlook." $0.35.
SHAKESPEARE'S MACBETH. T. M. Parrott, Princeton University. $0.40.
MILTON'S MINOR POEMS. M. A. Jordan, Smith College. $0.35.
ADDISON'S SIR ROGER DE COVERLEY PAPERS. C. T. Winchester, Wesleyan University. $0.40.
GOLDSMITH'S VICAR OF WAKEFIELD. James A. Tufts, Phillips Exeter Academy. $0.45.
BURKE'S SPEECH ON CONCILIATION. William MacDonald, Brown University. $0.35.
COLERIDGE'S ANCIENT MARINER. George E. Woodberry, Columbia University. $0.30.
SCOTT'S IVANHOE. Francis H. Stoddard, New York University, $0.50.
SCOTT'S LADY OF THE LAKE. R. M. Alden, Leland Stanford Jr. University. $0.40.
MACAULAY'S MILTON. Rev. E. L. Gulick, Lawrenceville School. $0.35.
MACAULAY'S ADDISON. Charles F. McClumpha, University of Minnesota. $0.35.
MACAULAY'S ADDISON AND JOHNSON. In one volume (McClumpha and Clark). $0.45.
MACAULAY'S LIFE OF JOHNSON. J. S. Clark, Northwestern University. $0.35.
CARLYLE'S ESSAY ON BURNS. Edwin Mims, Trinity College, North Carolina. $0.35.
GEORGE ELIOT'S SILAS MARNER. W. L. Cross, Yale University. $0.40.
TENNYSON'S PRINCESS. K. L. Bates, Wellesley College. $0.40.
TENNYSON'S GARETH AND LYNETTE, LANCELOT AND ELAINE, and THE PASSING OF ARTHUR. Henry van Dyke, Princeton University. $0.35.
EMERSON'S ESSAYS. Henry van Dyke, Princeton University. $0.35.
FRANKLIN'S AUTOBIOGRAPHY. Albert Henry Smyth, Central High School, Philadelphia.
GASKELL'S CRANFORD. Charles E. Rhodes, Lafayette High School, Buffalo. $0.40.

AMERICAN BOOK COMPANY

NEW ROLFE SHAKESPEARE
Edited by WILLIAM J. ROLFE, Litt.D.
40 volumes, each, $0.56

THE popularity of Rolfe's Shakespeare has been extraordinary. Since its first publication in 1870-83 it has been used more widely, both in schools and colleges, and by the general reading public, than any similar edition ever issued. It is to-day the standard annotated edition of Shakespeare for educational purposes.

¶ As teacher and lecturer Dr. Rolfe has been constantly in touch with the recent notable advances made in Shakespearian investigation and criticism; and this revised edition he has carefully adjusted to present conditions.

¶ The introductions and appendices have been entirely rewritten, and now contain the history of the plays and poems; an account of the sources of the plots, with copious extracts from the chronicles and novels from which the poet drew his material; and general comments by the editor, with selections from the best English and foreign criticism.

¶ The notes are very full, and include all the historical, critical, and illustrative material needed by the teacher, as well as by the student, and general reader. Special features in the notes are the extent to which Shakespeare is made to explain himself by parallel passages from his works; the frequent Bible illustrations; the full explanations of allusions to the manners and customs of the period; and descriptions of the localities connected with the poet's life and works. Attention is given to Shakespeare's grammar and metre, and to textual variations when these are of unusual importance and interest.

¶ New notes have also been substituted for those referring to other volumes of the edition, so that each volume is now absolutely complete in itself. The pictorial illustrations are all new, those retained from the old edition being re-engraved. The form of the books has also been modified, the page being made smaller to adjust them to pocket use.

AMERICAN BOOK COMPANY

CHEMISTRIES

By F. W. CLARKE, Chief Chemist of the United States Geological Survey, and L. M. DENNIS, Professor of Inorganic and Analytical Chemistry, Cornell University

| Elementary Chemistry . $1.10 | Laboratory Manual . . $0 50 |

THESE two books are designed to form a course in chemistry which is sufficient for the needs of secondary schools. The TEXT-BOOK is divided into two parts, devoted respectively to inorganic and organic chemistry. Diagrams and figures are scattered at intervals throughout the text in illustration and explanation of some particular experiment or principle. The appendix contains tables of metric measures with English equivalents.

¶ Theory and practice, thought and application, are logically kept together, and each generalization is made to follow the evidence upon which it rests. The application of the science to human affairs, its utility in modern life, is also given its proper place. A reasonable number of experiments are included for the use of teachers by whom an organized laboratory is unobtainable. Nearly all of these experiments are of the simplest character, and can be performed with home-made apparatus.

¶ The LABORATORY MANUAL contains 127 experiments, among which are a few of a quantitative character. Full consideration has been given to the entrance requirements of the various colleges. The left hand pages contain the experiments, while the right hand pages are left blank, to include the notes taken by the student in his work. In order to aid and stimulate the development of the pupil's powers of observation, questions have been introduced under each experiment. The directions for making and handling the apparatus, and for performing the experiments, are simple and clear, and are illustrated by diagrams accurately drawn to scale.

AMERICAN BOOK COMPANY

OUTLINES OF BOTANY
$1.00

By ROBERT GREENLEAF LEAVITT, A.M., of the Ames Botanical Laboratory. Prepared at the request of the Botanical Department of Harvard University

Edition with Gray's Field, Forest, and Garden Flora $1.80
Edition with Gray's Manual of Botany 2.25

THIS book covers the college entrance requirements in botany, providing a course in which a careful selection and a judicious arrangement of matter is combined with great simplicity and definiteness in presentation.

¶ The course offers a series of laboratory exercises in the morphology and physiology of phanerogams; directions for a practical study of typical cryptogams, representing the chief groups from the lowest to the highest; and a substantial body of information regarding the forms, activities, and relationships of plants and supplementing the laboratory studies.

¶ The work begins with the study of phanerogams, taking up in the order the seed, bud, root, stem, leaf, flower, and fruit, and closing with a brief but sufficient treatment of cryptogams. Each of the main topics is introduced by a chapter of laboratory work, followed by a descriptive chapter. Morphology is treated from the standpoint of physiology and ecology. A chapter on minute structure includes a discussion of the cell, while another chapter recapitulates and simplifies the physiological points previously brought out.

¶ The limitations of the pupil, and the restrictions of high school laboratories, have been kept constantly in mind. The treatment is elementary, yet accurate; and the indicated laboratory work is simple, but so designed as to bring out fundamental and typical truths. The hand lens is assumed to be the chief working instrument, yet provision is made for the use of the compound microscope where it is available.

AMERICAN BOOK COMPANY

ELEMENTS OF POLITICAL ECONOMY

By J. LAURENCE LAUGHLIN, Ph.D., Head Professor of Political Economy, University of Chicago

$1.20

IN the present edition the entire work is thoroughly revised, and as regards both theory and practical data is entirely in accord with the times. The treatment is sufficiently plain for even high school students.

¶ The book is in two parts: Part I, pertaining to the principles of political economy and containing chapters on the many phases of production, exchange, and distribution; and Part II, treating of such important topics as socialism, taxation, the national debt, free trade and protection, bimetallism, United States notes, banking, the national banking system, the labor problem, and coöperation.

¶ The work is equally suitable for a short or a long course, and contains many valuable practical exercises which are intended to stimulate thought on the part of the student. A large bibliography, footnotes, and references are included.

¶ Throughout the main purpose is to present a fair and impartial discussion of the important questions of the day, and to give a large amount of useful, practical information, rather than to devote extended space to abstract theory.

¶ Among the important features of the new edition are a discussion of the law of satiety, final utility, and its relationship to expenses of production in the theory of value; an explanation of the industrial system wherein the time element has created a different organization from that of primitive society; an adjustment of consumption to the general economic principles; an enlarged statement of the development of division of labor; and a brief discussion of large production and so-called "trusts."

AMERICAN BOOK COMPANY